KOVELS'
DEPRESSION
GLASS &
DINNERWARE
PRICE LIST

SEVENTH EDITION

KOVELS'
DEPRESSION GLASS & DINNERWARE PRICE LIST

Ralph and Terry Kovel

THREE RIVERS PRESS • NEW YORK

Published by Three Rivers Press, New York, New York.
Member of the Crown Publishing Group.

Random House, Inc., New York, Toronto, London, Sydney, Auckland
www.randomhouse.com

THREE RIVERS PRESS is a registered trademark and the Three Rivers Press colophon is a trademark of Random House, Inc.

Printed in the United States of America

Library of Congress Cataloging-in-Publication Data
Kovel, Ralph M.
Kovels' depression glass & dinnerware price list / Ralph and Terry Kovel. — 7th ed.
p.   cm.
Includes bibliographical references.
1. Depression glass—Catalogs.   2. Ceramic tableware—United States—History—
20th century—Catalogs.   I. Title: Depression glass & dinnerware price list.   II. Title:
Kovels' depression glass and dinnerware price list.   III. Kovel, Terry H.   IV. Title
NK5439.D44 K67   2001
738'0973'075—dc21   2001023458

ISBN 0-609-80640-8

Seventh Edition

10 9 8 7 6 5 4 3 2 1

Contents

Acknowledgments

The prices and pictures in this book are compiled with the help of many dealers, collectors, and companies. Thank you to Auntie Q's Antiques & Collectibles; Backward Glances; Barbara Balin; Van Beurden; Dennis Bialek; Florianna Bieros; Black Run Antiques; Blondie's Antiques; Jim & Carolyn Bosley; Nelda Brewer; Lee Broadwin; Diane Brouhle; C & K Collectibles; C. & L. Glassware; John & Judy Carroll; Jeanne Ceyler; Cheshire Cat Collectibles, Francee Boches; John Crawford; Curio Cabinet Antiques; D. & W. Collectibles; Victoria S. Digity; Dis-N-Dat Glass Shop; Elaine Dorrer; Dr. Bob Antiques; Dorothy Dupes; Mary D. Every; First Class Glass; Mark Fors; Diane Gentile; Jeanne Geyler; Glass Connection; Glass, Antiques or Not; Grandma's China Closet; Grapevine Antiques; Gray Goose Antiques; Tracy Green; Gschwend Glass; H. L. Collectibles; Arline Haenisch; Hardtimes Glassware; William Hatchett; Itz the Pitz, Chicago; Alex James; Frank Jay; Kaleidoscope; Harold Keller; Kemmerer's Depression Glass; Key's Glass Kottage; Kevin Kiley Antiques; Dan Kramer; L & T Collectibles; Ruby Lane; Made Especially for You by Jane Ellen; Dolores M. Makkers; Bill & Annette Mason; Nostalgic Glassware; Arlyn & Len Ols; Nadine Pankow; Polly Anne's Depression Glassware; R & M Antiques; Dave & Penny Renner; C. & D. Rizzo; Frances & Jarry Rosenau, Times Treasures Antiques; Roselle Scleifman; Gary Senavites; Roni Sionakides; Strawser Auctions; Sugartree Antiques; Symphony of Glass; Tanis May; The Archive-Antiques & Collectibles; Charles Toberman; Dan Tucker; Twentieth Century Designs; Walnut Mercantile; Waltz Time Antiques; Charlie & Loretta Weeks; Larry D. Wells; and Delmer H. Youngen. Thanks also to the nameless dealers with booths filled with Depression glass or dinnerware who allowed us to record their prices for the book.

The pictures for the book came from a variety of sources. Most of the glass and some of the dinnerware were photographed by Benjamin Margalit, who works with us on many books. He has mastered the trick of photographing glass so that the pattern will show. Special thanks to Liam Sullivan and the imaging department at Replacements Ltd. They furnished many of the pictures of dinnerware patterns from their huge stock of dishes. To find out if they have replacements for a glass or dinnerware pattern, call 1-800-REPLACE.

And of course we thank the staff at Crown: Dorothy Harris, our editor, and Pam Stinson-Bell and John Sharp, who push this book through the production stages. Thanks also to Merri Ann Morrell, our hardworking compositor at Precision Graphics. Thanks to our staff, Debbie Bedell, Kitty Busher, Grace DeFrancisco, Marcia Goldberg, Katie Karrick, Liz Lillis, Benjamin Margalit, Nancy Saada, Cherrie Smrekar, Edie Smrekar, Virginia Warner, and Ann Wochner. They are the ones who record the prices and proofread the results. Karen Kneisley is our computer-picture editor who has managed to make this a twenty-first–century book by turning all of the photos and slides into digital images that make each pattern easier to identify. But most of all thanks to Gay Hunter, the "coordinator," who keeps all of us working to meet the deadlines. She spots the problems before they become too big and turns our early manuscripts into a mass of colored Post-it notes that flag the problems for all of us to solve. The book is not considered finished until the last bit of colored paper has been removed. Our entire staff works hard to be sure the book is as accurate as possible. Once again, thank you.

DEPRESSION GLASS

DEPRESSION GLASS

Introduction

This book is a price report. Prices are actual offerings in the marketplace during the last year, not average prices. The high and low prices represent different sales. Prices reported are not those from garage or house sales. They are from dealers and collectors who understand the Depression glass market and who sell at shops, shows, on the Internet, or through national advertising.

This is a book for beginners as well as for serious collectors of Depression glass. We have included those patterns, both Depression and "elegant" patterns of glass, most often offered for sale. Most of the pattern names used are from the original glass factories' catalogs. We have gone beyond the *exact* definition of the term "Depression glass" and list patterns made between 1925 and 1970, including many newly popular patterns.

Opaque glass was popular in the 1930s. Each of the colors was given a special name by the company that produced it. "Monax" or "Ivrene" are opaque white glasswares. Opaque green glass was known by a variety of names. "Jade Green" is a generic name used by many companies. "Jade-ite" was the green used by Anchor Hocking; Jeannette Glass Company called their green kitchenware "Jadite." "Delphite," an opaque blue glass, is sometimes spelled "Delfite" in the ads. We have chosen to use the "Delphite" spelling.

A few forms are used consistently in the wording of entries. It is always a sugar & creamer, not a creamer & sugar. A pickle dish is listed as a pickle. An open salt dish is listed as a salt, but a saltshaker has its full name or is part of a salt and pepper set. Some pieces were made for dual use. A high sherbet may have been called a champagne goblet by some factories. We use the term preferred by the factory. Most glassware with a stem is called a goblet in this book, with the exception of sherbet and oyster cocktail glasses. A tumbler can have a flat or footed bottom but not a stem. A shot glass is listed here as a whiskey. We usually list not only the size of a plate but also what it is commonly called, thus the listing would be "plate, dinner, 10 in." The size of a dinner plate varies slightly with each pattern, and we have used the actual size. A plate meant to sit under a dish is listed as an underplate, not a liner. If there is a pair of candlesticks or salts or compotes, the word "pair" is included as the last word in the listing. Sometimes individual parts, such as covers for butter dishes, are sold. These items are listed, for instance, as "butter, cover only." When a dealer says a piece is "Book One" or "Book Two," it is a pattern of glassware in the books *A Guidebook to Colored Glassware of the 1920s and 1930s* and *Colored Glassware of the Depression Era 2* by Hazel Marie Weatherman. Book 2 is still in print. (See References, page 125.)

This book is not an in-depth study of Depression glass. The beginner who needs more information about patterns, manufacturers, color groups, or how and where to buy should use the books listed, the factory list, and the club and publication list we have included. E-mail and Web site addresses are included when available. All of these lists follow the last glass price entries.

This year, if a reproduction of a pattern is known, it has been included in the paragraph describing the pattern in the Depression glass listing. Hundreds of patterns, many not listed in other price books, are included here. The best way to learn about Depression glass is to attend the regional and national shows devoted to glass. Your local newspaper or the collectors' publications listed in this book will print the dates and locations.

Ceramic and Melmac dinnerware and the prices for these pieces can be found in separate sections of this book.

Ralph and Terry Kovel
Accredited Senior Appraisers
American Society of Appraisers
April 2001

DEPRESSION GLASS

Color Names

Here are some of the names used by companies to describe the glassware colors:

AMBER	Apricot, Desert Gold, Golden Glow, Mocha, Topaz
BLUE-GREEN	Limelight, Teal Blue, Ultramarine, Zircon
CHARCOAL GRAY	Dawn, Smoke
CLEAR	Crystal
DEEP BLUE	Cobalt, Dark Blue, Deep Blue, Regal Blue, Ritz Blue, Royal Blue, Stiegel Blue
GREEN	Avocado, Emerald, Evergreen, Forest Green, Imperial Green, Moongleam, Nu-Green, Olive, Pistachio, Springtime Green, Stiegel Green, Verde
LIGHT BLUE	Azure, Moonlight Blue, Willow Blue
MEDIUM BLUE	Capri Blue, Madonna, Ritz Blue
OPAQUE BLACK	Black, Ebony
OPAQUE BLUE	Delphite
OPAQUE GREEN	Jade, Jade-ite, Jadite
OPAQUE OFF-WHITE	Azure-ite, Chinex, Clambroth, Cremax, Ivrene
OPAQUE PINK	Crown Tuscan, Shell Pink, Rose-ite

OPAQUE WHITE	Anchorwhite, Milk Glass, Milk White, Monax
PINK	Azalea, Cheri-Glo, Flamingo, LaRosa, Nu-Rose, Peach-Blo, Rose, Rose Glow, Rose Marie, Rose Pink, Rose Tint, Wild Rose
PURPLE	Alexandrite, Amethyst, Black Amethyst, Burgundy, Hawthorne, Heatherbloom, Moroccan Amethyst, Mulberry, Orchid, Wisteria
RED	Carmen, Royal Ruby, Ruby Red
YELLOW	Canary, Chartreuse, Gold Krystol, Marigold, Sahara, Topaz

1700 LINE

Anchor Hocking Glass Corporation, Lancaster, Ohio, made the 1700 line from 1946 to 1958. The plain dishes were made in Ivory, Jade-ite, and Milk White. Other related patterns are listed in the Fire-King section in this book.

Ivory
Cup, St. Denis, 9 Oz. 6.00

Jade-ite
Cup & Saucer, 8 Oz. 18.00
Cup & Saucer, St. Denis,
9 Oz. 22.00
Saucer 8.00

ACCORDION PLEATS
See Round Robin

ADAM

Adam, sometimes called Chain Daisy or Fan & Feather, is a glass pattern made from 1932 to 1934 by the Jeannette Glass Company, Jeannette, Pennsylvania. Pink glass sets are the most common, but Crystal, Delphite, and Green pieces were also made. A few pieces are known in Yellow, but this does not seem to have been a standard production color. Reproductions have been made.

Crystal
Ashtray, 4 1/2 In. 14.00
Coaster, 3 1/4 In. 20.00

Green
Ashtray,
4 1/2 In. ..... 22.00 to 42.00
Berry Bowl,
4 3/4 In. ..... 22.00 to 23.00
Bowl, Cereal,
5 3/4 In. ..... 62.00 to 65.00
Bowl, Cover, 9 In. 52.00
Bowl, Vegetable, Oval,
10 In. 45.00
Butter, Cover . 345.00 to 425.00
Butter, No Cover 65.00
Cake Plate, Footed,
10 In. .... 26.00 to 36.00
Candlestick, 4 In.,
Pair 115.00
Candy Jar, Cover,
2 1/2 In. 120.00
Coaster, 3 1/4 In. 20.00
Creamer ...... 22.00 to 25.00
Cup .... 23.00 to 25.00
Cup & Saucer .. 28.00 to 35.00
Grill Plate, 9 In. . 10.00 to 27.00
Pitcher, Square, 32 Oz.,
8 In. 33.00
Plate, Dinner, Square,
9 In. .... 22.00 to 35.00
Plate, Salad, Square,
7 3/4 In. ..... 11.00 to 20.00
Plate, Sherbet, 6 In. 8.00
Platter,
11 3/4 In. .... 24.00 to 38.00
Relish, 2 Sections, 8 In. .. 22.00
Saucer, Square,
6 In. .... 6.00 to 8.00
Sherbet, 3 In. ... 33.00 to 44.00
Sugar 22.00
Sugar, Cover 75.00
Tumbler, 7 Oz.,
4 1/2 In. ..... 24.00 to 40.00
Tumbler, Iced Tea, 9 Oz.,
5 1/2 In. ..... 55.00 to 70.00
Vase, 7 1/2 In. .. 85.00 to 95.00

Pink
Ashtray, 4 1/2 In. 30.00
Berry Bowl,
4 3/4 In. ..... 15.00 to 30.00
Bowl, 7 3/4 In. .. 28.00 to 38.00
Bowl, 9 In. 40.00
Bowl, Cereal,
5 3/4 In. ..... 65.00 to 70.00
Bowl, Cover,
9 In. .... 75.00 to 80.00
Bowl, Vegetable,
Oval, 10 In. ... 30.00 to 40.00
Butter, Cover .. 95.00 to 145.00
Cake Plate, Footed,
10 In. .... 25.00 to 35.00
Candlestick, 4 In.,
Pair .... 100.00 to 125.00
Candy Jar, Cover,
2 1/2 In. ... 120.00 to 125.00
Creamer ...... 22.00 to 48.00
Creamer, Cover 75.00
Cup .... 24.00 to 33.00
Cup & Saucer .. 30.00 to 40.00
Grill Plate, 9 In. . 16.00 to 28.00
Pitcher, Round, 32 Oz.,
8 In. .... 38.00 to 45.00
Pitcher, Square, 32 Oz.,
8 In. .... 48.00 to 60.00
Plate, Dinner, Square,
9 In. .... 34.00 to 40.00
Plate, Salad, Square,
7 3/4 In. ..... 15.00 to 24.00
Plate, Sherbet,
6 In. .... 10.00 to 20.00
Platter,
11 3/4 In. .... 25.00 to 37.00
Relish, 2 Sections,
8 In. .... 20.00 to 24.00
Salt & Pepper,
Footed ..... 80.00 to 110.00
Saucer, 6 In. ...... 6.00 to 8.00
Sherbet, 3 In. ... 27.00 to 39.00
Sugar 17.00
Sugar, Cover ... 45.00 to 72.00
Tumbler, 7 Oz.,
4 1/2 In. ..... 30.00 to 42.00
Tumbler, Iced Tea, 9 Oz.,
5 1/2 In. ..... 60.00 to 90.00
Vase, 7 1/2 In. 450.00

AKRO AGATE

Picture a marble cake with an irregular mixture of

colors running through the batter. This is what Akro Agate usually looks like— a marbleized mixture of clear and opaque colored glass. The Akro Agate Company, Clarksburg, West Virginia, originally made children's marbles. The marbleized children's sets and accessories were made in many colors from 1932 to 1951. Lemonade & Oxblood is a marbleized yellow and red glass.

Amber
Candlestick, Short 100.00

Azure Blue
Ashtray, Shell 5.00
Basket, 2 Handles 42.00
Creamer, Interior Panel,
Darts, 1 3/8 In. 50.00
Creamer, Stacked
Disc & Interior Panel,
1 3/8 In. 35.00
Cup, Concentric Ring,
1 1/4 In. 15.00
Cup, Interior Panel,
1 3/8 In. 40.00
Powder Jar, Scotty
Dog 175.00
Saucer, Interior Panel,
2 3/4 In. 8.00
Saucer, Interior Panel,
3 1/8 In. 20.00

Black
Jardiniere, 5 In. 1500.00
Planter, Oval, Ribbed,
Scalloped Top, 6 In. . . 375.00
Planter, Rectangular,
Ribbed, 8 In. 750.00

Black & White
Bowl, Utility, Tab
Handles, 7 1/4 In. 425.00
Planter, Rectangular,
8 In. 345.00

Blue & Maroon
Bowl, Utility, Tab
Handles, 7 1/4 In. 500.00

Blue & White
Ashtray, Leaf 8.00

Cigarette Holder,
2 3/4 In. 25.00
Cup & Saucer, Interior
Panel, 3 1/8 In. 49.00
Planter, Oval, 6 In. 15.00
Plate, Interior Panel,
3 1/4 In. 10.00
Sugar & Creamer, Interior
Panel, 1 3/8 In. 85.00

Dark Green
Planter, Graduated Dart,
5 1/4 In. 195.00

Green & White
Ashtray, Shell 5.00
Bowl, Graduated Dart,
Scalloped Top,
5 1/4 In. 25.00
Bowl, Ribs & Flutes,
5 1/4 In. 65.00
Cigarette Holder,
2 3/4 In. 20.00
Cup, Interior Panel,
1 3/8 In. 18.00
Cup & Saucer, Interior
Panel, 3 1/8 In. 55.00
Flowerpot, 1 7/8 In. 80.00
Plate, Interior Panel,
4 1/4 In. 20.00
Saucer, Interior Panel,
2 3/4 In. . . . . . . 6.00 to 7.00
Teapot, Interior Panel,
2 5/8 In. 45.00

Green Luster
Cup, Interior Panel,
1 3/8 In. 20.00
Plate, Interior Panel,
3 1/4 In. . . . . . . 6.00 to 7.00
Teapot, Interior Panel,
2 5/8 In. 65.00

Ivory
Flowerpot, Graduated Dart,
Granddaddy, 5 1/4 In. . . 75.00

Lemonade
Saucer, Octagon,
2 3/4 In. 6.00

Lilac
Cup, Chiquita, 1 1/2 In. . . 35.00

Maroon & White
Vase, Graduated Dart,
8 3/4 In. 50.00

Opaque Blue
Bowl, Graduated Darts
Inside, 6 In. 30.00

Bowl, Ribs & Flutes,
5 1/4 In. 40.00
Cup, Stacked Disc,
1 1/4 In. . . . . . . 4.00 to 15.00
Mortar & Pestle, Cover . . 45.00
Pitcher, Stacked Disc,
2 7/8 In. 14.00
Plate, Raised Daisy,
3 In. 10.00
Sugar, Stacked Disc,
1 1/4 In. 10.00
Teapot, Stacked Disc,
2 3/8 In. 6.00
Teapot, White Cover, Stacked
Disc, 2 3/8 In. 75.00

Opaque Green
Bowl, Cereal, Octagonal,
3 3/8 In. 15.00
Bowl, Cereal, Octagonal,
Closed Handle,
2 1/4 In. 6.00
Bowl, Ribs & Flutes,
5 1/4 In. 30.00
Creamer, Chiquita,
1 1/2 In. 9.00
Creamer, Stacked Disc,
1 1/4 In. 22.00
Cup, Chiquita, 1 1/2 In. . . . 4.00
Cup, Concentric Rib,
1 1/4 In. 9.00
Cup, Concentric Ring,
1 1/4 In. 6.00
Cup, Octagonal, Open
Handle, 1 1/2 In. 15.00
Cup, Stacked Disc,
1 1/4 In. 6.00
Cup & Saucer, Chiquita,
3 1/8 In. . . . . . . 6.50 to 8.00
Cup & Saucer, Interior
Panel, 3 1/8 In. 55.00
Pitcher, Water, Stacked
Disc 10.00
Plate, Chiquita, 3 3/4 In. . . 8.00
Plate, Concentric Rib,
4 1/4 In. 8.00
Plate, Concentric Ring,
3 1/4 In. . . . . . . 1.50 to 6.00
Plate, Octagonal,
4 1/4 In. . . . . . . 7.00 to 7.50
Plate, Stacked Disc,
3 1/4 In. 4.00
Saucer, Chiquita,
3 1/8 In. 3.00
Saucer, Interior Panel,
3 1/8 In. 20.00

Sugar, Chiquita, 1 1/2 In. . . 7.00

Sugar & Creamer,
Chiquita, 1 1/2 In. 18.00

Teapot, Cover,
Chiquita, 2 3/4 In. 17.00

Teapot, Stacked Disc,
2 3/8 In. 9.00

Teapot, Stacked Disc,
No Cover, 2 3/8 In. 15.00

Teapot, White Cover, Stacked
Disc, 2 3/8 In. 12.00

Vase, Fluted, 5 1/2 In. . . 125.00

Opaque Jade

Bowl, Graduated Dart,
Scalloped Top,
5 1/4 In. . . . . . 45.00 to 95.00

Bowl, Graduated Darts
Inside, 6 In. 30.00

Bowl, No Darts, 6 In. . . 100.00

Bowl, Rib, Scalloped
Top, 5 1/4 In. 35.00

Jardiniere, White Mottled,
Square Mouth 45.00

Plate, Concentric Ring,
4 1/4 In. 19.00

Opaque Pink

Mortar & Pestle, Cover . . 45.00

Saucer, Concentric Ring,
2 3/4 In. 6.00

Orange & White

Bowl, Graduated Darts
Inside, 6 In. 35.00

Jar, Mexicali, Hat
Cover, Marked,
3 In. . . . . 22.00 to 40.00

Oxblood & White

Cigarette Holder,
2 3/4 In. 60.00

Pink

Tumbler, Stacked Disc &
Interior Panel, 2 In. 14.00

Pink Luster

Cup, Interior Panel,
1 3/8 In. 30.00

Plate, Interior Panel,
4 1/4 In. 10.00

Teapot, Cover, Interior
Panel, 2 5/8 In. 55.00

Pumpkin

Bowl, Graduated
Dart, 5 1/4 In. 75.00

Bowl, Ribs & Flutes,
5 1/4 In. 65.00

Bowl, Utility, Tab
Handles, 9 In. 85.00

Cup, Concentric Ring,
1 3/8 In. . . . . 25.00 to 39.00

Cup, Octagonal, Open
Handle, 1 1/2 In. 20.00

Cup, Octagonal, Open
Handle, 1 1/4 In. 20.00

Flowerpot, 1 7/8 In. . . . 145.00

Jardiniere, Graduated Dart,
5 In. . . . . 85.00 to 95.00

Vase, Graduated Dart,
6 In. 750.00

Vase, Graduated Dart,
8 3/4 In. 100.00

Royal Blue

Bowl, Graduated Dart,
Scalloped Top,
5 1/4 In. . . . 125.00 to 195.00

Cigarette Holder,
2 3/4 In. 20.00

Flowerpot, 1 7/8 In. . . . 135.00

Jardiniere, Graduated
Dart, 5 In. 125.00

Powder Jar, Colonial
Lady Cover 750.00

Tomato

Bowl, Ribs & Flutes,
5 1/4 In. 95.00

Topaz

Plate, Interior Panel,
4 1/4 In. 7.00

Transparent Blue

Cup, Chiquita,
1 1/2 In. . . . . . 8.00 to 14.00

Cup & Saucer, Chiquita,
3 1/8 In. 12.50

Sugar & Creamer,
Chiquita, 1 1/2 In. 22.00

Transparent Cobalt

Creamer, Chiquita,
1 1/2 In. 9.00

Creamer, Stacked Disc
& Interior Panel,
1 3/8 In. 50.00

Cup & Saucer, Stacked
Disc & Interior Panel,
3 1/8 In. 75.00

Sugar, Cover, Stacked Disc
& Interior Panel,
1 3/8 In. 100.00

Tea Set, Stacked Disc &
Interior Panel,
8 Piece 225.00

Transparent Green

Cup, Stippled Band,
1 1/2 In. 20.00

Cup, Stippled Band,
1 1/4 In. 15.00

Cup & Saucer, Stippled
Band, 2 3/4 In. 20.00

Plate, Interior Panel,
3 1/4 In. 9.00

Plate, Stippled Band,
3 1/4 In. 7.50

Teapot, Interior Panel,
2 3/8 In. . . . . 28.00 to 29.00

Tumbler, Interior Panel,
2 In. 20.00

Tumbler, Stippled Band,
1 11/16 In. 11.00

Water Set, Stippled
Band, 7 Piece 125.00

Transparent Topaz

Bowl, Cereal, Interior
Panel, 3 3/8 In. 18.00

Creamer, Stippled Band,
1 1/2 In. 22.00

Cup, Stippled Band,
1 1/2 In. . . . . 15.00 to 18.00

Cup & Saucer, Stippled
Band, 2 3/4 In. 20.00

Plate, Stippled Band,
4 1/4 In. . . . . . 8.00 to 9.00

Saucer, Stippled Band,
2 3/4 In. 4.00

Teapot, Cover, Stippled
Band, 2 5/8 In. 49.00

Tumbler, Stippled Band,
1 11/16 In. 10.00

Turquoise

Bowl, Graduated Dart,
Scalloped Top,
5 1/4 In. 165.00

Planter, Ribbed, Scalloped
Top, Oval, 6 In. 30.00

Planter, Ribbed, Scalloped Top,
Rectangular, 8 In. 85.00

White

Ashtray, Metal Lion,
7 1/2 x 4 In. 48.00

Bowl, Cereal, Octagonal,
3 3/8 In. 25.00

Bowl, Graduated Dart,
Scalloped Top,
5 1/4 In. 125.00

Powder Jar, Colonial
Lady 75.00

Puff Box, Cover 35.00

Saucer, Concentric
Ring, 2 5/8 In. 10.00

Teapot, Stacked Disc,
2 3/8 In. 7.00

Tumbler, Stacked Disc,
2 In. 7.00

Yellow

Bowl, Graduated Darts
Inside, 6 In. 40.00

Milk Bottle Cover,
2 3/8 In. 1000.00

Planter, Ribbed
Rectangular, 8 In. 75.00

Planter, Ribbed, Scalloped
Top, Oval, 6 In. 25.00

Saucer, Chiquita,
3 1/8 In. 12.00

Saucer, Octagonal, Open
Handle, 3 3/8 In. 8.00

Saucer, Raised Daisy,
2 1/2 In. 13.00

Sugar, Stacked Disc &
Interior Panel,
1 1/4 In. 12.00

Sugar & Creamer,
Octagonal, Closed
Handle, 1 1/2 In. 35.00

Vase, Graduated Dart,
8 3/4 In. 350.00

ALICE

An 8 1/2-inch plate, cup, and
saucer were apparently
the only pieces made in
the Alice pattern. The pattern was made by the
Anchor Hocking Glass
Corporation, Lancaster,
Ohio, from 1945 to 1949
in Ivory, Jade-ite, and
Opaque White with a red
or blue border. Other
related patterns are listed
in the Fire-King section in
this book.

Ivory

Saucer, 5 7/8 In. 2.00

Jade-ite

Plate, 8 1/2 In. .. 38.00 to 65.00

Saucer, 5 1/8 In. 3.00

White

Cup & Saucer, Blue
Trim .... 14.00 to 25.00

Plate, 8 1/2 In. 37.00

Saucer, Blue Trim,
5 7/8 In. .... 2.00 to 3.00

AMERICAN

American is a pattern
made to resemble the
pressed glass of an earlier
time. It was introduced by
Fostoria Glass Company,
Moundsville, West Vir-
ginia, in 1915 and remained
in production until the factory closed in 1986. Most
pieces were made of clear,
colorless glass known as
Crystal. A few pieces are
known in Amber, Blue,
Green, Milk Glass, Red,
and Yellow. It is similar to
Cubist pattern. Many
pieces of American pat-
tern were reproduced
after 1987.

Amber

Bonbon, 3-Footed, 7 In. . 125.00

Blue

Vase, Crystal Foot,
9 3/4 In. 110.00

Crystal

Ashtray, Square, 5 In. .. 100.00

Biscuit Jar 800.00

Bottle, Ketchup,
Stopper 160.00

Bowl, 3-Footed, 10 In. ... 52.00

Bowl, Centerpiece,
Rays, 11 In. 150.00

Bowl, Deep, 4 3/4 In. ... 25.00

Bowl, Deep,
8 In. ...... 95.00 to 150.00

Bowl, Flared, 5 1/2 In. ... 12.00

Bowl, Floating Garden,
Oval, 9 In. 50.00

Bowl, Footed,
7 In. 20.00

Bowl, Oval,
9 In. 32.00

Bowl, Preserve, 2 Handles,
Cover 100.00

Bowl, Salad, 11 In. 66.00

Bowl, Square, Handles,
4 1/2 In. 10.00

Bowl, Tricornered,
4 1/2 In. ..... 10.00 to 15.00

Bowl, Trophy, 2 Handles,
8 1/2 In. 72.00

Bowl, Trophy, Stem ... 115.00

Bowl, Vegetable, Oval,
11 3/4 In. 65.00

Box, Cosmetic, Round,
1 1/2 In. 750.00

Box, Hairpin, Cover ... 2000.00

Butter, Cover,
6 In. ...... 130.00 to 145.00

Butter, Cover, 1/4 lb. 32.00

Cake Stand, 2 Piece 125.00

Cake Stand, Square 75.00

Candleholder, Bell
Base 125.00

Candlestick, 2-Light,
4 1/4 In., Pair 135.00

Candlestick, 2-Light,
Bell Base, Pair 275.00

Candlestick, 2-Light,
Prisms, 9 1/2 In. 110.00

Candlestick, Eiffel
Tower 175.00

Candlestick, Square Step,
Pair 175.00

Candy Box, Open,
7 x 5 In. 500.00

Candy Dish, Cover,
7 In. 40.00

Candy Dish, Handle,
6 1/4 In. 29.00

Compote, 9 1/2 In. 75.00

Compote, Cheese 65.00

Creamer ...... 15.00 to 16.00

Cruet, 5 Oz. 30.00

Cruet, 7 Oz. 46.00

Cup 6.00

Cup & Saucer 11.00
Decanter, Gin 125.00
Dish, Banana Split 1200.00
Dish, Jelly, Cover,
  Footed, 6 3/4 In. 25.00
Dish, Jelly, Flared,
  5 x 3 In. 60.00
Finger Bowl 50.00
Goblet, Claret, Low,
  6 Oz., 4 1/4 In. 9.00
Goblet, Water, Hexagonal Foot,
  10 Oz., 7 In. .. 15.00 to 16.00
Goblet, Wine, Hexagonal Foot,
  2 1/2 Oz., 4 3/8 In. 10.00
Hair Receiver 750.00
Hat, 2 1/8 In. 15.00
Hat, 3 In. 25.00
Humidor, Cigar, Large .. 500.00
Ice Tub, 5 1/2 In. 25.00
Jam Jar, Cover, Spoon .. 125.00
Ladle 50.00
Mug, Beer, 12 Oz. 100.00
Mustard, Cover 65.00
Nappy, Handle, 5 In. 20.00
Oyster Cocktail, 4 1/2 Oz.,
  3 1/2 In. ..... 12.00 to 16.00
Perfume Bottle 100.00
Pickle Jar, 4 1/2 In. 600.00
Pin Tray,
  5 In. ...... 140.00 to 150.00
Pin Tray, Handles,
  6 In. 35.00
Pitcher, 1 Qt. 28.00
Pitcher, 1/2 Gal., 8 In. ... 45.00
Pitcher, 3 Pt. 80.00
Pitcher, English, 30 Oz. . 375.00
Pitcher, Ice Lip, 3 Pt.,
  6 1/2 In. ..... 45.00 to 60.00
Pitcher, Ice Lip, Straight
  Side, 1/2 Gal. 90.00
Plate, Bread & Butter,
  6 In. 8.00
Plate, Dinner,
  9 1/2 In. ..... 20.00 to 39.00
Plate, Ice Cream, Brick .. 75.00
Plate, Salad, 7 In. 8.00
Plate, Salad,
  8 1/2 In. ..... 12.00 to 17.00
Platter, Oval,
  10 In. .... 45.00 to 55.00
Platter, Oval, 12 In. 57.00
Puff Box, Round,
  2 7/8 In. 250.00

Punch Bowl,
  14 1/2 In. 250.00
Punch Bowl, 18 In. ... 1000.00
Relish, 3 Sections, Oval,
  6 In. .... 40.00 to 50.00
Relish, 3 Sections, Oval,
  11 In. 65.00
Relish, 4 Sections,
  Rectangular, 9 In. 70.00
Ring Tree 750.00
Rose Bowl, 3 1/2 In. 32.00
Rose Bowl, 5 In. 25.00
Salt, Spoon 15.00
Salt & Pepper 18.00
Salt & Pepper, Individual,
  Tray 70.00
Salt & Pepper, Straight,
  Pewter Lids 60.00
Sandwich Server, Center
  Handle, 9 In. .. 14.00 to 22.00
Sandwich Tray, 2 Handles,
  12 In. 35.00
Sauceboat 3.00
Saucer 3.00
Sherbet, 4 1/2 Oz.,
  4 1/2 In. ...... 6.00 to 14.00
Sherbet, 5 Oz.,
  3 1/4 In. ...... 6.00 to 14.00
Sherbet, Handles,
  4 1/2 Oz., 3 1/2 In. ... 150.00
Spooner ...... 45.00 to 59.00
Straw Jar,
  12 In. ..... 175.00 to 325.00
Sugar, Cover, Barrel,
  6 1/4 In. 50.00
Sugar, Footed 6.00
Sugar, Individual,
  2 1/4 In. ...... 5.00 to 12.00
Sugar & Creamer,
  Hexagonal 1500.00
Sugar & Creamer,
  Oval Tray 30.00
Sugar Cuber 250.00
Sundae, 6 Oz., 3 1/8 In. ... 9.00
Syrup, Bakelite
  Handle 150.00
Syrup, Drip-Cut,
  Cover .... 45.00 to 95.00
Torte Plate, 18 In. 90.00
Torte Plate, 20 In. 250.00
Torte Plate, Oval,
  13 In. 45.00
Tray, 5 Sections, Blue
  Frame 325.00

Tray, 5 Sections,
  Frame 160.00
Tray, Cloverleaf 250.00
Tray, Handles, 9 In. 48.00
Tray, Rectangular,
  10 1/2 In. 100.00
Tray, Square, 4 Sections,
  10 In. 150.00
Tumbler, Footed, 9 Oz.,
  4 3/4 In. 13.00
Tumbler, Iced Tea,
  Footed, 12 Oz.,
  5 3/4 In. ..... 12.00 to 20.00
Tumbler, Juice, Footed, 5 Oz.,
  4 3/4 In. ..... 12.00 to 14.00
Tumbler, Whiskey, 2 Oz.,
  2 1/2 In. ..... 10.00 to 15.00
Vase, Bud, Flared, Hexagonal
  Foot, 8 1/2 In. 28.00
Vase, Flared, 7 1/4 In. ... 87.00
Vase, Flared, 9 1/2 In. .. 250.00
Vase, Footed, 6 3/4 In. .. 40.00
Vase, Square Foot, 6 In. . 28.00
Vase, Square Foot,
  9 3/4 In. 80.00
Vase, Sweet Pea 75.00
Wedding Bowl, Cover,
  Large 1000.00
Wedding Bowl, Cover,
  Small 125.00

Pink

Creamer, Individual 8.00
Sugar, Individual 9.00

Red

Bonbon, 3-Toed, 7 In. .. 125.00

AMERICAN BEAUTY
See English Hobnail

❖

**Glass becomes cloudy if
not kept completely dry
when not in use. That's
why decanters and vases
often discolor. Drain
them upside down.**

❖

AMERICAN LADY

American Lady stemware was made to complement American tableware by Fostoria Glass Company, Moundsville, West Virginia, from 1933 to 1973. Items were made in Crystal or with Crystal bases and Amethyst, Burgundy, Empire Green, or Regal Blue bowls.

Crystal
Goblet, Claret, 3 1/2 Oz., 4 5/8 In.	18.00
Goblet, Cocktail, 3 1/2 Oz., 4 In.	14.00
Goblet, Water, 10 Oz., 6 1/8 In.	13.00 to 18.00
Goblet, Wine, 2 1/2 Oz., 4 1/8 In.	12.00

AMERICAN PIONEER

Panels of hobnail-like protrusions and plain panels were used in the design of American Pioneer. It was made by Liberty Works, Egg Harbor, New Jersey, from 1931 to 1934. Crystal, Green, and Pink dishes are easily found. Amber is rare.

Amber
Sherbet, 4 3/4 In.	50.00

Crystal
Candy Dish, Cover, 1 1/2 Lb.	99.00
Cup	5.00 to 10.00
Cup & Saucer	14.00
Dish, Mayonnaise, Underplate, Spoon	55.00
Goblet, 8 Oz.	20.00
Ice Bucket, 6 In.	55.00
Plate, Luncheon, 8 In.	5.00 to 10.50
Saucer	5.00
Sherbet, 4 1/2 In.	15.00
Sugar & Creamer	37.50 to 40.00
Tumbler, 12 Oz., 5 In.	45.00

Green
Bowl, Handles, 9 In.	40.00 to 48.00
Candlestick, 6 1/2 In., Pair	145.00
Candy Jar, 1 1/2 Lb.	170.00
Cheese Dish	50.00
Console, 10 3/4 In.	70.00
Cup	9.00 to 15.00
Cup & Saucer	12.00 to 17.00
Dish, Mayonnaise, Footed, 4 In.	90.00 to 115.00
Goblet, Cocktail, 4 In.	65.00
Goblet, Water, 8 Oz.	50.00
Ice Bucket, 6 In.	85.00
Pitcher, 5 In.	100.00
Plate, 2 Handles, 11 1/2 In.	35.00 to 55.00
Plate, Luncheon, 8 In.	10.00 to 16.00
Sherbet, 3 1/2 In.	22.00
Sherbet, 4 3/4 In.	50.00
Sugar, 2 3/4 In.	30.00
Sugar & Creamer, 2 3/4 In.	60.00
Sugar & Creamer, 3 1/2 In.	65.00
Tumbler, 12 Oz., 5 In.	75.00
Tumbler, Pilsner, 6 In.	150.00
Vase, Cupped, 8 In.	165.00

Pink
Bowl, Cover, 8 3/4 In.	75.00
Console, 10 3/4 In.	75.00
Creamer	27.00
Cup	6.00
Cup & Saucer	10.00 to 16.00
Goblet, Cocktail, 4 In.	55.00
Goblet, Water, 8 Oz.	55.00
Plate, Bread & Butter, 6 In.	15.00
Plate, Luncheon, 8 In.	6.00 to 14.00
Saucer	5.00
Sherbet, 4 3/4 In.	39.00 to 40.00
Sugar, 2 3/4 In.	30.00
Sugar & Creamer, 2 3/4 In.	60.00
Tumbler, 8 Oz., 4 In.	35.00
Vase, Flared, 7 3/4 In.	75.00 to 115.00

AMERICAN SWEETHEART

In 1930 Macbeth-Evans Glass Company introduced American Sweetheart. At first it was made of pink glass, but soon other colors were added. The pattern continued in production until 1936. Blue, Cremax, Monax, Pink, and Red pieces were made. Sometimes a gold, green, pink, platinum, red, or smoky black trim was used on Monax pieces. There is a center design on most plates, but some

Monax plates are found with plain centers. One of the rarest items in this pattern is the Monax sugar bowl lid. The bowls are easy to find, but the lids seem to have broken.

Blue
Console,
18 In. . . . . 1700.00 to 2000.00
Plate, Salad,
8 In. . . . . . 115.00 to 180.00
Salver, 12 In. 380.00
Sugar &
Creamer . . . 485.00 to 625.00

Cremax
Berry Bowl,
9 In. . . . . . . 45.00 to 48.00
Bowl, Cereal,
6 In. . . . . 10.00 to 19.00

Monax
Berry Bowl,
9 In. . . . . 70.00 to 85.00
Bowl, Cereal,
6 In. . . . . 19.00 to 24.00
Bowl, Vegetable, Oval,
11 In. . . . . . . 80.00 to 110.00
Chop Plate,
11 In. . . . . . . 22.00 to 28.00
Chop Plate, 12 In. 22.00
Creamer,
Footed . . . . . . 11.00 to 20.00
Cup . . . . 10.00 to 14.00
Cup & Saucer . . 10.00 to 18.00
Plate, Bread & Butter,
6 In. . . . . 7.00 to 10.00
Plate, Dinner,
9 3/4 In. . . . . 27.00 to 30.00
Plate, Dinner,
10 1/4 In. . . . . 25.00 to 40.00
Plate, Luncheon,
9 In. . . . . 11.00 to 18.00
Plate, Salad,
8 In. . . . . 9.00 to 16.00
Platter, 15 1/2 In. 235.00
Platter, Oval,
13 In. . . . . . . 45.00 to 89.50
Salt & Pepper,
Footed . . . . . 485.00 to 525.00
Salver, 12 In. . . . 20.00 to 32.00
Saucer . . . . 2.00 to 4.50
Sherbet,
4 1/4 In. . . . . . 22.00 to 28.00

Sherbet, Gold Trim,
4 1/4 In. 22.00
Soup, Cream,
4 1/2 In. . . . . 90.00 to 135.00
Soup, Dish,
9 1/2 In. . . . . 85.00 to 100.00
Sugar,
Cover . . . . . 525.00 to 600.00
Sugar, Footed . . . . 8.00 to 20.00
Sugar & Creamer,
Footed . . . . . . 18.00 to 35.00
Tidbit, 2 Tiers . . 55.00 to 95.00
Tidbit, 3 Tiers 325.00

Pink
Berry Bowl,
3 3/4 In. . . . . . 85.00 to 95.00
Berry Bowl,
9 In. . . . . 45.00 to 75.00
Bowl, Cereal,
6 In. . . . . 15.00 to 29.00
Bowl, Vegetable, Oval,
11 In. . . . . . . 65.00 to 95.00
Creamer,
Footed . . . . . . 15.00 to 24.00
Cup . . . . 18.00 to 24.00
Cup & Saucer . . 19.00 to 21.00
Pitcher, 60 Oz.,
7 1/2 In. 1250.00
Pitcher, 80 Oz.,
8 In. . . . . . . 795.00 to 975.00
Plate, Bread & Butter,
6 In. . . . . 4.25 to 13.50
Plate, Dinner,
9 3/4 In. . . . . 38.00 to 49.00
Plate, Dinner,
10 1/4 In. . . . . 40.00 to 45.00
Plate, Luncheon, 9 In. . . . 16.00
Plate, Salad,
8 In. . . . . 11.00 to 20.00
Platter, Oval,
13 In. . . . . . . 50.00 to 70.00
Salt & Pepper, Footed . . 575.00
Salver, 12 In. . . . 20.00 to 35.00
Saucer . . . . 4.00 to 5.00
Sherbet,
3 3/4 In. . . . . 17.00 to 36.00
Sherbet,
4 1/4 In. . . . . 20.00 to 25.00
Soup, Cream,
4 1/2 In. . . . 80.00 to 125.00
Soup, Dish,
9 1/2 In. . . . . 73.00 to 90.00
Sugar, Footed . . . 20.00 to 24.00

Tumbler, Juice, 5 Oz.,
3 1/2 In. . . . 95.00 to 110.00
Tumbler, Water, 9 Oz.,
4 1/4 In. . . . 85.00 to 125.00
Tumbler, Water, 10 Oz.,
4 3/4 In. . . . 145.00 to 175.00

Red
Console,
18 In. . . . . 1400.00 to 1800.00
Creamer, Footed 165.00
Cup . . . . 90.00 to 110.00
Cup & Saucer 150.00
Plate, Salad,
8 In. . . . . . . 100.00 to 125.00
Salver, 12 In. . 205.00 to 230.00
Sugar, Footed 150.00
Sugar & Creamer,
Footed 290.00
Tidbit,
2 Tiers . . . . . 320.00 to 425.00

ANNIVERSARY

Pink Anniversary pattern was made from 1947 to 1949, but it is still considered Depression glass by collectors. Crystal pieces are shown in a 1949 catalog. In the 1970s, Crystal and Iridescent, a carnival-glass-like amber color, were used. The pattern was the product of the Jeannette Glass Company, Jeannette, Pennsylvania.

Crystal
Berry Bowl, 4 7/8 In. 2.50
Berry Bowl, Silver Trim,
4 7/8 In. 3.50
Bowl, Fruit, 9 In. 16.00

Butter, Cover ... 25.00 to 30.00

Cake Plate,
12 1/2 In. ...... 6.00 to 8.50

Candy Dish,
Cover .... 22.00 to 35.00

Creamer .... 5.00 to 6.00

Cup .... 4.00 to 5.00

Cup & Saucer .... 3.00 to 6.00

Goblet, Water, 10 Oz.,
6 1/8 In. 23.00

Goblet, Wine, 2 1/2 Oz. .. 10.00

Pickle, 9 In. 6.00

Plate, Dinner,
9 In. .... 5.00 to 6.00

Plate, Sherbet,
6 1/4 In. .... 3.00 to 4.00

Plate, Silver Trim,
6 1/4 In. 2.00

Relish, 2 Sections,
8 In. 5.00

Sandwich Server,
12 1/2 In. 13.00

Sherbet 7.00

Soup, Dish,
7 3/8 In. .... 6.00 to 8.00

Sugar, Cover 11.00

Sugar & Creamer 8.00

Iridescent

Compote,
3-Footed ...... 5.00 to 6.00

Creamer 6.00

Plate, Sherbet, 6 1/4 In. ... 3.00

Sugar & Creamer,
Cover 16.00

Pink

Berry Bowl,
4 7/8 In. ..... 10.00 to 11.00

Bowl, Fruit, 9 In. 35.00

Butter, Cover 60.00

Candy Dish, Cover 65.00

Creamer,
Footed ...... 10.00 to 16.00

Cup .... 9.00 to 11.00

Goblet, Wine,
2 1/2 Oz. ..... 17.00 to 28.50

Plate, Sherbet,
6 1/4 In. 5.00

Plate, Dinner, 9 In. 18.00

Sandwich Server,
12 1/2 In. 24.00

Vase, 6 1/2 In. 35.00

ANNIVERSARY ROSE

Anniversary Rose was made by Anchor Hocking Glass Corporation, Lancaster, Ohio, in 1964 and 1965. The white dishes have pink and green rose decals and gold edges.

Bowl, 4 5/8 In. 6.00

Cup & Saucer .... 6.00 to 8.00

Plate, Dinner 9.00

APPLE BLOSSOM
See Dogwood

ARDITH

Paden City Glass Manufacturing Co., Paden City, West Virginia, opened its etching department in 1924. The Ardith etching has flowers that look like cherry blossoms. It was used on many of Paden City's patterns and is available in many colors, including Black, Blue, Green, Pink, and Yellow.

Black

Candlestick, 5 1/2 In. 95.00

Creamer 65.00

Vase, Elliptical, 5 In. ... 150.00

Green

Candlestick 95.00

Candy Dish, Square,
Cover 150.00

Gravy Boat 80.00

Pink

Plate, Dinner,
10 3/4 In. .. 125.00 to 135.00

Vase, 8 In. 250.00

Yellow

Bowl, Footed, 11 In. 55.00

Cup 35.00

ARDITH
See also Crow's Foot

AUNT POLLY

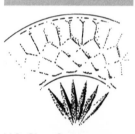

U.S. Glass Company, a firm with factories in Indiana, Ohio, Pennsylvania, and West Virginia, made Aunt Polly glass. Luncheon sets can be found in Blue, Green, and Iridescent. Pink pieces have been reported. The pattern was made in the late 1920s until c.1935.

Blue

Berry Bowl, 4 3/4 In. 18.00

Berry Bowl, Master,
7 7/8 In. ..... 50.00 to 60.00

Bowl, Oval,
8 3/8 In. 150.00

Butter,
Cover ..... 225.00 to 250.00

Candy Dish, 2 Handles,
Footed 43.00
Creamer 49.00
Cup 15.00
Cup & Saucer 24.00
Pickle, 2 Handles,
Oval, 7 1/4 In. 135.00
Pitcher, 48 Oz.,
8 In. 275.00
Plate, Luncheon,
8 In. 25.00
Sherbet . . . . 10.00 to 16.00
Tumbler,
8 Oz. . . . . 32.00 to 37.00

Green

Butter,
Cover . . . . 270.00 to 284.00
Candy Dish, 2 Handles,
Footed 33.00
Sherbet 13.00
Sugar, Cover 55.00

AURORA

The Hazel Atlas Glass Company made Aurora pattern glass in the late 1930s. Fewer than ten different pieces were made in Cobalt Blue and Pink, an even smaller quantity in Crystal and Green.

Cobalt Blue

Bowl, Cereal,
5 3/8 In. . . . . . 13.00 to 20.00
Bowl, Deep,
4 1/2 In. . . . . . 45.00 to 80.00
Creamer,
4 1/2 In. . . . . . 15.00 to 30.00
Cup . . . . 15.00 to 22.00
Cup & Saucer . . 15.00 to 25.00
Plate,
6 1/2 In. . . . . . 12.00 to 15.00
Saucer . . . . 5.00 to 8.00
Tumbler, 10 Oz.,
4 3/4 In. . . . . . 18.00 to 29.00

Pink

Bowl, Cereal,
5 3/8 In. . . . . . 12.00 to 30.00
Cup . . . . 14.00 to 15.00
Saucer 6.00

AVOCADO

Although the center fruit looks like a pear, the pattern has been named Avocado. It was made originally from 1923 to 1933 by the Indiana Glass Company, Dunkirk, Indiana, primarily in Green and Pink. Some Crystal pieces were also produced. In 1974, Tiara reissued a line of pitchers and tumblers in Amethyst, Blue, Frosted Pink, Green, Pink, and Red. By 1982, pieces were made in Amber. The pattern is sometimes called Sweet Pear or No. 601.

Crystal

Bowl, 2 Handles, Oval,
8 In. 18.00
Bowl, 9 1/2 In. 52.00
Bowl, Deep, 9 1/2 In. . . . 20.00
Bowl, Salad,
7 1/2 In. . . . . . 12.00 to 18.00
Pickle, 9 In. 15.00

Green

Bowl, 2 Handles,
5 1/4 In. 35.00
Bowl, 2 Handles, Oval,
8 In. . . . . 30.00 to 36.00
Bowl, Handle,
7 In. . . . . 25.00 to 32.00
Bowl, Salad,
7 1/2 In. . . . . . 55.00 to 65.00
Cup 42.00
Pickle, 9 In. 42.00

Plate, Luncheon,
8 1/4 In. . . . . . 20.00 to 30.00
Plate, Sherbet,
6 3/8 In. . . . . . 15.00 to 18.00
Relish, Footed,
6 In. . . . . 33.00 to 39.00
Saucer 28.00
Sherbet . . . . 60.00 to 75.00
Sugar, Footed . . . 35.00 to 45.00

Pink

Bowl, 2 Handles,
5 1/4 In. 28.00
Bowl, Deep, 9 1/2 In. . . 165.00
Bowl, Handle,
7 In. . . . . 28.00 to 35.00
Bowl, Salad, 7 1/2 In. . . . 50.00
Cup 45.00
Cup & Saucer 55.00
Plate, Luncheon,
8 1/4 In. . . . . . 19.00 to 24.00
Plate, Sherbet,
6 3/8 In. . . . . . 18.00 to 25.00
Saucer 22.00
Tumbler, Footed 20.00

B PATTERN
See Dogwood

BALLERINA
See Cameo

BAMBOO OPTIC

Bamboo Optic pattern was made by Liberty Works of Egg Harbor, New Jersey, about 1929. Green and Pink luncheon sets and other pieces were made. The pattern resembles Octagon.

Green

Bowl, 4 1/4 In. 7.00
Cup . . . . 5.00 to 7.00
Cup & Saucer 8.00

Sandwich Server, Center
Handle, 10 1/2 In. 45.00
Sugar & Creamer 26.00

Pink
Creamer 13.00
Sandwich Server, Center
Handle, 10 1/2 In. 59.00
Soup, Dish, 7 1/4 In. 95.00

BANDED CHERRY
See Cherry Blossom

BANDED FINE RIB
See Coronation

BANDED PETALWARE
See Petalware

BANDED RAINBOW
See Ring

BANDED RIBBON
See New Century

BANDED RINGS
See Ring

BAROQUE

Fostoria Glass Company of Moundsville, West Virginia, made Baroque, or No. 2496, from 1936 to 1966. The dishes have molded fleur-de-lis-shaped handles and ridges. The pattern was made in Amber, Amethyst, Azure (blue), Cobalt Blue, Crystal, Green, Pink, Red, and Topaz (yellow). The same

molds were used to make other glass patterns decorated with etched designs.

Azure
Bowl, 2 Sections,
6 1/2 In. 25.00
Candy Dish, Cover 140.00
Compote, 4 3/4 In. 30.00
Creamer 22.00
Cup & Saucer 32.00
Plate, Dinner, 9 1/2 In. . . 75.00
Salt & Pepper 135.00
Soup, Cream,
Underplate 325.00
Sugar 15.00
Tumbler, Iced Tea,
14 Oz., 5 7/8 In. 130.00
Tumbler, Old Fashioned,
6 1/2 Oz., 3 1/2 In. . . . 125.00
Tumbler, Water, Footed,
9 Oz., 5 1/2 In. 23.00
Vase, 6 1/2 In. 115.00
Vase, 7 In. . . . 125.00 to 150.00

Crystal
Bowl, 4-Footed,
2 Handles, 10 1/2 In. . . 15.00
Bowl, Flared, 12 In. 22.00
Bowl, Jelly, Cover 40.00
Candlestick, 2-Light,
4 1/2 In. 15.00
Candlestick, 2-Light,
Prisms, 4 1/2 In.,
Pair . . . . 90.00 to 155.00
Candlestick,
5 1/2 In., Pair 50.00
Cup 9.00
Goblet, Water, 9 Oz.,
6 3/4 In. 42.00
Plate, Bread & Butter,
6 In. 10.00
Plate, Dinner, 9 1/2 In. . . 65.00
Platter, 14 In. 40.00
Saucer 4.00
Tumbler, Iced Tea,
14 Oz., 5 3/4 In. 40.00

Topaz
Candlestick, 5 1/2 In.,
Pair 80.00
Nut Dish, Footed, 7 In. . . 25.00

BASKET
See No. 615

BEADED BLOCK

Imperial Glass Company, Bellaire, Ohio, made Beaded Block from the 1920s to the 1950s. It was made in Crystal, Green, Ice Blue, Pink, Red, and White, as well as several opalescent colors, including Amber, Blue, Canary (vaseline), and Green. Iridescent Marigold pieces were also made. The molds originally had stippling in the blocks, leading collectors to call the early pieces "Frosted Block." Some Iridescent Pink pieces made recently have been found marked with the IG trademark used from 1951 to 1977.

Amber
Plate, 8 3/4 In. . . 18.00 to 20.00
Plate, Square, 7 3/4 In. . . . 8.00

Blue
Vase, 6 In. . . . . . 17.00 to 45.00

Crystal
Creamer, Footed 25.00
Pitcher, 1 Pt.,
5 1/4 In. . . . . 90.00 to 100.00
Sugar, Footed 22.00
Sugar & Creamer,
Footed . . . . 45.00 to 49.00

Green
Creamer, Footed 29.00
Plate, Square, 7 3/4 In. . . 25.00

Iridescent
Bowl, Flared, 7 1/2 In. 40.00

Pink
Bowl, 5 3/4 In. 38.00
Parfait 28.00

Vase, 5 1/4 In. . . 18.00 to 22.00
Vase, Frank Tea &
   Spice Co., 5 1/4 In. 75.00

BEADED EDGE

Collectors call Westmore-
land Glass Company's No.
22 pattern Beaded Edge.
The dishes are a plain
shape with "beads" around
the edges. The pattern
was produced mostly in
Milk Glass from the late
1930s to the 1950s and is
often decorated with
enameled flowers, birds,
or fruit. Crystal and other
colors can be found, too.

Crystal
Bowl, Scalloped Rim 9.00
Plate, Bread & Butter,
   6 In. 9.00
Plate, Dinner,
   10 1/2 In. 12.00
Plate, Luncheon,
   8 1/2 In. 8.00
Plate, Salad, 7 In. 10.00

Milk Glass
Bowl, 5 In. 5.00
Bowl, Oval, Crimped,
   Blackberries, 6 In. 22.00
Cup, Blackberry 12.00
Cup, Cherry 12.00
Cup & Saucer 7.00
Plate, Blackberries,
   7 1/2 In. 15.00
Plate, Cherries, 7 In. 15.00
Plate, Peaches, 7 1/2 In. . . 15.00
Plate, Plums, 7 1/2 In. . . . 15.00
Plate, Salad, Apple,
   7 In. 14.00

Plate, Strawberries,
   7 1/2 In. . . . . . 12.00 to 15.00

BERWICK
See Bubble

BEVERAGE WITH
  SAILBOATS
See White Ship

BIG RIB
See Manhattan

BLACK FOREST

Black Forest was first
made in 1930 by Paden
City Glass Manufacturing
Company, Paden City,
West Virginia. The etching
pictures a moose and
trees. The dishes were
distributed by Van Deman
& Son, New York City,
and came in Amber, Black
with gold, Cobalt Blue,
Green, Light Blue, Pink,
and Red.

Black
Bowl, 11 In. 170.00
Bowl, Handles, 10 In. . . 100.00
Vase, 6 1/2 In. 175.00
Vase, 10 In. 200.00

Green
Console,
   13 In. . . . . 250.00 to 300.00
Sandwich Tray, Center
   Handle 80.00
Vase, 10 In. 300.00

Pink
Bowl, Fruit,
   11 3/4 In. 250.00

Candlestick, Footed, 2 In.,
   Pair 125.00

BLOCK
See Block Optic

BLOCK OPTIC

Block Optic, sometimes
called Block, was made
from 1929 to 1933 by the
Hocking Glass Company,
Lancaster, Ohio. Slight
variations in the design of
some pieces, like creamers
and sugars, show that the
pattern was redesigned at
times. Green is the most
common color, followed
by Crystal, Pink, and Yellow. Amber and Blue ex-
amples are harder to find.
Some pieces were made
with a black stem or a
black flat foot.

Amber
Candlestick, 1 3/4 In.,
   Pair 35.00
Console, Rolled Edge,
   11 3/4 In. 55.00

Crystal
Candy Jar, Cover 50.00
Goblet, 9 Oz.,
   5 3/4 In. . . . . . 12.00 to 28.00
Goblet, Wine, 4 1/2 In. . . . 8.00
Pitcher, 54 Oz.,
   8 1/2 In. . . . . . 30.00 to 50.00
Pitcher, 80 Oz., 8 In. 60.00
Plate, Dinner, 9 In. 10.00
Plate, Sherbet, 6 In. 2.00

Sandwich Server,
10 1/4 In. 20.00

Sherbet, 5 1/2 Oz.,
3 1/4 In. 5.00

Sherbet, 6 Oz.,
4 3/4 In. . . . . . . 7.00 to 14.00

Green

Berry Bowl,
4 1/4 In. . . . . . 10.00 to 31.00

Berry Bowl, Master,
8 1/2 In. . . . . . 30.00 to 80.00

Bottle, Water 15.00

Bowl, Cereal,
5 1/4 In. . . . . . 12.00 to 22.00

Bowl, Salad, 7 1/4 In. . . 165.00

Butter, Cover . . . 30.00 to 55.00

Candlestick, 1 3/4 In.,
Pair 130.00

Candy Jar, Cover,
2 1/4 In. . . . . . 65.00 to 70.00

Candy Jar, Cover,
6 1/4 In. . . . . . 50.00 to 65.00

Console, Rolled Edge,
11 3/4 In. 120.00

Console, Rolled Edge,
14 In. 45.00

Creamer, Cone . . 14.00 to 15.00

Cup, Black Foot 25.00

Cup, Curly Handle 7.00

Cup, Medium 8.00

Cup, Plain
Handle . . . . 7.00 to 17.00

Cup, Small . . . . 5.00 to 7.50

Cup & Saucer,
Large . . . . 13.00 to 17.00

Cup & Saucer,
Small . . . . . . 17.00 to 18.00

Dish, Mayonnaise,
Footed . . . . 35.00 to 80.00

Goblet, 9 Oz., 5 3/4 In. . . 30.00

Goblet, Wine, 4 1/2 In. . . 43.00

Ice Tub . . . . 63.00 to 85.00

Mug . . . . 35.00 to 60.00

Pitcher, 54 Oz.,
8 1/2 In. 65.00

Pitcher, 80 Oz., 8 In. . . . 125.00

Pitcher, Bulbous, 54 Oz.,
7 5/8 In. 85.00

Plate, Dinner,
9 In. . . . . 22.00 to 30.00

Plate, Dinner, Gold Trim,
9 In. 10.00

Plate, Dinner, Snowflake
Design, 9 In. 26.00

Plate, Luncheon,
8 In. . . . . 4.50 to 13.00

Plate, Sherbet,
6 In. . . . . 2.00 to 6.50

Plate, Sherbet, Gold
Trim, 6 In. 3.00

Salt & Pepper,
Footed . . . . . . 35.00 to 96.00

Salt & Pepper,
Squat . . . . . 100.00 to 135.00

Saltshaker, Footed 28.00

Saltshaker, Squat 59.00

Sandwich Server,
10 1/4 In. . . . . 25.00 to 50.00

Saucer,
6 1/8 In. . . . . . 11.00 to 17.00

Saucer, Frosted,
5 3/4 In. 11.00

Sherbet, 5 1/2 Oz.,
3 1/4 In. . . . . . . 6.00 to 12.50

Sherbet, 6 Oz.,
4 3/4 In. . . . . . 15.00 to 17.00

Sherbet, Cone . . . . 4.00 to 8.50

Sherbet, Gold Trim,
6 Oz., 4 3/4 In. 20.00

Sugar, Cone . . . . 11.00 to 14.00

Sugar, Squat 15.00

Sugar & Creamer,
Cone . . . . 25.00 to 35.00

Sugar & Creamer,
Squat . . . . 35.00 to 40.00

Tumbler, 5 Oz.,
3 1/2 In. 26.00

Tumbler, 12 Oz.,
4 7/8 In. . . . . . 24.00 to 25.00

Tumbler, 15 Oz.,
5 1/4 In. 50.00

Tumbler, Whiskey,
2 Oz., 2 1/4 In. 20.00

Pink

Bowl, Salad, 7 In. 60.00

Candlestick, 1 3/4 In.,
Pair . . . . 50.00 to 80.00

Candy Jar,
Cover, 2 1/4 In. 65.00

Candy Jar,
Cover, 6 1/4 In. 165.00

Console, Rolled Edge,
11 3/4 In. . . . 60.00 to 122.00

Creamer, Cone . . 12.00 to 16.00

Creamer,
Squat . . . . . . 13.00 to 16.00

Cup . . . . 3.00 to 9.00

Cup, Curly Handle 7.00

Cup, Plain Handle 7.00

Cup & Saucer . . 16.00 to 18.00

Goblet, Cocktail,
4 In. . . . . 40.00 to 48.00

Goblet, Water, 9 Oz.,
5 3/4 In. . . . . . 29.00 to 40.00

Goblet, Wine, 4 1/2 In. . . 48.00

Pitcher, Bulbous,
54 Oz., 7 5/8 In. 75.00

Plate, Luncheon,
8 In. . . . . 5.00 to 15.00

Plate, Sherbet,
6 In. . . . . 3.00 to 6.00

Saltshaker,
Footed . . . . 40.00 to 45.00

Sandwich Server,
10 1/4 In. . . . . 25.00 to 30.00

Sandwich Server, Center
Handle 108.00

Saucer, 6 1/8 In. . . 8.75 to 10.00

Sherbet, 5 Oz.,
3 1/4 In. . . . . . . 7.50 to 9.00

Sherbet, 6 Oz.,
4 3/4 In. . . . . . 18.00 to 20.00

Sugar, Cone . . . . 13.00 to 15.00

Sugar, Squat 11.00

Sugar & Creamer, Cone . . 30.00

Sugar & Creamer, Squat . 15.00

Tumbler, 3 Oz.,
2 5/8 In. 25.00

Tumbler, 5 Oz.,
3 1/2 In. . . . . . 25.00 to 30.00

Tumbler, 9 1/2 Oz.,
3 13/16 In. . . . 15.00 to 18.00

Tumbler, 10 Oz.,
5 In. . . . . 15.00 to 26.00

Tumbler, 11 Oz.,
5 In. . . . . 15.00 to 20.00

Tumbler, 12 Oz.,
4 7/8 In. . . . . . 28.00 to 30.00

Tumbler, Footed, 3 Oz.,
3 1/4 In. 65.00

Tumbler, Footed,
9 Oz. . . . . 16.00 to 22.00

Tumbler, Footed,
10 Oz., 6 In. 48.00

Tumbler, Whiskey,
1 Oz., 1 5/8 In. 48.00

Tumbler, Whiskey,
2 Oz., 2 1/4 In. 40.00

Yellow

Candy Jar, Cover,
2 1/4 In. . . . . . 25.00 to 75.00

Creamer, Cone 16.00

Creamer, Squat 15.00
Cup .... 6.50 to 12.00
Cup & Saucer .. 15.00 to 16.00
Goblet, Thin, 9 Oz.,
   7 1/4 In. ..... 40.00 to 42.00
Plate, Dinner,
   9 In. .... 45.00 to 55.00
Plate, Luncheon,
   8 In. .... 6.75 to 10.00
Plate, Sherbet, 6 In. 3.50
Salt & Pepper, Footed .. 104.00
Sherbet, 5 1/2 Oz.,
   3 1/4 In. 10.00
Sherbet, 6 Oz.,
   4 3/4 In. ..... 18.00 to 24.00
Sugar, Cone 14.00
Sugar, Squat .... 14.00 to 15.00
Sugar &
   Creamer ..... 29.00 to 40.00
Sugar & Creamer,
   Footed 35.00
Tumbler, Footed, 9 Oz. .. 28.00

BLUE MOSAIC

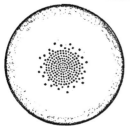

Blue Mosaic dinnerware was made by Anchor Hocking Glass Corporation, Lancaster, Ohio, from 1966 to 1969. The opaque white dishes have a circular mosaic decal. The cup, sugar, and creamer are solid fired-on blue and do not have a decal. Other related patterns are listed in the Fire-King section in this book.

Bowl, Vegetable,
   8 1/4 In. 12.00
Cup 5.00

Plate, Dinner, 10 In. 4.00
Plate, Salad, 7 1/4 In. 5.00
Saucer 1.00
Snack Plate, Oval, 10 In. .. 8.00

BOOPIE
See Bubble

BOUQUET & LATTICE
See Normandie

BOWKNOT

The Bowknot pattern remains a mystery, although it probably dates from the late 1920s. The manufacturer is still unidentified. The swags and bows of the pattern were mold-etched. There does not seem to be a full dinner set of this pattern. Only the 7-inch plate, cup, sherbet, two sizes of bowls, and two types of 10-ounce tumblers have been found. Green pieces are found easily. The pattern was also made in Crystal.

Green
Berry Bowl, 4 1/2 In. 24.00
Cup .... 11.00 to 16.00
Plate, Salad,
   7 In. .... 12.00 to 18.00
Sherbet .... 21.00 to 24.00
Tumbler, Footed, 10 Oz.,
   5 In. .... 25.00 to 28.00

BRIDAL BOUQUET
See No. 615

❖

Never leave a note outside explaining you're not at home. It invites burglars.

❖

BUBBLE

Names of Depression glass patterns can be depressingly confusing. Bubble is also known as Bullseye, the original name given by Anchor Hocking Glass Corporation, and as Provincial or Early American Line from 1960s ads. The stemware made to match the dishes was called Boopie, Berwick, or Inspiration in ads. The pattern was made from 1941 to 1968 in Crystal, Forest Green, Iridescent, Jade-ite, Pink, Royal Ruby, Sapphire Blue, White, and fired-on colors. Some Desert Gold (amber) pieces have been seen. The dishes, excluding items made in Forest Green and Royal Ruby, are heat-proof. The 4 1/2- and 8-inch bowls were reissued in Royal Ruby by Anchor Hocking. They are marked with the anchor trademark. Other related patterns are listed in the Fire-King section in this book.

Crystal
Berry Bowl,
   4 In. .... 3.00 to 12.00
Berry Bowl, Master,
   8 3/8 In. ...... 5.00 to 12.00
Bowl, Cereal,
   5 1/4 In. .... 5.00 to 8.00
Bowl, Fruit,
   4 1/2 In. .... 3.50 to 8.00

Candlestick, Colored
Flowers 95.00
Candlestick,
Pair .... 10.00 to 28.00
Creamer .... 6.00 to 10.00
Cup .... 3.00 to 8.00
Goblet, Cocktail,
3 1/2 Oz. .... 2.00 to 4.00
Goblet, Cocktail,
4 1/2 Oz. 4.00
Goblet, Green Stem,
9 1/2 Oz. 13.00
Goblet, Water,
9 Oz. .... 5.00 to 8.00
Plate, Bread & Butter,
6 3/4 In. .... 1.00 to 4.00
Plate, Dinner,
9 3/8 In. .... 6.00 to 8.00
Saucer 2.00
Sherbet, 6 Oz. 3.00
Sherbet, 9 Oz. 7.00
Sherbet, Green Stem,
6 Oz. 9.00
Soup, Dish,
7 3/4 In. ...... 7.00 to 14.00
Sugar .... 9.00 to 12.00
Sugar & Creamer 15.00
Tumbler, Footed,
8 Oz. 15.00
Tumbler, Iced Tea, Footed,
14 Oz. .... 15.00 to 25.00
Tumbler, Juice,
6 Oz. 10.00
Tumbler, Juice, Footed,
4 Oz. .... 4.50 to 6.50
Tumbler, Juice, Footed,
5 Oz. 11.00
Tumbler, Old Fashioned,
Footed, 8 Oz. 9.00
Tumbler, Water, 9 Oz. ... 13.00

Desert Gold
Goblet, Cocktail,
3 1/2 Oz. 10.00
Plate, 6 In. 5.00

Forest Green
Berry Bowl, Master,
8 3/8 In. 20.00
Bowl, Cereal,
5 1/4 In. ..... 15.00 to 25.00
Candlestick 79.00
Creamer .... 9.00 to 18.00
Cup .... 9.00 to 10.00
Cup & Saucer .. 15.00 to 22.00

Goblet, Cocktail,
4 1/2 Oz. ..... 12.00 to 19.00
Goblet, Juice, 4 Oz. 15.00
Goblet, Water,
9 Oz. .... 13.00 to 20.00
Plate, Bread & Butter,
6 3/4 In. 15.00
Plate, Dinner,
9 3/8 In. ..... 25.00 to 30.00
Saucer 4.00
Sherbet, 6 Oz. ... 9.00 to 12.00
Sugar .... 9.00 to 18.00
Sugar &
Creamer ..... 29.00 to 45.00

Iridescent
Bowl, Fruit, 4 1/2 In. 5.00

Jade-ite
Berry Bowl, Shallow,
8 1/2 In. 35.00

Pink
Berry Bowl, Master,
8 3/8 In. ..... 14.00 to 35.00
Saucer 48.00

Royal Ruby
Berry Bowl, 4 3/4 In. 7.00
Berry Bowl, Master,
8 3/8 In. ..... 18.00 to 25.00
Bowl, Fruit,
4 1/2 In. ..... 12.00 to 13.00
Cup .... 8.00 to 12.00
Cup & Saucer .. 12.00 to 18.00
Goblet, Cocktail,
3 1/2 Oz. 18.00
Goblet, Cocktail,
4 1/2 Oz. 15.00
Goblet, Water, 9 Oz. 18.00
Pitcher, Ice Lip,
64 Oz. .... 55.00 to 72.00
Plate, Dinner,
9 3/8 In. ..... 24.00 to 30.00
Sherbet, 6 Oz. 15.00
Tumbler, Iced Tea, 12 Oz.,
4 1/2 In. ..... 10.00 to 16.00
Tumbler, Juice,
6 Oz. .... 8.00 to 12.00
Tumbler, Lemonade, 16 Oz.,
5 7/8 In. ..... 15.00 to 22.00
Tumbler, Old Fashioned, 8 Oz.,
3 1/4 In. ..... 15.00 to 17.00
Tumbler, Water,
9 Oz. 12.00

Sapphire Blue
Berry Bowl, 4 In. 10.00

Berry Bowl, Master,
8 3/8 In. ..... 12.00 to 22.00
Bowl, Cereal,
5 1/4 In. ..... 11.00 to 22.00
Bowl, Fruit,
4 1/2 In. ..... 10.00 to 16.00
Creamer ...... 25.00 to 45.00
Cup .... 3.50 to 5.50
Cup & Saucer ... 4.50 to 10.00
Grill Plate,
9 3/8 In. ..... 20.00 to 25.00
Plate, Bread & Butter,
6 3/4 In. .... 2.00 to 7.00
Plate, Dinner,
9 3/8 In. ...... 6.00 to 12.00
Platter, Oval,
12 In. .... 11.00 to 21.00
Saucer .... .75 to 3.00
Soup, Dish,
7 3/4 In. ..... 11.00 to 19.00
Sugar .... 14.00 to 29.00
Sugar &
Creamer ..... 60.00 to 62.50

White
Berry Bowl, Master,
8 3/8 In. ..... 6.50 to 10.00
Bowl, Fruit,
4 1/2 In. 4.50
Creamer .... 3.00 to 9.00
Sugar 6.00
Sugar &
Creamer ...... 8.00 to 15.00

BULLSEYE
See Bubble

BURPLE

Burple is not a mistype,
but a real name used by
the factory. Anchor Hock-
ing Glass Corporation,
Lancaster, Ohio, made
Crystal, Forest Green, and
Ruby Red dessert sets in
this pattern in the 1940s.

There are also two sizes of bowls.

Crystal
Berry Bowl, Master,
8 1/2 In. 10.00
Bowl, Fruit,
4 1/2 In. . . . . . . 2.50 to 4.50

Forest Green
Berry Bowl, Master,
8 1/2 In. . . . . . 12.00 to 30.00
Bowl, Fruit,
4 1/2 In. . . . . . . 5.00 to 7.00

BUTTERFLIES & ROSES
See Flower Garden with Butterflies

BUTTONS & BOWS
See Holiday

CABBAGE ROSE
See Sharon

CABBAGE ROSE
WITH SINGLE ARCH
See Rosemary

CAMEO

Cameo is also called Ballerina or Dancing Girl because the most identifiable feature of the etched pattern is the silhouette of the dancer. This pattern must have sold well when made by Hocking Glass Company from 1930 to 1934, because many different pieces were made, from dinner sets and servers to cookie jars and lamps. The pattern was

made in Crystal, sometimes with a platinum trim, and in Green, Pink, and Yellow. In 1981, reproductions were made of both Green and Pink salt and pepper shakers. Children's dishes have recently been made in Green, Pink, and Yellow; there were never any old Cameo children's dishes.

Crystal
Bottle, Water 35.00
Bowl, Cereal, Platinum
Trim, 5 1/2 In. 7.00
Cup, Platinum Trim 6.00
Plate, Salad, Platinum
Trim, 7 In. 4.00
Sherbet, 3 1/8 In. 16.00
Tumbler, 11 Oz., 5 In. . . . 22.00

Green
Berry Bowl, Master,
8 1/4 In. . . . . . 40.00 to 45.00
Bowl, Cereal,
5 1/2 In. . . . . . 35.00 to 45.00
Bowl, Salad,
7 1/4 In. 90.00
Bowl, Vegetable, Oval,
10 In. . . . . . . 22.00 to 45.00
Butter,
Cover . . . . . 250.00 to 280.00
Cake Plate, 3-Footed,
10 In. . . . . . . 25.00 to 40.00
Candlestick, 4 In.,
Pair . . . . . . 150.00 to 165.00
Candy Jar, Cover,
4 In. . . . . . . 90.00 to 105.00
Candy Jar, Cover,
6 1/4 In. 250.00
Compote, 5 In. . 39.00 to 65.00
Console, 3-Footed,
11 In. . . . . . . 85.00 to 95.00
Cookie Jar 47.00
Cookie Jar, Cover 65.00
Creamer, 3 1/4 In. 25.00
Creamer,
4 1/4 In. . . . . 30.00 to 75.00
Cup . . . . 12.00 to 17.00
Cup & Saucer . . 19.00 to 26.00
Decanter, Frosted,
Stopper, 10 In. 30.00

Decanter, Stopper Only . . 65.00
Decanter, Stopper,
10 In. . . . . . 135.00 to 245.00
Dish,
Mayonnaise . . . 42.00 to 50.00
Goblet, Water,
6 In. . . . . . . 65.00 to 75.00
Goblet, Wine,
4 In. . . . . . . 75.00 to 120.00
Grill Plate,
10 1/2 In. . . . . 12.00 to 18.00
Ice Bowl, 3 x
5 1/2 In. . . . 200.00 to 210.00
Jam Jar, Cover, 2 In. . . . 245.00
Pitcher, 20 Oz.,
5 3/4 In. 475.00
Pitcher, 36 Oz., 6 In. 60.00
Pitcher, 56 Oz.,
8 1/2 In. . . . . . 60.00 to 85.00
Plate, Closed Handles,
10 1/2 In. . . . . 13.00 to 28.00
Plate, Dinner,
9 1/2 In. . . . . . 20.00 to 29.50
Plate, Luncheon,
8 In. . . . . 9.00 to 15.00
Plate, Sherbet,
6 In. . . . . 4.00 to 8.00
Plate, Square,
8 1/2 In. . . . . . 50.00 to 75.00
Platter, Oval, Closed Handles,
12 In. . . . . . . 20.00 to 30.00
Relish, 3 Sections, Footed,
7 1/2 In. . . . . . 27.00 to 45.00
Salt & Pepper . . . 78.00 to 90.00
Saltshaker . . . . . 45.00 to 55.00
Sandwich Server,
10 In. . . . . . . 10.00 to 20.00
Saucer, 6 In. 4.00
Sherbet,
3 1/8 In. . . . . . 15.00 to 18.00
Sherbet,
4 7/8 In. . . . . . 35.00 to 45.00
Soup, Cream,
4 3/4 In. . . . 195.00 to 200.00
Soup, Dish, Rim,
9 In. . . . . 74.00 to 79.00
Sugar,
3 1/4 In. . . . . . 20.00 to 25.00
Sugar,
4 1/4 In. . . . . . 30.00 to 32.00
Tray, Domino,
7 In. . . . . . . 250.00 to 275.00
Tumbler, 10 Oz.,
4 3/4 In. 44.00

Tumbler, 11 Oz.,
   5 In. . . . . 39.00 to 50.00
Tumbler, Footed, 10 Oz.,
   4 3/4 In. 50.00
Tumbler, Footed, 11 Oz.,
   5 3/4 In. . . . . . 70.00 to 87.00
Tumbler, Juice, 5 Oz.,
   3 3/4 In. . . . . . 30.00 to 45.00
Tumbler, Juice, Footed, 3 Oz.,
   3 3/8 In. . . . . 75.00 to 110.00
Tumbler, Water, 9 Oz.,
   4 In. . . . . 33.00 to 35.00
Tumbler, Water, Footed,
   9 Oz., 5 In. . . . 30.00 to 35.00
Vase,
   5 3/4 In. . . . 275.00 to 375.00
Vase, 8 In. . . . . . 40.00 to 65.00

Pink

Bowl, Cereal, 5 1/2 In. . . . 285.00
Console, 3-Footed,
   11 In. 120.00
Salt & Pepper 1200.00
Sandwich Server, 10 In. . . 75.00
Sugar & Creamer 365.00

Yellow

Bowl, 4 In. 8.00
Bowl, Cereal,
   5 1/2 In. . . . . . 40.00 to 48.00
Bowl, Vegetable, Oval . . . 50.00
Candy Jar, Cover,
   4 In. 115.00
Creamer . . . . 14.00 to 18.00
Cup . . . . 5.00 to 10.00
Cup & Saucer . . 14.00 to 18.00
Goblet, Wine, 2 7/8 In. . . 10.00
Grill Plate,
   10 1/2 In. . . . . 10.00 to 17.00
Grill Plate, Closed Handles,
   10 1/2 In. . . . . 12.00 to 14.00
Plate, Dinner,
   9 1/2 In. . . . . . . 9.00 to 15.00
Plate, Luncheon, 8 In. . . . 11.00
Plate, Sherbet,
   6 In. . . . . 3.00 to 6.00
Platter, Oval, Closed Handle,
   12 In. . . . . 48.00 to 50.00
Saucer 3.50
Sherbet, 3 1/8 In. 40.00
Sherbet,
   4 7/8 In. . . . . . 40.00 to 42.00
Soup, Cream, 4 3/4 In. 8.00
Sugar,
   3 1/4 In. . . . . . 18.00 to 20.00

Sugar & Creamer 45.00
Tumbler, Footed,
   9 Oz., 5 In. 27.00

CANDLEWICK

Candlewick was made by Imperial Glass Company, Bellaire, Ohio, from 1936 to 1984. A few pieces are still being made. Many similar patterns have been made by other companies. The beaded edge is the only design. Although the glass was first made in Crystal, it has also been produced in Black, Nut Brown, Sunshine Yellow, Ultra Blue, and Verde (green). Some pieces of Crystal are decorated with gold. Pieces have been found in Amber, Lavender, Pink, Red, and with fired-on gold, red, blue, or green beading. Some sets were made with cuttings, etchings, and hand-painted designs. Reproductions have been made.

Black

Bowl, Lily, 4-Footed,
   7 In. 550.00
Plate, 2 Handles, 7 In. . . 375.00

Crystal

Ashtray, 4 In. . . . 12.00 to 18.00
Ashtray, 5 In. 8.00

Ashtray,
   6 In. . . . . . 135.00 to 165.00
Ashtray, Eagle 65.00
Ashtray, Heart Shape,
   4 In. . . . . 9.00 to 10.00
Ashtray, Rectangular,
   4 1/2 x 3 In. 8.50
Basket, Handle,
   5 In. . . . . . 255.00 to 325.00
Bonbon, Brass Base,
   6 In. 20.00
Bonbon, Sterling Base,
   6 In. 30.00
Bowl, 10 1/2 In. 60.00
Bowl, 12 In. 90.00
Bowl, 2 Handles,
   8 1/4 In. 45.00
Bowl, 2 Handles,
   10 In. 115.00
Bowl, 2 Sections,
   6 1/2 In. . . . . . 28.00 to 45.00
Bowl, 2 Sections, Oval,
   11 In. . . . . 450.00 to 550.00
Bowl, 3-Footed, 6 In. 75.00
Bowl, 3-Footed, 10 In. . . 175.00
Bowl, Float, 11 In. 45.00
Bowl, Float,
   12 In. . . . . . . 55.00 to 60.00
Bowl, Fruit, 5 In. 20.00
Bowl, Heart, 5 1/2 In. . . . 45.00
Bowl, Heart, 9 In. 225.00
Bowl, Heart, Handle,
   5 In. 35.00
Bowl, Heart, Handle,
   6 In. 45.00
Bowl, Ivy, Footed,
   7 In. 275.00
Bowl, Round, 2 Sections,
   6 1/2 In. 22.00
Bowl, Salad,
   10 In. . . . . 40.00 to 50.00
Bowl, Square, 5 In. 150.00
Bowl, Square, 7 In. 160.00
Bowl, Sterling Base,
   10 In. 325.00
Butter, Cover, 6 In. 44.00
Butter & Jam, 3 Sections,
   10 1/2 In. 210.00
Cake Plate, Birthday,
   72 Candleholders,
   14 In. 500.00
Cake Stand, 11 In. 85.00
Cake Stand, Sterling
   Base, 10 In. 65.00

Candleholder, Beaded
Handle, 3 1/2 In. 42.00
Candleholder, Flower
Insert, 5 In., 2 Piece . . 125.00
Candleholder, Flower
Insert, 9 In.,
2 Piece . . . . 275.00 to 295.00
Candlestick, Mushroom . . 40.00
Candlestick, Square,
Pair 195.00
Candy Box, Cover, 3 Sections,
7 In. . . . . . 100.00 to 135.00
Candy Dish, Cover,
7 In. 150.00
Celery Dish, 2 Handles,
13 1/2 In. 25.00
Celery Dish, Oval,
8 3/8 In. 33.00
Chip & Dip, 2 Sections,
14 In. 650.00
Cocktail Muddler 39.00
Compote,
5 In. . . . . . 135.00 to 145.00
Compote, 7 In. 125.00
Compote, Sterling Base . . 30.00
Creamer, 2 3/4 In. 28.00
Creamer, 3 In. 33.00
Cruet, Handle, 4 Oz. 95.00
Cup . . . . 8.00 to 10.00
Cup & Saucer 18.00
Cup & Saucer, After
Dinner . . . . . . 25.00 to 32.00
Decanter, Stopper,
18 Oz. . . . . 650.00 to 1100.00
Deviled Egg Server,
Center Heart Handle,
11 1/2 In. 175.00
Dish, Mayonnaise, 2 Sections,
Underplate 80.00
Dish, Mayonnaise,
3 Sections 65.00
Dish, Mayonnaise,
Ladle 50.00
Goblet, 10 Oz. . . 23.00 to 30.00
Goblet, Cordial, 1 Oz. . . . 40.00
Goblet, Water,
9 Oz. . . . . 20.00 to 30.00
Goblet, Wine,
4 Oz. . . . . 28.00 to 30.00
Ice Tub,
7 In. . . . . . 195.00 to 205.00
Icer, Seafood Insert,
2 Piece . . . . 90.00 to 135.00
Knife 550.00

Ladle, Marmalade,
3 Beads 16.00
Ladle, Punch 85.00
Marmalade, Cover, Footed,
Spoon, Underplate . . . 100.00
Pitcher,
40 Oz. . . . . . 195.00 to 325.00
Pitcher,
80 Oz. . . . . . 210.00 to 320.00
Plate, 2 Handles,
10 In. . . . . 38.00 to 45.00
Plate, 2 Handles,
5 1/2 In. 25.00
Plate, 2 Handles,
Crimped, 10 In. 30.00
Plate, 4 1/2 In. 9.00
Plate, Bread & Butter,
6 In. . . . . 9.00 to 11.00
Plate, Canape, 6 In. 17.00
Plate, Crimped Edge,
Handles, 12 In. 58.00
Plate, Salad, 7 In. 12.00
Plate, Salad,
8 In. . . . . 9.00 to 15.00
Plate, Salad, Kidney,
8 1/4 In. 18.00
Plate, Service, 12 In. 55.00
Punch Bowl, Cover . . . 1395.00
Punch Cup 8.00
Punch Set, Bowl,
Underplate, Cups,
Ladle, 15 Piece 300.00
Relish, 13 In. 48.00
Relish, 2 Sections,
6 1/2 In. . . . . 18.00 to 25.00
Relish, 2 Sections, 8 In. . . 30.00
Relish, 3 Sections,
3-Footed 125.00
Relish, 4 Sections, 4 Handles,
8 1/2 In. . . . . 30.00 to 35.00
Relish, 5 Sections,
13 In. 75.00
Salt & Pepper, Beaded
Foot . . . . . . 25.00 to 35.00
Salt & Pepper, Beaded
Stem 100.00
Salt & Pepper, Tray 36.00
Sauce Bowl, Underplate,
5 In. 45.00
Saucer 3.00
Sherbet, 6 Oz.,
5 1/4 In. . . . . . .17.00 to 24.00
Soup, Cream,
Underplate 48.00

Sugar & Creamer, Beaded
Handle 45.00
Sugar & Creamer,
Individual 16.00
Sugar & Creamer,
Plain Foot 38.00
Sugar & Creamer, Tray . . 25.00
Teacup 10.00
Teacup & Saucer 25.00
Torte Plate,
14 In. . . . . 25.00 to 45.00
Tray, 2 Handles,
12 x 10 In. 25.00
Tray, 8 In. 45.00
Tray, Cupped 235.00
Tray, Oval, 9 In. 50.00
Tumbler,
12 Oz. . . . . 16.00 to 25.00
Tumbler, 14 Oz. 32.00
Tumbler, Juice, 5 Oz. . . . 14.00
Tumbler, Water, 9 Oz. . . . 14.00
Vase, 8 1/2 In. 450.00
Vase, Crimped Edge,
6 In. 65.00
Vase, Fan, Beaded
Handles, 8 1/2 In. 75.00
Vase, Flip, 8 In. 365.00
Vase, Fluted Rim,
2 Handles, 8 In. 45.00

Red
Bowl, 8 1/2 In. 450.00
Goblet, Crystal Stem
& Foot, 6 In. 100.00

Ultra Blue
Plate, Divided, 7 1/4 In. . . 45.00

CANTERBURY

Duncan & Miller Glass
Company, Washington,
Pennsylvania, introduced
Canterbury in 1937. The
pattern was made in Cape
Cod (opalescent blue),

Chartreuse, Cranberry (opalescent pink), Crystal, Ebony, Jasmine (opalescent yellow), Ruby, Sapphire, and with etchings. Tiffin Glass Company bought some of Duncan's molds in 1955 and continued to make Canterbury.

Crystal

Bowl, 9 In.	30.00
Candlestick, 3 In., Pair	26.00
Cup & Saucer	13.00
Plate, 7 1/2 In.	10.00
Rose Bowl, 6 In.	23.00
Torte Plate, 14 In.	25.00

CAPE COD

Cape Cod was a pattern made by the Imperial Glass Company, Bellaire, Ohio, from 1932. It is usually found in Crystal, but was also made in Amber, Azalea (pink), Black, Evergreen, Heritage Blue, Milk Glass, Ritz Blue, Ruby, and Verde (green). In 1978 the dinner set was reissued. The cruet was reissued in 1986 without the rayed bottom.

Amber

Sherbet	10.00

Crystal

Bottle, Bitters, 4 Oz.	60.00
Bowl, 2 Sections, Oval, 11 In.	95.00
Bowl, Baked Apple, 6 In.	10.00
Bowl, Fruit, 6 In.	7.50 to 10.00

Bowl, Heart, Underplate, 5 In.	12.00
Bread Plate, 12 1/2 In.	7.00
Coaster, 4 1/2 In.	10.00
Coaster, With Spoon Rest	12.00
Console, 13 In.	50.00
Creamer, Footed, 4 3/4 In.	15.00
Cup	7.00
Cup & Saucer	7.00 to 8.00
Decanter, 24 Oz.	65.00
Decanter, 30 Oz.	75.00
Goblet, Claret, 5 Oz.	11.00 to 15.00
Goblet, Cocktail, 3 1/2 Oz.	8.00
Goblet, Cordial, 1 1/2 Oz.	5.00 to 10.00
Goblet, Parfait, 6 Oz.	10.00
Goblet, Sundae, 6 Oz.	7.00
Goblet, Water, 8 Oz.	10.00
Goblet, Water, 9 Oz.	10.00
Goblet, Water, 10 Oz.	10.00
Goblet, Wine, 3 Oz.	5.00 to 8.00
Mug, Beer, 12 Oz.	45.00
Oyster Cocktail	8.00
Pepper Mill	28.00
Plate, 7 In.	8.00
Plate, Cupped, 16 In.	55.00
Plate, Dinner, 10 In.	38.00
Plate, Salad, 8 In.	7.00 to 10.00
Punch Cup	5.50
Salt & Pepper	20.00
Saltshaker, Footed, 4 In.	7.50
Sherbet, 6 Oz., 3 1/2 In.	12.00 to 15.00
Sherbet, 6 Oz., 5 In.	8.00 to 9.00
Sugar & Creamer, Footed, 4 1/4 In.	17.50
Sugar & Creamer, Footed, Tray	35.00
Tumbler, Iced Tea, Footed, 12 Oz.	10.00 to 12.00
Tumbler, Juice, 6 Oz.	10.00
Tumbler, Water, Footed, 10 Oz.	10.00 to 13.00

Ritz Blue

Parfait, 6 Oz.	20.00

CAPRI BLUE

Capri Blue is the name of medium blue glass made in the 1960s by Hazel Atlas, a division of Continental Can Company, Clarksburg, West Virginia. The modern-looking dishes were made in several shapes, including Daisy, El Dorado, Gothic, Moderne, Scanda, Seashell, Simplicity, Skol, Spiral, Swirl, and Twist. Skol was made in other colors, too, and is listed in its own section in this book.

Berry Bowl, Hobnail, 4 7/8 In.	5.00
Berry Bowl, Seashell, 4 7/8 In.	9.00
Bowl, Cereal, Hobnail, 5 1/2 In.	10.00
Bowl, Oval, Simplicity, 9 1/2 In.	18.00 to 19.00
Bowl, Salad, Simplicity, 10 3/4 In.	25.00
Bowl, Seashell, 4 3/4 In.	7.50 to 10.00
Bowl, Seashell, 9 In.	29.00
Bowl, Square, Simplicity, 5 3/4 In.	10.00
Bowl, Square, Simplicity, 10 3/4 In.	29.00
Candy Jar, Cover, Simplicity	35.00
Cup, Seashell	5.50
Cup & Saucer, Hobnail	5.00 to 8.00
Saucer	2.50
Snack Set, Seashell, Cup, Fan Tray, 10 In.	14.00
Tumbler, Simplicity, 5 Oz., 3 In.	6.00
Tumbler, Simplicity, 9 Oz., 4 1/4 In.	6.50
Vase, Swirl, 8 1/2 In.	35.00

CAPRICE

Caprice was advertised in 1936 as the most popular crystal pattern in America. It was made until 1953. Over 200 pieces were included in the line. Frosted pieces are called Alpine Caprice, the name given by the maker, Cambridge Glass Company, Cambridge, Ohio. The sets were made in Amber, Amethyst, Blue, Cobalt Blue, Crystal, Emerald Green, Light Green, Milk Glass, Moonlight Blue, and Pink. Reproductions are being made in Cobalt Blue and Moonlight Blue.

Amber

Decanter, 35 Oz. 250.00
Tumbler, Straight,
  12 Oz. 60.00
Vase, 8 1/2 In. 100.00

Crystal

Ashtray, 4 In. 10.00
Bowl, 4-Footed, 10 In. . . . 15.00
Bowl, Fruit, 4-Footed, 2
  Handles, Oval, 11 In. . . 42.00
Bowl, Fruit, 5 In. 26.00
Candlestick, 2 1/2 In.,
  Pair 35.00
Candlestick, 3-Light,
  Pair 145.00
Creamer, 3 In. 12.00
Cruet, Tray, 5 Oz. 110.00
Cup & Saucer 15.00
Dish, Mayonnaise,
  Underplate 36.00
Goblet, Claret, Thin,
  4 1/2 Oz. 55.00
Goblet, Wine, 2 1/2 Oz. . . 25.00
Ice Bucket 25.00

Plate, 4-Footed, 14 In. . . . 38.00
Plate, Bread & Butter,
  6 1/2 In. 24.00
Plate, Dinner, 9 1/2 In. . . 40.00
Saucer 3.00
Sherbet, 6 Oz. 12.00
Sugar, 3 1/2 In. 8.00
Sugar & Creamer,
  2 1/2 In. 28.00
Tray, Oval, 9 In. 22.00
Tumbler, Footed,
  10 Oz. . . . . . . 16.00 to 18.00
Tumbler, Iced Tea, Footed,
  12 Oz. . . . . . . 15.00 to 22.00
Tumbler, Juice, 5 Oz. . . . 15.00
Tumbler, Juice, Footed,
  5 Oz. . . . . 12.00 to 18.00

Moonlight Blue

Ashtray, Shell, Footed,
  2 1/4 In. 20.00
Ashtray, Triangular,
  3 In. . . . . 10.00 to 12.00
Bonbon, Oval, Footed,
  6 In. . . . . 60.00 to 65.00
Bonbon, Square,
  2 Handles, 6 In. 45.00
Bowl, Belled, 4-Footed,
  9 1/2 In. 150.00
Bowl, Belled, 4-Footed,
  12 1/2 In. . . . 92.00 to 95.00
Bowl, Crimped,
  10 1/2 In. 175.00
Bowl, Crimped, 4-Footed,
  13 In. 145.00
Bowl, Crimped, Square,
  8 1/2 In. 200.00
Bowl, Fruit, 5 3/4 In. 8.50
Bowl, Square, 4-Footed,
  8 In. 150.00
Candlestick, 2 1/2 In.,
  Pair 75.00
Candlestick, 7 In., Pair . . 160.00
Cigarette Box Cover,
  3 1/2 In. 75.00
Compote . . . . . 24.00 to 45.00
Cup & Saucer . . 15.00 to 50.00
Dish, Mayonnaise,
  Underplate 35.00
Goblet, Cocktail,
  3 1/2 Oz. 45.00
Goblet, Water, 9 Oz. 58.00
Goblet, Wine, 3 Oz. 195.00
Ice Bucket 190.00

Pitcher, Ball,
  32 Oz. . . . . . 375.00 to 500.00
Pitcher, Ball, 80 Oz. . . . 360.00
Plate, 16 In. 110.00
Plate, 4-Footed, 14 In. . . 100.00
Plate, Bread & Butter,
  6 1/2 In. 27.00
Plate, Cabaret,
  11 1/2 In. 89.00
Plate, Cabaret, 4-Footed,
  14 In. 90.00
Plate, Dinner, 9 1/2 In. . . 175.00
Relish, 3 Sections,
  8 1/2 In. . . . . . 51.00 to 96.00
Relish, Club 98.00
Relish, Ruffled Top,
  7 1/2 x 1 3/4 In. 35.00
Rose Bowl, 4-In. Flower
  Frog, 6 In. 450.00
Rose Bowl, 4-Footed,
  6 In. 120.00
Rose Bowl, 4-Footed,
  8 In. 250.00
Salt & Pepper,
  Tray . . . . . . 125.00 to 140.00
Sherbet, Thin, 6 Oz. 25.00
Sugar & Creamer,
  Individual 35.00
Tumbler, 5 Oz. . . 55.00 to 85.00
Tumbler, Footed,
  10 Oz. . . . . . . 35.00 to 40.00
Tumbler, Footed, 3 Oz. . . 70.00
Tumbler, Footed,
  5 Oz. . . . . 30.00 to 40.00
Tumbler, Iced Tea,
  12 Oz. . . . . 115.00 to 150.00
Tumbler, Iced Tea, Footed,
  12 Oz. . . . . . . 55.00 to 60.00
Tumbler, Water, Straight,
  9 Oz. 90.00

Pink

Plate, Luncheon,
  8 1/2 In. 35.00

The safest way to store plates is vertically in a rack. Stacking puts too much weight on the dishes on the bottom.

CARIBBEAN

The rippled design of Caribbean is slick and modern in appearance and has attracted many collectors. It was made by Duncan & Miller Glass Company, Washington, Pennsylvania, from 1936 to 1955. Sets were made in Amber, Blue, Crystal, Crystal with Ruby trim, and Red glass. The Duncan & Miller catalogs identify the line as No. 112.

Blue
Cheese Stand 45.00
Pitcher, 16 Oz.,
    4 3/4 In. . . . 275.00 to 300.00
Plate, Luncheon, Opalescent,
    8 1/2 In. 50.00

Crystal
Punch Bowl, 10 In. 100.00
Punch Cup, Amber
    Handle 13.00
Relish, 4 Sections,
    9 1/2 In. 45.00

CENTAUR

The Egyptian sphinx included in the border gave this pattern its original name of Sphinx. Collectors now call it Centaur. It was made by the Lancaster Glass Company, Lancaster, Ohio, in the 1930s. Black, Green, and Yellow glass was made.

Black
Powder Box 175.00

Powder Box, Yellow
    Base 45.00

CENTURY

Century pattern was made by Fostoria Glass Company from 1926 until 1986. It is a plain pattern with a slightly rippled rim. Full dinner sets were made of Crystal.

Crystal
Ashtray, 2 3/4 In. 12.00
Bonbon, 3-Footed,
    7 1/4 In. 24.00
Bowl, 2 Handles, 12 In. . . 36.00
Bowl, Flared, 8 In. 35.00
Bowl, Footed, 11 In. 45.00
Bowl, Fruit, 5 In. 30.00
Bowl, Handle, 5 In. 19.00
Cake Stand, 12 1/4 In. . . . 60.00
Candlestick, 3-Light,
    Prisms, 9 In. 165.00
Candlestick, 4 1/2 In. 55.00
Compote, 4 3/8 In. 14.00
Cruet, Stopper, Oil 60.00
Cup & Saucer . . 16.00 to 18.00
Dish, Preserve, Footed . . . 22.00
Goblet, 10 Oz. 24.00
Goblet, Cocktail,
    3 1/2 Oz., 4 1/2 In. 31.00
Party Set, Cup & Plate . . . 28.00
Pitcher, 16 Oz.,
    6 1/8 In. . . . . . 60.00 to 75.00
Pitcher, 48 Oz.,
    7 1/8 In. 100.00
Plate, Bread & Butter,
    6 1/2 In. 6.00
Plate, Muffin, 9 In. 30.00
Plate, Salad, 7 In. 8.00
Plate, Salad, Crescent,
    7 1/2 In. 37.00
Relish, 3 Sections,
    11 1/8 In. 32.00
Sandwich Server, Center
    Handle, 11 1/2 In. 35.00

Sherbet, 5 1/2 Oz.,
    4 1/2 In. 11.00
Sugar, Footed, 4 In. 12.00
Sugar & Creamer 22.00
Tidbit, 3-Footed,
    8 1/8 In. 25.00
Torte Plate,
    14 In. . . . . . . 30.00 to 33.00
Tray, 2 Handles,
    9 1/8 In. 36.00
Vase, Handle, 7 In. 75.00

CHAIN DAISY
See Adam

CHANTILLY

As late as the 1960s the Jeannette Glass Company, Jeannette, Pennsylvania, made a pattern called Chantilly that is collected by Depression glass buffs. It was made in Crystal and Pink.

Crystal
Bowl, 4-Footed, 13 In. . . . 70.00
Bowl, Footed,
    11 1/2 In. 85.00
Candlestick 100.00
Ice Tub 145.00

Pink
Decanter, 12 Oz. 375.00
Relish, 3 Sections, 9 In. . . 70.00

CHARM

Charm is a pattern of Fire-King dinnerware made

from 1950 to 1954. The square-shaped dishes were made by Anchor Hocking Glass Corporation of Lancaster, Ohio. The dinnerware was made in Azure-ite (opaque blue-white), Forest Green, Jade-ite (opaque green), and Royal Ruby. Collectors often refer to the color name rather than the pattern name when describing these pieces. It is sometimes called Square. Other related patterns are listed in the Fire-King section in this book.

Azure-Ite
Cup	. . . . 4.00 to 6.50
Cup & Saucer	. . . . 3.00 to 9.00
Plate, Dinner, 9 1/4 In.	. . 20.00
Plate, Salad, 6 5/8 In.	. . . . . 7.00
Saucer	. . . . 1.00 to 4.00

Forest Green
Bowl, Dessert, 4 3/4 In.	. . . . . . 7.00 to 10.50
Bowl, Salad, 7 3/8 In.	. . . 20.00
Creamer	. . . . 4.00 to 12.00
Cup	. . . . 5.00
Cup & Saucer	. . . 6.00 to 10.00
Plate, Dinner, 9 1/4 In.	. . . . . 32.00 to 38.00
Plate, Luncheon, 8 3/8 In.	. . . . . . 6.00 to 12.50
Plate, Salad, 6 5/8 In.	. . . . . 10.00 to 11.00
Platter, 11 In.	. . . . 28.00
Soup, Dish, 6 In.	. . . . . . 18.00 to 25.00
Sugar	. . . . 6.00 to 10.00
Sugar & Creamer	. . . . 15.00

Jade-ite
Bowl, Dessert, 4 3/4 In.	. . 16.00
Cup	. . . . 12.00
Plate, Luncheon, 8 3/8 In.	. . . . 35.00
Plate, Salad, 6 5/8 In.	. . . . 30.00
Platter, 11 In.	. . . . 55.00
Saucer, 5 3/8 In.	. . . . 6.00

Royal Ruby
Bowl, Dessert, 4 3/4 In.	. . . . . . 8.00 to 10.00
Cup	. . . . 5.00 to 7.00
Cup & Saucer	. . . . 11.00
Cup & Saucer, Large	. . . . 7.00
Plate, Luncheon, 8 3/8 In.	. . . . . 10.00 to 14.00
Saucer	. . . . 3.00 to 4.00

CHEROKEE ROSE

The Tiffin glass factory can be traced back to the 1840s, when Joseph Beatty made glass in Steubenville, Ohio. The factory failed and was purchased by Alexander Beatty in 1851. He was joined by his sons and moved to Tiffin, Ohio, in 1888. The company became part of U.S. Glass Company in 1892 and was still operating in 1963 when U.S. Glass went bankrupt. Employees bought the plant and it went through several changes of ownership until it closed in 1980. Cherokee Rose was one of the popular glass patterns made by Tiffin in the 1940s and 1950s. The glass was made only in Crystal.

Crystal
Goblet, Cocktail, 3 1/2 In.	. . . . 20.00
Sherbet, 5 1/2 Oz.	. . . . . . 20.00
Tumbler, Iced Tea, Footed, 10 1/2 Oz.	. . . . 35.00

CHERRY
See Cherry Blossom

CHERRY BLOSSOM

Cherry Blossom is one of the most popular Depression glass patterns. It has been called Banded Cherry, Cherry, or Paneled Cherry Blossom by some collectors. The pattern was made by the Jeannette Glass Company, in Jeannette, Pennsylvania, from 1930 to 1939. Full dinner sets, serving pieces, and a child's set were made in a wide range of colors. Pieces were made in Crystal, Delphite (opaque blue), Green, Jadite, Pink, and Red. Molds were changed a number of times, resulting in several shapes and styles for some pieces. Reproductions have been made.

Crystal
Child's Set, 14 Piece	. . . 305.00

Delphite
Berry Bowl, 4 3/4 In.	. . . . 16.00
Berry Bowl, Master, 8 1/2 In.	. . . . 48.00
Bowl, 2 Handles, 9 In.	. . . 35.00
Child's Set, 14 Piece	. . . 325.00 to 425.00
Creamer	. . . . 20.00 to 25.00
Creamer, Child's	. . . . . . 48.00 to 50.00
Cup	. . . . 20.00

Cup, Child's . . . . 39.00 to 45.00
Cup & Saucer 50.00
Cup & Saucer,
   Child's . . . . . . 45.00 to 55.00
Plate, Child's,
   6 In. . . . . 10.00 to 25.00
Plate, Dinner, 9 In. 25.00
Plate, Sherbet,
   6 In. . . . . 10.00 to 13.00
Sandwich Tray, Handles,
   10 1/2 In. 24.00
Saucer . . . . 6.00 to 10.00
Saucer, Child's . . . 7.00 to 8.00
Sugar . . . . 20.00 to 25.00
Sugar, Child's 50.00
Tumbler, 9 Oz.,
   4 1/4 In. 22.00
Tumbler, Footed,
   5 Oz. 20.00
Tumbler, Footed, 9 Oz.,
   4 3/8 In. 25.00
Tumbler, Scalloped Foot,
   8 Oz., 4 1/2 In. 25.00 to 30.00

Green

Berry Bowl,
   4 3/4 In. . . . . . 20.00 to 24.00
Berry Bowl, Master,
   8 1/2 In. . . . . . 50.00 to 60.00
Bowl, Cereal,
   5 3/4 In. . . . . . 46.00 to 52.00
Bowl, Fruit, 3-Footed,
   10 1/2 In. . . 100.00 to 120.00
Bowl, Vegetable, Oval,
   9 In. . . . . 40.00 to 52.00
Butter, Cover . . 85.00 to 125.00
Butter, No
   Cover . . . . . . 35.00 to 45.00
Cake Plate, 3-Footed,
   10 1/4 In. 43.00
Coaster . . . . 12.00 to 20.00
Creamer . . . . 20.00 to 25.00
Cup & Saucer . . 28.00 to 34.00
Grill Plate, 9 In. . 30.00 to 40.00
Mug, 7 Oz. 350.00
Pitcher, 42 Oz.,
   8 In. . . . . 60.00 to 75.00
Pitcher, Footed, 36 Oz.,
   8 In. . . . . 72.00 to 97.00
Plate, Dinner,
   9 In. . . . . 27.00 to 28.00
Plate, Salad,
   7 In. . . . . 22.00 to 27.00
Plate, Sherbet,
   6 In. . . . . 6.00 to 10.00

Platter, Oval,
   11 In. . . . . . . 50.00 to 60.00
Platter, Oval,
   13 In. . . . . . . 55.00 to 75.00
Sandwich Server,
   10 1/2 In. . . . . 33.00 to 40.00
Saucer . . . . 4.00 to 7.00
Sherbet . . . . 18.00 to 24.00
Soup, Dish,
   7 3/4 In. . . . 80.00 to 100.00
Sugar . . . . 17.00 to 22.00
Sugar, Cover . . . 20.00 to 45.00
Sugar & Creamer,
   Cover 49.00
Tumbler, 9 Oz.,
   4 1/4 In. . . . . . 24.00 to 26.00
Tumbler, Footed, 4 Oz.,
   3 3/4 In. . . . . . 20.00 to 30.00
Tumbler, Footed, 9 Oz.,
   4 1/2 In. 24.00
Tumbler, Scalloped Foot,
   8 Oz., 4 1/2 In. 43.00

Pink

Berry Bowl,
   4 3/4 In. . . . . . 19.00 to 30.00
Berry Bowl, Master,
   8 1/2 In. . . . . . 50.00 to 61.00
Bowl, 2 Handles,
   9 In. . . . . 53.00 to 69.00
Bowl, 3-Footed,
   10 1/2 In. 90.00
Bowl, 8 1/2 In. 56.00
Bowl, Cereal,
   5 3/4 In. . . . . . 40.00 to 65.00
Bowl, Fruit, 3-Footed,
   10 1/2 In. 125.00
Bowl, Vegetable, Oval,
   9 In. . . . . 55.00 to 60.00
Butter, Cover . . 90.00 to 125.00
Butter, No Cover 20.00
Cake Plate, 3-Footed,
   10 1/4 In. . . . . 33.00 to 65.00
Child's Set,
   14 Piece . . . 410.00 to 435.00
Coaster, 6 In. . . . 14.00 to 17.00
Creamer . . . . 20.00 to 50.00
Creamer, Child's 50.00
Cup . . . . 20.00 to 45.00
Cup & Saucer . . 23.00 to 50.00
Grill Plate,
   9 In. . . . . 32.00 to 44.00
Pitcher, 36 Oz.,
   6 3/4 In. . . . . . 55.00 to 90.00
Pitcher, 42 Oz., 8 In. 87.00

Pitcher, Footed, 36 Oz.,
   6 3/4 In. 90.00
Pitcher, Footed,
   8 In. . . . . 89.00 to 90.00
Pitcher, Scalloped Foot, 36 Oz.,
   6 3/4 In. . . . . 65.00 to 100.00
Plate, Child's,
   6 In. . . . . 12.50 to 24.00
Plate, Dinner,
   9 In. . . . . 24.00 to 30.00
Plate, Salad,
   7 In. . . . . 25.00 to 32.00
Plate, Sherbet,
   6 In. . . . . 7.00 to 9.00
Platter, 2 Sections,
   13 In. . . . . . . 72.00 to 95.00
Platter, Oval,
   11 In. . . . . . . 49.00 to 60.00
Platter, Oval, 13 In. 125.00
Salt & Pepper 85.00
Sandwich Server, Handles,
   10 1/2 In. . . . . 30.00 to 45.00
Saucer . . . . 5.00 to 6.00
Saucer, Child's 9.50
Sherbet . . . . 17.50 to 24.00
Soup, Dish,
   7 3/4 In. . . . 95.00 to 125.00
Sugar . . . . 6.00 to 14.00
Sugar, Cover . . . 24.00 to 45.00
Sugar & Creamer,
   Cover 60.00
Tumbler, 4 Oz.,
   3 1/2 In. 22.00
Tumbler, 9 Oz.,
   4 1/4 In. 24.00
Tumbler, Iced Tea, 12 Oz.,
   5 In. . . . . 88.00 to 95.00
Tumbler, Juice, Footed, 4 Oz.,
   3 3/4 In. . . . . . 19.00 to 24.00
Tumbler, Scalloped Foot, 8 Oz.,
   4 1/2 In. . . . . . 35.00 to 45.00
Tumbler, Water, Footed, 9 Oz.,
   4 1/2 In. . . . . . 20.00 to 45.00

**Stains on glass can
sometimes be removed
by rubbing the stain
with a cut lemon or
a cloth dipped in
turpentine.**

CHERRY-BERRY

Two similar patterns, Cherry-Berry and Strawberry, can be confusing. If the fruit pictured is a cherry, then the pattern is called Cherry-Berry. If a strawberry is used, then the pattern has that name. The dishes were made by the U.S. Glass Company around 1927 in Crystal, Green, Iridescent Amber, and Pink.

Crystal
Berry Bowl, Deep,
7 1/2 In. 17.00

Green
Berry Bowl, Deep,
7 1/2 In. 32.00
Compote, 5 3/4 In. 35.00
Cup 25.00
Plate, Sherbet, 6 In. 11.00
Sherbet 10.00
Sugar, Cover Only,
Large 55.00
Sugar, Small 20.00

Pink
Berry Bowl, 4 In. 12.00
Sherbet . . . . 11.00 to 12.00

CHERRY-BERRY
See also Strawberry

❖

You can remove paper stickers from glass by spraying them with oil.

❖

CHINEX CLASSIC

Chinex Classic and Cremax are similar patterns made by the Macbeth-Evans Division of Corning Glass Works from about 1938 to 1942. Chinex and Cremax are both words with two meanings. Each is the name of a pattern and the name of a color used for other patterns. Chinex is ivory-colored; Cremax is a bit whiter. Chinex Classic, the dinnerware pattern, has a piecrust edge, and just inside the edge is an elongated feathered scroll. It may have a floral or scenic decal in the center, colored edging, or both. The Cremax pattern has the piecrust edge, but no scroll design.

Ivory
Creamer 5.00
Cup & Saucer . . . . 5.00 to 7.00
Plate, Dinner,
9 3/4 In. . . . . . . 5.00 to 9.00
Plate, Sherbet, 6 1/4 In. . . . 2.75
Sandwich Server,
11 1/2 In. 8.50
Saucer 2.00
Sugar & Creamer 11.00

Ivory With Decal
Bowl, Cereal, Castle,
Blue Trim, 5 3/4 In. . . . 15.00
Bowl, Cereal, Flowers,
5 3/4 In. . . . . 5.00 to 8.00
Bowl, Floral, 9 In. 25.00
Bowl, Vegetable, Castle,
Blue Trim, 9 In. 38.00
Butter, Cover,
Flowers . . . . . . 35.00 to 65.00
Cup, Castle, Blue Trim . . 15.00
Cup, Flowers 6.00
Cup & Saucer, Castle 5.00
Cup & Saucer, Flowers . . 11.00
Plate, Dinner, Castle, Blue Trim,
9 3/4 In. . . . . . 15.00 to 20.00
Plate, Dinner, Castle, Pink
Trim, 9 3/4 In. 22.00
Plate, Dinner, Floral,
9 3/4 In. . . . . . . 8.00 to 9.00
Plate, Sherbet, Castle,
Blue Trim, 6 1/4 In. 7.50
Plate, Sherbet, Flowers,
6 1/4 In. . . . . . . 3.50 to 4.50
Sandwich Server, Castle,
Pink Trim, 11 1/2 In. . . 30.00
Sandwich Server, Floral,
11 1/2 In. . . . 12.00 to 14.00
Saucer, Castle, Blue Trim . 6.00
Saucer, Floral 4.00
Saucer, Pink Trim 6.00
Sherbet, Castle, Blue
Trim . . . . 25.00 to 29.00
Sherbet, Flowers 11.00
Soup, Dish, Castle, Blue Trim,
7 3/4 In. . . . . . 35.00 to 40.00
Soup, Dish, Flowers,
7 3/4 In. . . . . . 19.50 to 20.00

CHINTZ

Several companies made etchings named Chintz. Fostoria Glass Company, Moundsville, West Virginia, used a Chintz etching on Baroque, No. 338, and other blanks. The all-over etched design pictures branches of leaves and flowers. Fostoria made Crystal pieces from 1940 to 1973. Other Chintz patterns, featuring flowers and butterflies, were made by A. H. Heisey & Company from 1931 to 1938 in Alexandrite (orchid), Crystal, Flamingo (pink), Moongleam (green), and Sahara (yellow). Tiffin Glass Company made stemware with a Chintz etching. Pieces listed in this book are Fostoria Chintz.

Bell 200.00
Bonbon, Tricornered,
    4 5/8 In. 23.00
Bowl, 2 Handles,
    10 1/2 In. . . . 75.00 to 125.00
Bowl, Flared,
    11 1/2 In. . . . 78.00 to 100.00
Cake Plate, 2 Handles,
    10 1/2 In. . . . . 50.00 to 55.00
Candlestick, 3-Light,
    6 In., Pair 125.00
Celery Dish, 11 In. 75.00
Creamer 18.00
Cruet, Oil 85.00
Cup & Saucer 35.00
Goblet, Champagne, 6 Oz.,
    5 1/2 In. . . . . . 15.00 to 38.00
Goblet, Claret, 4 1/2 Oz.,
    5 3/8 In. . . . . . 40.00 to 45.00
Goblet, Cocktail, 4 Oz.,
    5 In. . . . . 25.00 to 30.00
Goblet, Cordial, 1 Oz.,
    3 7/8 In. . . . . 50.00 to 120.00
Goblet, Water, 9 Oz.,
    7 5/8 In. . . . . . 25.00 to 45.00
Oyster Cocktail, 4 Oz.,
    3 3/8 In. 30.00
Pitcher, Footed,
    48 Oz. 725.00
Plate, Bread & Butter,
    6 In. 12.00
Plate, Dinner, 9 1/2 In. . . 75.00
Plate, Salad,
    7 1/2 In. . . . . . 14.00 to 25.00

Relish, 3 Sections,
    10 In. . . . . 40.00 to 45.00
Salt & Pepper 90.00
Sherbet, 6 Oz.,
    4 3/8 In. . . . . . 22.00 to 27.00
Sugar & Creamer 50.00
Sugar & Creamer, Tray,
    Individual 135.00
Tumbler, Iced Tea, 13 Oz.,
    6 In. . . . . 34.00 to 37.00
Tumbler, Juice, Footed, 5 Oz.,
    4 5/8 In. . . . . . 29.00 to 30.00
Tumbler, Water, 9 Oz.,
    7 5/8 In. 30.00

CHRISTMAS CANDY

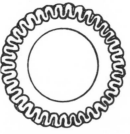

Christmas Candy, sometimes called Christmas Candy Ribbon or No. 624, was made by the Indiana Glass Company, Dunkirk, Indiana, in 1937. The pattern, apparently only made in luncheon sets, was made in Crystal, dark Emerald Green, a light green called Seafoam Green, and a bright blue called Teal Blue.

Crystal
Creamer 10.00
Cup . . . . 5.00 to 8.00
Plate, Luncheon, 8 In. 7.00
Sugar, 3 In. . . . . . 8.50 to 10.00
Sugar & Creamer 35.00

Teal Blue
Cup 35.00
Cup & Saucer 60.00

Plate, Bread & Butter,
    6 In. . . . . 12.50 to 16.00
Plate, Luncheon, 8 In. . . . 35.00
Sandwich Server,
    11 1/4 In. 125.00
Saucer 15.00

CHRISTMAS CANDY
    RIBBON
See Christmas Candy

CIRCLE

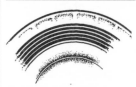

Circles ring the Circle pattern made by Hocking Glass Company, Lancaster, Ohio, beginning in 1929. It is found in Crystal, Green, and Pink. It can be distinguished from the similar Hocking pattern called Ring by the number of groupings of rings—Circle has only one set, Ring has several sets with four rings in each group.

Crystal
Goblet, Water, 8 Oz. 7.50
Goblet, Wine, 4 1/2 In. . . . 8.50
Goblet, Wine, Gold Trim,
    4 1/2 In. 15.00
Sherbet, Gold Trim,
    3 1/8 In. 4.00
Tumbler, Juice, 4 Oz.,
    3 1/2 In. 5.00

Green
Cup . . . . 4.00 to 6.00
Cup & Saucer . . . . 3.50 to 7.00
Goblet, Water, 8 Oz. 15.00
Goblet, Wine,
    4 1/2 In. 15.00
Pitcher, 80 Oz. 40.00
Plate, Luncheon,
    8 1/4 In. . . . . . . 6.00 to 8.00

Plate, Sherbet,
6 In. . . . . 2.50 to 5.00
Sherbet, 3 1/8 In. . . 4.00 to 5.00
Sherbet,
4 3/4 In. . . . . . 6.00 to 11.00
Tumbler, Iced Tea,
10 Oz., 5 In. 20.00

Pink

Cup & Saucer 10.00
Plate, Sherbet, 6 In. 4.00
Sherbet, 3 1/8 In. 10.00

CIRCULAR RIBS
See Circle

CLASSIC
See Chinex Classic

CLEO

In 1930 the Cambridge Glass Company, Cambridge, Ohio, introduced an etched pattern called Cleo. Many pieces are marked with the Cambridge C in a triangle. Sets were made in Amber, Blue, Crystal, Green, Pink, and Yellow.

Amber

Butter 10.00
Pitcher, 62 Oz. 260.00
Plate, Salad, 7 In. 10.00

Blue

Sugar Sifter, Glass
Cover 1500.00

Green

Plate, Luncheon,
8 1/2 In. 22.00
Sugar Sifter,
Metal Cover 395.00

Pink

Compote, 10 1/2 In. 275.00
Plate, Decagon, 12 In. . . . 68.00

CLOVERLEAF

Three-leaf clovers form part of the border of Cloverleaf pattern made by Hazel Atlas Glass Company from 1930 to 1936. It was made in Black, Crystal, Green, Pink, and Topaz (yellow).

Black

Ashtray, 4 In. . . . 45.00 to 60.00
Creamer,
3 5/8 In. . . . . 19.00 to 25.00
Cup . . . . 20.00 to 22.00
Cup & Saucer . . 23.00 to 29.50
Plate, Luncheon,
8 In. . . . . 12.00 to 19.50
Plate, Sherbet,
6 In. . . . . 39.00 to 45.00
Salt & Pepper . . 90.00 to 115.00
Saltshaker . . . . . 40.00 to 45.00
Saucer . . . . 2.00 to 7.00
Sherbet . . . . 20.00 to 25.00
Sugar, 3 5/8 In. . 15.00 to 28.00
Sugar & Creamer,
3 5/8 In. . . . . 30.00 to 50.00

Crystal

Plate, Luncheon, 8 In. . . . 14.00

Green

Bowl, Dessert,
4 In. . . . . 28.00 to 50.00
Candy Dish, Cover 200.00
Cup . . . . 9.00 to 14.00
Cup & Saucer 20.00
Grill Plate, 10 1/4 In. 25.00

Plate, Luncheon,
8 In. . . . . 8.00 to 20.00
Plate, Sherbet,
6 In. . . . . 7.00 to 15.00
Salt & Pepper 85.00
Saucer . . . . 3.00 to 8.50
Sherbet . . . . 10.00 to 15.00
Sugar & Creamer,
3 5/8 In. 35.00
Tumbler, 9 Oz.,
4 In. . . . . 60.00 to 63.00
Tumbler, Footed, 10 Oz.,
5 3/4 In. 45.00

Pink

Bowl, Dessert, 4 In. 35.00
Cup . . . . 7.00 to 12.00
Cup & Saucer . . 12.00 to 16.00
Plate, Luncheon,
8 In. . . . . 10.00 to 14.00
Saucer 8.00
Sherbet . . . . 9.00 to 12.50
Tumbler, 9 Oz., 4 In. 26.50

Topaz

Creamer 20.00
Plate, Luncheon, 8 In. . . . 14.00
Plate, Sherbet, 6 In. 10.00
Salt & Pepper . 120.00 to 140.00
Saltshaker 70.00
Saucer . . . . 4.00 to 5.00
Sugar . . . . 16.00 to 23.00
Tumbler, Footed, 10 Oz.,
5 3/4 In. . . . . 35.00 to 45.00

COIN

Fostoria Glass Company, Moundsville, West Virginia, made the Coin pattern from 1958 to 1982. It resembles the early pressed glass patterns, U.S. Coin and Columbian Coin. Dishes and accessories were made in Amber, Blue, Crystal, Empire Green, Olive, and Ruby. The four coins, usually frosted, depict a torch, a colonial man, an eagle, and the Liberty Bell. Lancaster Colony reissued some Coin pieces without frosted coins in the 1990s.

Amber
Candy Dish, Cover,
6 3/8 In. . . . . . 35.00 to 49.50

Blue
Candlestick, 8 In., Pair . . 55.00

Crystal
Cake Plate, Footed,
10 In. 135.00

Olive
Bowl, Oval, 9 In. 33.50
Candlestick, 4 1/2 In.,
Pair 33.50
Candlestick, 8 In.,
Pair 55.00
Candy Dish, Cover,
6 3/8 In. . . . . . 27.50 to 33.50
Cigarette Urn, 3 3/8 In. . . 22.50
Tumbler, Iced Tea, Footed,
14 Oz. 60.00
Vase, Bud, 8 In. 27.50

COLONIAL

Sometimes this pattern is called Knife & Fork, although Colonial is the more common name. It was made by Hocking Glass Company, Lancaster, Ohio, from 1934 to 1938. Crystal, Green, and Pink pieces are more common than Opaque White.

Crystal
Butter, Cover . . . 40.00 to 49.00
Butter, No Cover 25.00
Creamer . . . . 17.00 to 25.00

Cup 8.00
Goblet, Claret, 4 Oz.,
5 1/4 In. 20.00
Goblet, Cocktail, 3 Oz.,
4 In. . . . . 10.00 to 17.50
Goblet, Cordial, 1 Oz.,
3 3/4 In. . . . . . 20.00 to 27.50
Goblet, Water, 8 1/2 Oz.,
5 3/4 In. . . . . . 22.00 to 25.00
Goblet, Wine, 2 1/2 Oz.,
4 1/2 In. . . . . . 10.00 to 18.00
Pitcher, 54 Oz., 7 In. 40.00
Pitcher, 68 Oz.,
7 3/4 In. . . . . . 40.00 to 55.00
Plate, Dinner, 10 In. 33.00
Plate, Luncheon,
8 1/2 In. . . . . . 5.00 to 12.00
Plate, Sherbet,
6 In. 4.00
Platter, Oval,
12 In. 20.00
Salt & Pepper 65.00
Saucer 8.00
Sherbet,
3 3/8 In. . . . . . . 7.00 to 10.00
Sugar, 4 1/2 In. 10.00
Sugar, Cover . . . 28.00 to 35.00
Tumbler, Footed, 3 Oz.,
3 1/4 In. . . . . . . 7.00 to 14.00
Tumbler, Footed, 5 Oz.,
4 In. . . . . 18.00 to 22.00

Green
Berry Bowl,
4 1/2 In. . . . . . 15.00 to 20.00
Berry Bowl, Master,
9 In. . . . . 30.00 to 40.00
Butter, Cover . . . 25.00 to 60.00
Butter, Cover
Only . . . . 22.50 to 30.00
Cheese Dish, Cover 765.00
Cup . . . . 14.00 to 15.00
Cup & Saucer 17.00
Goblet, Claret, 4 Oz.,
5 1/4 In. . . . . . 20.00 to 40.00
Goblet, Cordial, 1 Oz.,
3 3/4 In. . . . . . 27.00 to 30.00
Goblet, Water, 8 Oz.,
5 3/4 In. . . . . . 30.00 to 32.00
Goblet, Wine, 2 1/2 Oz.,
4 1/2 In. . . . . . 25.00 to 30.00
Grill Plate,
10 In. . . . . 23.00 to 30.00
Plate, Luncheon,
8 1/2 In. . . . . . . 9.00 to 17.00

Plate, Sherbet,
6 In. . . . . 6.00 to 9.00
Platter, Oval,
12 In. . . . . 25.00 to 30.00
Saltshaker 75.00
Saucer 8.00
Sherbet,
3 3/8 In. . . . . . 12.00 to 18.00
Soup, Cream, 4 1/2 In. . . . 85.00
Spooner . . . . . 120.00 to 125.00
Sugar,
4 1/2 In. . . . . . 15.00 to 20.00
Sugar, Cover . . . 40.00 to 50.00
Sugar & Creamer 40.00
Sugar & Creamer,
Cover 65.00
Tumbler, Juice, 5 Oz.,
3 In. 32.00
Tumbler, Lemonade,
15 Oz. 80.00
Tumbler, Water, 9 Oz.,
4 In. 20.00
Tumbler, Whiskey, 1 1/2 Oz.,
2 1/2 In. . . . . . 15.00 to 20.00

Opaque White
Cup 7.00
Cup, Pastel Trim 5.00
Cup & Saucer 11.00
Cup & Saucer,
After Dinner 18.00

Pink
Berry Bowl, 4 1/2 In. 16.00
Bowl, Vegetable, Oval,
10 In. 45.00
Cup . . . . 10.00 to 12.00
Grill Plate,
10 In. . . . . 28.00 to 30.00
Pitcher, 54 Oz.,
7 In. . . . . 40.00 to 50.00
Pitcher, 68 Oz.,
7 3/4 In. 75.00
Plate, Dinner,
10 In. . . . . 38.50 to 78.00
Plate, Luncheon,
8 1/2 In. 11.00
Plate, Sherbet,
6 In. . . . . 6.00 to 7.00
Platter, Oval,
12 In. . . . . 33.00 to 42.00
Salt & Pepper 155.00
Saucer 2.00
Sherbet,
3 3/8 In. . . . . . 11.00 to 13.00

Sherbet, 3 In. 19.00
Soup, Cream,
  4 1/2 In. 90.00
Soup, Dish,
  7 In. . . . . . 65.00 to 85.00
Spooner 145.00
Tumbler, Footed, 5 Oz.,
  4 In. . . . . 29.00 to 35.00
Tumbler, Footed, 10 Oz.,
  5 In. 50.00
Tumbler, Juice, 5 Oz.,
  3 In. 22.00
Tumbler, Juice, Footed, 3 Oz.,
  3 1/4 In. . . . . . 14.00 to 22.00
Tumbler, Water, 9 Oz.,
  4 In. . . . . 19.00 to 28.00
Tumbler, Water, Footed,
  10 Oz., 5 1/4 In. 50.00
Tumbler, Whiskey, 1 1/2 Oz.,
  2 1/2 In. . . . . 12.00 to 20.00

COLONIAL BLOCK

A small set of dishes, mostly serving pieces, was made in Colonial Block pattern by Hazel Atlas Glass Company, a firm with factories in Ohio, Pennsylvania, and West Virginia. The dishes were made in the 1930s in Black, Crystal, Green, and Pink, and in the 1950s in White.

Crystal
Bowl, 4 In. 6.00
Bowl, 7 1/2 In. 16.00
Butter, Cover . . . 25.00 to 40.00
Sugar . . . . 6.00 to 15.00

Green
Bowl, 4 In. 8.00
Butter . . . . 10.00 to 45.00

Candy Dish,
  Cover . . . . 40.00 to 42.00
Candy Jar,
  Cover 35.00
Creamer 12.00
Goblet . . . . 9.75 to 12.00
Sherbet . . . . 5.00 to 10.00
Sugar, Cover 25.00
Tumbler, Footed, 5 Oz.,
  5 3/4 In. 10.00

Pink
Bowl, 7 In. 25.00
Goblet . . . . 11.00 to 15.00
Sherbet . . . . 8.00 to 9.00

White
Sugar 10.00

COLONIAL FLUTED

Federal Glass Company made Colonial Fluted or Rope pattern from 1928 to 1933. Luncheon sets were made primarily in Green, although Crystal pieces were also produced.

Green
Berry Bowl,
  4 In. . . . . 11.00 to 12.00
Berry Bowl, Master,
  7 1/2 In. . . . . . 22.00 to 25.00
Bowl, Cereal,
  6 In. . . . . 14.00 to 18.00
Cup 8.00
Cup & Saucer 15.00
Plate, Luncheon,
  8 In. . . . . 6.00 to 10.00
Plate, Sherbet,
  6 In. . . . . 3.00 to 5.00
Saucer 2.00

Sherbet . . . . 7.00 to 8.00
Sugar, Footed 14.00

COLONY

Colony was made by Fostoria Glass Company from 1926 to 1979. It evolved from an earlier Fostoria pattern, Queen Anne. Red candlesticks and bowls were sold in the 1980s under the Maypole name, and matching vases and other pieces were made by Viking. Colony was originally made in Amber, Blue, Crystal, Green, and Yellow. Reproductions have been made.

Crystal
Berry Bowl, 4 1/2 In. 32.00
Bonbon, 3-Footed, 7 In. . . 22.00
Bonbon, 6 In. 15.00
Bowl, Cereal, 5 In. 40.00
Bowl, Fruit, 14 In. 85.00
Bowl, Handle,
  8 1/2 In. . . . . . 35.00 to 40.00
Bowl, Rolled Rim,
  Handle, 4 7/8 In. 14.00
Bowl, Vegetable, Oval,
  10 In. 35.00
Cake Plate, 2 Handles,
  10 In. 25.00
Candlestick, 2-Light,
  6 1/2 In., Pair 50.00
Candlestick, 3 1/4 In. . . . 27.00
Candlestick, Prisms,
  14 1/2 In. 190.00
Candy Dish, Cover,
  6 1/2 In. 70.00
Celery Dish, 9 5/8 In. . . . 45.00

Compote, Cover,
6 3/8 In. 60.00
Creamer, 3 1/4 In. 14.00
Cup . . . . 9.00 to 10.00
Cup & Saucer . . . 9.00 to 11.00
Dish, Mayonnaise,
Underplate 23.00
Goblet, Cocktail,
3 1/2 Oz., 4 In. 12.00
Goblet, Water, 9 Oz.,
5 1/8 In. . . . . . 13.00 to 17.00
Goblet, Wine, 3 1/4 Oz.,
4 1/4 In. . . . . . 24.00 to 30.00
Ice Bucket, 6 1/4 In. . . . 195.00
Oyster Cocktail, 4 Oz.,
3 3/8 In. 14.00
Plate, Bread & Butter,
6 In. 6.00
Plate, Dinner, 9 In. 32.50
Plate, Luncheon,
8 In. 13.00
Plate, Salad,
7 In. . . . . 7.50 to 12.00
Platter, 12 In. 47.00
Punch Bowl 795.00
Punch Cup 30.00
Relish, 2 Sections,
Handle, 7 In. 24.00
Relish, 2 Sections,
Oblong, 7 1/2 In. 20.00
Sandwich Server, Center Handle,
11 1/2 In. . . . 38.00 to 45.00
Sherbet, 5 Oz.,
3 5/8 In. . . . . . . 9.00 to 10.00
Soup, Cream,
5 In. . . . . 90.00 to 95.00
Soup, Dish, 7 In. 4.00
Torte Plate, 13 In. 45.00
Torte Plate,
15 In. . . . . . . 65.00 to 75.00
Tray, Muffin, 2 Handles,
8 3/8 In. 35.00
Tumbler, Iced Tea,
12 Oz., 4 7/8 In. 39.00
Tumbler, Iced Tea, Footed,
12 Oz., 5 3/4 In. 24.00
Tumbler, Juice, Footed, 5 Oz.,
4 1/2 In. . . . . . 23.00 to 24.00
Vase, 12 In. 225.00
Vase, Bud, Flared,
6 In. 12.00
Vase, Flared,
7 1/2 In. 50.00

COLUMBIA

Columbia pattern can be found in Crystal but is rare in Pink. It was made by Federal Glass Company, Columbus, Ohio, from 1938 to 1942.

Crystal
Bowl, Cereal,
5 In. . . . . 10.00 to 22.00
Bowl, Ruffled Edge,
10 1/2 In. . . . . 17.00 to 23.00
Bowl, Salad,
8 1/2 In. . . . . . 12.50 to 24.00
Butter, Cover . . . 19.00 to 25.00
Butter, Metal Cover 17.00
Butter, No Cover 5.00
Chop Plate,
11 In. . . . . 7.00 to 15.00
Cup . . . . 7.00 to 10.00
Cup & Saucer . . . 6.00 to 14.00
Plate, Bread & Butter,
6 In. . . . . 3.00 to 6.00
Plate, Luncheon,
9 1/2 In. . . . . . . 7.50 to 12.00
Saucer . . . . 2.00 to 4.00
Snack Plate,
8 3/4 In. . . . . . 30.00 to 35.00
Soup, Dish,
8 In. . . . . 20.00 to 29.00
Tumbler, Juice, Dot Etch,
4 Oz., 2 7/8 In. 30.00
Tumbler, Water,
9 Oz. 30.00
Tumbler, Water,
Gold Band, 9 Oz. 28.00

Pink
Cup & Saucer 58.00
Plate, Luncheon,
9 1/2 In. 45.00

CORONATION

Coronation was made, primarily in berry sets, by Anchor Hocking Glass Corporation, Lancaster, Ohio, from 1936 to 1940. Most pieces are Pink, but there are also Crystal, Green, and Royal Ruby sets. The pattern is sometimes called Banded Fine Rib or Saxon. Some of the pieces are confused with those in Old Colony pattern.

Crystal
Berry Set,
7 Piece 75.00

Pink
Berry Bowl, 2 Handles,
4 1/4 In. . . . . . . 7.50 to 8.50
Berry Bowl, 2 Handles,
Master, 8 In. . . 15.00 to 20.00
Cup . . . . 5.50 to 6.50
Cup & Saucer . . 10.00 to 14.00
Plate, Luncheon,
8 1/2 In. 24.00
Plate, Sherbet,
6 In. . . . . 2.00 to 5.50
Saucer . . . . 2.00 to 8.00
Sherbet . . . . 7.00 to 18.00
Tumbler, Footed, 10 Oz.,
5 In. . . . . 32.00 to 36.00

Royal Ruby
Berry Bowl, 2 Handles,
4 1/4 In. . . . . . . 6.00 to 12.00
Berry Bowl, 2 Handles,
Master, 8 In. . . 18.00 to 28.00
Bowl, 2 Handles,
6 1/2 In. . . . . . 18.00 to 23.00

CRACKED ICE

Cracked Ice is an Art Deco–looking geometric pattern made by Indiana Glass Company in the 1930s. It was made in Green and Pink.

Pink
Sugar, Cover 25.00
Tumbler, Footed 22.00

CREMAX

Cremax and Chinex Classic are confusing patterns. Cremax dishes have a pie-crust edge but no scroll design like the one on Chinex. Also, the names Cremax and Chinex refer to colors as well as patterns. Cremax, made by the Macbeth-Evans Division of Corning Glass Works, was made from 1938 to 1942. It is a cream-colored opaque glass, sometimes decorated with floral or brown-tinted decals or with a colored rim.

Bowl, Cereal,
  5 3/4 In. 3.50
Cup 4.00
Cup, Gold Trim 4.50
Cup & Saucer 15.00
Cup & Saucer,
  After Dinner 15.00
Cup & Saucer, After
  Dinner, Fired-On
  Blue . . . . 18.00 to 25.00
Cup & Saucer, After
  Dinner, Fired-On
  Green . . . . . . 18.00 to 35.00
Cup & Saucer, After
  Dinner, Fired-On
  Pink . . . . 18.00 to 25.00
Cup & Saucer, After
  Dinner, Fired-On
  Yellow . . . . . 18.00 to 25.00
Plate, Bread & Butter,
  Green Trim, 6 1/4 In. . . . 4.50
Plate, Bread & Butter,
  Pink Trim, 6 1/4 In. 3.50
Plate, Bread & Butter,
  Yellow Trim, 6 1/4 In. . . 3.50
Plate, Dinner,
  9 3/4 In. . . . . . . 4.50 to 10.00
Plate, Dinner, Pink Trim,
  9 3/4 In. 8.00
Sandwich Server, Pink Trim,
  11 1/2 In. 13.00
Saucer, Pink Trim 3.50
Sugar, Fired-On
  Blue 18.00

CRINOLINE
See Ripple

CRISS CROSS

The Criss Cross pattern is named for the embossed intersecting lines on the outside of the pieces. Kitchen items were made in Crystal, Green, Pink,

---

and Ritz Blue by Hazel Atlas Glass Company in the 1930s. Some Crystal pieces are coated with fired-on colors.

Crystal
Bottle, Water, 64 Oz.,
  10 In. 79.00
Bottle, Water, Orange
  Hard Plastic Lid,
  64 Oz., 10 In. 46.00
Bowl, Cereal,
  5 1/4 In. 29.00
Bowl, Cereal, Fired-On White,
  5 1/4 In. 16.00
Butter, 1/4 Lb. 38.00
Creamer 29.00
Jar, Food Mixer,
  Baby's Face 50.00
Mixing Bowl, Fired-On White,
  9 5/8 In. 50.00
Refrigerator Dish,
  Cover, 4 x 4 In. 25.00
Refrigerator Dish,
  Cover, 8 x 8 In. 59.00

Green
Butter, Cover,
  1 Lb. . . . . 55.00 to 65.00
Candy Dish, Cover 38.00
Creamer 16.00
Reamer, Large 50.00
Reamer, Small 35.00
Refrigerator Dish,
  Cover, 8 In. 50.00
Refrigerator Dish,
  Cover Only, 8 x 8 In. . . 32.00

CROCHETED CRYSTAL

Crocheted Crystal dishes are a variation of Laced Edge. Imperial Glass Company made the pattern from 1943 to the early

1950s for Sears, Roebuck & Company.

Bowl, Narcissus,
7 1/2 In. 49.00
Bowl, Salad,
10 1/2 In. 48.00
Cake Stand, 12 In. . . . 55.00
Candlestick, 2-Light,
Pair 40.00
Punch Bowl,
14 In. 95.00

CROW'S FOOT

Crow's Foot is the popular name for Paden City Glass Manufacturing Company's Lines 412 and 890. The pattern was made in the 1930s in Amber, Amethyst, Black, Crystal, Pink, Ritz Blue, Ruby, White, and Yellow. See the Ardith, Nora Bird, and Peacock & Wild Rose sections for Crow's Foot pieces with etchings.

Black
Vase, Cupped,
10 1/4 In. 145.00

Ritz Blue
Bowl, 8 In. 125.00
Compote, 6 1/2 In. 75.00
Console Set, Gold Trim,
3 Pieces 185.00

Ruby
Bowl, Square, 2 Handles,
8 1/2 In. 50.00
Cheese Stand 65.00
Creamer 18.00
Cup & Saucer 15.00
Cup & Saucer,
Square . . . . . . 12.00 to 19.00
Sandwich Server,
2 Handles, 11 In. 40.00
Saucer, Round 8.00
Soup, Cream 28.00
Sugar 18.00
Sugar & Creamer 35.00
Vase, Flared, 8 In. 125.00

White
Candlestick, Keyhole,
5 3/4 In., Pair 250.00

CRYSTOLITE

A. H. Heisey & Company made Crystolite from 1938 to 1957. The extensive pattern line was made mostly in Crystal. A few pieces can be found in Sahara (yellow) and Zircon (light turquoise). Many pieces are marked with the Diamond H logo.

Crystal
Bowl, 2 Sections,
2 Handles, 6 In. 18.00
Candlestick, 3-Light 30.00
Candlestick, Footed,
Pair 50.00
Candy Dish, Cover,
Floral Etch, 7 In. 55.00
Cheese Stand 25.00
Cigarette Box, Cover,
4 In. 35.00
Cup 18.00
Cup & Saucer 25.00
Jam Jar, Footed,
4 1/2 In. 32.00
Mustard, Cover,
2 1/2 In. . . . . . 40.00 to 42.00
Plate, 2 Handles, 7 In. . . . 20.00
Plate, Salad, 7 In. 15.00
Saucer 6.00
Sugar & Creamer, Tray . . 40.00

CUBE
See Cubist

CUBIST

Cubist, or Cube, molded with the expected rectangular and diamond pattern, was made by Jeannette Glass Company from 1929 to 1933. It was made first in Crystal and Pink. Later, Green replaced Crystal, and Amber, Blue, Canary Yellow, Pink, Ultramarine, and White were added. Various shades of some of the colors were made. It has been made recently in Amber, Avocado, and Opaque White.

Amber
Bowl, Dessert, 4 1/2 In. . . . 8.00

Crystal
Bowl, Dessert, 4 1/2 In. . . . 3.00
Plate, Sherbet, 6 In. 6.50
Powder Jar, 3-Footed 6.00
Saucer 2.50
Sugar, 3 In. 3.50
Tray, For Sugar &
Creamer 4.00

Green
Bowl, Dessert,
4 1/2 In. . . . . . . 6.00 to 10.00
Bowl, Salad, 6 1/2 In. . . . 16.00
Butter, Cover . . . 65.00 to 80.00
Butter, No Cover 20.00
Candy Jar, Cover,
6 1/2 In. . . . . . 29.00 to 36.50
Coaster . . . . 7.00 to 10.00
Creamer . . . . 7.00 to 14.00
Cup 9.00

Plate, Luncheon,
8 In. 11.00
Plate, Sherbet,
6 In. . . . . 3.00 to 4.00
Powder Jar, Cover,
3-Footed . . . . . 28.00 to 38.00
Powder Jar,
No Cover 27.50
Salt & Pepper . . . 30.00 to 50.00
Saltshaker 20.00
Saucer . . . . 3.00 to 4.00
Sherbet . . . . 7.00 to 11.00
Sugar . . . . 8.00 to 10.00
Sugar, Cover . . . 22.00 to 30.00
Sugar & Creamer 20.00
Sugar & Creamer,
Cover 28.00
Tumbler, Water, 9 Oz.,
4 In. . . . . 70.00 to 75.00

Pink
Bowl, Dessert,
4 1/2 In. . . . . . . 7.00 to 14.00
Bowl, Salad,
6 1/2 In. . . . . . 10.00 to 15.00
Butter, Cover . . . 50.00 to 75.00
Butter, No Cover 20.00
Candy Jar, Cover,
6 1/2 In. . . . . . 27.00 to 35.00
Coaster . . . . 7.00 to 10.00
Creamer,
2 5/8 In. . . . . 2.00 to 5.00
Creamer,
3 1/2 In. . . . . . 10.00 to 16.00
Pitcher, 45 Oz.,
8 3/4 In. . . . 225.00 to 235.00
Plate, Luncheon,
8 In. 10.00
Plate, Sherbet,
6 In. . . . . 3.00 to 5.00
Powder Jar, Cover,
3-Footed . . . . . 28.00 to 35.00
Salt & Pepper . . . 20.00 to 35.00
Saucer 3.00
Sherbet . . . . 8.00 to 11.00
Sugar, 2 3/8 In. . . . 2.00 to 6.00
Sugar, 3 1/2 In. 7.00
Sugar, Cover . . . 22.00 to 25.00
Sugar & Creamer,
2 3/8 In. 10.00
Sugar & Creamer,
3 1/2 In. 15.00
Tumbler, Water, 9 Oz.,
4 In. 74.00

CUPID

There is an etched pair of Cupids on the pattern with the name Cupid. The pattern was made in the 1930s by the Paden City Glass Manufacturing Company of Paden City, West Virginia. It was made in Black, Green, Light Blue, Pink, and Yellow. Some pieces have gold trim.

Green
Cake Stand 245.00
Compote, 6 1/4 In. 250.00
Dish, Mayonnaise,
Underplate 230.00
Ice Bucket, 6 In. 325.00
Ice Tub, 4 3/4 In. 295.00
Sugar, Footed, 4 1/4 In. . 185.00
Tray, Center Handle,
10 3/4 In. 225.00
Tray, Oval, Footed,
10 7/8 In. 360.00

Pink
Bowl, Rolled Edge,
10 1/2 In. . . 350.00 to 400.00
Compote, 6 1/4 In. 325.00
Creamer, Footed, 5 In. . . 175.00
Tray, Oval, Footed,
10 7/8 In. 380.00

DAISY
See No. 620

DAISY PETALS
See Petalware

DANCING GIRL
See Cameo

DECAGON

Decagon, named for its 10-sided outline, was made by the Cambridge Glass Company of Cambridge, Ohio. The pattern, dating from the 1930s, was made in Amber, Black, Carmen (red), Emerald Green, Moonlight Blue (light blue), and Peach-Blo (pink), and Royal Blue.

Amber
Creamer 15.00
Cup & Saucer 10.00
Goblet, Claret, 4 Oz. 40.00
Goblet, Cordial, 1 Oz. . . . 45.00
Gravy Boat, 2 Spouts 55.00
Nut Dish 28.00
Plate, 8 In. 15.00
Plate, Bread & Butter,
6 1/4 In. . . . . 3.00 to 8.00
Server, Center Handle,
11 In. 12.00
Soup, Cream,
Underplate 32.00
Soup, Dish,
3 3/4 In. 23.00
Tumbler, Water, Footed,
8 Oz. 12.00
Tumbler, Whiskey,
Footed, 2 1/2 Oz. 18.00

Emerald Green
Bonbon, 2 Handles,
6 1/2 In. 14.00
Bowl, Cranberry,
3 1/2 In. 25.00
Candlestick, 3 1/2 In. 30.00
Compote, 6 In. 45.00
Creamer, Scalloped 18.00
Cup 5.00
Cup & Saucer 13.00
Nut Dish, 2 1/2 In. 38.00
Plate, Service,
2 Handles, 15 In. 65.00
Sherbet, 6 Oz., Low 16.00

Moonlight Blue
Candlestick, 4 In. 38.00
Finger Bowl 30.00
Goblet, Cocktail,
3 1/2 Oz. . . . . . 26.00 to 40.00
Goblet, Cordial, 1 Oz. . . . 80.00

Plate, Bread & Butter,
6 1/4 In. 7.50

Sandwich Server, Center
Handle, 12 In. 33.00

Sherbet, 6 Oz., Low 16.00

Tumbler, Footed,
10 Oz. 25.00

Tumbler, Iced Tea, Footed,
12 Oz. 35.00

Tumbler, Juice, Footed,
5 Oz. 20.00

Peach-Blo

Bowl, Cranberry, Belled,
3 1/2 In. 15.00

Bowl, Vegetable, Oval,
10 1/2 In. 50.00

Candy Dish, Cover 116.00

Creamer . . . . . . 13.00 to 15.00

Cup & Saucer 13.00

Dish, Cereal, Flat Rim,
6 In. 29.00

Goblet, Cocktail,
3 1/2 Oz. 30.00

Goblet, Water, 9 Oz. 25.00

Parfait, 5 1/8 In. 38.00

Pitcher, Cover, 11 In. . . . 117.00

Plate, Dinner, 9 1/2 In. . . 25.00

Plate, Salad, 8 1/4 In. 28.00

Plate, Service, 12 1/2 In. . 70.00

Sandwich Server, Center
Handle, 12 In. 30.00

Sherbet, 6 Oz.,
High . . . . 13.00 to 22.00

Tumbler, Iced Tea,
Footed, 12 Oz. 33.00

Tumbler, Whiskey,
Footed, 2 1/2 Oz. 23.00

Royal Blue

Bowl, 11 3/4 In. 55.00

Goblet, Water, 9 Oz. 30.00

Tumbler, Juice, Footed,
5 Oz. 25.00

❖

**When ordering antiques
by mail, do not send
cash; send a check or
charge them. Keep a
copy of your order.**

❖

DELLA ROBBIA

Della Robbia is a heavy
glass pattern with raised
pears and apples as part of
the design. It was made by
Westmoreland Glass
Company, Grapeville,
Pennsylvania, from 1926
to the 1960s. The pattern
was made mostly in Crys-
tal. Amber, Green, Milk
Glass, and Roselin were
also found. Crystal pieces
often have fruit stained in
natural colors.

Crystal

Bowl, Footed,
12 In. 155.00

Bowl, Bell Shape, Handle,
8 In. 185.00

Bowl, Heart Shape,
8 In. 200.00

Bowl, Heart Shape,
Handle, 8 In. 90.00

Candlestick, 2-Light,
Pair 125.00

Candlestick, 4 In., Pair . . 65.00

Candy Box,
Cover . . . . . . 80.00 to 115.00

Candy Dish, Cover, Footed,
Scalloped 150.00

Compote,
6 1/2 In. . . . . . 25.00 to 65.00

Compote, 8 In. 200.00

Goblet, Champagne,
6 Oz. . . . . 23.00 to 35.00

Goblet, Water, 8 Oz.,
6 In. . . . . 17.00 to 25.00

Plate, Luncheon,
9 In. . . . . 35.00 to 50.00

Plate, Salad,
7 1/4 In. 20.00

Punch Set,
15 Piece 795.00

Sugar & Creamer 55.00

Torte Plate,
14 In. . . . . . . 85.00 to 110.00

Tumbler, Footed, 8 Oz.,
4 3/4 In. 15.00

Tumbler, Iced Tea,
12 Oz. 15.00

Tumbler, Iced Tea, Footed,
Belled, 12 Oz. 15.00

Milk Glass

Goblet, Water, 8 Oz.,
6 In. 15.00

DEWDROP

Dewdrop was made in
1954 and 1955 by Jean-
nette Glass Company,
Jeannette, Pennsylvania.
It is available only in
Crystal.

Bowl, 4 3/4 In. 5.00

Bowl,
8 1/2 In. . . . . . 12.00 to 20.00

Bowl, 10 3/8 In. 24.00

Creamer 8.00

Cup 4.00

Punch Bowl 15.00

Punch Bowl,
Base Only . . . . . 9.00 to 10.00

Punch Cup 4.00

Punch Set, Bowl, Cups,
11 Piece 65.00

Punch Set, Bowl, Cups,
Underplate, 14 Piece . . . 90.00

Relish, Leaf Shape 8.00

Relish, Leaf Shape,
Gold Trim 6.00

Snack Plate,
With Cup . . . . . . 6.00 to 8.00

Sugar, Cover . . . . 8.00 to 14.00

Tray, Lazy Susan,
13 In. . . . . 22.00 to 29.00

DIAMOND
See Windsor

DIAMOND PATTERN
See Miss America

DIAMOND QUILTED

Collectors use the names Diamond Quilted or Flat Diamond for the No. 414 line made by Imperial Glass Company, Bellaire, Ohio, in the 1920s and early 1930s. It was made in Amber, Black, Blue, Crystal, Green, Pink, and Red. Dinner sets, luncheon sets, and serving pieces, including a large punch bowl, were made, but not all items were made in all colors.

Amber

Bowl, Handle, 5 1/2 In.	25.00
Creamer	9.00
Plate, Luncheon, 8 In.	9.00
Sherbet	10.00

Black

Candlestick, Pair	50.00
Creamer	20.00
Sherbet	14.00
Soup, Cream, 4 3/4 In.	23.00
Sugar & Creamer	30.00

Blue

Bowl, 7 In.	21.00 to 24.00
Bowl, Ruffled Edge, 7 In.	22.00 to 24.00
Bowl, Handle, 5 1/2 In.	24.00
Candlestick, Pair	49.00
Creamer	19.00
Plate, Luncheon, 8 In.	16.00
Plate, Sherbet, 6 In.	9.00 to 9.50
Sherbet	14.00
Soup, Cream, 4 3/4 In.	20.00 to 23.00
Sugar	20.00
Sugar & Creamer	45.00

Green

Bowl, 10 In.	20.00
Bowl, Ruffled Edge, 7 In.	18.00
Candlestick, Pair	23.00 to 30.00
Creamer	8.00 to 10.00
Cup	10.00
Plate, Luncheon, 8 In.	6.00 to 12.00
Plate, Sherbet, 6 In.	4.00
Saucer	6.00
Sherbet	4.50 to 10.00
Soup, Cream, 4 3/4 In.	12.50
Sugar	13.00
Sugar & Creamer	24.00

Pink

Bowl, 7 In.	17.00 to 20.00
Bowl, Handle, 5 1/2 In.	20.00
Bowl, Rolled Edge, 11 In.	24.00
Creamer	10.00 to 15.00
Cup & Saucer	20.00
Plate, Luncheon, 8 In.	6.00 to 12.00
Sherbet	8.00
Soup, Cream, 4 3/4 In.	25.00

Red

Bowl, Ruffled Edge, 7 In.	35.00

DIANA

Diana is one of the many Depression glass patterns with swirls in the glass. Federal Glass Company, Columbus, Ohio, made this pattern, sometimes called Swirled Sharp Rib, from 1937 to 1941. It was made in Amber, Crystal, Green, and Pink, and can be distinguished from other swirled patterns by the two sets of swirls used—one in the center of the piece, another on the rim. A Pink bowl was reproduced in 1987.

Amber

Bowl, Fruit, 11 In.	12.00 to 22.00
Coaster	13.00
Cup & Saucer	9.00 to 10.00
Plate, Luncheon, 9 1/2 In.	5.00
Salt & Pepper	116.00
Sugar	12.00
Tumbler, Water, 9 Oz., 4 1/8 In.	29.00

Crystal

Bowl, Cereal, 5 In.	4.00 to 8.00
Bowl, Fruit, 11 In.	20.00
Bowl, Salad, 9 In.	14.00 to 17.00
Bowl, Scalloped Edge, 12 In.	10.00 to 14.50
Candy Dish, Cover	22.00
Candy Dish, Gold Metal Holder	14.50
Creamer, Oval	9.50
Cup	6.00
Cup, After Dinner	14.50
Cup, Gold Trim	5.00
Cup & Saucer	8.50 to 12.00
Cup & Saucer, After Dinner	10.00 to 15.00
Cup & Saucer, After Dinner, Gold Trim	12.00
Junior Set, 6 Cups, 6 Saucers, Rack	100.00 to 125.00
Plate, Bread & Butter, 6 In.	1.00 to 2.00
Plate, Luncheon, 9 1/2 In.	6.00 to 16.00
Platter, Oval, 12 In.	12.00
Salt & Pepper	30.00 to 80.00
Saltshaker	15.00
Sandwich Server, 11 3/4 In.	5.00 to 14.50
Saucer	2.00 to 4.00
Saucer, After Dinner	4.00

Saucer, After Dinner,
Gold Trim 4.50

Soup, Cream,
5 1/2 In. . . . . . 10.00 to 12.00

Sugar, Oval 10.00

Green
Sherbet 12.00

Pink
Bowl, Cereal,
5 In. . . . . 8.00 to 22.00

Bowl, Fruit,
11 In. . . . . 40.00 to 44.00

Bowl, Salad,
9 In. . . . . 20.00 to 32.00

Candy Dish,
Cover . . . . 50.00 to 55.00

Coaster 7.00

Creamer 19.00

Cup, After
Dinner . . . . 25.00 to 40.00

Cup & Saucer,
After Dinner . . 39.00 to 50.00

Plate, Bread & Butter,
6 In. . . . . 4.00 to 8.00

Platter, Oval,
12 In. . . . . 25.00 to 37.50

Salt & Pepper . . . 82.00 to 92.00

Saucer . . . . 4.00 to 6.00

Saucer, After Dinner 10.00

Saucer, Cup Ring 10.50

Soup, Cream,
5 1/2 In. . . . . . 35.00 to 45.00

Tea Set, Child's,
Metal Holder 400.00

Tumbler, 9 Oz.,
4 1/8 In. . . . . . 45.00 to 60.00

DOGWOOD

Dogwood is decorated with a flower that has been given many names. Collectors have called this pattern Apple Blossom, B pattern, Magnolia, or Wildrose. It was made

from 1930 to 1934 by Macbeth-Evans Glass Company. It is found in Cremax, Crystal, Green, Monax, Pink, and Yellow. Some Pink pieces are trimmed with gold. Some pieces were made with such thin walls, the factory redesigned the molds to make the pieces thicker.

Cremax
Berry Bowl, Master,
8 1/2 In. 40.00

Cup 50.00

Crystal
Ashtray, 4 In. 20.00

Plate, Luncheon, 8 In. . . . 15.00

Green
Ashtray, 4 In. 15.00

Bowl, Fruit, 10 1/4 In. . . 350.00

Cake Plate,
13 In. . . . . . 120.00 to 225.00

Cup . . . . 35.00 to 65.00

Cup & Saucer, Thin 54.00

Grill Plate, 10 1/2 In. 45.00

Pitcher, 80 Oz., 8 In. . . . 595.00

Plate, Bread & Butter,
6 In. 14.00

Plate, Luncheon,
8 In. . . . . 8.00 to 16.00

Saucer . . . . 7.00 to 13.00

Sugar & Creamer, Thin . 120.00

Tumbler, Decorated,
10 Oz., 4 In. 120.00

Tumbler, Decorated,
11 Oz., 4 3/4 In. 140.00

Pink
Berry Bowl, Master,
8 1/2 In. . . . . . 59.00 to 78.00

Bowl, Cereal,
5 1/2 In. . . . . . 32.00 to 42.00

Bowl, Cereal, Flat Rim,
5 1/2 In. . . . . . 74.00 to 85.00

Bowl, Fruit, 10 1/4 In. . . 750.00

Cake Plate, Solid Foot,
13 In. . . . . . 130.00 to 200.00

Creamer, Thick,
Footed . . . . . . 22.00 to 30.00

Creamer, Thin . . 17.00 to 32.00

Cup, Thick . . . . . 17.00 to 18.00

Cup, Thin . . . . . 16.00 to 30.00

Cup & Saucer,
Thick . . . . . . 20.00 to 33.00

Cup & Saucer,
Thin . . . . 20.00 to 33.00

Grill Plate,
10 1/2 In. . . . . 19.00 to 45.00

Pitcher, Decorated, 80 Oz.,
8 In. . . . . . . 250.00 to 285.00

Plate, Bread & Butter,
6 In. . . . . 8.00 to 24.00

Plate, Dinner,
9 1/4 In. . . . . . 35.00 to 48.00

Plate, Luncheon,
8 In. . . . . 35.00 to 39.00

Platter, Oval,
12 In. . . . . . 750.00 to 800.00

Salver, 12 In. . . . 30.00 to 45.00

Saucer, Thick . . . . . 4.00 to 8.00

Saucer, Thin . . . . . 4.00 to 8.00

Sherbet . . . . 32.00 to 45.00

Sugar, Footed . . . 15.00 to 22.00

Sugar, Thin, 2 1/2 In. 18.00

Sugar & Creamer, Thick,
Footed,
3 1/4 In. . . . . . 41.00 to 45.00

Sugar & Creamer, Thin,
Flat . . . . 40.00 to 60.00

Tumbler, 10 Oz.,
4 In. . . . . 45.00 to 65.00

Tumbler, 11 Oz.,
4 3/4 In. . . . . . 45.00 to 55.00

Tumbler, 12 Oz.,
5 In. . . . . 65.00 to 90.00

Tumbler, Molded
Band . . . . 25.00 to 35.00

Yellow
Plate, Luncheon, 8 In. . . . 75.00

DORIC

Doric was made by Jeannette Glass Company, Jeannette, Pennsylvania, from 1935 to 1938. The molded pattern has also inspired another name for the pattern, Snowflake. It was made in Delphite (opaque blue), Green, Pink, and Yellow. A few White pieces may have been made.

Delphite

Sherbet, Footed,
  3 1/2 In. . . . . . 10.00 to 18.00

Green

Berry Bowl,
  4 1/2 In. . . . . . 10.00 to 14.00
Berry Bowl, Master,
  8 1/4 In. . . . . . 30.00 to 38.00
Butter, Cover 90.00
Butter, Cover
  Only . . . . 45.00 to 52.50
Cake Plate, 3-Footed,
  10 In. 30.00
Candy Dish, 3 Sections . . 18.00
Candy Dish, 3 Sections,
  Cover . . . . . . 42.00 to 45.00
Coaster, 3 In. 20.00
Creamer . . . . . . 14.00 to 15.00
Cup 15.00
Cup & Saucer . . 18.00 to 20.00
Pitcher, 32 Oz.,
  5 1/2 In. 45.00
Plate, Dinner,
  9 In. . . . . 18.00 to 19.00
Plate, Sherbet,
  6 In. . . . . . . 5.00 to 16.00
Platter, Oval, 12 In. 35.00
Relish, Oblong, 8 In. 20.00
Relish, Square,
  4 In. . . . . 13.00 to 18.00
Salt & Pepper 55.00
Saltshaker 20.00
Sandwich Server, 2 Handles,
  10 In. . . . . . . 29.00 to 33.00
Saucer 5.00
Shaker 20.00
Sherbet . . . . 16.00 to 17.00
Sugar, Cover 45.00
Tray, 2 Handles,
  Square, 8 In. 30.00

Pink

Berry Bowl,
  4 1/2 In. . . . . . 9.00 to 14.00

Berry Bowl, Master,
  8 1/2 In. 35.00
Bowl, Cereal,
  5 1/2 In. . . . . 85.00 to 110.00
Bowl, Vegetable, Oval,
  9 In. . . . . 40.00 to 49.00
Cake Plate, 3-Footed,
  10 In. . . . . . . 25.00 to 35.00
Candy Dish,
  3 Sections . . . . 10.00 to 15.00
Candy Dish, 3 Sections,
  Cover 45.00
Coaster, 3 In. 24.00
Creamer . . . . . . 14.00 to 21.00
Cup . . . . 9.00 to 11.00
Cup & Saucer . . 13.00 to 18.00
Grill Plate,
  9 In. . . . . 22.00 to 30.00
Pitcher, 32 Oz.,
  5 1/2 In. . . . . 25.00 to 60.00
Plate, Dinner,
  9 In. . . . . 10.00 to 28.00
Plate, Sherbet, 6 In. 7.00
Platter, Oval,
  12 In. . . . . . . 35.00 to 40.00
Relish, Oblong, 8 In. 18.00
Relish, Square,
  4 In. . . . . 15.00 to 22.00
Salt & Pepper . . . 35.00 to 40.00
Saucer . . . . 3.00 to 6.00
Sherbet . . . . 14.00 to 16.00
Sugar, Cover . . . 20.00 to 35.00
Tray, 2 Handles,
  10 In. . . . . . . 22.00 to 29.00
Tray, 2 Handles,
  Square, 8 In. 42.00
Tumbler, 9 Oz.,
  4 1/2 In. . . . . . 75.00 to 90.00
Tumbler, Footed, 10 Oz.,
  4 In. . . . . . . 75.00 to 100.00

DORIC & PANSY

Doric & Pansy features the snowflake design of Doric

alternating with pansies. It, too, was made by Jeannette Glass Company, but only in 1937 and 1938. It was made in Crystal, Pink, and Ultramarine. The Ultramarine varied in color from green to blue. Collectors pay more for the blue shades. A set of child's dishes called Pretty Polly Party Dishes was made in this pattern.

Pink

Berry Bowl,
  4 1/2 In. 10.00
Child's Set,
  14 Piece 295.00
Creamer, Child's 42.00
Cup, Child's 40.00
Cup & Saucer,
  Child's . . . . . . 42.00 to 48.00
Plate, Child's . . . 12.00 to 25.00
Plate, Sherbet,
  6 In. . . . . 7.00 to 13.00
Saucer, Child's 10.00
Sugar, Child's . . 28.00 to 42.00
Sugar & Creamer,
  Child's 80.00

Ultramarine

Butter, Cover 595.00
Child's Set,
  14 Piece . . . 295.00 to 425.00
Creamer, Child's 65.00
Cup & Saucer . . 20.00 to 25.00
Cup & Saucer,
  Child's . . . . . . 55.00 to 58.00
Plate, Child's . . . 12.00 to 13.00
Plate, Dinner, 9 In. 40.00
Plate, Sherbet, 6 In. 13.00
Salt &
  Pepper . . . . . 415.00 to 600.00
Saucer 8.00
Saucer, Child's . . . 6.00 to 10.00
Sugar . . . . 60.00 to 145.00
Sugar, Child's 59.00
Tumbler, 9 Oz.,
  4 1/2 In. . . . 120.00 to 125.00

DORIC WITH PANSY
See Doric & Pansy

DOUBLE SHIELD
See Mt. Pleasant

DOUBLE SWIRL
See Swirl

DRAPE & TASSEL
See Princess

DUTCH
See Windmill

DUTCH ROSE
See Rosemary

EARLY AMERICAN
  HOBNAIL
See Hobnail

EARLY AMERICAN PRESCUT

Early American Prescut was made by Anchor Hocking Glass Corporation, Lancaster, Ohio, from 1960 to 1998. The pieces have an imitation cut glass design and were made in Crystal, Honey Gold, Laser Blue, Royal Ruby, and with tints (Amber, Avocado, Blue, and Ruby). There are other imitation cut glass patterns that are easily confused with Early American Prescut. All of the pieces in Anchor Hocking's pattern have ten-point stars except the punch cups and Lazy Susan inserts.

Avocado
Bowl, Dip, 5 1/2 In. 12.00

Crystal
Ashtray, 4 In. 5.00
Ashtray, 7 3/4 In. 15.00
Bowl, 10 3/4 In. 12.00
Bowl, 3-Footed, 6 3/4 In. . . 5.00
Bowl, 7 1/4 In. 6.00
Bowl, 8 3/4 In. 9.00
Bowl, Oval, 9 x 4 In. 7.00
Bowl, Salad, 10 3/4 In. . . 12.00
Bowl, Smooth Rim,
  4 1/4 In. 22.00
Butter, Cover 6.00
Candleholders, Pair 60.00
Candlestick, 2-Light,
  7 In. 60.00
Candy Dish, Cover,
  5 1/4 In. . . . . 3.00 to 6.00
Candy Dish, Cover,
  7 1/4 In. 15.00
Candy Dish, Cover,
  Metal Finial, 7 1/4 In. . . 27.00
Candy Jar, Cover,
  7 1/4 In. . . . . . 10.00 to 12.00
Coaster . . . . 2.00 to 3.00
Creamer 3.00
Cruet, Stopper,
  7 3/4 In. . . . . . . 5.00 to 10.00
Cup 3.00
Egg Plate,
  11 3/4 In. . . . . 42.00 to 69.00
Pitcher, 60 Oz. 17.00
Punch Set, Bowl, Cups,
  Ladle, Box, 14 Piece . . 45.00
Relish, 2 Sections, Tab
  Handles, 10 In. 7.00
Relish, 3 Sections, Oval,
  8 1/2 In. 3.00
Salt & Pepper . . . . 8.00 to 9.00
Snack Plate,
  10 In. . . . . . . 10.00 to 12.00
Sugar, Cover . . . . 4.00 to 10.00
Syrup 23.00
Tray, Hostess,
  6 1/2 x 12 In. 13.00
Tumbler, Water,
  10 Oz., 4 1/2 In. 7.00
Vase, 8 1/2 In. 7.00
Vase, 10 In. . . . . 12.00 to 13.00

Honey Gold
Bowl, 3-Footed, 6 3/4 In. . . 9.00

EARLY AMERICAN ROCK
  CRYSTAL
See Rock Crystal

EARLY AMERICAN
  SANDWICH GLASS
See Sandwich Duncan
  & Miller

ELONGATED
  HONEYCOMB
See Colony

ENGLISH HOBNAIL

Westmoreland Glass Company, Grapeville, Pennsylvania, made English Hobnail pattern from the 1920s through 1983. It is similar to Miss America except for more-rounded hobs and the absence of the typical Hocking sunburst ray on the base. English Hobnail was made in Amber, Cobalt Blue, Crystal, Green, Ice Blue, Light Laurel Green, Milk Glass, Pink, Red, and Turquoise. Some pieces were flashed with black or ruby. There is much variation in the shading, and a darker amber was reissued in the 1960s. Red and Pink reproduction pieces were made in the 1980s.

Amber
Bonbon, Handle,
  6 1/2 In. 95.00

Bowl, Grapefruit,
6 1/2 In. 24.00

Finger Bowl, 4 1/2 In. . . . 24.00

Cobalt Blue

Bonbon, Handle,
6 1/2 In. 155.00

Crystal

Bonbon, Handle,
6 1/2 In. 19.50

Bowl, Footed, Oval,
9 In. 55.00

Bowl, Grapefruit,
6 1/2 In. 12.00

Bowl, Ruffled Edge,
5 1/2 In. 24.00

Candlestick, 5 1/2 In.,
Pair 45.00

Candy Jar, Cover, 1/2 Lb.,
9 In. . . . . 40.00 to 50.00

Cheese Dish, Cover,
6 In. 49.50

Creamer, Square Foot . . . 12.00

Cup . . . . 3.00 to 6.50

Cup, After Dinner 20.00

Cup & Saucer . . . 9.00 to 19.00

Dish, Mayonnaise, 6 In. . . 14.50

Goblet, Champagne,
4 Oz. 10.00

Goblet, Cocktail, 3 Oz. . . 10.00

Goblet, Cordial, 1 Oz. . . . 12.00

Goblet, Water,
8 Oz. . . . . 10.00 to 27.50

Goblet, Wine, Square
Foot, 2 Oz. . . . 10.00 to 12.00

Ice Tub, 2 Handles,
4 In. 49.00

Ivy Ball, Crimped Top,
Footed, 6 1/2 In. 45.00

Jardiniere, 5 1/2 In. 65.00

Nut Dish, Footed,
Individual . . . 10.00 to 26.00

Oyster Cocktail, Square
Foot, 5 Oz. . . . 8.50 to 12.00

Pitcher, 32 Oz. 60.00

Plate, Bread & Butter,
5 1/2 In. . . . . . . 5.00 to 7.50

Plate, Luncheon,
8 1/2 In. . . . . . 8.00 to 12.00

Plate, Luncheon, Square,
8 3/4 In. 10.00

Plate, Square,
6 In. . . . . 6.00 to 10.00

Rose Bowl, 5 In. 20.00

Salt & Pepper, Round
Foot . . . . 20.00 to 40.00

Salt & Pepper, Square
Foot 20.00

Salt Dip, Footed,
Triangular 25.00

Sherbet, High 12.50

Sherbet, Round Foot,
High 8.00

Sherbet, Round Foot,
Low 7.00

Sherbet, Square Foot,
High . . . . 8.00 to 9.50

Sherbet, Square Foot,
Low 6.00

Soup, Cream, 2 Handles,
6 1/2 In. 13.00

Soup, Cream, 2 Handles,
Underplate 21.00

Sugar, Hexagonal
Foot . . . . 8.00 to 12.50

Sugar & Creamer, Hexagonal
Foot . . . . 17.00 to 27.00

Tidbit, 2 Tiers 30.00

Tumbler, 5 Oz. 10.00

Tumbler, 8 Oz. 10.00

Tumbler, 12 Oz. 12.00

Tumbler, Footed,
5 Oz. . . . . 10.00 to 18.00

Tumbler, Footed,
7 Oz. 10.00

Tumbler, Footed,
12 Oz. . . . . 14.00 to 24.00

Tumbler, Square Foot,
11 Oz. 15.00

Vase, 6 1/2 In. 25.00

Green

Candy Dish, Cover,
3-Footed, Frosted,
Painted Flowers 24.00

Candy Jar, 1/2 Lb.,
9 In. 89.00

Nut Dish, Triangular,
Footed 48.00

Ice Blue

Bonbon, Handle,
6 1/2 In. 155.00

Bottle, Toilet, 5 Oz. 65.00

Goblet, Water, 9 Oz. 75.00

Vase, Ivy, Square Foot,
6 1/2 In. 89.00

Milk Glass

Ashtray, Hat 20.00

Basket, 6 In. 60.00

Candleholder, Pair 22.00

Cruet, 5 In. 23.00

Goblet, Water, 8 Oz. 12.00

Rose Bowl, 6 In. 18.00

Sugar, Footed 8.00

Pink

Bottle, Toilet, 5 Oz. 46.00

Bowl, 6 In. 16.00

Jam Jar, Cover 55.00

Plate, Luncheon, 8 In. . . . 17.00

Salt & Pepper 48.00

Saltshaker, Footed,
Triangular 25.00

Saltshaker, Open Foot . . . 25.00

Sherbet, High 12.00

Sugar 7.00

Red

Bonbon, Handle, 6 1/2 In. 99.50

Turquoise

Basket 140.00

ENGLISH HOBNAIL
See also Miss America

FAIRFAX

Fairfax was made by Fostoria Glass Company, Fostoria, Ohio, from 1927 to 1960. The name Fairfax refers to a glass blank and to an etching pattern. The same glass blanks were used for other etched designs including June, Trojan, and Versailles. The undecorated blank, also known as No. 2375, is popular with collectors. The same shapes were used to make other patterns with etched designs. The glass was made in

Amber, Azure (blue), Black, Crystal, Gold Tint, Green, Orchid, Rose (pink), Ruby, Topaz, and Wisteria.

Amber
Cup & Saucer 8.00
Sauceboat 20.00

Azure
Baker, Oval, 9 1/4 In. . . . 60.00
Candy Dish, Cover,
   3-Footed 100.00
Compote, 7 In. 60.00
Cup, Footed 10.00
Cup & Saucer 15.00
Cup & Saucer, Footed . . . 18.00
Goblet, Cocktail, 3 Oz.,
   5 1/4 In. 24.00
Ice Bucket 60.00
Nut Dish 30.00
Plate, Bread & Butter,
   6 In. 5.00
Plate, Salad, 7 1/2 In. 8.00
Sauceboat, Underplate . . 100.00
Sugar 13.00
Sugar & Creamer 50.00
Tumbler, Footed, 9 Oz.,
   5 1/4 In. 26.00
Tumbler, Footed, 12 Oz.,
   6 In. 32.00

Crystal
Goblet, Water, 10 Oz.,
   8 1/4 In. 18.00
Sherbet, 6 In.. . . . . 12.00

Green
Cup & Saucer,
   After Dinner 20.00
Cup & Saucer, Footed . . . 12.00
Icer 20.00
Pitcher 225.00
Sauceboat, Underplate . . . 95.00
Saucer 4.00

Orchid
Plate, Dinner, 10 1/2 In. . . 50.00
Soup, Cream 20.00

Rose
Butter 110.00
Creamer 15.00
Cup & Saucer 15.00
Grill Plate, 10 1/4 In. 50.00

Icer, 2 Piece 49.00
Plate, Bread & Butter,
   6 In. 5.00
Plate, Salad, 7 1/2 In. 6.00
Plate, Salad, 8 3/4 In. . . . 10.00

Topaz
Bowl, Lemon, 2 Handles,
   9 In. 16.00
Cup 5.00
Cup & Saucer,
   After Dinner 12.00
Icer . . . . 20.00 to 25.00
Sherbet, 6 Oz.,
   6 In. . . . . 12.00 to 14.00
Sweetmeat, 2 Handles . . . 18.00
Tumbler, Footed,
   5 Oz., 4 1/2 In. 9.00

FAN & FEATHER
See Adam

FINE RIB
See Homespun

FIRE-KING

Fire-King Oven Glass, Fire-King Ovenware, and the related Anchorglass dinnerware were all made by Anchor Hocking Glass Corporation, Lancaster, Ohio, from 1941 through 1992. Most of the glass is heat resistant. Fire-King Oven Glass was made in plain Ivory or in Ivory, Jade-ite, and transparent Sapphire Blue with an embossed lacy pattern. A matching dinnerware set, called Philbe, is harder to find. It was made in Blue, Crystal, Green, and Pink. Fire-King Ovenware was

made by Anchor Hocking from the late 1940s through the 1960s. Plain dinnerware listed in this section is also known as Restaurant Ware. It was made in Azure-ite, Crystal, Ivory, Jade-ite, Pink, Rose-ite, and White (later called Anchorwhite). Some pieces were decorated with gold trim, fired-on colors, or decals. Anchor-glass dinnerware sets were made in patterns named 1700 Line, Alice, Anniversary Rose, Blue Mosaic, Bubble, Charm, Early American Prescut, Fleurette, Game Bird, Gray Laurel, Jane-Ray, Meadow Green, Peach Lustre, Primrose, Sheaf of Wheat, Soreno, Swirl Fire-King, Three Bands, Turquoise Blue, Wexford, and Wheat. These are listed in this book in their own sections.

Azure-Ite
Bowl, Blossom,
   5 1/4 In. 10.00
Relish, 3 Sections,
   Gold Trim 10.00

Crystal
Batter Bowl, 3/4-In.
   Band 50.00
Batter Bowl, 1-In. Band . . 70.00
Bowl, Cereal, 8 Oz. 35.00
Bowl, Chili, 5 In. 25.00
Candy Dish, Maple
   Leaf 30.00
Candy Dish, Shell 35.00
Custard Cup 6.00
Custard Cup, Fired-On
   White 4.50
Flower Pot, Ruffled 30.00
Measuring Cup, 16 Oz. . . 14.00
Mixing Bowl, Ribbed,
   5 1/2 In. 65.00

Mixing Bowl, Ribbed,
7 1/4 In. 65.00

Pie Plate,
50th Anniversary 30.00

Refrigerator Dish,
Cover, 4 x 8 In. 6.00

Skillet, Spout,
7 In. 165.00

Ivory

Batter Bowl 16.00

Batter Bowl, 2 Handles . . 14.00

Bowl, Cereal,
16 Oz. . . . . 2.00 to 5.00

Bowl, Chili,
5 In. . . . . 5.00 to 10.00

Bowl, Vegetable,
8 1/2 In. 5.00

Cake Stand,
Gold Trim . . . . 15.00 to 18.00

Casserole, Cover, 2-Handled
Server, 8 1/2 In. 32.00

Casserole, Cover, Peach
Blossom, 1 1/2 Qt. 25.00

Casserole, Electric Warmer,
1 1/2 Qt. 24.00

Casserole, Tab Handles,
5 1/4 In. 3.00

Creamer . . . . 4.00 to 6.00

Cup & Saucer 3.00

Cup & Saucer, Tulip 6.00

Custard Cup, Cover, Peach
Blossom, Ruffled Edge,
6 Oz. 8.00

Custard Cup, Flared 7.00

Loaf Pan, Fruit,
5 x 9 In. 15.00

Mixing Bowl, Beaded
Edge, 6 In. 8.00

Mixing Bowl, Black Dots,
Splashproof, 2 Qt.,
7 5/8 In. 88.00

Mixing Bowl, Black Dots,
Splashproof, 3 Qt.,
8 1/2 In. 50.00

Mixing Bowl, Black Dots,
Splashproof, 4 Qt.,
9 1/2 In. 55.00

Mixing Bowl, Colonial, Peach
Blossom, 7 3/8 In. 15.00

Mixing Bowl, Colonial, Peach
Blossom, 8 5/8 In. 18.00

Mixing Bowl, Fruit,
6 In. 15.00

Mixing Bowl, Modern Tulip,
3 Qt., 8 1/4 In. 20.00

Mixing Bowl, Red Dots,
Splashproof, 1 Qt.,
6 1/2 In. 50.00

Mixing Bowl, Red Dots,
Splashproof, 2 Qt.,
7 5/8 In. 55.00

Mixing Bowl, Swirl,
7 In. 5.00

Mixing Bowl, Tulip,
4 Qt., 9 1/2 In. 28.00

Mixing Bowl, Tulip,
Set Of 3 . . . . 75.00

Mug . . . . 4.00 to 6.00

Mug, Peach Blossom 8.00

Plate, Dinner,
9 1/8 In. . . . . 3.00 to 5.00

Plate, Salad, 7 3/4 In. 2.00

Refrigerator Dish, Cover,
4 x 4 In. 27.00

Refrigerator Dish, Cover,
4 x 8 In. 43.00

Relish, 3 Sections,
Gold Trim . . . . 8.00 to 13.00

Relish, Oval, 3 Sections,
11 1/8 In. 4.00

Saucer 1.00

Sugar & Creamer 5.00

Utility Pan, Fruit,
10 1/2 x 6 1/2 In. 15.00

Warming Plate,
2 Tab Handles 14.00

Jade-ite

Batter Bowl . . . . 40.00 to 45.00

Beater,
Electric . . . . 125.00 to 135.00

Bowl, Beaded Edge,
7 In. 30.00

Bowl, Breakfast, 10 Oz.,
4 7/8 In. . . . . . 14.00 to 40.00

Bowl, Cereal, 8 Oz. 20.00

Bowl, Cereal, 16 Oz. 19.00

Bowl, Cereal, Rim,
8 Oz. . . . . 25.00 to 37.00

Bowl, Deep,
10 Oz. . . . . . . 48.00 to 125.00

Bowl, Deep,
15 Oz. . . . . 35.00 to 42.00

Bowl, Fruit,
4 3/4 In. . . . . . 10.00 to 20.00

Bowl, Grapefruit, 8 Oz.,
6 1/4 In. 24.00

Butter, Crystal Cover . . . 125.00

Cup, After Dinner 49.00

Cup & Saucer . . . 8.00 to 18.00

Cup & Saucer,
After Dinner 95.00

Cup & Saucer, Heavy,
7 Oz. 18.00

Custard Cup 135.00

Eggcup 50.00

Grill Plate,
9 5/8 In. . . . . 27.00 to 38.00

Juicer, For Mixer 45.00

Mixing Bowl, Beaded Edge,
4 7/8 In. 20.00

Mixing Bowl, Beaded Edge,
7 1/8 In. 12.00

Mixing Bowl, Swedish
Modern, 5 In. 70.00

Mug, Chocolate, Straight,
6 Oz. . . . . 26.00 to 35.00

Mug, Coffee,
7 Oz. . . . . 9.00 to 12.00

Mug, Heavy, 7 Oz. 21.00

Mug, Shaving 14.00

Pie Plate 14.00

Pie Plate, Embossed,
10 1/2 In. 650.00

Pitcher, Milk,
20 Oz. . . . . . . 80.00 to 93.00

Pitcher, Milk, Bead & Bar,
20 Oz. . . . . . 450.00 to 470.00

Plate, Bread & Butter,
5 1/2 In. 150.00

Plate, Bread & Butter,
6 3/4 In. . . . . . 15.00 to 16.00

Plate, Dinner,
9 In. . . . . 26.00 to 27.00

Plate, Indentation, Oval,
8 7/8 In. . . . . 92.00 to 140.00

Plate, Luncheon, 8 In. . . . 80.00

Plate, Salad,
6 3/4 In. . . . . . 10.00 to 15.00

Platter, Oval,
9 1/2 In. . . . . 85.00 to 115.00

Platter, Oval,
11 1/2 In. . . . . 39.00 to 52.00

Reamer, Grapefruit 400.00

Refrigerator Dish,
Cover, 4 x 8 In. 60.00

Refrigerator Dish, Cover,
Embossed, 4 x 4 In. . . . 65.00

Saucer 5.00

Saucer, After Dinner 32.00

Saucer, Deep,
6 In. 5.00

Skillet, 1 Spout,
7 In. . . . . . . 120.00 to 150.00

Skillet, 2 Spouts,
7 In. . . . . . . 189.00 to 200.00

Soup, Dish, Flanged,
9 In. . . . . . 123.00 to 155.00

Sapphire Blue

Bottle, Nurser,
4 Oz. . . . . 15.00 to 20.00

Bowl, Cereal,
5 3/8 In. . . . . . 23.00 to 25.00

Bowl, Utility, 6 7/8 In. . . 20.00

Bowl, Utility, 10 1/8 In. . . 25.00

Casserole, 10 Oz.,
4 3/4 In. 6.50

Casserole, 2 Handles,
9 3/4 In. 15.00

Casserole, 8 1/2 In. 15.00

Casserole, Cover, 10 Oz.,
4 3/4 In. 13.50

Casserole, Knob Cover,
6 1/2 In. 9.00

Casserole, Pie Plate
Cover, 1 1/2 Quart 19.00

Casserole, Tab Handles,
8 1/4 In. 6.00

Custard Cup,
6 Oz. . . . . 4.00 to 5.25

Custard Cup,
12 Oz. . . . . 4.00 to 5.00

Loaf Pan,
9 x 5 In. . . . . . 15.00 to 22.00

Measuring Cup, 1 Spout,
8 Oz. . . . . 22.00 to 30.00

Mixing Bowl, 8 3/8 In. . . 25.00

Mixing Bowl,
10 1/8 In. 35.00

Mixing Bowl, Measuring,
2 Spouts, 16 Oz. 35.00

Mug, 7 Oz. 25.00

Mug, 8 Oz. 37.00

Percolator Top, 2 1/8 In. . . 5.00

Pie Plate, 8 3/8 In. 7.50

Pie Plate,
9 5/8 In. . . . . . 9.50 to 11.00

Pie Plate, Cover,
6 3/4 In. 10.00

Pie Plate, Juice Saver,
10 3/8 In. . . 130.00 to 180.00

Refrigerator Dish,
Cover, 4 x 5 In. 18.00

Refrigerator Dish,
Cover, 5 x 9 In. 30.00

Roaster, 8 3/4 In. 45.00

Roaster, Cover,
10 3/8 In. 130.00

Table Server,
2 Tab Handles 24.00

Utility Pan,
6 1/2 x 10 1/2 In. 35.00

White

Bowl, Breakfast, 10 Oz. . . 9.00

Cake Plate, Gold Trim,
Footed, 10 In. 12.00

Cup, Bachelor Buttons 3.00

Cup & Saucer,
Bachelor Buttons 6.00

Mug, Coffee, 7 Oz. 5.00

Planter 8.00

Plate, Salad, 6 3/4 In. 15.00

Relish, 3 Sections,
Gold Trim 11.00

Tom & Jerry Set, Bowl,
Red & Green Decal,
8 Cups 60.00

FLANDERS

Flanders dinnerware was
made at the U.S. Glass
Company's Tiffin, Ohio,
plant from 1914 to 1935.
It was made in Crystal and
in Mandarin (yellow) or
Pink with crystal trim.

Crystal

Sherbet, 4 1/2 In. 20.00

Pink

Console, Footed, 11 In. . 275.00

Goblet, Water, 8 1/4 In. . . 72.00

FLAT DIAMOND
See Diamond Quilted

FLEURETTE

Fleurette is a white Fire-
King pattern with decal
decoration. It was made
by Anchor Hocking Glass
Corporation, Lancaster,
Ohio, from 1958 to 1961.
Other related patterns are
listed in the Fire-King section in this book.

Bowl, Dessert,
4 5/8 In. . . . . 3.00 to 5.00

Bowl, Vegetable,
8 1/4 In. 12.50

Creamer 4.00

Cup, 8 Oz. 4.00

Cup, Snack, 5 Oz. . 2.00 to 3.00

Cup & Saucer . . . . 2.50 to 4.00

Plate, Dinner,
9 1/8 In. . . . . 3.50 to 6.00

Platter, Oval,
12 In. . . . . 8.00 to 15.00

Saucer 1.00

Snack Tray, Cup 7.00

Soup, Dish,
6 5/8 In. . . . . . . 5.00 to 12.50

Sugar & Creamer,
Cover 18.00

❖

**Sometimes glasses get a
cloudy look from the
lime deposits in hard
water. Cover the cloudy
part with wet potato
peelings for 24 hours.
Rinse, dry.**

❖

FLORAGOLD

The iridescent marigold color of carnival glass was copied in this 1950s pattern made by Jeannette Glass Company, Jeannette, Pennsylvania. The pattern is called Floragold or Louisa, the name of the original carnival glass pattern that was copied. Pieces were made in Crystal, Ice Blue, Iridescent, Reddish Yellow, and Shell Pink.

Crystal
Berry Bowl, Ruffled Edge,
  5 1/2 In. 8.00
Bowl, Cereal, 5 1/2 In. . . 40.00
Bowl, Fruit, Ruffled Edge,
  12 In. 8.00
Bowl, Ruffled Edge,
  9 1/2 In. 8.00
Bowl, Square,
  4 1/2 In. . . . . . . 5.00 to 7.00
Bowl, Square, 8 1/2 In. . . 12.00
Bowl, Square, Ruffled Edge,
  8 1/2 In. 8.00
Candy Dish, 4-Footed,
  5 1/4 In. 10.00
Candy Dish, Cover 50.00
Candy Dish, Handle,
  5 In. 12.00
Creamer 9.00
Cup 5.00
Cup & Saucer . . 15.00 to 19.00
Pitcher, 64 Oz. 37.00
Plate, Dinner,
  8 1/2 In. . . . . . 40.00 to 45.00
Plate, Indented,
  13 1/2 In. . . . . 50.00 to 75.00

Platter, 11 1/2 In. 18.00
Saucer, 5 1/4 In. 15.00
Sherbet 15.00
Sugar, Cover 23.00
Sugar & Creamer,
  Cover 26.00
Tumbler, Footed,
  10 Oz. . . . . . . 18.00 to 20.00
Tumbler, Footed,
  11 Oz. 18.00
Vase,
  Ruffled . . . . 370.00 to 575.00

Iridescent
Ashtray, Square, 4 In. . . . 10.00
Berry Bowl, Ruffled Edge,
  5 1/2 In. 8.00
Bowl, Cereal,
  5 1/2 In. . . . . . 40.00 to 55.00
Bowl, Ruffled Edge,
  8 1/2 In. . . . . . . 8.00 to 20.00
Bowl, Ruffled Edge,
  9 1/2 In. . . . . . . 8.00 to 14.00
Bowl, Salad, 9 1/2 In. . . . 45.00
Bowl, Square,
  4 1/2 In. . . . . . . 5.00 to 8.00
Butter, Cover, 1/4 Lb. . . . 25.00
Butter, Cover, 6 1/4 In. . . 45.00
Butter, Cover,
  Rectangular . . . 25.00 to 30.00
Butter, Cover,
  Round . . . . . . 45.00 to 55.00
Butter, Round 15.00
Candy Dish, 4-Footed,
  5 1/4 In. . . . . . . 8.00 to 15.00
Candy Dish, Handle 8.00
Cheese Dish,
  Cover Only 30.00
Coaster, 4 In. . . . . 6.00 to 10.00
Creamer . . . . 9.00 to 15.00
Cup . . . . 5.00 to 9.00
Cup & Saucer . . 15.00 to 23.00
Pitcher, 64 Oz. . . 36.00 to 55.00
Plate,
  13 1/2 In. . . . . 23.00 to 28.00
Plate, 5 3/4 In. 14.00
Plate, Dinner,
  8 1/2 In. . . . . . 40.00 to 45.00
Plate, Indented,
  13 1/2 In. . . . . 50.00 to 75.00
Plate, No Indent,
  13 1/2 In. 18.00
Plate, Sherbet,
  5 1/4 In. . . . . . 12.00 to 14.00

Platter, Oval,
  11 1/4 In. . . . . 22.00 to 30.00
Salt & Pepper . . . 48.00 to 50.00
Saucer . . . . 12.00 to 15.00
Sherbet, Footed 18.00
Sugar . . . . 7.00 to 10.00
Sugar, Cover . . . 16.00 to 23.00
Tumbler, Footed,
  15 Oz. 125.00
Tumbler, Footed,
  Banded, 11 Oz. 20.00
Tumbler, Water, Footed,
  10 Oz. . . . . . . 20.00 to 26.00
Vase,
  Footed . . . . . 300.00 to 550.00

Reddish Yellow
Tray, 13 1/2 In. 24.00

FLORAL

Poinsettia blossoms are the decorations on Floral patterns made by Jeannette Glass Company from 1931 to 1935. Green is the most common color, although the pattern was also made in Amber, Crystal, Delphite, Green, Jadite, Pink, Red, and Yellow. Reproductions have been made.

Crystal
Vase, 8 Sides,
  6 7/8 In. 295.00

Green
Berry Bowl,
  4 In. . . . . 18.00 to 30.00
Bowl, Vegetable, Cover,
  Round, 8 In. . . 56.00 to 70.00

Bowl, Vegetable, Cover Only,
8 In. 38.00

Bowl, Vegetable, Oval,
9 In. . . . . 27.00 to 30.00

Butter,
Cover . . . . 110.00 to 130.00

Butter,
No Cover . . . . 20.00 to 25.00

Candlestick, 4 In. 50.00

Candlestick, 4 In.,
Pair . . . . . . 100.00 to 125.00

Candy Jar,
Cover . . . . . . 42.00 to 50.00

Coaster,
3 1/4 In. . . . . 10.00 to 19.00

Creamer . . . . . . 12.00 to 20.00

Cup . . . . 14.00 to 15.00

Cup & Saucer . . 20.00 to 28.00

Pitcher, 24 Oz.,
5 1/2 In. . . . 595.00 to 650.00

Pitcher, Cone, Footed,
32 Oz., 8 In. . . 38.00 to 45.00

Pitcher, Lemonade,
48 Oz., 10 1/4 In. 255.00

Plate, Dinner,
9 In. . . . . 22.00 to 28.00

Plate, Salad,
8 In. . . . . 15.00 to 20.00

Plate, Sherbet,
6 In. . . . . 9.00 to 25.00

Platter, Oval,
10 3/4 In. . . . . 19.00 to 30.00

Refrigerator Dish,
Cover Only, 4 7/8 In. . . 35.00

Refrigerator Dish, Cover,
Square, 4 In. 80.00

Relish, 2 Sections,
Oval . . . . 15.00 to 28.00

Salt & Pepper, Footed,
4 In. . . . . 42.00 to 62.00

Saltshaker . . . . . 25.00 to 26.00

Saucer . . . . 12.00 to 14.00

Sherbet . . . . 17.00 to 24.00

Sugar, Cover . . . 31.00 to 35.00

Sugar,
No Cover . . . . . 9.00 to 18.00

Sugar & Creamer 27.00

Sugar & Creamer,
Cover 60.00

Tray, Dresser, Oval,
9 1/4 In. 595.00

Tray, Square, 6 In. 38.00

Tumbler, Flat, 9 Oz.,
4 1/2 In. 230.00

Tumbler, Footed, 3 Oz.,
3 1/2 In. 265.00

Tumbler, Juice, Footed,
5 Oz., 4 In. . . . 22.00 to 28.00

Tumbler, Lemonade,
Footed, 9 Oz.,
5 1/4 In. . . . . 50.00 to 60.00

Tumbler, Water, Footed, 7 Oz.,
4 3/4 In. . . . . 22.00 to 30.00

Vase, 8 Sides,
6 7/8 In. 500.00

Vase, Flared,
3-Footed 700.00

Jadite

Refrigerator Dish,
Square, 5 In. 48.00

Pink

Berry Bowl,
4 In. . . . . 22.00 to 30.00

Bowl, Salad, 7 1/2 In. . . . 39.00

Bowl, Vegetable,
Cover, 8 In. . . . 50.00 to 85.00

Bowl, Vegetable,
Oval, 9 In. . . . . 25.00 to 35.00

Butter, Cover . . 95.00 to 125.00

Butter,
No Cover . . . . 25.00 to 40.00

Candlestick, Pair 125.00

Candy Dish,
Cover . . . . . . 43.00 to 50.00

Coaster,
3 1/4 In. . . . . 14.00 to 20.00

Compote, Footed,
9 In. 1995.00

Creamer . . . . . . 15.00 to 21.00

Cup . . . . 12.00 to 16.00

Cup & Saucer . . 24.00 to 35.00

Pitcher, Cone, Footed,
32 Oz., 8 In. . . 45.00 to 60.00

Pitcher, Juice, Cone,
32 Oz., 8 In. . . 42.00 to 45.00

Pitcher, Lemonade,
48 Oz., 10 1/4 In. 295.00

Plate, 6 In. . . . . . 6.00 to 10.00

Plate, 8 In. . . . . 14.00 to 19.00

Plate, Dinner,
9 In. . . . . 19.00 to 35.00

Plate, Salad,
8 In. . . . . 8.00 to 18.00

Plate, Sherbet,
6 In. . . . . 8.00 to 10.00

Platter, Oval,
10 3/4 In. . . . . 19.00 to 28.00

Platter, Rim,
11 In. . . . . . . 85.00 to 175.00

Relish, 2 Sections,
Oval . . . . 18.00 to 28.00

Salt & Pepper,
6 In. . . . . 35.00 to 75.00

Saltshaker,
6 In. . . . . 30.00 to 33.00

Saucer . . . . 13.00 to 15.00

Sherbet . . . . 17.00 to 25.00

Sugar 10.00

Sugar, Cover . . . 20.00 to 48.00

Sugar, Cover Only 20.00

Sugar & Creamer,
Cover . . . . 46.00 to 60.00

Tray, Square, Closed Handles,
6 In. . . . . 25.00 to 45.00

Tumbler, Juice, Footed,
5 Oz., 4 In. 27.00

Tumbler, Lemonade, 9 Oz.,
5 1/4 In. . . . . . 50.00 to 75.00

Tumbler, Water, Footed, 7 Oz.,
4 3/4 In. . . . . . 20.00 to 35.00

FLORAL & DIAMOND BAND

Floral & Diamond Band was made by the U.S. Glass Company from the late 1920s until c.1937. It features a large center flower and an edging of pressed diamond bands. Luncheon sets were made in varying shades of Green and Pink, but Black, Crystal, and Yellow were also used. Some Crystal pieces are Iridescent Marigold.

Crystal
Compote, 5 1/2 In. 20.00

Green
Berry Bowl, 4 1/2 In. 14.00
Creamer 18.00
Pitcher, 42 Oz. 145.00
Sherbet . . . . 5.00 to 10.00
Sugar, Cover 80.00
Tumbler, Iced Tea,
    5 In. 55.00
Tumbler, Water,
    4 In. . . . . 25.00 to 30.00

Pink
Butter,
    Cover . . . . . 150.00 to 175.00
Pitcher, 42 Oz. 135.00
Tumbler, Iced Tea,
    5 In. 35.00
Tumbler, Water, 4 In. . . . 25.00

FLORAL RIM
See Vitrock

FLORENTINE NO. I

Florentine No. I, also called Poppy No. I, is neither Florentine in appearance nor decorated with recognizable poppies. The plates are hexagonal and have scalloped edges, differentiating them from Florentine No. 2, which has round pieces. The pattern was made by the Hazel Atlas Glass Company from 1932 to 1935 in Cobalt Blue, Crystal,

Green, Pink, and Yellow. Reproductions have been made.

Cobalt Blue
Berry Bowl, 5 In. 38.00
Creamer, Ruffled Edge . . 68.00

Crystal
Ashtray 16.00
Berry Bowl, 5 In. 10.00
Creamer . . . . 5.00 to 13.00
Creamer,
    Ruffled Edge . . 30.00 to 46.00
Cup . . . . 8.00 to 10.00
Cup & Saucer . . 12.00 to 13.00
Grill Plate, 10 In. 12.00
Pitcher, Footed,
    36 Oz., 6 1/2 In. 40.00
Plate, Dinner,
    10 In. . . . . 6.00 to 16.00
Plate, Luncheon,
    8 1/2 In. . . . . . 7.00 to 12.00
Plate, Sherbet,
    6 In. . . . . 4.00 to 6.00
Platter, Oval,
    11 1/2 In. 20.00
Salt & Pepper,
    Footed 38.00
Saucer 4.00
Saucer, Silver Trim 3.00
Sherbet, Footed,
    3 Oz. . . . . 8.00 to 10.00
Soup, Cream . . . 10.00 to 25.00
Sugar 10.00
Sugar, Ruffled Edge 40.00
Sugar &
    Creamer . . . . . 10.00 to 20.00
Sugar & Creamer,
    Ruffled Edge . . 35.00 to 65.00
Tumbler, Footed,
    5 1/4 Oz., 3 1/4 In. 16.00
Tumbler, Thin,
    8 Oz., 4 3/16 In. 16.00
Tumbler, Thin,
    10 Oz., 4 3/4 In. 19.00
Vase, 6 In. . . . . . 28.00 to 40.00

Green
Bowl, Vegetable,
    Oval, 9 1/2 In. 50.00
Butter, Cover 155.00
Creamer 12.00
Creamer, Ruffled Edge . 100.00
Cup . . . . 8.00 to 13.00

Cup & Saucer . . 16.00 to 20.00
Grill Plate,
    10 1/4 In. 20.00
Pitcher, Footed, 36 Oz.,
    6 1/2 In. . . . . . 45.00 to 65.00
Plate, Dinner,
    10 In. . . . . 18.00 to 25.00
Plate, Luncheon,
    8 1/2 In. . . . . . 8.00 to 15.00
Plate, Sherbet,
    6 In. . . . . 4.00 to 12.00
Platter, Oval,
    11 1/2 In. . . . . 24.00 to 28.00
Salt & Pepper . . . 18.00 to 60.00
Saltshaker . . . . . 20.00 to 43.00
Saucer 5.00
Sherbet . . . . 10.00 to 14.00
Sugar 10.00
Tumbler, Juice, Footed,
    5 Oz., 3 3/8 In. 22.00
Tumbler, Water, Footed,
    10 Oz., 4 3/4 In. 36.00

Pink
Ashtray, 5 1/2 In. 95.00
Berry Bowl,
    5 In. . . . . 19.00 to 28.00
Berry Bowl, Master,
    8 1/2 In. . . . . . 34.00 to 50.00
Bowl, Cereal, 6 In. 50.00
Butter, Cover 169.00
Compote, Ruffled Edge,
    3 1/2 In. . . . . . 25.00 to 50.00
Creamer,
    Footed . . . . . . 20.00 to 24.00
Cup . . . . 9.00 to 14.00
Cup & Saucer . . 9.00 to 23.00
Nut Cup, Ruffled Edge,
    5 In. . . . . 20.00 to 25.00
Pitcher, 48 Oz.,
    7 1/2 In. 135.00
Pitcher, Juice, Footed,
    36 Oz., 6 1/2 In. 50.00
Plate, Dinner,
    10 In. . . . . 14.00 to 36.00
Plate, Luncheon,
    8 1/2 In. . . . . . 12.00 to 17.00
Plate, Sherbet,
    6 In. . . . . 8.00 to 13.00
Salt & Pepper . . . 59.00 to 65.00
Sherbet,
    Footed . . . . . . 10.00 to 15.00
Sugar . . . . 12.00 to 38.00
Sugar, Cover 45.00

Sugar, Ruffled Edge,
Open . . . . 50.00 to 60.00

Sugar & Creamer,
Cover 65.00

Sugar & Creamer,
Open . . . . 35.00 to 45.00

Tumbler, Juice, Footed, 5 Oz.,
3 3/4 In. . . . . . 26.00 to 55.00

Vase, 6 In. 35.00

Yellow

Ashtray, 5 1/2 In. 28.00

Berry Bowl, Master,
8 1/2 In. 45.00

Bowl, Vegetable, Oval,
9 1/2 In. . . . . . 49.00 to 60.00

Butter, Cover 165.00

Creamer 18.00

Cup . . . . 8.00 to 9.00

Grill Plate, 10 In. 16.00

Pitcher, Footed, 36 Oz.,
6 1/2 In. 48.00

Plate, Dinner,
10 In. 14.00

Platter, Oval,
11 1/2 In. . . . . 22.00 to 35.00

Salt & Pepper . . . 45.00 to 60.00

Sherbet, Footed,
3 Oz. 14.00

FLORENTINE NO. 2

Florentine No. 2, some-times called Poppy No. 2 or Oriental Poppy, was also made by Hazel Atlas Glass Company from 1934 to 1937. It has round plates instead of hexagonal plates, and larger and more prominent flowers than Florentine No. 1. It was made in Amber, Co-balt Blue, Crystal, Green, Ice Blue, and Pink. Amber is so light that many peo-ple refer to it as Yellow. Reproductions have been made.

Amber

Ashtray,
3 3/4 In. . . . . . 16.00 to 32.00

Ashtray,
5 1/2 In. . . . . . 22.00 to 42.00

Berry Bowl,
4 1/2 In. . . . . . 22.00 to 25.00

Berry Bowl,
8 In. . . . . 33.00 to 50.00

Bowl, Cereal,
6 In. . . . . 35.00 to 62.00

Bowl, Vegetable, Cover,
Oval, 9 In. . . . . 45.00 to 85.00

Butter,
Cover . . . . . 140.00 to 185.00

Butter, No Cover 50.00

Candlestick, Pair,
2 3/4 In. . . . . 40.00 to 85.00

Candy Dish,
Cover . . . . . 165.00 to 175.00

Candy Dish,
No Cover . . . . 55.00 to 75.00

Coaster, 3 1/4 In. 22.00

Creamer . . . . 10.00 to 15.00

Cup . . . . 8.00 to 10.00

Cup & Saucer . . 14.00 to 25.00

Custard
Cup . . . . . . 125.00 to 145.00

Gravy Boat . . . . 55.00 to 105.00

Gravy Boat, Underplate,
11 1/2 In. . . . 88.00 to 135.00

Grill Plate,
10 1/4 In. . . . . 15.00 to 20.00

Parfait, 6 In. . . . . 59.00 to 68.00

Pitcher, Cone, Footed, 28 Oz.,
7 1/2 In. . . . . . 19.00 to 39.00

Pitcher, Footed, 28 Oz.,
7 1/2 In. . . . . . 19.00 to 50.00

Pitcher, Water, Straight
Side, 48 Oz. 335.00

Plate, 6 1/4 In. 36.00

Plate, Dinner,
10 In. . . . . 12.00 to 25.00

Plate, Luncheon,
8 1/2 In. . . . . . . 8.00 to 27.00

Plate, Sherbet,
6 In. . . . . 5.00 to 9.00

Platter, Oval,
11 In. . . . . 11.00 to 25.00

Relish, 3 Sections,
10 In. . . . . 28.00 to 45.00

Salt & Pepper . . . 48.00 to 65.00

Saltshaker . . . . . 30.00 to 60.00

Saucer . . . . 4.00 to 8.00

Sherbet, Footed . . 8.00 to 14.00

Soup, Cream,
4 3/4 In. . . . . . 20.00 to 45.00

Sugar . . . . 10.00 to 20.00

Sugar, Cover . . . 35.00 to 40.00

Sugar, Cover Only 20.00

Sugar & Creamer,
Cover . . . . 25.00 to 70.00

Sugar & Creamer,
Open 21.00

Tray,
Condiment . . 92.00 to 135.00

Tumbler, Footed, 5 Oz.,
3 1/4 In. . . . . . 17.00 to 28.00

Tumbler, Footed, 5 Oz.,
4 In. . . . . 18.00 to 30.00

Tumbler, Footed, 9 Oz.,
4 1/2 In. . . . . . 20.00 to 39.00

Tumbler, Iced Tea, 12 Oz.,
5 In. . . . . 38.00 to 60.00

Tumbler, Juice, Footed, 5 Oz.,
3 3/8 In. . . . . . 18.00 to 29.00

Tumbler, Water, 9 Oz.,
4 In. . . . . 20.00 to 35.00

Tumbler, Water, Footed, 9 Oz.,
4 1/2 In. . . . . . 35.00 to 40.00

Underplate, For Gravy Boat,
11 1/2 In. . . . . 45.00 to 54.00

Vase, 6 In. . . . . . 60.00 to 62.00

Crystal

Ashtray, 3 3/4 In. 25.00

Berry Bowl,
4 1/2 In. . . . . . 11.00 to 16.00

Butter, Cover 110.00

Candlestick,
2 3/4 In. 22.00

Candy Dish 120.00

Compote, Ruffled Edge,
3 1/2 In. . . . . . 18.00 to 25.00

Creamer, Footed 10.00

Cup . . . . 5.00 to 9.00

Cup & Saucer . . . 9.00 to 16.00

Custard Cup 75.00

Parfait, 6 In. 35.00

Pitcher, 48 Oz.,
7 1/2 In. .... 50.00 to 60.00

Pitcher, 76 Oz.,
8 1/4 In. .... 70.00 to 120.00

Plate, Dinner,
10 In. .... 10.00 to 18.00

Plate, Luncheon,
8 1/2 In. .... 4.00 to 9.00

Plate, Sherbet,
6 In. .... 4.00 to 25.00

Platter, Oval,
11 In. .... 22.00 to 23.00

Salt & Pepper ... 40.00 to 42.00

Saltshaker ..... 15.00 to 20.00

Saucer 5.00

Sherbet 10.00

Soup, Cream,
4 3/4 In. ..... 10.00 to 18.00

Sugar .... 9.00 to 12.00

Sugar & Creamer,
Metal Cover 20.00

Tumbler, Footed, Juice,
5 Oz., 3 3/8 In. 10.00

Tumbler, Iced Tea,
12 Oz., 5 In. 20.00

Tumbler, Water,
9 Oz., 4 In. ... 10.00 to 20.00

Vase, 6 In. ..... 28.00 to 35.00

Green

Ashtray,
5 1/2 In. ..... 19.00 to 30.00

Berry Bowl,
4 1/2 In. ..... 12.00 to 15.00

Berry Bowl,
8 In. 30.00

Bowl, 5 1/2 In. 55.00

Bowl, Vegetable, Oval,
Cover, 9 In. 80.00

Butter, Cover 140.00

Candy Dish 40.00

Candy Jar, Cover 150.00

Coaster,
3 1/4 In. ..... 14.00 to 18.00

Creamer .... 9.00 to 10.00

Cup .... 8.00 to 10.00

Cup & Saucer ... 5.00 to 20.00

Gravy Boat 60.00

Parfait, 6 In. 35.00

Pitcher, 76 Oz.,
8 1/4 In. 215.00

Pitcher, Cone Footed,
28 Oz., 7 1/2 In. 49.00

Pitcher, No Ice Lip, 48 Oz.,
7 1/2 In. 125.00

Plate, Dinner,
10 In. .... 16.00 to 20.00

Plate, Luncheon,
8 1/2 In. ...... 8.00 to 15.00

Plate, Sherbet,
6 In. .... 4.00 to 9.00

Platter, Oval,
11 In. .... 16.00 to 25.00

Salt & Pepper ... 42.00 to 60.00

Saltshaker,
Footed .... 8.00 to 25.00

Saucer .... 4.00 to 10.00

Sherbet, Footed .. 8.00 to 14.00

Soup, Cream,
4 3/4 In. ...... 6.00 to 20.00

Sugar, Cover 39.00

Sugar &
Creamer ..... 17.00 to 40.00

Tumbler, Cocktail,
5 Oz., 4 In. ... 17.00 to 18.00

Tumbler, Footed, 5 Oz.,
3 1/4 In. ..... 15.00 to 24.00

Tumbler, Footed, 9 Oz.,
4 1/2 In. ..... 30.00 to 35.00

Tumbler, Iced Tea,
12 Oz., 5 In. 40.00

Tumbler, Juice, 5 Oz.,
3 3/8 In. ..... 14.00 to 16.00

Tumbler, Water, 9 Oz.,
4 In. .... 13.00 to 16.00

Underplate, For Gravy Boat,
11 1/2 In. 45.00

Pink

Berry Bowl,
4 1/2 In. 17.00

Candy Dish,
Cover ..... 145.00 to 155.00

Candy Dish,
No Cover ... 25.00 to 100.00

Compote, Ruffled Edge,
3 1/2 In. ..... 20.00 to 48.00

Pitcher, 48 Oz.,
7 1/2 In. ... 135.00 to 175.00

Plate, Dinner, 10 In. 35.00

Plate, Luncheon,
8 1/2 In. 24.00

Relish, 3 Sections,
10 In. 28.00

Sherbet, 6 In. 13.00

Soup, Cream .... 12.00 to 25.00

Tumbler, Iced Tea,
9 Oz., 4 In. 18.00

FLOWER
See Princess Feather

FLOWER &
LEAF BAND
See Indiana Custard

FLOWER BASKET
See No. 615

FLOWER GARDEN WITH BUTTERFLIES

There really is a butterfly hiding in the flower on this U.S. Glass Company pattern called Flower Garden with Butterflies, Butterflies & Roses, Flower Garden, or Wildrose with Apple Blossom. It was made in the late 1920s in a variety of colors, including Amber, Black, Blue, Canary Yellow, Crystal, Green, and Pink.

Blue

Ashtray 295.00

Candy Dish,
Cover 430.00

Canary Yellow

Candy Dish, Cover,
Heart 1500.00

Crystal

Dish, Mayonnaise,
Footed, Yellow Band,
4 3/4 In. 65.00

Green
Powder Jar, Footed 215.00
Tray, Rectangular,
11 3/4 x 7 3/4 In. 95.00

Pink
Cup & Saucer 225.00
Powder Jar, Cover,
7 1/2 In. 215.00

FLOWER RIM
See Vitrock

FOREST GREEN

Its Forest Green color identifies this pattern. Anchor Hocking Glass Corporation, Lancaster, Ohio, made this very plain pattern from 1950 to 1965. Other patterns were also made in this same deep green color, but these are known by their pattern names. Related Anchor Hocking patterns are listed in the Fire-King section in this book.

Ashtray, Hexagonal,
5 3/4 In. ..... 10.00 to 12.00
Ashtray, Square,
3 1/2 In. .... 4.00 to 7.00
Ashtray, Square,
4 3/8 In. 6.00
Batter Bowl, Spout 40.00
Bowl, Deep,
5 1/4 In. ...... 8.00 to 12.00
Bowl, Dessert,
4 3/4 In. ...... 5.00 to 14.00
Bowl, Popcorn 23.00

Bowl, Salad, 7 3/8 In. 15.00
Bowl, Vegetable, Oval,
8 1/2 In. ..... 23.00 to 34.00
Centerpiece, Cover 135.00
Cup & Saucer ..... 5.00 to 9.00
Dish, Maple Leaf
Shape .... 8.00 to 10.00
Dish, Shell 14.00
Dish, Triangular 8.50
Mixing Bowl,
6 In. .... 9.00 to 17.00
Pitcher, Juice,
22 Oz. .... 23.00 to 26.00
Plate, Dinner,
9 1/2 In. ..... 33.00 to 45.00
Plate, Luncheon,
8 3/8 In. ...... 9.00 to 11.00
Plate, Salad,
6 3/4 In. ..... 11.50 to 12.00
Platter, Rectangular,
8 x 11 .... 22.00
Popcorn Set 135.00
Punch Cup ...... 2.50 to 4.00
Punch Set, 13 Piece 110.00
Punch Set,
14 Piece .... 75.00 to 165.00
Relish, Handle 13.00
Sherbet, Flat 8.00
Snack Plate Set, 2 Piece .. 10.00
Soup, Dish,
6 In. .... 18.00 to 20.00
Sugar .... 6.00 to 12.00
Sugar & Creamer 16.00
Tumbler, 5 Oz.,
3 1/2 In. .... 6.00 to 8.50
Tumbler, 9 1/2 Oz.,
Tall .... 6.00 to 7.00
Tumbler, 11 Oz.,
5 In. .... 7.00 to 8.00
Tumbler, 14 Oz.,
5 In. 7.50
Tumbler, Fancy, 9 Oz.,
4 1/4 In. .... 4.00 to 5.00
Tumbler, Iced Tea, 15 Oz.,
6 1/2 In. ..... 10.00 to 14.00
Tumbler, Iced Tea,
32 Oz. .... 17.00 to 18.00
Tumbler, Long Boy, 15 Oz.,
6 1/2 In. ..... 10.00 to 13.00
Tumbler, Table,
9 Oz., 4 In. 6.00
Vase, 6 3/8 In. .... 6.00 to 7.00
Vase, 9 In. 1.00
Vase, Ivy, 4 In. 5.00

FORTUNE

Anchor Hocking Glass Corporation, Lancaster, Ohio, made Fortune pattern in 1937 and 1938. The simple design was made in Crystal or Pink.

Crystal
Cake Plate, 3-Footed,
11 1/2 In. 25.00
Candy Dish,
Cover ...... 15.00 to 22.00

Pink
Berry Bowl, 4 In. .. 8.00 to 9.00
Bowl, Cereal, 5 1/4 In. .. 22.00
Bowl, Handle,
4 1/2 In. ...... 7.00 to 10.00
Bowl, Rolled Rim,
5 1/4 In. 17.00
Candy Dish, Cover Only . 19.00
Cup 11.00
Cup & Saucer 15.00
Tumbler, Juice, 5 Oz.,
3 1/2 In. 10.00
Tumbler, Water, 9 Oz.,
4 In. .... 12.00 to 14.00

FROSTED BLOCK
See Beaded Block

❖

If a decorative glass dinner plate is scratched, it will look better for display if it is coated with a non-yellowing floor wax and then lightly buffed. Of course, then you can't use it for food.

❖

FRUITS

Pears, grapes, apples, and other fruits are displayed in small bunches on pieces of Fruits pattern. Hazel Atlas Glass Company and several other companies made this pattern about 1931 to 1933. Pieces are known in Crystal, Green, Iridescent finish, and Pink.

Green
Bowl, 5 In. 40.00
Cup . . . . 6.00 to 11.00
Cup & Saucer . . 12.00 to 16.00
Pitcher, 7 In. 140.00
Plate, Luncheon,
    8 In. . . . . 11.00 to 20.00
Saucer 6.00
Tumbler, 12 Oz., 5 In. . . 199.50

Pink
Cup 7.00
Sherbet . . . . 12.00 to 15.00

GAME BIRD

Game Bird, sometimes called Wild Bird, was made by Anchor Hocking Glass Corporation, Lancaster, Ohio, from 1959

to 1962. The opaque white glass was decorated with a decal of a Canada goose, mallard duck, ring-necked pheasant, or ruffled grouse. Other related patterns are listed in the Fire-King section in this book.

Canada Goose
Bowl, Dessert, 4 5/8 In. . . . 5.00
Mug, 8 Oz. . . . . . . 4.00 to 7.50
Plate, Bread & Butter,
    6 1/4 In. 10.00
Plate, Dinner, 9 1/8 In. . . . 6.50
Tumbler, Iced Tea,
    11 Oz. 12.00

Mallard Duck
Ashtray, 5 1/4 In. 15.00
Bowl, Dessert, 4 5/8 In. . . . 5.00
Mug, 8 Oz. 8.00
Plate, Bread & Butter,
    6 1/4 In. 10.00
Tumbler, Iced Tea,
    11 Oz. 12.00

Ring-Necked Pheasant
Bowl, Dessert, 4 5/8 In. . . . 5.00
Mug, 8 Oz. . . . . . . 4.00 to 8.00
Plate, Dinner, 9 1/8 In. . . . 6.50
Platter, 9 x 12 In. 50.00
Tumbler, Iced Tea,
    11 Oz. 12.00

Ruffled Grouse
Ashtray 18.00
Bowl, Dessert, 4 5/8 In. . . . 5.00
Mug, 8 Oz. 8.00
Plate, Bread & Butter,
    6 1/4 In. 10.00
Plate, Dinner, 9 1/8 In. . . . 6.50
Tumbler, Iced Tea,
    11 Oz., 5 In. . . 12.00 to 13.00

GAZEBO

Paden City Glass Manufacturing Company made

glass with the Gazebo etching in the 1930s. It looks like the Ardith etching, but has a gazebo between the flowers. Dishes were made in Black, Blue, Crystal, and Yellow.

Blue
Candy Dish, Cover,
    Pedestal 145.00

Crystal
Candlestick, 3-Light 65.00
Tray, Center Handle,
    Swan Head 100.00

GEORGIAN

Georgian, also known as Lovebirds, was made by the Federal Glass Company, Columbus, Ohio, from 1931 to 1936. The pattern shows alternating sections with birds in one and a basket of flowers in the next. Some dishes have no lovebirds. Dinner sets were made mostly in Crystal, although Green pieces were also manufactured. Notice that it is mold-etched and in no way resembles the Fenton glass pattern called Georgian. Reproductions have been made.

Crystal
Berry Bowl, 4 1/2 In. 10.00
Berry Bowl, Master,
    7 1/2 In. 1200.00
Creamer 85.00

Cup 12.00
Cup & Saucer . . 13.00 to 15.00
Sherbet . . . . 10.00 to 12.00
Sugar & Creamer,
    Footed, 3 In. 19.00
Tumbler, Iced Tea,
    12 Oz., 5 1/4 In. 12.50
Tumbler, Juice, 4 In. 10.00
Tumbler, Water,
    9 Oz., 4 In. 11.00

Green

Berry Bowl,
    4 1/2 In. . . . . . . 8.00 to 12.00
Berry Bowl, Master,
    7 1/2 In. . . . . . 65.00 to 70.00
Bowl, Cereal,
    5 3/4 In. . . . . . 26.00 to 45.00
Bowl, Deep,
    6 1/2 In. 75.00
Bowl, Salad, Oval,
    9 In. . . . . 70.00 to 75.00
Butter, Cover . . . 85.00 to 95.00
Creamer, Footed,
    3 In. . . . . 10.00 to 22.00
Creamer, Footed,
    4 In. . . . . 10.00 to 25.00
Cup . . . . 8.00 to 12.00
Cup & Saucer . . 10.00 to 45.00
Plate, 8 In. . . . . . 10.00 to 12.00
Plate, Center Design,
    9 1/4 In. 23.00
Plate, Dinner,
    9 1/4 In. . . . . . 18.00 to 40.00
Plate, Luncheon,
    8 In. . . . . 8.00 to 15.00
Plate, Sherbet,
    6 In. . . . . 5.00 to 10.00
Saucer . . . . 3.00 to 8.00
Sherbet,
    Footed . . . . . . 12.00 to 18.00
Sherbet, Underplate 28.00
Sugar, Cover, Footed,
    3 In. . . . . 61.00 to 80.00
Sugar, Footed,
    3 In. . . . . 9.00 to 15.00
Sugar, Footed,
    4 In. . . . . 10.00 to 16.00
Sugar & Creamer,
    Footed 36.00
Tumbler, Iced Tea, 12 Oz.,
    5 1/4 In. . . . 135.00 to 185.00
Tumbler, Juice,
    4 In. . . . . 65.00 to 75.00

Tumbler, Water, 9 Oz.,
    4 In. . . . . 65.00 to 69.00

GLADIOLA
See Royal Lace

GOLF BALL

Morgantown Glass Works, Inc., Morgantown, West Virginia, made Golf Ball stemware and accessories in the late 1920s and early 1930s. The items came in a wide variety of colors with crystal stems and feet. The pattern name comes from the faceted ball that is part of the stem.

Ritz Blue
Tumbler, Cocktail,
    14 Oz., 4 1/8 In. 45.00

Spanish Red
Goblet, Champagne,
    7 Oz., 5 In. 50.00
Goblet, Cordial,
    3 7/16 In. 60.00
Tumbler, Cocktail, 4 Oz.,
    4 1/8 In. 40.00

GRAPE

Grape design is sometimes confused with the pattern known as Woolworth. Both have grapes in the pattern. Grape was made by Standard Glass Manufacturing Company, Lancaster, Ohio, in the 1930s. Full dinnerware sets were made in Green, Rose, and Topaz.

Green
Pitcher, Water,
    8 1/2 In. 100.00
Sherbet, 3 1/4 In. 15.00
Tumbler, 5 1/8 In. 20.00

Tumbler, Juice,
    3 3/4 In. 15.00

Rose
Goblet, Champagne 35.00

GRAY LAUREL

CRCR Gray Laurel is a Fire-King dinnerware made by Anchor Hocking Glass Corporation in 1953. The pattern has a laurel leaf design around the edge of the plates and bowls and on the side of the cups. The pieces are Gray. The same pattern of laurel leaves was made in a lustrous orange-yellow color from 1952 to 1963 and was known as Peach Lustre.

Creamer, Footed 8.00
Cup, 8 Oz. 5.00
Cup & Saucer, Footed 8.00
Plate, Dinner, 9 1/8 In. . . 10.00
Plate, Salad, 7 3/8 In. 10.00

GREEK KEY

Greek Key is one of A. H. Heisey & Company's oldest and most easily recognizable patterns. Some pieces were made until 1938. Other companies made glassware with a similar border, but most Heisey pieces are marked with the Diamond H logo.

Nappy, 4 1/2 In. 20.00

Nappy, 5 1/2 In. 25.00

Sherbet, Footed,
3 In. . . . . 25.00 to 30.00

Tub, Cover, Tab Handles,
6 In. x 4 In. 100.00

HAIRPIN
See Newport

HANGING BASKET
See No. 615

HARP

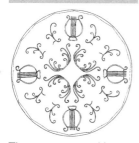

The pattern name Harp describes the small lyre-shaped instruments that are included on the borders of these pieces of glass. This Jeannette Glass Company pattern was made from 1954 to 1957. Pieces are found in Crystal, Crystal with gold trim, Light Blue, and Pink.

Crystal

Cake Stand,
9 In. . . . . 20.00 to 25.00

Coaster, With
Ashtray . . . . 4.00 to 8.50

Cup . . . . 14.00 to 30.00

Cup & Saucer . . 35.00 to 50.00

Plate, 7 In. . . . . . 12.00 to 22.00

Saucer 12.00

Tray, Rectangular 35.00

Vase, Gold Trim,
7 1/2 In. 25.00

Light Blue

Cake Stand,
9 In. . . . . 40.00 to 45.00

Cup & Saucer 54.00

Pink

Cake Stand,
9 In. . . . . 35.00 to 45.00

HEIRLOOM

Heirloom is a ribbed, free-form pattern made in opalescent colors by the Fostoria Glass Company, Moundsville, West Virginia, in the 1950s and 1960s. The pieces were pressed in molds and then stretched with tools.

Pink Opal

Bowl, Oblong, 13 In. 45.00

Bowl, Square, 5 1/2 In. . . 20.00

Candle Bowl,
9 1/2 In. 40.00

HERITAGE

Federal Glass Company, Columbus, Ohio, made Heritage from the 1930s through the 1960s. Evidently the serving pieces were made in blue, light green, and pink, but the plates and dinnerware pieces were made only in Crystal. Amber and Crys-

tal reproduction bowls were made in 1987.

Crystal

Berry Bowl,
5 In. . . . . 7.00 to 10.00

Berry Bowl, Master,
8 1/2 In. . . . . . 15.00 to 40.00

Bowl,
10 1/2 In. . . . . 15.00 to 18.00

Creamer,
Footed . . . . . . 24.00 to 33.00

Cup . . . . 5.00 to 7.00

Cup & Saucer . . . 7.00 to 12.00

Plate, Dinner,
9 1/4 In. . . . . . 12.00 to 14.50

Plate, Luncheon,
8 In. . . . . 9.00 to 13.00

Sandwich Server,
12 In. . . . . 14.00 to 17.00

Saucer 4.00

Sugar, Footed . . . 20.00 to 25.00

Sugar & Creamer,
Footed 55.00

HEX OPTIC
See Hexagon Optic

HEXAGON OPTIC

Hexagon Optic, also called Honeycomb or Hex Optic, has an accurate, descriptive name. Green or Pink sets of kitchenware were made in this pattern by Jeannette Glass Company, Jeannette, Pennsylvania, from 1928 to 1932. Around 1960, some Iridescent sets and some Ultramarine (blue-green) pieces were made.

Green

Cup, Open
Handle . . . . 4.50 to 6.00

Ice Bucket,
    Metal Handle 20.00
Pitcher, Sunflower
    Base, 5 In. 25.00
Salt & Pepper 30.00
Saucer 2.50
Tumbler, Footed,
    5 3/4 In. 8.00
Tumbler, Footed,
    9 Oz., 3 3/4 In. 8.00

Pink

Cup 4.00
Cup & Saucer 6.00
Pitcher, Footed, 48 Oz.,
    9 In. .... 50.00 to 240.00
Salt & Pepper 40.00
Sherbet, Footed, 5 Oz. ... 12.00
Tumbler, Footed,
    5 3/4 In. ..... 10.00 to 12.00
Tumbler, Footed,
    9 Oz., 3 3/4 In. 6.00
Tumbler, Iced Tea,
    Footed, 7 In. .... 6.00 to 7.00

HINGE
See Patrician

HOBNAIL

Hobnail is the name of this pattern, although many similar patterns have been made with similar hobbed decorations. Hocking Glass Company, Lancaster, Ohio, made this pattern from 1934 to 1936, and it can be distinguished from other hobbed patterns by a honeycomb design with long sides and pointed ends. Mostly Crystal or Pink beverage sets were made. Some pieces have

red rims or black feet.

Crystal

Bowl, 5 1/2 In. 6.50
Bowl, 7 In. ..... 10.00 to 11.00
Cup .... 4.00 to 7.50
Cup & Saucer 7.00
Decanter, Stopper 40.00
Decanter Set, Stopper,
    Red Trim, 7 Whiskey
    Tumblers, 8 Piece 40.00
Plate, 6 In. 3.00
Plate, 8 1/2 In. .... 3.50 to 6.00
Sherbet 4.00
Sugar &
    Creamer ..... 15.00 to 20.00
Tumbler, 5 1/4 In. 30.00
Tumbler, Footed, 5 Oz. ... 6.00
Tumbler, Whiskey, 1 1/2 Oz.,
    2 1/2 In. ...... 4.50 to 5.00
Tumbler, Wine, Footed, 3 Oz.,
    3 1/2 In. ...... 5.00 to 7.00
Water Set, Red Trim, 67-Oz.
    Pitcher, 9-Oz. Tumblers,
    5 Piece 75.00

Pink

Cup .... 5.00 to 8.00
Cup & Saucer 10.00
Pitcher, Water, 67 Oz. ... 35.00
Plate, 6 In. .... 4.00 to 8.00
Plate, Sherbet, 6 In. 2.50

HOBNAIL
See also Moonstone

HOLIDAY

Holiday is one of the later Depression glass patterns. It was made from 1947 through 1949 by Jeannette Glass Company. The pattern is found in dinnerware sets of Crystal,

Iridescent, and Pink. A few pieces of opaque Shell Pink were made. The pattern is sometimes also called Buttons & Bows or Russian.

Crystal

Creamer 12.00
Plate, Bread & Butter,
    6 In. 7.00
Tumbler, Juice, Footed,
    4 In. 7.50

Iridescent

Pitcher, 16 Oz.,
    4 3/4 In. 23.00
Platter, Oval, 11 3/8 In. .. 13.00
Tumbler, Juice, Footed,
    4 In. .... 12.00 to 16.00

Pink

Berry Bowl,
    5 1/8 In. ..... 13.00 to 16.00
Berry Bowl, Master,
    8 1/2 In. ..... 30.00 to 33.00
Bowl, 7 3/4 In. 60.00
Bowl, Vegetable,
    Oval, 9 1/2 In. 29.00
Butter .... 8.00 to 20.00
Butter, Cover ... 36.00 to 60.00
Butter, Cover Only 35.00
Cake Plate, Footed,
    10 1/2 In. .. 110.00 to 125.00
Candlestick,
    3 In. .... 35.00 to 50.00
Candlestick, 3 In., Pair .. 100.00
Console,
    10 3/4 In. .. 140.00 to 225.00
Creamer,
    Footed ...... 12.00 to 22.00
Cup .... 5.00 to 12.00
Cup & Saucer .. 13.00 to 22.00
Pitcher 40.00
Pitcher, Milk, 16 Oz.,
    4 3/4 In. ..... 59.00 to 82.00
Pitcher, Water, 52 Oz.,
    6 3/4 In. ..... 40.00 to 45.00
Plate, Bread & Butter,
    6 In. 7.00
Plate, Dinner,
    9 In. .... 12.00 to 38.00
Plate, Sherbet,
    6 In. .... 5.50 to 7.00
Platter, 11 3/8 In. 30.00

Platter, Oval, 11 3/8 In. . . 29.00
Sandwich Tray,
   10 1/2 In. . . . . 16.00 to 24.00
Saucer . . . . 4.00 to 5.00
Sherbet . . . . 7.00 to 12.00
Soup, Dish, 7 3/4 In. 59.00
Sugar . . . . 10.00 to 11.00
Sugar, Cover . . . 25.00 to 40.00
Sugar & Creamer,
   Cover . . . . . . 40.00 to 42.00
Tumbler, 4 In. . . 17.00 to 27.00
Tumbler, Iced Tea,
   Footed, 6 In. 195.00
Tumbler, Juice,
   Footed, 4 In. 60.00
Tumbler, Water, Footed,
   10 Oz., 4 In. . . 16.00 to 27.00

HOMESPUN

Homespun, often called
Fine Rib, is a cause of confusion. Jeannette Glass
Company made Crystal
and Pink pieces in this pattern in 1939 and 1940.
Similar pieces made by
Hazel Atlas Glass Com-
pany are listed in the
Homespun Lookalike sec-
tion. Homespun made by
Jeannette Glass Company
is listed here.

Crystal
Platter, Closed Handles,
   13 In. 21.00
Sandwich Tray,
   10 1/2 In. 20.00
Tumbler, Iced Tea, 12 1/2 Oz.,
   5 3/8 In. . . . . . 14.00 to 24.00
Tumbler, Juice, Footed,
   5 Oz., 4 In. . . . . 8.00 to 12.00

Tumbler, Water, Flared,
   8 Oz., 4 1/8 In. 10.00

Pink
Berry Bowl,
   4 1/2 In. . . . . . 12.00 to 20.00
Berry Bowl, Master,
   8 1/4 In. . . . . . 24.00 to 40.00
Bowl, Cereal, Closed Handles,
   5 In. . . . . 35.00 to 55.00
Butter 15.00
Creamer 12.00
Cup, Child's 49.00
Cup & Saucer . . 16.00 to 30.00
Plate, Child's . . 13.00 to 18.00
Plate, Dinner,
   9 1/4 In. . . . . . 18.00 to 28.00
Plate, Sherbet,
   6 In. . . . . 6.00 to 12.50
Platter, Closed Handles,
   13 In. . . . . 12.00 to 25.00
Saucer . . . . 10.00 to 27.00
Saucer, Child's 10.00
Sherbet . . . . 18.00 to 28.00
Sugar . . . . 10.00 to 20.00
Sugar, Cover 39.00
Sugar & Creamer 25.00
Teapot, Cover,
   Child's . . . . 125.00 to 250.00
Tumbler, 7 Oz.,
   3 7/8 In. 25.00
Tumbler, Banded,
   9 Oz., 4 1/4 In. 25.00
Tumbler, Footed,
   5 Oz., 4 In. . . . 10.00 to 15.00
Tumbler, Footed,
   15 Oz., 6 3/8 In. 33.00
Tumbler, Juice, Footed,
   5 Oz., 4 In. . . . . 8.00 to 15.00
Tumbler, Water, Flared,
   8 Oz., 4 1/8 In. 25.00

❖

*If you have an alarm
system, set it each
time you leave the
house, not just at night.
Most home burglaries
take place during the
day or early evening.*

❖

HOMESPUN LOOKALIKE

Hazel Atlas Glass Com-
pany made tumblers and
pitchers with fine ribs that
are confused with the
Homespun pattern by
Jeannette. Homespun
lookalikes were made in
Crystal, Pink, and Ritz
Blue in the 1930s. Home-
spun by Jeannette is listed
in its own section in this
book.

Crystal
Pitcher, Juice, Tilt,
   40 Oz. 35.00

Ritz Blue
Pitcher, Juice 50.00
Pitcher, Juice, Tilt,
   40 Oz. . . . . . . 55.00 to 60.00
Pitcher, Tilt,
   80 Oz. . . . . . 100.00 to 120.00
Tumbler, Iced Tea,
   12 Oz., 5 In. 30.00
Tumbler, Juice, 5 Oz.,
   3 1/4 In. 14.00
Tumbler, Water, 9 Oz.,
   4 In. 17.00

HONEYCOMB
See Hexagon Optic

HORIZONTAL
FINE RIB
See Manhattan

HORIZONTAL RIBBED
See Manhattan

HORIZONTAL ROUNDED
BIG RIB
See Manhattan

HORIZONTAL SHARP
BIG RIB
See Manhattan

HORSESHOE
See No. 612

INDIANA CUSTARD

This design makes its original pattern name, Flower & Leaf Band, clear, but collectors prefer to call this pattern Indiana Custard. It is an opaque glassware of Custard, or Ivory, made by the Indiana Glass Company. Primarily luncheon sets were made from the 1930s to the 1950s. Some pieces have bands that are decorated with pastel colors or decal designs. The same pattern was made of Milk Glass in 1957. It was called Orange Blossom.

Berry Bowl,
5 1/2 In. . . . . . 11.00 to 14.00
Berry Bowl, Master,
9 In. 39.00
Bowl, Cereal,
6 1/2 In. 30.00
Bowl, Vegetable,
Oval, 9 1/2 In. 39.00

Butter, Cover 69.00
Creamer . . . . 6.00 to 18.00
Cup 17.00
Cup & Saucer . . 20.00 to 50.00
Plate, Bread & Butter,
5 3/4 In. 8.00
Plate, Dinner,
9 3/4 In. . . . . . 28.00 to 34.00
Plate, Luncheon,
8 7/8 In. 20.00
Plate, Salad,
7 1/2 In. . . . . . 18.00 to 20.00
Platter, Oval,
11 1/2 In. 42.00
Saucer . . . . 8.00 to 12.00
Sherbet . . . . . 110.00 to 125.00
Soup, Dish,
7 1/2 In. 39.00
Sugar 12.00
Sugar, Cover . . . 31.00 to 42.00
Sugar & Creamer,
Cover 59.00

IRIS

The design of Iris is unusually bold for Depression glass. Molded representations of stalks of iris fill the center of a ribbed plate. Other pieces in the pattern show fewer irises, but the flower is predominant. Edges of pieces may be ruffled or beaded. It was made by Jeannette Glass Company, Jeannette, Pennsylvania, from 1928 to 1932 and then again in the 1950s and 1970s. Early pieces were made in Crystal, Green, Iridescent, and Pink; later pieces were made in Blue-Green, Green, Red-Yellow, and White. Red after dinner

cups and saucers can be found. The pattern is also called Iris & Herringbone. Reproduction candy vases and coasters have been made in a variety of colors since 1977.

Crystal

Berry Bowl, Beaded Edge,
4 1/2 In. . . . . . 41.00 to 60.00
Berry Bowl Set, Beaded,
8 Piece 115.00
Bowl, 11 In. . . . 45.00 to 80.00
Bowl, Beaded,
8 In. . . . . . . 100.00 to 125.00
Bowl, Cereal, 5 In. 115.00
Bowl, Cereal, Ruffled Edge,
5 In. . . . . . . 125.00 to 168.00
Bowl, Ruffled Edge,
5 In. . . . . 8.00 to 15.00
Bowl, Ruffled Edge,
9 1/2 In. . . . . . 14.00 to 20.00
Bowl, Ruffled Edge,
11 In. 28.00
Bowl, Vegetable,
Straight 85.00
Butter, Cover . . . 42.00 to 65.00
Butter,
No Cover . . . . 12.00 to 22.00
Candlestick,
2-Light . . . . . . 18.00 to 25.00
Candlestick, 2-Light,
Pair . . . . 40.00 to 50.00
Candy Jar,
Cover . . . . . 185.00 to 235.00
Candy Jar, Cover Only . . 125.00
Coaster . . . . . . 100.00 to 150.00
Creamer,
Footed . . . . . . 12.00 to 15.00
Cup . . . . 16.00 to 20.00
Cup, After
Dinner . . . . . . 40.00 to 55.00
Cup & Saucer . . 27.00 to 32.00
Cup & Saucer, After
Dinner . . . . . 230.00 to 250.00
Goblet, Cocktail, 3 Oz.,
4 1/4 In. 30.00
Goblet, Cocktail, 4 Oz.,
5 1/2 In. . . . . . 28.00 to 30.00
Goblet, Water, 8 Oz.,
5 3/4 In. . . . . . 20.00 to 38.00
Goblet, Wine, 3 Oz.,
4 1/4 In. . . . . . 10.00 to 19.00

Nut Set . . . . . . 65.00 to 115.00
Pitcher, 8 1/2 In. 79.00
Pitcher, Water,
 9 1/2 In. . . . . . 38.00 to 75.00
Plate, Dinner,
 9 In. . . . . 50.00 to 75.00
Plate, Luncheon,
 8 In. . . . . . 110.00 to 145.00
Plate, Sherbet,
 5 1/2 In. . . . . . 15.00 to 20.00
Sandwich Server,
 11 3/4 In. . . . . 28.00 to 45.00
Sauce Bowl, Ruffled Edge,
 5 In. . . . . 9.00 to 14.00
Saucer . . . . 10.00 to 15.00
Sherbet, Footed,
 2 1/2 In. . . . . . 28.00 to 33.00
Sherbet, Footed,
 4 In. . . . . 20.00 to 27.00
Soup, Dish,
 7 1/2 In. . . . 165.00 to 182.00
Sugar 12.00
Sugar, Cover . . . 25.00 to 38.00
Sugar &
 Creamer . . . . . 23.00 to 27.00
Sugar & Creamer,
 After Dinner 240.00
Sugar & Creamer,
 Cover . . . . 28.00 to 50.00
Tumbler,
 4 In. . . . . . . 150.00 to 175.00
Tumbler, Iced Tea, Footed,
 6 In. . . . . 18.00 to 45.00
Vase, 9 In. . . . . . 25.00 to 35.00

Iridescent

Berry Bowl, 4 1/2 In. 10.00
Berry Bowl, Beaded,
 4 1/2 In. 26.00
Berry Bowl, Beaded,
 Master, 8 In. . . 12.00 to 35.00
Berry Bowl, Ruffled Edge,
 4 1/2 In. . . . . . 30.00 to 33.00
Bowl, 11 1/2 In. 14.00
Bowl, Cereal, 5 In. 28.00
Bowl, Ruffled Edge,
 9 1/2 In. . . . . . 13.00 to 16.00
Bowl, Ruffled Edge,
 11 In. . . . . 14.00 to 55.00
Butter, Cover . . . 27.00 to 55.00
Candlestick,
 2-Light . . . . . . 24.00 to 25.00
Candlestick, 2-Light,
 Pair 50.00

Creamer,
 Footed . . . . . . 10.00 to 16.00
Cup . . . . 14.00 to 18.00
Cup, After Dinner 50.00
Cup & Saucer . . 20.00 to 30.00
Cup & Saucer,
 Ringed 25.00
Goblet, Cocktail, 4 Oz.,
 4 1/4 In. . . . . 27.00 to 30.00
Goblet, Water, 8 Oz.,
 5 3/4 In. 30.00
Goblet, Wine,
 4 In. . . . . 18.00 to 39.00
Nut Set 140.00
Pitcher, Water, Footed,
 9 1/2 In. . . . . 42.00 to 60.00
Plate, 6 In. 12.00
Plate, Dinner,
 9 In. . . . . 30.00 to 52.00
Plate, Sherbet,
 5 1/2 In. . . . . 12.00 to 15.00
Sandwich Server,
 11 3/4 In. . . . . 27.00 to 40.00
Sauce Bowl, Ruffled Edge,
 5 In. . . . . 25.00 to 28.00
Saucer . . . . 8.00 to 12.00
Sherbet, Footed,
 2 1/2 In. . . . . 14.00 to 19.00
Soup, Dish,
 7 1/2 In. . . . . 60.00 to 72.00
Sugar, Cover . . . 13.00 to 28.00
Tumbler, Iced Tea,
 Footed, 6 In. . . 16.00 to 45.00
Vase, 9 In. . . . . . 20.00 to 35.00
Wine, 4 In. 30.00

Red

Cup & Saucer, After
 Dinner 460.00

Red-Yellow

Bowl, Ruffled Edge,
 11 In. 24.00
Butter 12.50
Creamer 12.00

White

Vase, 9 In. . . . . . 15.00 to 20.00

IRIS & HERRINGBONE
See Iris

IVEX
See Chinex Classic;
 Cremax

JADITE

Jadite is a color as well as
a pattern. Kitchenware
was made in Jadite from
1936 to 1938 by Jeannette
Glass Company. All of the
pieces of kitchenware
made of Jadite by Jean-
nette were also made of a
blue glass called Delphite,
but it is incorrect to call
any but the green dishes
by the name Jadite. The
opaque green made by
Anchor Hocking Glass
Corporation is called Jade-
ite and is listed in the Fire-
King section in this book.

Batter Jug 45.00
Butter . . . . . . 135.00 to 250.00
Canister, Coffee, Metal
 Cover, 40 Oz. 300.00
Canister, Tea, Metal
 Cover, 16 Oz. 210.00
Measuring Cup Set,
 4 Piece 250.00
Reamer, Grapefruit 400.00
Shaker, Flour 110.00
Shaker, Sugar 110.00

❖

**Look in your hardware
store for the new glues
that can fix almost any-
thing. Buy the proper
one to fix transparent
glass. There will be one
that will work.**

❖

JAMESTOWN

Jamestown was made by the Fostoria Glass Company from 1958 to 1982. It was made in Amber, Amethyst, Blue, Crystal, Green, Pink, and Red.

Amber
Cup 12.00
Goblet, Juice, 5 Oz.,
  4 3/4 In. 10.00

Amethyst
Goblet, 9 1/2 Oz.,
  5 3/4 In. 16.00
Goblet, Juice, 5 Oz.,
  4 3/4 In. 21.00
Tumbler, 9 Oz.,
  4 1/4 In. 18.00

Blue
Goblet, Iced Tea,
  11 Oz., 6 In.. . . . . 17.00
Goblet, Iced Tea,
  12 Oz., 6 In. 25.00
Goblet, Juice, 5 Oz.,
  4 3/4 In. 26.00
Goblet, Water, 9 1/2 Oz.,
  5 3/4 In. 25.00
Goblet, Wine, 4 Oz.,
  4 5/16 In. 24.00
Sherbet, 6 1/2 Oz.,
  4 1/4 In. 17.00

Crystal
Goblet, Iced Tea,
  11 Oz., 6 In. 19.00
Goblet, Juice,
  5 Oz., 4 3/4 In. 21.00
Goblet, Wine,
  4 Oz., 4 5/16 In. 20.00
Tumbler, Water,
  9 Oz., 4 1/4 In. 18.00

Green
Bowl, Dessert, 4 1/2 In. . . 13.00

Goblet, Water, 10 Oz.,
  5 7/8 In. 21.00
Sherbet, 6 1/2 Oz.,
  4 1/4 In. 13.00

Pink
Goblet, Juice, 5 Oz.,
  4 3/4 In. . . . . . 26.00 to 28.00
Goblet, Water,
  10 Oz., 5 7/8 In. 25.00
Goblet, Wine,
  4 Oz., 4 5/16 In. 34.00
Plate, 8 In. 24.00
Sherbet, 6 1/2 Oz.,
  4 1/4 In. 18.00

Red
Goblet, Juice,
  5 Oz., 4 3/4 In. 28.00
Goblet, Wine,
  4 Oz., 4 5/16 In. 30.00
Tumbler,
  12 Oz., 5 1/8 In. 30.00

JANE-RAY

Jane-Ray is a plain dinnerware with ribbed edge made mostly in Jade-ite from 1945 to 1963 by Anchor Hocking Glass Corporation, Lancaster, Ohio. Crystal, Ivory, Peach Lustre, and Vitrock pieces were also made. Other related patterns are listed in the Fire-King section in this book.

Jade-ite
Bowl, Dessert,
  4 7/8 In. . . . . . 13.00 to 14.50
Bowl, Oatmeal,
  5 7/8 In. . . . . . 25.00 to 28.00
Bowl, Vegetable,
  8 1/4 In. . . . . . 35.00 to 45.00
Creamer . . . . 14.00 to 23.00

Cup . . . . 7.00 to 8.00
Cup & Saucer . . 10.00 to 20.00
Cup & Saucer, After
  Dinner . . . . . . 95.00 to 115.00
Plate, Dinner,
  9 1/8 In. . . . . . 10.00 to 20.00
Plate, Salad,
  7 3/4 In. . . . . . 12.00 to 22.00
Platter, Oval,
  12 In. . . . . 35.00 to 45.00
Saucer . . . . 2.00 to 3.00
Saucer, After
  Dinner . . . . . . 10.00 to 45.00
Soup, Dish,
  7 5/8 In. . . . . . 28.00 to 35.00
Starter Set, Box,
  18 Piece 150.00
Sugar, Cover . . . 35.00 to 50.00
Sugar & Creamer,
  Cover 40.00

JANICE

Janice was made by New Martinsville Glass Co., New Martinsville, West Virginia, from 1926 to 1944. Dishes came in Amethyst, Blue, Cobalt Crystal, Emerald, Light Blue, and Ruby. Viking Glass Company purchased the New Martinsville factory in 1944 and continued to make Janice pieces until 1970. Dalzell-Viking made Janice pieces from 1996 to 1998. The recent pieces were made in Cobalt Blue, Crystal, and Red.

Cobalt Blue
Bowl, Fruit, 11 In. 295.00
Cup & Saucer 22.00
Platter 50.00

Sherbet 18.00
Tumbler, Footed,
    10 Oz. 20.00
Tumbler, Water, Footed . . 35.00
Vase, 3 1/2 In. 25.00

Crystal
Sugar & Creamer,
    Tray 45.00

Red
Celery Dish, Swan,
    11 In. . . . . . 125.00 to 225.00
Cup & Saucer 30.00
Tumbler, Footed, 10 Oz. . 35.00
Vase, 8 In. 165.00

JUBILEE

In the early 1930s, the Lancaster Glass Company, Lancaster, Ohio, made this luncheon set decorated with etched flowers. It was made in Pink and in a yellow shade, called Topaz. Collectors will find many similar patterns. The original Lancaster Jubilee has twelve petals and an open center on each flower.

Pink
Bowl, 3-Footed,
    Curved, 11 1/2 In. 275.00
Goblet, Water, 10 Oz.,
    6 In. . . . . . . 150.00 to 195.00
Pitcher, Water 995.00

Topaz
Bowl, 3-Footed, Curved,
    11 1/2 In. . . 295.00 to 350.00
Creamer . . . . . . 16.00 to 24.00
Cup . . . . 12.00 to 16.00
Cup & Saucer . . 16.00 to 25.00
Dish, Mayonnaise,
    Spoon, ... 210.00
Goblet, Water, 10 Oz.,
    6 In. . . . . 33.00 to 50.00

Plate, Luncheon,
    8 3/4 In. . . . . 12.00 to 17.00
Plate, Salad,
    7 In. . . . . 12.00 to 16.00
Saucer . . . . 6.00 to 8.00
Sugar . . . . 16.00 to 24.00
Sugar & Creamer 44.00
Tray, Center Handle,
    11 In. 275.00
Tray, Handles,
    11 In. . . . . . . 45.00 to 55.00

JUNE

June is one of very few patterns that can be dated with some accuracy from the color. Fostoria Glass Company, Fostoria, Ohio, made full dinnerware sets in various colors. From 1928 to 1944, the glass was Azure, Green, or Rose. Crystal was made from 1928 to 1952. If your set is Topaz, it dates from 1929 to 1938. Gold-tinted glass was made from 1938 to 1944. Color pieces with crystal stems or bases were made only from 1931 to 1944. Reproductions have been made in Azure (blue), Crystal, Rose (pink), and Topaz (yellow).

Azure
Ashtray 75.00
Bowl, Cereal,
    6 In. 70.00

Bowl, Footed,
    12 In. . . . . 125.00 to 180.00
Candlestick, 3 In., Pair . . 75.00
Candy Dish, Cover,
    3 Sections 695.00
Cup, After Dinner 70.00
Cup & Saucer 45.00
Goblet, 10 Oz.,
    8 1/4 In. . . . . . 65.00 to 75.00
Plate, Breakfast,
    8 3/4 In. 25.00
Plate, Salad, 7 1/4 In. 9.00
Sherbet, 4 1/4 In. 30.00
Sherbet, 6 In. 35.00
Soup, Cream,
    Handles, 6 In.. . . . . 45.00
Tumbler, Iced Tea,
    Footed, 12 Oz. 68.00
Vase, Flip, 8 In. 1100.00

Crystal
Goblet, Cocktail, 3 Oz. . . 18.00
Goblet, Water, 10 Oz.,
    8 1/4 In. 30.00
Oyster Cocktail, 3 Oz. . . . 24.00
Sherbet, 6 Oz.,
    4 1/4 In. 22.00
Tumbler, 12 Oz.,
    6 In. 40.00
Tumbler, Juice, Footed,
    5 Oz. 25.00

Rose
Baker, Oval, 9 1/2 In. . . 175.00
Candy Dish, Cover 575.00
Candy Dish, Cover,
    3 Sections, Low 625.00
Centerpiece, 12 In. 275.00
Cup, After Dinner 70.00
Finger Bowl, Underplate,
    2 In. 200.00
Goblet, Claret, 4 Oz.,
    6 In. 175.00
Goblet, Wine, 3 Oz.,
    5 3/8 In. 118.00
Pitcher, 48 Oz. 1200.00
Plate, Dinner,
    10 1/4 In. 165.00
Sugar & Creamer 185.00
Tumbler, Footed,
    2 1/2 Oz. 175.00
Tumbler, Iced Tea, Crystal
    Foot, 12 Oz., 6 In. 85.00
Tumbler, Water, Footed,
    9 Oz. 50.00

Vase, Flip,
8 In. . . . . . 900.00 to 975.00

Topaz

Baker, Oval, 9 1/2 In. . . 125.00

Bouillon, Footed,
3 3/4 In. 24.00

Bowl, Dessert, Handles,
Large 95.00

Bowl, Footed, 12 In. . . . 125.00

Bowl, Whipped Cream,
Handles 35.00

Cake Plate, Handle,
10 1/2 In. 75.00

Candy Dish, Cover,
1/2 Lb. 370.00

Cruet, Handle,
Stopper 700.00

Goblet, Claret,
4 Oz., 6 In. 80.00

Goblet, Wine, 3 Oz.,
5 1/2 In. . . . . . 50.00 to 65.00

Lemon Dish, Handles,
9 In. 34.00

Parfait, 5 1/4 In. 70.00

Plate, Bread & Butter,
6 In. 15.00

Plate, Salad,
7 1/2 In. . . . . . 14.00 to 16.00

Relish, 2 Sections,
8 1/2 In. 50.00

Salt & Pepper 109.00

Sherbet, 6 Oz.,
4 1/4 In. 27.00

Tumbler, 12 Oz., 6 In. . . . 40.00

Tumbler, Iced Tea,
12 Oz., 6 In. 40.00

Vase, Fan, 8 1/2 In. 450.00

Vase, Flip,
8 In. . . . . . 450.00 to 575.00

KING'S CROWN

King's Crown was origi-
nally known as Thumb-
print when Tiffin Glass

Company (U.S. Glass
Company Factory R, Tiffin,
Ohio) introduced it in
1891. Tiffin started to call
the pattern King's Crown
in the 1940s and contin-
ued to make it until the
1960s. In the 1970s, Indiana Glass Company
bought the molds and
changed them slightly. The
Tiffin items came in Cobalt
Blue; Crystal; Crystal with
ruby, cranberry, or amber
stain; Green; and Mulberry.
Indiana items came in
Amber, Avocado Green,
Cobalt Blue, and iridized
carnival colors. Tiara
Exclusives sold King's
Crown in Imperial Blue.

Amber

Bowl, Salad, 9 In. 35.00

Candleholder, 3 In.,
Pair 40.00

Goblet, Water,
9 Oz. 8.00

Snack Plate, Indentation,
9 3/4 In. 5.00

Snack Set, 2 Piece 10.00

Torte Plate,
14 1/2 In. 28.00

Crystal

Bowl, Salad, 9 1/4 In. . . . 85.00

Goblet, Claret, Ruby
Stain, 4 Oz. 9.00

Goblet, Juice, Ruby
Stain, 4 Oz. 12.00

Goblet, Water, Ruby
Stain, 9 Oz. 12.00

Goblet, Wine, 2 Oz. 8.00

Goblet, Wine, Ruby
Stain, 2 Oz. 13.00

Plate, Salad, Ruby
Stain, 7 3/4 In. 12.00

Saucer 9.00

Sherbet, Ruby Stain 10.00

Sugar &
Creamer . . . . . 32.00 to 50.00

Sugar & Creamer, Ruby
Stain . . . . 42.00 to 65.00

Tumbler, Juice, Ruby Stain,
Footed, 4 Oz. 10.00

Green

Cup 5.00

Finger Bowl 6.00

Sherbet 5.00

Snack Set, 2 Piece 10.00

KNIFE & FORK
See Colonial

LACE EDGE
See Old Colony

LACED EDGE

Imperial Glass Company,
Bellaire, Ohio, made Laced
Edge in the early 1930s.
The pattern is similar to
Hocking's Old Colony.
The biggest difference is
the shape of the lace. The
openings around Imperial's
edges are triangular, while
Hocking's are circular.
Laced Edge often has a
waffle design on the out-
side of the dishes and
comes in Amber, Crystal,
Green, Ritz Blue, Rose
Pink, Sea Foam (opales-
cent green or blue), and
Steigel Green. In the
1940s, Laced Edge was
sold as Crocheted Crystal
by Sears, Roebuck & Com-
pany. Crocheted Crystal is
listed in its own section in

this book. Imperial continued to make Laced Edge until the 1970s.

Sea Foam Blue

Bowl, 5 5/8 In. 44.00
Candleholder,
Plain 75.00
Cup 15.50
Cup & Saucer 50.00
Plate, 8 In. 37.00
Saucer, 5 1/4 In. 15.50
Tumbler, 8 Oz.,
4 In. 31.00
Vase, 4-Footed,
5 In. 40.00

LACY DAISY
See No. 618

LAKE COMO

At first glance, Lake Como looks more like ceramic than glass. It is Opaque White with blue decal decorations picturing a lake and part of an ancient ruin. It was made by Hocking Glass Company from 1934 to 1937.

Bowl, Cereal,
6 In. 30.00
Bowl, Vegetable,
9 1/2 In. 45.00
Creamer 35.00
Cup & Saucer . . 45.00 to 49.00
Plate, Bread & Butter,
7 1/4 In. . . . . . 20.00 to 24.00
Plate, Dinner,
9 1/4 In. . . . . . 35.00 to 37.00
Platter, 11 In. 79.00
Salt & Pepper . . . 35.00 to 49.00
Sugar . . . . 35.00 to 37.00
Sugar & Creamer 69.00

LARIAT

A. H. Heisey & Company, Newark, Ohio, made the Lariat pattern in Crystal from 1941 to 1957. The design is named for the looped "rope" around the border of the dishes. Heisey made the pattern to compete with Imperial's Candlewick. Lariat was produced by Imperial for six years after the Heisey factory closed in 1957.

Ashtray, 4 In. 12.00
Candy Box, Cover,
Footed, 7 In. 95.00
Cup & Saucer 25.00
Goblet, 10 Oz. 22.00
Plate, Salad,
8 In. . . . . 15.00 to 22.00
Punch Cup 6.00
Relish, 3 Sections,
11 In. . . . . . . 24.00 to 36.00
Vase, Fan, Footed,
7 In. 100.00

LAUREL

Opaque glass was used by McKee Glass Company, Jeannette, Pennsylvania, to make Laurel dinnerware in the 1930s. The pattern, with a raised band of flowers and leaves as the only

decoration, is sometimes called Raspberry Band. A few pieces have decals of a dog in the center. That group is called Scottie Dog. The dinnerware was made in French Ivory, Jade Green, Powder Blue, or White Opal. A child's set was made with a colored rim.

French Ivory

Berry Bowl,
5 In. . . . . 7.00 to 10.00
Berry Bowl, Master,
9 In. 30.00
Bowl, Cereal,
6 In. . . . . 8.00 to 10.00
Candlestick, 4 In. 14.00
Candlestick, 4 In.,
Pair 40.00
Cheese Dish,
Cover . . . . . . 45.00 to 55.00
Cheese Dish,
Cover Only 30.00
Creamer . . . . 8.50 to 15.00
Cup & Saucer, Red Rim,
Child's 55.00
Plate, Dinner,
9 1/8 In. . . . . 12.00 to 18.00
Plate, Sherbet, 6 In. 5.00
Platter, Oval,
10 3/4 In. 23.00
Sherbet . . . . 9.00 to 12.00
Tea Set, Red Rim,
Child's, 14 Piece 350.00

Jade Green

Bowl, Vegetable,
Oval, 9 3/4 In. 55.00
Cup 12.00
Goblet, Champagne,
5 In. 70.00
Plate, Dinner, 9 1/8 In. . . 25.00
Saucer 8.50
Sugar, Footed 13.00

Powder Blue

Berry Bowl, Master,
9 In. 50.00

White Opal

Plate, Red Rim,
Child's 22.00
Salt & Pepper 49.00

LELA BIRD

Paden City Glass Manufacturing Company, Paden City, West Virginia, made dishes with the Lela Bird etching in the 1930s. It was made in a variety of colors.

Green
Cake Plate, 10 In. 125.00
Cheese & Cracker 64.00
Pink
Tray, Center Handle ... 125.00

LIDO

Lido pattern was made by the Federal Glass Company of Columbus, Ohio, in the mid-1930s. The glass was offered in Crystal, Golden Glow, Green, or Rose Glow.

Crystal
Tumbler, Juice, 5 Oz.,
 4 3/4 In. 16.00
Golden Glow
Tumbler, Iced Tea,
 Footed, 15 Oz. 22.00

LILY MEDALLION
See American Sweetheart

LINCOLN DRAPE
See Princess

LINCOLN INN

Lincoln Inn was made by the Fenton Glass Company, Williamstown, West Virginia, from 1928 until about 1936. The ridged dinnerware sets were made of Amber, Amethyst, Black, Cobalt Blue, Crystal, Green, Jade Green, Light Blue, Pink, and Red. A recent copy of the Lincoln Inn pitcher was made by Fenton Glass Company in Iridescent carnival glass.

Cobalt Blue
Plate, Dinner, 9 1/4 In. .. 35.00
Tumbler, Footed, 9 Oz. .. 40.00
Crystal
Goblet, Water 15.00
Goblet, Wine 16.00
Pitcher,
 7 1/4 In. ... 625.00 to 725.00
Plate, 8 In. 7.00
Plate, 12 In. 5.00
Sherbet,
 4 3/4 In. ..... 10.00 to 13.00
Sherbet, Footed 14.00
Tumbler, Footed,
 5 Oz. 15.00
Tumbler, Footed,
 9 Oz. 18.00
Tumbler, Iced Tea, Footed,
 12 Oz. .... 19.00 to 22.00

Tumbler, Juice,
 Footed, 4 Oz. 13.00
Pink
Tumbler, Footed,
 9 Oz. 20.00
Red
Sherbet, 4 3/4 In. 22.00
Tumbler, Footed, 9 Oz. .. 30.00

LINE 191
See Party Line

LINE 300
See Peacock & Wild Rose

LITTLE HOSTESS
See Moderntone Little
 Hostess Party Set

LOOP
See Old Colony

LORAIN
See No. 615

LOUISA
See Floragold

LOVEBIRDS
See Georgian

LYDIA RAY
See New Century

MADRID

Madrid has probably had more publicity than any other Depression glass pattern. It was originally made by the Federal Glass Company, Columbus, Ohio, from 1932 to 1939, using the molds developed for Sylvan, an earlier Federal pattern. Madrid was made first in Green, then in Amber; Madonna Blue and Pink pieces were made for a limited time. In 1976 Federal Glass reworked the molds and made full sets of amber glass called Recollection. These can be identified by a small "76" worked into the pattern. In 1982, Crystal pieces of Recollection were made. In more recent years, Blue, Crystal, and Pink pieces have been reproduced by the Indiana Glass Company. Madrid is sometimes called Paneled Aster, Primus, or Winged Medallion.

Amber

Bowl, Cereal,
   7 In. . . . . 18.00 to 20.00
Bowl, Salad, Deep,
   9 1/2 In. 30.00
Bowl, Vegetable,
   Oval, 10 In. . . . 10.00 to 20.00
Butter, Cover . . . 70.00 to 80.00
Butter, Cover Only 38.00
Cake Plate, 11 1/4 In. . . . 14.00
Candlestick,
   2 1/2 In. . . . . . 11.00 to 13.00
Console, Low,
   11 In. . . . . . . 15.00 to 35.00
Cookie Jar,
   Cover . . . . 45.00 to 60.00
Cookie Jar,
   Cover Only 30.00
Creamer,
   Footed . . . . . . 6.00 to 20.00
Cup . . . . 4.50 to 8.00
Cup & Saucer . . . 5.00 to 12.00
Grill Plate,
   10 1/2 In. . . . . . 6.00 to 12.00

Jam Dish, 7 In. 25.00
Mold, Jell-O,
   2 1/8 In. . . . . 11.00 to 25.00
Pitcher, 80 Oz.,
   8 1/2 In. . . . . 69.00 to 75.00
Pitcher, Juice, 36 Oz.,
   5 1/2 In. . . . . 40.00 to 50.00
Pitcher, Square, 60 Oz.,
   8 In. . . . . 45.00 to 50.00
Plate, Dinner,
   10 1/2 In. . . . . 65.00 to 75.00
Plate, Luncheon,
   8 7/8 In. . . . . . 5.00 to 12.00
Plate, Salad,
   7 1/2 In. . . . . . 4.00 to 13.00
Plate, Sherbet,
   6 In. . . . . 3.00 to 7.00
Platter, Oval,
   11 1/2 In. . . . 15.00 to 25.00
Relish, 10 1/4 In. 15.00
Salt & Pepper,
   3 1/2 In. 55.00
Salt & Pepper, Flat,
   3 1/2 In. 28.00
Salt & Pepper, Footed,
   3 1/2 In. 150.00
Sauce Bowl, 5 In. . . 5.00 to 9.00
Saucer . . . . 2.00 to 4.00
Sherbet, Cone . . . . 6.00 to 8.00
Sherbet, Round . . 6.00 to 8.00
Soup, Cream,
   4 3/4 In. . . . . . 16.00 to 18.00
Soup, Dish,
   7 In. . . . . 12.00 to 16.00
Sugar . . . . 5.00 to 15.00
Sugar, Cover . . . 45.00 to 65.00
Sugar & Creamer,
   Cover . . . . 35.00 to 63.00
Tumbler, 5 Oz.,
   3 3/4 In. . . . . . 14.00 to 22.00
Tumbler, 9 Oz.,
   4 1/4 In. . . . . 12.00 to 22.00
Tumbler, 12 Oz.,
   5 1/2 In. . . . . 20.00 to 25.00
Tumbler, Footed,
   5 Oz., 4 In. 20.00
Tumbler, Footed, 10 Oz.,
   5 1/2 In. . . . . 15.00 to 38.00

Crystal

Butter 15.00
Cup 4.00
Grill Plate, 10 1/2 In. 9.00
Mold, Jell-O, 2 1/8 In. 6.00

Pitcher, 80 Oz.,
   8 1/2 In. 75.00
Plate, Dinner,
   10 1/2 In. . . . . 20.00 to 60.00
Salt & Pepper,
   Footed, 3 1/2 In. 45.00
Sherbet, Cone 9.00
Soup, Dish, 7 In. 10.00
Sugar 7.00
Sugar, Cover 65.00
Tumbler, 5 Oz.,
   3 7/8 In. 16.00

Green

Bowl, Vegetable, Oval,
   10 In. . . . . . . 24.00 to 25.00
Butter 37.00
Butter, Cover . . 90.00 to 104.00
Creamer,
   Footed . . . . . . 14.00 to 20.00
Cup 8.50
Cup & Saucer 13.00
Grill Plate,
   10 1/2 In. . . . . 18.00 to 23.00
Jam Dish, 7 In. 40.00
Pitcher, Square, 60 Oz.,
   8 In. . . . . . . 140.00 to 155.00
Plate, Luncheon,
   8 7/8 In. . . . . . . 9.00 to 12.00
Platter, Oval, 11 1/2 In. . . 20.00
Salt & Pepper . . . 65.00 to 71.00
Salt & Pepper, Footed . . 125.00
Saltshaker, Footed 55.00
Sauce Bowl,
   5 In. . . . . 8.00 to 10.00
Saucer 5.00
Sherbet . . . . 12.00 to 15.00
Sherbet, Cone . . . 11.00 to 12.00
Soup, Dish, 7 In. 25.00
Sugar 15.00
Sugar, Cover . . 25.00 to 85.00
Tumbler, 12 Oz.,
   5 1/2 In. . . . . 50.00 to 55.00

Madonna Blue

Cup & Saucer 11.00
Pitcher, Square, 60 Oz.,
   8 In. . . . . . 175.00 to 225.00
Plate, Dinner, 10 1/2 In. . . 65.00
Plate, Luncheon,
   8 7/8 In. 28.00
Plate, Salad, 7 1/2 In. 25.00
Salt & Pepper, Footed,
   3 1/2 In. . . . 150.00 to 195.00

Sherbet . . . . 20.00 to 28.00

Tumbler, 5 Oz.,
3 7/8 In. 45.00

Tumbler, 9 Oz.,
4 1/4 In. 22.00

Tumbler, 12 Oz.,
5 1/2 In. . . . . . 45.00 to 65.00

Tumbler, Footed,
5 Oz., 3 7/8 In. 40.00

Pink

Bowl, 11 In. 13.00

Cake Plate,
11 1/4 In. . . . . 10.00 to 20.00

Candlestick,
2 1/4 In., Pair 24.00

Cookie Jar, Cover 35.00

Cup & Saucer . . 12.00 to 15.00

Relish, 2 Sections,
10 1/4 In. 15.00

Sauce Bowl, 5 In. 11.00

Saucer 7.00

Tumbler, 9 Oz.,
4 1/4 In. . . . . 20.00 to 23.00

MAGNOLIA
See Dogwood

MANHATTAN

Manhattan is another
modern-looking pattern
with a design made of
molded circles. It was
made by Anchor Hocking
Glass Corporation from
1938 to 1941, primarily in
Crystal. A few Green, Iridescent, Pink, and Red
pieces also are known.
The pattern has been
called many names, such
as Horizontal Fine Rib,
Horizontal Ribbed, Hori-
zontal Rounded Big Rib,

Horizontal Sharp Big Rib,
and Ribbed. A similar line,
called Park Avenue, was
made in Blue and Crystal
by Anchor Hocking from
1987 to 1993.

Crystal

Ashtray, Round,
4 In. . . . . 9.00 to 15.00

Ashtray, Square,
4 1/2 In. 18.00

Berry Bowl, Handles,
5 3/8 In. 18.00

Berry Bowl, Master,
7 1/2 In. . . . . . 25.00 to 30.00

Bowl, Closed Handles,
8 In. 20.00

Bowl, Fruit, Open
Handle, 9 1/2 In. 48.00

Candlestick, 4 1/2 In.,
Pair 15.00

Candlestick, Square,
4 1/2 In. 7.50

Candlestick, Square, 4 1/2 In.,
Pair . . . . 15.00 to 25.00

Candy Dish, 3-Footed . . . 37.50

Candy Dish,
Cover . . . . . . 35.00 to 42.00

Coaster,
3 1/2 In. . . . . . 15.00 to 25.00

Compote,
5 3/4 In. . . . . . 33.00 to 45.00

Cookie Jar, Cover 35.00

Creamer, Oval 8.00

Cup 18.00

Cup & Saucer . . 25.00 to 39.00

Goblet, Wine, 4 In. 6.00

Pitcher, Tilted,
24 Oz. . . . . 35.00 to 50.00

Pitcher, Tilted,
80 Oz. 50.00

Plate, Dinner,
10 1/4 In. . . . . 20.00 to 30.00

Plate, Salad,
8 1/2 In. . . . . . 15.00 to 24.00

Plate, Sherbet,
6 In. . . . . 5.00 to 10.00

Relish, 4 Sections,
14 In. . . . . 22.00 to 30.00

Relish Insert, Triangular,
3 3/4 In. . . . . . . 8.00 to 15.00

Relish Tray, 5 Clear Inserts,
14 In. . . . . 20.00 to 29.50

Relish Tray, 5 Red Inserts,
14 In. . . . . . . 57.00 to 80.00

Salt & Pepper,
Square, 2 In. 30.00

Sandwich Tray,
14 In. . . . . 29.00 to 33.00

Sauce Bowl, Handles,
4 1/2 In. . . . . . 7.00 to 12.00

Sherbet . . . . 10.00 to 14.00

Sugar, Oval . . . . 8.00 to 12.00

Sugar & Creamer 25.00

Tumbler, Footed,
10 Oz. . . . . 17.00 to 22.00

Vase, 8 In. . . . . . 25.00 to 33.00

Pink

Berry Bowl, Handles,
5 3/8 In. . . . . . 22.00 to 35.00

Bowl, Closed Handles,
8 In. 20.00

Bowl, Fruit, Open
Handles, 9 1/2 In. 75.00

Candy Dish,
3-Footed . . . . . 12.00 to 18.00

Compote,
5 3/4 In. . . . . . 45.00 to 65.00

Creamer, Oval . . 15.00 to 18.00

Pitcher, Tilted,
80 Oz. . . . . 70.00 to 95.00

Relish Insert,
Triangular, 3 3/4 In. . . . 13.00

Salt & Pepper, 2 In. 55.00

Sauce Bowl, Handles,
4 1/2 In. 10.00

Sherbet . . . . 18.00 to 26.00

Sugar, Oval . . . . 10.00 to 15.00

Sugar & Creamer 35.00

Tumbler, Footed,
10 Oz. . . . . 24.00 to 29.00

Red

Relish Insert, Triangular,
3 3/4 In. . . . . . . 4.50 to 8.00

MANY WINDOWS
See Roulette

**Glass plates that are
cloudy can sometimes
be cleaned with silver
polish and a plastic
scouring pad.**

MARTHA WASHINGTON

The Cambridge Glass Company of Cambridge, Ohio, started manufacturing Martha Washington pattern in 1932. The glass was made in Amber, Crystal, Forest Green, Gold Krystol, Heatherbloom, Royal Blue, and Ruby.

Crystal
Powder Jar 70.00

Royal Blue
Goblet, Cocktail, 8 In. . . . 40.00

MAYFAIR
See Rosemary

MAYFAIR FEDERAL

The Mayfair patterns can easily be recognized, but if you are buying by mail, the names are sometimes confusing. Mayfair Federal is the pattern sometimes called Rosemary Arches. It was made in Amber, Crystal, or Green by Federal Glass Company in 1934, but was discontinued because of a patent conflict

with Hocking's Mayfair pattern, referred to as Mayfair Open Rose.

Amber
Bowl, Vegetable, Oval,
10 In. 15.00
Plate, Dinner,
9 1/2 In. . . . . . . 9.00 to 18.00
Plate, Salad, 6 3/4 In. 6.00
Soup, Cream, 5 In. 19.00
Sugar, Footed 9.00
Sugar & Creamer 18.00
Tumbler, 9 Oz.,
4 1/2 In. . . . . . 28.00 to 30.00

Crystal
Plate, Dinner, 9 1/2 In. . . 12.00

MAYFAIR OPEN ROSE

Mayfair Open Rose was made by Hocking Glass Company from 1931 to 1937. It was made primarily in Light Blue and Pink, with a few Green and Yellow pieces. Crystal examples are rare. The cookie jar and the whiskey glass have been reproduced since 1982.

Green
Bowl,
11 3/4 In. . . . . 40.00 to 55.00
Bowl, Fruit,
Scalloped, 12 In. 55.00
Sandwich Server, Center
Handle . . . . . . 37.00 to 55.00

Light Blue
Bowl, 11 3/4 In. 125.00
Bowl, Cover, 10 In. 210.00
Bowl, Fruit, Scalloped,
12 In. . . . . 110.00 to 125.00
Bowl, Vegetable, 7 In. . . . 65.00

Bowl, Vegetable, 10 In. . . 80.00
Bowl, Vegetable, Oval,
9 1/2 In. 70.00
Butter, Cover 310.00
Cake Plate, Footed,
10 In. 90.00
Cake Plate, Handles,
12 In. 100.00
Candy Dish,
Cover . . . . . 295.00 to 350.00
Celery Dish,
2 Sections, 9 In. 65.00
Celery Dish, 2 Sections,
10 In. . . . . . 40.00 to 135.00
Cookie Jar, Cover 350.00
Creamer 103.00
Cup . . . . 50.00 to 65.00
Cup & Saucer . . 77.00 to 90.00
Goblet, Water,
5 3/4 In. 330.00
Grill Plate,
9 1/2 In. . . . . 40.00 to 66.00
Pitcher, 60 Oz., 8 In. . . . 195.00
Pitcher, 80 Oz.,
8 1/2 In. 350.00
Plate, Dinner, 9 1/2 In. . . 80.00
Plate, Luncheon,
8 1/2 In. . . . . 35.00 to 55.00
Plate, Off-Center Indent,
6 1/2 In. . . . . 25.00 to 45.00
Platter, Oval, 12 In. 75.00
Salt & Pepper 335.00
Saltshaker 175.00
Sandwich Server, Center
Handle . . . . . 65.00 to 125.00
Saucer, 5 3/4 In. . 27.00 to 35.00
Sherbet, 2 1/4 In. 195.00
Sherbet, Footed,
4 3/4 In. . . . . 80.00 to 110.00
Sherbet, Underplate,
Flat 300.00
Sugar, Footed 85.00
Sugar & Creamer 220.00
Tumbler, Footed,
10 Oz., 5 1/4 In. 175.00
Tumbler, Iced Tea, Footed,
15 Oz., 6 1/2 In. 385.00
Tumbler, Juice, 5 Oz.,
3 1/2 In. 225.00
Tumbler, Water, 9 Oz.,
4 1/4 In. 195.00
Vase, Sweet
Pea . . . . 105.00 to 150.00

Pink

Bowl,
11 3/4 In. .... 60.00 to 90.00

Bowl, Cereal,
5 1/2 In. ..... 28.00 to 35.00

Bowl, Hat 75.00

Bowl, Vegetable,
7 In. 31.00

Bowl, Vegetable,
10 In. .... 26.00 to 49.00

Bowl, Vegetable, Cover,
10 In. ..... 139.00 to 160.00

Bowl, Vegetable,
2 Handles, 10 In. 29.00

Bowl, Vegetable, Oval,
9 1/2 In. ..... 34.00 to 40.00

Butter, Cover ... 75.00 to 80.00

Butter, Cover Only 75.00

Cake Plate, 2 Handles,
12 In. ..... 35.00 to 80.00

Candy Dish,
Cover .... 55.00 to 85.00

Celery Dish,
10 In. .... 45.00 to 60.00

Celery Dish, 2 Sections,
9 In. 350.00

Cookie Jar,
Cover .... 55.00 to 60.00

Creamer,
Footed ...... 29.00 to 42.00

Cup .... 18.00 to 25.00

Cup & Saucer .. 31.00 to 55.00

Decanter,
Stopper .... 200.00 to 250.00

Goblet, Cocktail, 3 Oz.,
4 In. ...... 100.00 to 130.00

Goblet, Water, 9 Oz.,
5 3/4 In. ..... 75.00 to 95.00

Goblet, Water, Thin, 9 Oz.,
7 1/4 In. ... 410.00 to 425.00

Goblet, Wine, 3 Oz.,
4 1/2 In. ... 110.00 to 145.00

Grill Plate,
9 1/2 In. ..... 40.00 to 50.00

Pitcher, 37 Oz.,
6 In. .... 60.00 to 70.00

Pitcher, 60 Oz.,
8 In. .... 70.00 to 97.00

Pitcher, 80 Oz.,
8 1/2 In. ... 115.00 to 145.00

Plate, Dessert,
6 1/2 In. 16.00

Plate, Dinner,
9 1/2 In. ..... 58.00 to 65.00

Plate, Luncheon,
8 1/2 In. ..... 30.00 to 39.00

Plate, Sherbet,
6 1/2 In. ..... 12.00 to 20.00

Platter, Open Handles,
Oval, 12 In. .... 30.00 to 33.00

Relish, 4 Sections,
8 3/8 In. ..... 30.00 to 45.00

Salt & Pepper ... 70.00 to 85.00

Sandwich Server, Center
Handle ...... 43.00 to 65.00

Saucer .... 12.00 to 47.00

Sherbet, 3 In. ... 16.00 to 20.00

Sherbet,
4 3/4 In. ... 170.00 to 175.00

Sherbet, Underplate 300.00

Soup, Cream ... 48.00 to 70.00

Sugar, Footed ... 33.00 to 45.00

Sugar &
Creamer ..... 58.00 to 87.00

Tumbler, Footed, 10 Oz.,
5 1/4 In. ..... 45.00 to 48.00

Tumbler, Iced Tea, 13 1/2 Oz.,
5 1/4 In. ..... 50.00 to 80.00

Tumbler, Iced Tea,
Footed, 15 Oz.,
6 1/2 In. ..... 48.00 to 55.00

Tumbler, Juice, 5 Oz.,
3 1/2 In. ..... 51.00 to 80.00

Tumbler, Water, 9 Oz.,
4 1/4 In. ..... 25.00 to 45.00

Tumbler, Water, 11 Oz.,
4 3/4 In. 375.00

Tumbler, Whiskey,
1 1/2 Oz., 2 1/4 In. ... 125.00

Vase, Sweet
Pea ...... 120.00 to 245.00

MEADOW FLOWER
See No. 618

MEADOW GREEN

Anchor Hocking Glass
Corporation, Lancaster,
Ohio, made Meadow
Green dinnerware and
ovenware from 1967 to
1977. Most of the items
are made of opaque white
glass and have green and
golden yellow floral decals.
The cup, creamer, and
sugar have a solid fired-on
avocado green coating.
Other related patterns are
listed in the Fire-King section in this book.

Bowl, Cereal, 8 Oz.,
5 In. 5.00

Bowl, Dessert,
4 5/8 In. 4.00

Casserole, 2 Handles,
12 Oz. 6.00

Casserole, Cover,
1 1/2 Qt. 18.00

Custard Cup, 6 Oz. 3.00

Loaf Pan, 5 x 9 In. 9.00

Mug 7.00

Plate, Dinner, 10 In. 8.00

Soup, 6 5/8 In. 9.00

MEANDERING VINE
See Madrid

MISS AMERICA

Miss America, or Diamond
Pattern, was made by
Hocking Glass Company
from 1933 to 1936 in many
colors, including Crystal,
Green, Ice Blue, Jade-ite,
Pink, Red, and Ritz Blue.

It is similar to English Hobnail, but can be distinguished by the typical Hocking sunburst base and hobs that are more pointed than those of the Westmoreland pattern. In 1977, some reproduction butter dishes were made of Amberina, Crystal, Green, Ice Blue, Pink, and Red. Saltshakers, pitchers, and tumblers are also being reproduced.

Crystal

Bowl, Cereal,
6 1/4 In. . . . . . 8.00 to 17.00
Bowl, Curved In,
8 In. 65.00
Bowl, Vegetable,
Oval, 10 In. . . . 15.00 to 20.00
Cake Plate, Footed,
12 In. . . . . . . 24.00 to 40.00
Candy Jar, Cover,
11 1/2 In. . . . 55.00 to 165.00
Celery Dish,
10 1/2 In. . . . . 14.00 to 19.00
Coaster,
5 3/4 In. . . . . . 15.00 to 20.00
Compote, 5 In. . . 18.00 to 30.00
Creamer,
Footed . . . . 8.00 to 13.00
Cup . . . . 8.00 to 13.00
Cup & Saucer . . . 9.00 to 33.00
Goblet, 10 Oz. 15.00
Goblet, Juice, 5 Oz.,
4 3/4 In. . . . . . 24.00 to 35.00
Goblet, Water, 10 Oz.,
5 1/2 In. . . . . . 20.00 to 30.00
Goblet, Wine, 3 Oz.,
3 3/4 In. . . . . . 19.00 to 26.00
Grill Plate,
10 1/4 In. . . . . 10.00 to 15.00
Plate, Dinner,
10 1/4 In. . . . . 13.00 to 25.00
Plate, Salad,
8 1/2 In. . . . . . . 7.50 to 15.00
Plate, Sherbet,
5 3/4 In. . . . . . . 4.50 to 11.00
Platter, Oval,
12 1/4 In. . . . . 16.00 to 32.00
Relish, 4 Sections,
8 3/4 In. . . . . . . 7.00 to 13.00

Relish, Divided, Round,
11 3/4 In. . . . . 15.00 to 50.00
Salt & Pepper . . . 17.00 to 40.00
Saucer 4.00
Sherbet . . . . 6.00 to 16.00
Sugar . . . . 8.00 to 10.00
Sugar &
Creamer . . . . . 16.00 to 25.00
Tumbler, Juice, 5 Oz.,
4 In. . . . . 14.00 to 19.00
Tumbler, Water, 10 Oz.,
4 1/2 In. . . . . . 17.00 to 25.00

Green

Cup . . . . 15.00 to 20.00
Plate,
6 3/4 In. . . . . . 14.00 to 15.00
Salt & Pepper 250.00
Tumbler, Water, 10 Oz.,
4 1/2 In. 35.00

Pink

Bowl, Cereal,
6 1/4 In. . . . . . 24.00 to 35.00
Bowl, Curved In,
8 In. . . . . 89.00 to 115.00
Bowl, Vegetable, Oval,
10 In. . . . . 35.00 to 48.00
Butter 725.00
Cake Plate, Footed,
12 In. . . . . 45.00 to 62.00
Candy Jar, Cover,
11 1/2 In. . . 140.00 to 200.00
Celery Dish,
10 1/2 In. . . . . 33.00 to 47.00
Coaster,
5 3/4 In. . . . . . 35.00 to 55.00
Compote, 5 In. . . 30.00 to 39.00
Creamer . . . . 22.00 to 30.00
Cup . . . . 23.00 to 30.00
Cup & Saucer . . 25.00 to 40.00
Goblet, Juice, 5 Oz.,
4 3/4 In. . . . 100.00 to 135.00
Goblet, Water, 10 Oz.,
5 1/2 In. . . . . . 45.00 to 75.00
Goblet, Wine, 3 Oz.,
3 3/4 In. . . . 100.00 to 135.00
Grill Plate,
10 1/4 In. . . . . 25.00 to 35.00
Pitcher, 65 Oz.,
8 In. . . . . . . 175.00 to 325.00
Pitcher, Ice Lip, 65 Oz.,
8 1/2 In. . . . 255.00 to 265.00
Plate, Dinner,
10 1/4 In. . . . . 37.00 to 45.00

Plate, Salad,
8 1/2 In. . . . . . 23.00 to 45.00
Plate, Sherbet,
5 3/4 In. . . . . . 10.00 to 17.00
Platter, Oval,
12 1/4 In. . . . . 39.00 to 50.00
Relish, 4 Sections, Round,
8 3/4 In. . . . . . 25.00 to 35.00
Salt & Pepper . . . 60.00 to 75.00
Saltshaker 38.00
Saucer . . . . 6.00 to 10.00
Sherbet . . . . 14.00 to 22.00
Sugar . . . . 23.00 to 25.00
Sugar &
Creamer . . . . . 42.00 to 50.00
Tumbler, Iced Tea, 14 Oz.,
5 3/4 In. . . . . 80.00 to 135.00
Tumbler, Juice, 5 Oz.,
4 In. . . . . 60.00 to 125.00
Tumbler, Water, 10 Oz.,
4 1/2 In. . . . . . 35.00 to 45.00

MISS AMERICA
See also English Hobnail

MODERNE ART
See Tea Room

MODERNTONE

Moderntone, or Wedding Band, was made by Hazel Atlas Glass Company from 1935 to 1942. The simple pattern is popular today with Art Deco enthusiasts. It was made of Amethyst, Cobalt Blue, Crystal, and Pink glass. Green tumblers can be found, too. It was also made of an opaque, almost white glass called Platonite, which is listed here under Moderntone Platonite.

Amethyst

Berry Bowl,
  5 In. . . . . 23.00 to 25.00
Berry Bowl, Master,
  8 3/4 In. 80.00
Creamer 11.00
Cup . . . . 11.00 to 13.00
Cup & Saucer . . 10.00 to 17.00
Custard Cup 13.00
Plate, Dinner,
  8 7/8 In. . . . . 10.00 to 16.00
Plate, Luncheon,
  7 3/4 In. . . . . 12.00 to 14.00
Plate, Sherbet,
  5 3/4 In. . . . . . . 5.00 to 6.50
Platter, Oval, 12 In. 40.00
Punch Set, Chrome Stand,
  Ladle, Cups, 11 Piece . 110.00
Salt & Pepper 37.00
Saltshaker 23.00
Sandwich Server,
  10 1/2 In. 32.00
Saucer 6.00
Sherbet . . . . 13.00 to 15.00
Soup, Cream . . 16.00 to 22.00
Sugar . . . . 10.00 to 15.00
Sugar & Creamer,
  Cover . . . . 10.00 to 21.00
Tumbler, Juice,
  5 Oz. . . . . 40.00 to 45.00
Tumbler, Roly Poly 12.00

Cobalt Blue

Ashtray,
  7 3/4 In. . . . 111.00 to 245.00
Berry Bowl,
  5 In. . . . . 25.00 to 35.00
Berry Bowl, Master,
  8 3/4 In. . . . . 45.00 to 75.00
Bowl, Cereal,
  6 1/4 In. . . . . 55.00 to 75.00
Butter, Cover,
  Red Finial 40.00
Butter, Metal Cover,
  Black Knob 150.00
Butter Base 90.00
Creamer . . . . . . 10.00 to 17.00
Cup . . . . 11.00 to 13.00
Cup & Saucer . . 11.00 to 22.00

Custard Cup . . . . 18.00 to 25.00
Ice Bowl, Bail 35.00
Plate, Dinner,
  8 7/8 In. . . . . 15.00 to 25.00
Plate, Luncheon,
  7 3/4 In. . . . . 10.00 to 16.00
Plate, Salad,
  6 3/4 In. . . . . . 5.00 to 15.00
Plate, Sherbet,
  5 7/8 In. . . . . . 5.00 to 12.00
Platter, Oval,
  11 In. . . . . . . 52.00 to 60.00
Punch Set, 8 Cups 395.00
Salt & Pepper . . . 40.00 to 55.00
Saltshaker 25.00
Saltshaker,
  Pair . . . . 42.00 to 45.00
Sandwich Server,
  10 1/2 In. . . . . 60.00 to 70.00
Saucer . . . . 4.00 to 8.50
Sherbet . . . . 10.00 to 18.50
Soup, Cream . . . 12.00 to 26.00
Soup, Cream,
  Ruffled Edge . . 60.00 to 85.00
Sugar . . . . 10.00 to 13.00
Sugar, Footed 14.00
Sugar, Metal Cover 57.00
Sugar, Open 12.00
Sugar &
  Creamer . . . . . 18.00 to 28.00
Tumbler, Water,
  9 Oz. . . . . 32.00 to 45.00
Tumbler, Whiskey,
  1 1/2 Oz. . . . . . 45.00 to 60.00

Crystal

Soup, Dish 35.00
Tumbler, Water, 9 Oz. . . . 15.00
Tumbler, Whiskey,
  1 1/2 Oz. . . . . . . 8.00 to 16.00

Green

Cup & Saucer 21.00
Tumbler, Juice,
  5 Oz. . . . . 12.50 to 33.00
Tumbler, Water,
  9 Oz. . . . . 15.00 to 19.00
Tumbler, Whiskey,
  1 1/2 Oz. . . . . 17.00 to 18.00

Pink

Ashtray, Matchholder
  Center, 7 3/4 In. 85.00
Bowl, Rim, 8 In. 15.00
Cup 3.00
Cup & Saucer 22.00

Plate, Dinner,
  8 7/8 In. . . . . . . 6.00 to 7.50
Plate, Sherbet,
  5 1/4 In. 15.00
Saucer 1.00
Sherbet 6.00
Soup, Cream 12.00
Soup, Dish, 5 In. 7.00
Sugar 20.00
Tumbler, Water, 9 Oz. . . . 15.00

MODERNTONE LITTLE HOSTESS PARTY SET

The Moderntone Little Hostess Party Set was also made by Hazel Atlas Glass Company in the late 1940s. This is a child's set of dishes made in Platonite with fired-on colors. We have seen Beige, Blue, Chartreuse, Gray, Green, Maroon, Orange (rust), Pink, Turquoise, White, Yellow, and pastels, but other colors were probably made.

Beige

Plate, 5 1/4 In. 17.00

Blue

Cup 8.00
Plate, 5 1/4 In. 8.00
Saucer 7.00

Chartreuse

Creamer 15.00
Cup . . . . 10.00 to 15.00
Cup & Saucer 30.00
Plate, 5 1/4 In. 9.00
Sugar 15.00
Tea Set, 16 Piece, Box . . 225.00

Gray

Cup . . . . 8.00 to 14.00
Plate, 5 1/4 In. . . . 8.00 to 10.00
Saucer . . . . 7.00 to 8.00
Tea Set, 16 Piece, Box . . 225.00

Green

Cup . . . . 8.00 to 9.00

Plate, 5 1/4 In. . . . 9.00 to 12.00
Saucer . . . . 6.00 to 8.00
Tea Set, 16 Piece, Box . . 225.00

Maroon
Creamer 8.00
Cup 11.00
Plate, 5 1/4 In. . . . . 8.00 to 9.00
Tea Set, 16 Piece, Box . . 225.00
Teapot . . . . 95.00 to 115.00

Orange
Creamer 15.00
Cup 13.00
Plate, 5 1/4 In. . . . 8.00 to 12.00
Saucer 8.00
Sugar 15.00

Pastels
Salt & Pepper 18.50

Pink
Creamer . . . . 10.00 to 15.00
Cup 9.00
Plate, 5 1/4 In. 12.00
Saucer . . . . 7.00 to 12.00
Sugar . . . . 10.00 to 20.00

Turquoise
Plate, 5 1/4 In. . . . 8.00 to 17.00
Saucer 8.00

White
Cup 11.00

Yellow
Cup . . . . 4.00 to 13.00
Plate, 5 1/4 In. . . . 8.00 to 15.00
Saucer . . . . 7.00 to 8.00
Sugar 6.00

MODERNTONE PLATONITE

Moderntone Platonite was made by Hazel Atlas Glass Company from 1940 to the early 1950s. Platonite, an almost white glass, was covered with a variety of bright fired-on colors, including Black, Light or Dark Blue, Light or Dark Green, Orange, Red, Yellow, and White trimmed with a small colored rim. Clear glass pieces are listed in this book under Moderntone.

Dark Blue
Saltshaker 10.00
Sherbet, 3 In. 8.50

Gray
Cup & Saucer 10.00

Green
Berry Bowl, 5 In. 9.00
Bowl, Cereal, 5 In. 10.00
Cup 6.50
Plate, Dinner, 8 7/8 In. . . . 7.00
Plate, Salad, 6 3/4 In. 5.00
Sherbet . . . . 4.00 to 10.00
Soup, Cream . . . . 6.50 to 7.00
Sugar . . . . 5.00 to 10.00
Tumbler, 4 In. 10.00

Light Blue
Berry Bowl, No Rim,
  5 In. 5.00
Creamer 8.00
Cup 3.50
Plate, Dinner,
  8 7/8 In. . . . . . . 7.00 to 12.00
Plate, Sherbet,
  6 3/4 In. . . . . . . 4.50 to 5.00
Salt & Pepper 18.00
Saucer . . . . 2.00 to 3.00

Light Green
Plate, Salad, 6 3/4 In. 5.50
Sherbet 5.00

Orange
Plate, Salad, 7 In. 7.00
Salt & Pepper 23.00
Sandwich Server,
  10 1/2 In. 22.00
Sherbet, 3 In. . . . . 7.00 to 8.50

Pink
Bowl, Cereal,
  5 In. . . . . 10.00 to 12.00

Bowl, No Rim, 8 In. 23.00
Bowl, Rim, 8 In. 17.00
Bowl, Rim,
  9 In. . . . . 12.00 to 15.00
Cup 4.00
Cup & Saucer . . . . 5.00 to 6.00
Plate, Dinner,
  8 7/8 In. . . . . . . 5.00 to 12.00
Plate, Salad, 6 3/4 In. 5.00
Platter, Oval 15.00
Salt & Pepper . . . 16.00 to 23.00
Saucer, 5 1/2 In. 2.00
Sherbet, 3 In. . . . . 4.00 to 5.00
Soup, Dish, 5 In. 7.00
Sugar 5.00
Tumbler, 4 In. 10.00

Red
Cup 5.00
Cup & Saucer 22.00
Plate, Luncheon,
  7 3/4 In. 8.00
Plate, Salad, 6 3/4 In. 6.00
Saucer 3.00
Sherbet, Footed 17.00
Tumbler, Whiskey,
  Handle . . . . . . 15.00 to 19.00

Turquoise
Salt & Pepper 23.00
Sherbet, 3 In. 8.50

White
Plate, Dinner, Green Ring,
  9 In. 8.00
Salt & Pepper,
  Green Stripe 13.00
Salt & Pepper,
  Red Stripe . . . . 13.00 to 20.00
Saltshaker, 4 1/4 In. 12.00
Sherbet . . . . 4.00 to 6.00
Sherbet, Red Ring 5.00

Yellow
Creamer . . . . 5.00 to 10.00
Cup & Saucer . . . 5.00 to 18.00
Plate, Dinner,
  8 7/8 In. 12.00
Plate, Salad, 6 3/4 In. 5.00
Platter, Oval,
  11 1/2 In. . . . . 12.00 to 15.00
Salt & Pepper 16.00
Saucer 8.00
Sherbet, 3 In. . . . . 4.00 to 8.50
Sherbet, Footed, 3 In. 8.50

Soup, Cream . . . . 5.00 to 12.00
Tumbler, Water, 9 Oz. . . . 12.00

MOONDROPS

The New Martinsville Glass Manufacturing Company, New Martinsville, West Virginia, made Moondrops, Line No. 37, from 1932 until late 1936. Collectors like the pieces with fan-shaped knobs or stoppers. The pattern was made in Amber, Amethyst, Black, Cobalt Blue, Crystal, Evergreen, Ice Blue, Jade, Light Green, Medium Blue, Pink, Rose, Ruby, and Smoke.

Amber
Bowl, 7 1/2 In. 65.00
Bowl, Ruffled Edge, 3-Footed,
 9 1/2 In. . . . . . 23.00 to 55.00
Butter, Cover 275.00
Creamer, 3 3/4 In. 10.00
Cup 10.00
Cup & Saucer 11.00
Decanter, Stopper,
 7 3/4 In. 40.00
Goblet, Cordial,
 3/4 Oz., 2 7/8 In. 23.00
Pitcher, 53 Oz.,
 8 1/8 In. 155.00
Sherbet, 2 5/8 In. 11.00
Sugar & Creamer,
 3 3/4 In. 20.00
Whiskey, Handle, 2 Oz.,
 2 3/4 In. . . . . . . 8.00 to 12.00

Amethyst
Cup 10.00
Goblet, Cordial, 3/4 Oz.,
 2 7/8 In. 35.00
Tumbler, 9 Oz.,
 4 7/8 In. 20.00

Cobalt Blue
Bowl, Divided, Footed,
 8 1/2 In. 37.00
Butter, Cover 550.00
Butter, Crystal Cover . . . 165.00
Cup 15.00
Cup & Saucer . . 23.00 to 29.00
Goblet, Cordial, 3/4 Oz.,
 2 7/8 In. 50.00
Plate, Dinner, 9 1/2 In. . . 25.00
Plate, Luncheon,
 8 1/2 In. . . . . . 15.00 to 20.00
Plate, Sherbet, 6 1/8 In. . . . 7.00
Relish, 2 Sections,
 Footed 65.00
Sherbet, High, 4 1/2 In. . . 35.00
Tumbler, Juice, Footed, 3 Oz.,
 3 1/4 In. . . . . . 20.00 to 22.00
Vase, Ruffled Edge,
 7 3/4 In. 195.00
Whiskey, Handle,
 2 Oz., 2 3/4 In. 20.00
Whiskey, No Handle 18.00

Crystal
Berry Bowl, 5 1/4 In. 9.00
Bowl, Crimped,
 9 1/2 In. 24.00
Cocktail Measure,
 2 Oz. 200.00
Cup 7.00
Goblet, Cordial, 3 Oz.,
 2 7/8 In. 65.00
Perfume Bottle, Stopper . . 25.00
Relish, Divided,
 8 1/2 In. 13.00
Sugar, 2 3/4 In. 8.00
Sugar & Creamer 18.00
Tray, For Sugar & Creamer,
 7 1/2 In. 45.00
Whiskey, 2 Oz.,
 2 3/4 In. 13.00

Evergreen
Cup . . . . 7.00 to 10.00
Cup & Saucer 15.00
Whiskey, 2 Oz., 2 3/4 In. . . 9.00

Pink
Bowl, Vegetable, Oval,
 9 3/4 In. 18.00
Coaster 15.00
Plate, Sherbet, 6 1/8 In. . . 16.00

Ruby
Ashtray . . . . . . 29.00 to 35.00

Berry Bowl, 5 1/4 In. 30.00
Bowl, 3-Footed, 9 7/8 In. . 65.00
Bowl, Ruffled Edge,
 10 In. 85.00
Console, 12 In. 65.00
Creamer, Individual 18.00
Cup 16.00
Cup & Saucer . . 19.00 to 24.00
Decanter, Fan Stopper,
 Long Neck 165.00
Goblet, Cocktail, 4 Oz.,
 4 In. . . . . 20.00 to 33.00
Goblet, Cordial, 3/4 Oz.,
 2 7/8 In. 50.00
Goblet, Metal Stem, 3 Oz.,
 5 1/8 In. 15.00
Goblet, Water, 9 Oz.,
 6 1/4 In. 50.00
Goblet, Wine, 4 Oz.,
 4 In. . . . . 18.00 to 28.00
Mint Dish, 3-Footed,
 4 1/2 In. 95.00
Plate, Canape, 6 In. 20.00
Plate, Luncheon,
 8 1/2 In. 14.00
Plate, Salad, 7 1/8 In. 45.00
Relish, Divided,
 3-Footed, 8 1/2 In. 45.00
Sugar, Individual 18.00
Sugar & Creamer,
 2 3/4 In. . . . . . 33.00 to 35.00
Sugar & Creamer,
 3 1/2 In. . . . . . 15.00 to 40.00
Tumbler, Footed, 5 Oz.,
 3 5/8 In. 15.00
Tumbler, Juice, Footed, 3 Oz.,
 3 1/4 In. . . . . . 13.00 to 20.00
Tumbler, Water, 9 Oz.,
 4 7/8 In. 23.00
Whiskey, 2 Oz.,
 2 3/4 In. . . . . . 18.00 to 24.00
Whiskey, Handle, 2 Oz.,
 2 3/4 In. . . . . . 15.00 to 22.00

❖

Recycle ashtrays as drip-catching candle-holders, containers for change on your dresser, or as "bowls" for sugar packets.

❖

MOONSTONE

The opalescent hobnails on this crystal pattern give it the name Moonstone. It was made by Anchor Hocking Glass Corporation, Lancaster, Ohio, from 1941 to 1946. A few pieces are seen in Green. Reproductions have been made.

Berry Bowl, 5 1/2 In. 26.00
Bonbon, Heart Shape,
    Handles . . . . . . 12.00 to 18.00
Bowl,
    Cloverleaf . . . . 11.00 to 18.00
Bowl, Crimped,
    5 1/2 In. 10.00
Bowl, Crimped,
    9 1/2 In. . . . . . 20.00 to 30.00
Candleholder,
    Pair . . . . 10.00 to 25.00
Candy Dish, Lid 26.00
Cigarette Jar,
    Cover . . . . . . 22.00 to 28.00
Creamer . . . . 7.00 to 18.00
Cup 8.00
Cup & Saucer 15.00
Goblet, Footed,
    10 Oz. . . . . 24.00 to 26.00
Plate, Luncheon,
    8 In. . . . . 16.00 to 18.00
Plate, Sandwich,
    10 In. . . . . 22.00 to 34.00
Plate, Sherbet,
    6 1/4 In. . . . . . . 6.00 to 11.00
Puff Box, Cover,
    Round . . . . 25.00 to 27.00
Relish, Divided,
    7 3/4 In. 12.00
Relish, 2 Sections,
    7 3/4 In. . . . . . 10.00 to 16.00
Saucer 6.00
Soup, Dish 20.00

Sugar, Footed . . . . 5.00 to 18.00
Sugar &
    Creamer . . . . . 16.00 to 20.00
Vase, Bud, Footed,
    5 1/2 In. . . . . . 12.00 to 22.00

MOROCCAN AMETHYST

Moroccan Amethyst is the name of a color, not a shape. The smoky-purple glass was made by Hazel Atlas, a division of Continental Can Company, Clarksburg, West Virginia, in the 1960s. The modern-looking dishes were made in several shapes, including Apple, Moderne, Seashell, Simplicity, Square, Starlite, Swirl, Swirl Colonial, and Vanity. Alpine punch sets and snack sets are a combination of Moroccan Amethyst and Opaque White pieces. Many of these shapes were made in the color Capri Blue, which is listed in its own section in this book.

Bowl, 6 In. . . . . . 10.00 to 12.00
Bowl, Fruit, Octagonal,
    4 3/4 In. 9.00
Bowl, Oval,
    7 3/4 In. 16.00
Bowl, Rectangular,
    7 3/4 In. 18.00
Bowl, Rectangular,
    9 1/2 In. . . . . . 18.00 to 20.00
Bowl, Square, Deep,
    5 3/4 In. 10.00
Candy Dish, Cover,
    Tall . . . . 35.00 to 45.00
Cocktail Shaker,
    Cover 30.00
Cup & Saucer . . . 9.00 to 10.00
Goblet, Water,
    9 Oz., 5 1/2 In. 17.00
Goblet, Wine, 4 1/4 Oz.,
    4 In. 10.00

Ice Bucket, 6 In. 40.00
Plate, Bread & Butter,
    Octagonal, 5 3/4 In. . . . 12.50
Plate, Dinner, 9 3/4 In. . . 12.00
Sherbet, 7 1/2 Oz.,
    4 1/4 In. 12.00
Tumbler, Iced Tea, 16 Oz.,
    6 1/2 In. . . . . . 16.00 to 17.00
Tumbler, Juice, 4 Oz.,
    2 1/2 In. . . . . . . 8.00 to 12.50
Tumbler, Old Fashioned, 8 Oz.,
    3 1/4 In. . . . . . 12.00 to 15.00
Tumbler, Water,
    9 Oz. 10.00
Tumbler, Water, 11 Oz.,
    4 5/8 In. 12.00

MT. PLEASANT

Mt. Pleasant, sometimes called Double Shield, was made by L. E. Smith Company, Mt. Pleasant, Pennsylvania, from the mid-1920s to 1934. The pattern was made in Amber, Black Amethyst (a very deep purple that appears black unless held in front of a strong light), Cobalt Blue, Crystal, Green, Pink, and White. Some pieces have gold or silver trim.

Black Amethyst

Bowl, Center Handle,
    9 In. 40.00
Bulb Bowl, 3-Footed,
    5 3/4 In. 15.00
Cake Plate, Handles,
    10 In. 35.00
Candlestick, 2-Light 23.00
Candlestick, 2-Light,
    Pair . . . . 40.00 to 47.50

Creamer . . . . 19.00 to 20.00
Cup 12.00
Cup & Saucer . . 17.00 to 19.50
Dish, Mayonnaise,
   3-Footed . . . . . 28.00 to 32.00
Grill Plate,
   9 In. . . . . 6.00 to 24.00
Mint Dish, 6 In. 12.00
Mint Dish, Center
   Handle 22.00
Plate, 8 In. . . . . . 12.00 to 18.50
Plate, Scalloped,
   8 In. 15.00
Plate, Scalloped, Handles,
   7 In. . . . . 14.00 to 15.00
Saltshaker . . . . . 22.00 to 25.00
Sandwich Server, Center
   Handle . . . . . . 40.00 to 45.00
Saucer 5.00
Sherbet . . . . 16.00 to 22.50
Sugar . . . . 10.00 to 20.00

Cobalt Blue

Bowl, 3-Footed, Rolled
   Edge, 7 In. 25.00
Bowl, Fruit, Footed,
   4 7/8 In. 35.00
Bowl, Scalloped, Handles,
   8 In. 35.00
Bowl, Square, Handles,
   6 In. 20.00
Candlestick, 2-Light 24.00
Creamer 20.00
Cup . . . . 12.00 to 16.00
Cup & Saucer . . 18.00 to 23.00
Dish, Mayonnaise, 3-Footed,
   5 1/2 In. . . . . . 22.00 to 35.00
Grill Plate, 9 In. 18.00
Mint Dish, Center Handle,
   6 In. 25.00
Plate, Closed Handle,
   8 In. 18.00
Plate, Leaf,
   8 In. 18.00
Plate, Scalloped,
   8 In. . . . . 15.00 to 16.00
Plate, Scalloped, Handles,
   7 In. . . . . 15.00 to 20.00
Salt & Pepper . . . 50.00 to 65.00
Sherbet . . . . 15.00 to 20.00
Sugar 20.00
Sugar & Creamer 19.00
Tumbler,
   Footed . . . . 22.00 to 30.00

MT. VERNON

Mt. Vernon was made in
the late 1920s through the
1940s by the Cambridge
Glass Company, Cam-
bridge, Ohio. It was made
in Amber, Carmen (red),
Crystal, Emerald Green,
Heatherbloom, Royal
Blue, and Violet.

Amber

Oyster Cocktail, 4 Oz. 9.00

Carmen

Plate, Salad, 8 1/2 In. 12.00

Crystal

Goblet, Cordial, Footed,
   1 Oz. 20.00
Plate, Bread & Butter,
   6 3/8 In. 4.00
Punch Set, 14 Piece 125.00
Sugar & Creamer 12.00
Tumbler, 5 Oz. 12.00
Tumbler, Juice, Footed,
   3 Oz., 3 1/4 In. . . 8.00 to 9.00

NAVARRE

Fostoria Glass Company,
Fostoria, Ohio, made
Navarre pattern glass
from 1937 to 1980. It is an
etched pattern. Some of
the pieces were made on

the Baroque glass blank,
others on more modern
shapes. It was originally
made only in Crystal. A
few pieces were made in
the 1970s in Blue, Green,
or Pink.

Blue

Bell, Dinner . . . . 92.00 to 95.00
Goblet, Champagne,
   6 Oz., 5 5/8 In. 55.00
Goblet, Claret, 4 1/2 Oz.,
   6 1/2 In. . . . . . 70.00 to 80.00
Tumbler, Iced Tea,
   Footed, 13 Oz.,
   5 7/8 In. . . . . . 60.00 to 65.00

Crystal

Berry Bowl, Handle,
   4 3/8 In. 30.00
Bonbon, Handle 25.00
Bowl, Flame, Oval,
   12 1/2 In. 110.00
Bowl, Handle, Footed,
   12 In. 75.00
Candleholder 100.00
Candlestick, 2-Light,
   Pair 80.00
Candlestick, 3-Light,
   Pair 125.00
Candlestick, 5 1/2 In.,
   Pair 65.00
Candy Dish, Cover,
   3 Sections 175.00
Compote, 6 In. 45.00
Creamer 20.00
Cup & Saucer 25.00
Goblet, Champagne, 6 Oz.,
   5 5/8 In. . . . . . 22.00 to 25.00
Goblet, Cocktail,
   3 1/2 Oz., 6 In. 25.00
Goblet, Cordial,
   1 Oz., 3 7/8 In. 80.00
Goblet, Water,
   10 Oz., 7 5/8 In. 40.00
Oyster Cocktail 28.00
Pickle 15.00
Pitcher, 48 Oz. 650.00
Plate, 6 In. 13.00
Plate, Salad, 7 1/2 In. 16.00
Sauceboat,
   Underplate . 175.00 to 200.00
Sherbet, 6 Oz.,
   4 3/8 In. 26.00

Sherbet, 6 Oz.,
  5 5/8 In. . . . . . 20.00 to 28.00

Sugar & Creamer 45.00

Sugar & Creamer,
  Individual . . . . 42.00 to 46.00

Tumbler, Water, Footed, 10 Oz.,
  7 5/8 In. . . . . . 30.00 to 42.00

Vase, 5 In. 225.00

Vase, Footed, 10 In. 275.00

Pink

Bell, Dinner 135.00

Goblet, Claret, 4 Oz.,
  6 1/2 In. 80.00

Sherbet, 6 Oz., 5 5/8 In. . . 45.00

NEW CENTURY

New Century used to be called Lydia Ray by some collectors. It was made by Hazel Atlas Glass Company, a firm with factories in Ohio, Pennsylvania, and West Virginia, from 1930 to 1935. It has a series of ribs in the glass design. It is found in Amethyst, Cobalt Blue, Crystal, Green, and Pink. Ovide, another Hazel Atlas pattern, is sometimes incorrectly called New Century.

Amethyst

Plate, Salad, 8 1/2 In. 15.00

Tumbler, 5 Oz., 4 In. 15.00

Tumbler, 9 Oz.,
  4 1/4 In. . . . . . 15.00 to 20.00

Tumbler, 10 Oz., 5 In. . . . 18.00

Tumbler, 12 Oz.,
  5 1/4 In. 33.00

Tumbler, Iced Tea, 12 Oz.,
  5 1/4 In. . . . . . 20.00 to 31.00

Tumbler, Juice, 5 Oz.,
  3 1/2 In. . . . . . 12.00 to 19.50

Cobalt Blue

Pitcher 70.00

Tumbler, 5 Oz.,
  3 1/2 In. . . . . . 10.00 to 16.00

Tumbler, 10 Oz., 5 In. . . . 20.00

Tumbler, Iced Tea, 12 Oz.,
  5 1/4 In. . . . . . 20.00 to 30.00

Crystal

Goblet, Cocktail,
  3 1/4 Oz. 4.00

Plate, Dinner, 10 In. 18.00

Plate, Salad,
  8 1/2 In. . . . . . . 8.50 to 10.00

Salt & Pepper 35.00

Tumbler, Juice, Red, Black
  Trim, 5 Oz. 12.00

Green

Butter, Cover Only 25.00

Creamer . . . . 16.00 to 20.00

Cup 14.00

Decanter . . . . . 35.00 to 40.00

Pitcher, 60 Oz.,
  7 3/4 In. 35.00

Plate, Breakfast, 7 In. . . . 15.00

Plate, Dinner, 10 In. 27.50

Plate, Salad,
  8 1/2 In. . . . . . 12.00 to 15.00

Plate, Sherbet, 6 In. 9.00

Salt & Pepper . . . 36.00 to 45.00

Sherbet . . . . 8.00 to 13.00

Sugar, Cover 30.00

Sugar & Creamer,
  Cover 45.00

Tumbler, 9 Oz.,
  4 1/4 In. . . . . . 20.00 to 22.00

Pink

Tumbler, 9 Oz., 4 1/4 In. . . 16.00

❖

Switch dishwasher detergent brands periodically. This helps to keep the inside of the dishwasher and the dishes free of any chemical buildup.

❖

NEWPORT

Newport, or Hairpin, was made by Hazel Atlas Glass Company from 1936 to 1940. It is known in Amethyst, Cobalt Blue, Pink, Platonite (white), and a variety of fired-on colors. Reproductions have been made.

Amethyst

Berry Bowl,
  4 3/4 In. . . . . . 16.00 to 22.00

Berry Bowl, Master,
  8 1/2 In. 20.00

Bowl, 6 In. 10.00

Bowl, Cereal,
  5 1/4 In. . . . . . 32.00 to 36.00

Creamer 15.00

Cup . . . . 10.00 to 12.00

Cup & Saucer . . . 9.00 to 16.00

Plate, Dinner,
  8 13/16 In. . . . 30.00 to 32.00

Plate, Luncheon,
  8 1/2 In. . . . . . 15.00 to 16.00

Plate, Sherbet,
  5 7/8 In. . . . . . . 7.00 to 10.00

Saltshaker 25.00

Sandwich Server,
  11 3/4 In. 42.00

Saucer . . . . 3.50 to 5.00

Sherbet . . . . 13.00 to 15.00

Soup, Cream,
  4 3/4 In. . . . . . 18.00 to 24.00

Soup, Cream,
  Underplate 25.00

Sugar 15.00

Sugar, Footed 16.00

Sugar &
  Creamer . . . . . 30.00 to 31.00

Tumbler, 9 Oz.,
4 1/2 In. ..... 38.00 to 40.00

Cobalt Blue

Berry Bowl, Master,
8 1/2 In. 70.00

Bowl, Cereal,
5 1/4 In. ..... 45.00 to 55.00

Creamer .... 16.00 to 20.00

Cup .... 14.00 to 15.00

Cup & Saucer .. 18.00 to 22.00

Plate, Luncheon,
8 1/2 In. ..... 16.00 to 20.00

Plate, Sherbet,
5 7/8 In. ...... 8.00 to 16.00

Platter, Oval, 11 3/4 In. .. 55.00

Salt & Pepper 57.00

Saucer 5.00

Sherbet .... 16.00 to 19.00

Soup, Cream ... 20.00 to 25.00

Sugar .... 15.00 to 18.00

Sugar & Creamer 38.00

Tumbler, 9 Oz.,
4 1/2 In. ..... 40.00 to 50.00

Pink

Berry Bowl,
4 3/4 In. ..... 12.00 to 13.00

Cup 9.00

Plate, Sherbet, 5 7/8 In. ... 6.00

Platonite

Creamer 5.00

Salt & Pepper 18.00

Sandwich Plate, Pink,
11 1/2 In. 25.00

Sandwich Plate, Red,
11 1/2 In. 16.00

Sugar 5.00

Sugar, Fired-On Red 8.00

Sugar, Gold Edge 6.00

NO. 414
See Diamond Quilted

NO. 601
See Avocado

❖

**Restoring and reusing
old things is the purest
form of recycling.**

❖

NO. 610

Many patterns are listed both by the original pattern number and by a name. No. 610 is often called Pyramid or Rex. It was made from 1926 to 1932 by the Indiana Glass Company. Green and Pink were used more than Crystal, White, and Yellow. In 1974 and 1975 Tiara reissued the pattern in Black and Blue.

Black

Bowl, 4 3/4 In. 15.00

Bowl, 8 1/2 In. 39.00

Tumbler, 11 Oz. 35.00

Blue

Relish, 4 Sections 29.00

Crystal

Ashtray 15.00

Pickle, 9 1/2 In. 39.00

Plate, 9 3/8 In. 15.00

Green

Berry Bowl, 4 3/4 In. 24.00

Bowl, Oval, 9 1/2 In. 38.00

Creamer 25.00

Relish, 4 Sections 95.00

Sugar & Creamer,
Tray 235.00

Tumbler, 9 Oz. 6.50

Pink

Berry Bowl, Master,
8 1/2 In. 65.00

Bowl, Oval, 9 1/2 In. 65.00

Creamer 30.00

Pickle, 9 1/2 x
5 3/4 In. ..... 60.00 to 65.00

Sugar 30.00

Sugar & Creamer 125.00

Tumbler, 8 Oz. 60.00

Yellow

Berry Bowl,
4 3/4 In. ..... 50.00 to 75.00

Berry Bowl, Master,
8 1/2 In. ..... 75.00 to 80.00

Ice Bucket 275.00

Ice Bucket, Cover 1250.00

Pickle, 9 1/2 x
5 3/4 In. ..... 60.00 to 95.00

Pitcher, Water 495.00

Sugar & Creamer,
Tray 255.00

Tray, For Sugar &
Creamer 59.00

NO. 612

Indiana Glass Company, Dunkirk, Indiana, called this pattern No. 612, but collectors call it Horseshoe. It was made from 1930 to 1933 primarily in Green and Yellow, with a smaller number of Pink pieces. Sugar and creamer sets were also made in Crystal. Plates came in two styles, one with the center pattern, one plain.

Green

Berry Bowl,
4 1/2 In. ..... 28.00 to 55.00

Berry Bowl, Master,
9 1/2 In. ..... 38.00 to 60.00

Bowl, Cereal,
6 1/2 In. ..... 35.00 to 48.00

Butter 1195.00

Creamer, Square Foot,
4 1/8 In. . . . . 20.00 to 22.00
Cup . . . . 8.50 to 15.00
Cup & Saucer . . 12.00 to 23.00
Grill Plate,
10 3/8 In. . . 135.00 to 225.00
Pitcher, 64 Oz.,
8 1/2 In. 550.00
Plate, Luncheon,
9 3/8 In. . . . . . 13.00 to 20.00
Plate, Salad,
8 3/8 In. . . . . . 12.00 to 17.00
Plate, Sherbet,
6 In. . . . . 8.00 to 14.00
Platter, Oval, 10 3/4 In. . . 60.00
Relish, 3 Sections,
Footed . . . . 25.00 to 38.00
Sandwich Server,
11 1/2 In. 35.00
Sandwich Server, Center
Design, 11 1/2 In. 40.00
Sandwich Server, No
Center Design,
11 1/2 In. . . . . 25.00 to 30.00
Saucer . . . . 5.00 to 10.00
Sherbet . . . . 15.00 to 18.00
Sugar . . . . 16.00 to 20.00
Sugar, Square Foot,
3 3/4 In. . . . . . 17.00 to 25.00
Sugar & Creamer, Square
Foot . . . . 42.00 to 55.00
Tumbler, Water, Footed, 9 Oz.,
4 1/2 In. . . . . . 26.00 to 35.00

Pink
Pitcher, 64 Oz.,
8 1/2 In. 525.00

Yellow
Berry Bowl, 4 1/2 In. 30.00
Bowl, Cereal,
6 1/2 In. . . . . . 42.00 to 55.00
Bowl, Salad, 7 1/2 In. . . . 31.00
Bowl, Vegetable,
8 1/2 In. 38.00
Bowl, Vegetable, Oval,
10 1/2 In. . . . . 28.00 to 40.00
Creamer, Square
Foot . . . . 18.00 to 25.00
Cup . . . . 10.00 to 16.00
Cup & Saucer . . 18.00 to 25.00
Pitcher, 64 Oz.,
8 1/2 In. . . . 400.00 to 500.00
Plate, Dinner, 10 1/4 In. . . 90.00
Plate, Luncheon,
9 3/8 In. . . . . . 13.00 to 20.00

Plate, Salad,
8 3/8 In. . . . . . 11.00 to 15.00
Plate, Sherbet,
6 In. . . . . 8.00 to 10.00
Platter, Oval,
10 3/4 In. . . . . 28.00 to 40.00
Relish, 3 Sections,
Footed . . . . . . 23.00 to 40.00
Sandwich Server,
11 1/2 In. . . . . 15.00 to 35.00
Saucer 5.00
Sherbet . . . . 13.00 to 25.00
Sugar . . . . 17.00 to 25.00
Sugar & Creamer 45.00
Tumbler, Water, Footed, 9 Oz.,
4 3/4 In. . . . . . 30.00 to 36.00

NO. 615

No. 615 is often called Lorain. Others call it Basket, Bridal Bouquet, Flower Basket, or Hanging Basket. It was made by the Indiana Glass Company from 1929 to 1932 in Crystal, Green, and Yellow. Sometimes Crystal pieces have blue, green, red, or yellow borders. Reproduction pieces were made in Milk Glass or Olive Green.

Crystal
Cup & Saucer 15.00
Relish, 4 Sections, 8 In. . . 18.00
Sugar, Footed 20.00

Green
Creamer . . . . 19.00 to 25.00
Cup & Saucer . . 18.00 to 26.00
Plate, Dinner,
10 1/4 In. . . . . 50.00 to 70.00
Plate, Luncheon,
8 3/8 In. . . . . . 15.00 to 22.00

Plate, Salad,
7 3/4 In. . . . . . 12.00 to 13.00
Relish, 3 Sections 38.00
Saucer 5.00
Sherbet 28.00
Sugar 22.00
Tumbler, Water, Footed,
9 Oz., 4 3/4 In. 28.00

Yellow
Bowl, Vegetable, Oval,
9 3/4 In. . . . . 56.00 to 100.00
Creamer . . . . . . 28.00 to 35.00
Cup . . . . 15.00 to 20.00
Cup & Saucer . . 21.00 to 30.00
Plate, Dinner,
10 1/4 In. . . . . 75.00 to 88.00
Plate, Luncheon,
8 3/8 In. . . . . . 28.00 to 40.00
Plate, Salad,
7 3/4 In. . . . . . 12.00 to 28.00
Plate, Sherbet,
5 1/2 In. . . . . . 12.00 to 15.00
Platter, Oval,
11 1/2 In. . . . . 40.00 to 55.00
Relish, 3 Sections 38.00
Relish, 4 Sections,
8 In. . . . . 37.00 to 55.00
Saucer . . . . 5.00 to 7.00
Sherbet,
Footed . . . . . . 33.00 to 38.00
Sugar 30.00
Sugar, Open 28.00
Tray, 11 1/2 x 7 1/4 In. . . 85.00
Tumbler, Footed, 9 Oz.,
4 3/4 In. . . . . . 28.00 to 38.00

NO. 616

No. 616 is called Vernon by some collectors. It was made by Indiana Glass Company from 1930 to 1932. The pattern was made in Crystal, Green, and Yellow. Some Crystal pieces have a platinum trim.

Crystal
Tumbler, Footed, 5 In. . . . 22.00

Green
Tumbler, Footed, 5 In. . . . 45.00

Yellow

Cup 17.00
Plate, Luncheon, 8 In. . . . 10.00
Saucer 4.00

NO. 618

Another Indiana Glass
Company pattern made
from 1932 to 1937 was
No. 618, or Pineapple &
Floral. It is also called Lacy
Daisy, Meadow Flower,
or Wildflower. The pat-
tern was made of Amber,
Crystal, and fired-on
Green and Red. Repro-
ductions were made in
Olive Green in the late
1960s.

Amber

Bowl, Vegetable, Oval,
   10 In. 14.00
Compote 8.00
Creamer 11.00
Cup . . . . 9.00 to 10.00
Cup & Saucer . . 10.00 to 15.00
Plate, Dinner,
   9 3/8 In. . . . . . 11.00 to 15.00
Plate, Salad,
   8 3/8 In. . . . . 8.00 to 9.00
Plate, Sherbet,
   6 In. . . . . 4.00 to 5.00
Platter,
   11 1/2 In. . . . . 18.00 to 19.00
Saucer 5.00
Soup, Cream . . . 15.00 to 23.00
Sugar 11.00
Sugar &
   Creamer . . . . . 14.00 to 20.00

Crystal

Ashtray 16.00
Berry Bowl, 4 3/4 In. 35.00

Bowl, Cereal,
   6 In. . . . . 20.00 to 32.00
Bowl, Salad,
   7 In. . . . . 9.00 to 10.00
Bowl, Vegetable, Oval,
   10 In. . . . . . . 25.00 to 26.00
Butter, 5 In. 150.00
Compote, Footed 5.00
Creamer 7.00
Cup . . . . 10.00 to 15.00
Cup & Saucer . . 14.00 to 17.00
Plate, 11 1/2 In. 18.00
Plate, Dinner,
   9 3/8 In. . . . . . 15.00 to 25.00
Plate, Indentation,
   11 1/2 In. 25.00
Plate, Salad,
   8 3/8 In. . . . . . . 8.00 to 9.00
Plate, Sherbet,
   6 In. . . . . 7.00 to 8.00
Platter, Closed Handle,
   11 In. . . . . . . 15.00 to 18.00
Relish, Divided,
   11 1/2 In. . . . 17.00 to 20.00
Relish, 3 Sections,
   6 1/2 In. . . . . 18.00 to 25.00
Sandwich Server,
   11 1/2 In. 20.00
Saucer . . . . 4.00 to 5.00
Sherbet,
   Footed . . . . . . 14.00 to 23.00
Soup, Cream 20.00
Sugar . . . . 7.50 to 8.50
Sugar &
   Creamer . . . . . 16.00 to 20.00
Tumbler, Iced Tea,
   12 Oz., 5 In. 50.00
Tumbler, Water, 8 Oz.,
   4 1/4 In. . . . . 32.00 to 40.00
Vase, Cone Shape 55.00

NO. 620

No. 620, also known as
Daisy, was made by Indi-

ana Glass Company. In
1933 the pattern was
made in Crystal, and in
1940 in Amber. It was
reissued in the 1960s and
1970s in Dark Green and
Milk Glass. Some pieces
have a fired-on red color.

Amber

Berry Bowl, 4 1/2 In. 9.00
Bowl, Vegetable, Oval,
   10 In. . . . . . . 17.50 to 18.00
Cake Plate, 11 1/2 In. . . . 15.00
Creamer . . . . 7.00 to 9.00
Cup 5.00
Cup & Saucer . . . . 7.00 to 8.00
Plate, Dinner,
   9 3/8 In. . . . . . . 8.00 to 9.00
Plate, Luncheon,
   8 3/8 In. . . . . . . 6.00 to 7.00
Plate, Salad, 7 3/8 In. 7.50
Plate, Sherbet,
   6 In. . . . . 3.00 to 4.00
Platter,
   10 3/4 In. . . . 15.00 to 17.00
Relish, 3 Sections,
   8 3/8 In. . . . . 25.00 to 35.00
Sandwich Server,
   11 1/2 In. . . . 15.00 to 17.00
Saucer . . . . 2.00 to 5.00
Sherbet . . . . 8.00 to 9.00
Soup, Cream,
   4 1/2 In. . . . . . 8.75 to 14.00
Sugar . . . . 6.00 to 9.00
Sugar &
   Creamer . . . . . 15.00 to 16.00
Tumbler, Water, Footed,
   9 Oz. . . . . 18.00 to 25.00

Crystal

Bowl, Oval, 10 In. 26.00
Creamer 6.00
Cup . . . . 4.00 to 5.00
Grill Plate, 10 3/8 In. 4.00
Sandwich Server,
   11 1/2 In. 6.00
Sugar 6.00
Tumbler, Water, Footed,
   9 Oz. 10.00

Dark Green

Berry Bowl, Deep,
   7 1/2 In. . . . . . 9.00 to 10.00
Creamer . . . . 5.00 to 9.00

Cup . . . . 3.00 to 4.00

Cup & Saucer . . . . 5.00 to 8.00

Plate, Dinner,
9 3/8 In. 7.00

Plate, Salad,
7 3/8 In. 4.00

Saucer 1.50

Tumbler, Iced Tea, Footed,
12 Oz. . . . . 20.00 to 22.00

Tumbler, Water, 9 Oz. . . .10.00

Milk Glass

Sugar 5.00

NO. 622
See Pretzel

NO. 624
See Christmas Candy

NORA BIRD

The Nora Bird etching, made by Paden City Glass Manufacturing Company, Paden City, West Virginia, is a smaller version of the Peacock & Wild Rose etching by the same company. It was produced from 1920 to the 1930s in Amber, Black, Cobalt Blue, Crystal, Green, Light Blue, Pink, and Red.

Green

Candy Dish, Cover 350.00

Dish, Mayonnaise,
Spoon 120.00

Pink

Candlestick, Pair 125.00

Candy Dish,
Cover 325.00

Cup & Saucer 210.00

NORA BIRD
See also Crow's Foot

NORMANDIE

A few Depression glass patterns were made in Iridescent Marigold color, which has been collected as carnival glass. Normandie products made in this iridescence, called Sunburst, appear in the carnival glass listings as Bouquet & Lattice; when the pattern is in the other known colors, it is called Normandie. Look for it in Amber, Crystal, Pink, and Spring Green, as well as in the Iridescent color. Normandie was made by the Federal Glass Company from 1933 to 1940.

Amber

Berry Bowl,
5 In. . . . . 9.00 to 10.00

Berry Bowl, Master,
8 1/2 In. . . . . . 22.00 to 35.00

Bowl, Cereal,
6 1/2 In. . . . . . 15.00 to 22.00

Bowl, Vegetable, Oval,
10 In. 21.00

Cup . . . . 7.00 to 8.00

Cup & Saucer 12.00

Pitcher, 80 Oz.,
8 In. . . . . 70.00 to 90.00

Plate, Dinner,
11 In. . . . . . . 40.00 to 55.00

Plate, Salad,
7 3/4 In. 13.00

Platter, 11 3/4 In. 23.00

Salt & Pepper . . . 45.00 to 60.00

Saltshaker 25.00

Sherbet 7.00

Sugar, Open 7.00

Sugar & Creamer,
Open . . . . 23.00 to 38.00

Tumbler, Iced Tea, 12 Oz.,
5 In. . . . . 40.00 to 45.00

Tumbler, Juice,
5 Oz., 4 In 38.00

Tumbler, Water, 9 Oz.,
4 1/4 In. . . . . . 18.00 to 25.00

Crystal

Sherbet . . . . 5.00 to 7.00

Iridescent

Berry Bowl, 5 In. . . 5.00 to 7.00

Berry Bowl, Master,
8 1/2 In. 15.00

Bowl, Cereal,
6 1/2 In. . . . . . . 6.00 to 12.00

Bowl, Vegetable, Oval,
10 In. 18.00

Cup 6.00

Cup & Saucer . . . . 7.50 to 9.00

Grill Plate,
11 In. . . . . 8.00 to 15.00

Plate, Dinner, 11 In. 22.00

Plate, Sherbet,
6 In. . . . . 3.00 to 4.00

Saucer 3.00

Sherbet . . . . 4.00 to 7.00

Sugar 5.00

Pink

Berry Bowl, Master,
8 1/2 In. . . . . . 40.00 to 42.00

Cup . . . . 6.00 to 11.00

Cup & Saucer . . . 9.00 to 16.00

Pitcher, 80 Oz.,
8 In. 200.00

Plate, Sherbet,
6 In. . . . . 6.00 to 12.00

Platter, Oval,
11 3/4 In. 54.00

Salt & Pepper 98.00

Saucer 4.50

Sherbet . . . . 9.00 to 12.00

Tumbler, Water, 9 Oz.,
4 1/4 In. . . . . . 65.00 to 70.00

OATMEAL LACE
See Princess Feather

OCTAGON

Octagon, sometimes called Tiered Octagon or U.S. Octagon, was made by the U.S. Glass Company from 1927 to 1929. It was used by the Octagon Soap Company as a premium. The pieces were made in Crystal, Green, and Pink. Some pieces are found marked with the glass company trademark.

Green

Nut Dish, Individual 30.00
Plate, Salad, 7 in. 15.00

OLD CAFE

Old Cafe was made by the Hocking Glass Company, Lancaster, Ohio, from 1936 to 1940. Pieces are found in Crystal, Pink, and Royal Ruby.

Crystal

Candy Dish, Ruby
  Cover 13.00
Candy Jar, Tab Handles,
  8 In. 12.00
Dish, Olive 6.00
Plate, Sherbet, 6 1/2 In. ... 5.00
Vase, 7 1/4 In. 15.00

Pink

Berry Bowl, Tab Handle,
  3 3/4 In. 15.00
Bowl, Cereal,
  5 1/2 In. ..... 26.00 to 29.00
Bowl, Tab Handle,
  4 In. 10.00
Candy Dish, Low,
  8 In. .... 13.00 to 15.00

Cup .... 8.00 to 12.50
Dish, Olive ..... 7.00 to 8.00
Plate, Dinner,
  10 In. ...... 55.00 to 70.00
Relish 17.00
Sherbet 20.00
Tumbler, Juice,
  3 In. 20.00
Tumbler, Water,
  4 In. .... 22.00 to 29.00

Royal Ruby

Bowl, 5 In. 15.00
Bowl, Cereal,
  5 1/2 In. ..... 20.00 to 23.00
Candy Dish, Low,
  8 In. .... 15.00 to 25.00
Cup .... 8.00 to 15.00
Sherbet 25.00
Tumbler, 4 In. 35.00

OLD COLONY

To add to the confusion in the marketplace, this pattern, which was advertised as Old Colony, has also been called Colony, Lace Edge, Loop, Open Lace, or Open Scallop. In addition, the pattern is often confused with other similar patterns, such as Imperial's Laced Edge. Cups or tumblers may also be mixed up with Queen Mary or Coronation. The pattern listed here, made by Hocking Glass Company, Lancaster, Ohio, from 1935 to 1938, can usually

be identified by the familiar sunburst base common to many of Hocking's designs. Most pieces of Old Colony are Pink, although Crystal is also found.

Crystal

Bowl, Cereal,
  6 3/8 In. ..... 29.00 to 30.00
Bowl, Plain, 9 1/2 In. 30.00
Bowl, Ribbed,
  9 1/2 In. 33.00
Butter, Cover .. 90.00 to 100.00
Candlestick, Pair 80.00
Compote, Cover, Footed,
  7 In. 74.00
Console, 3-Footed,
  10 1/2 In. 375.00
Cup & Saucer 50.00
Dish, Mayonnaise 80.00
Flower Bowl, Frog 41.00
Plate, 4 Sections,
  13 In. 60.00
Plate, Dinner,
  10 1/2 In. 39.00
Plate, Luncheon,
  8 1/4 In. 28.00
Plate, Salad, 7 1/4 In. 27.00
Platter, 5 Sections,
  12 3/4 In. 42.00
Platter, Oval, 12 3/4 In. .. 44.00
Relish 3 Sections,
  7 1/2 In. 29.00
Saucer 13.00
Sherbet, Footed 129.00
Tumbler, 9 Oz.,
  4 1/2 In. 23.00
Tumbler, Straight,
  12 Oz. 50.00

Pink

Bowl, Cereal,
  6 3/8 In. ..... 25.00 to 39.00
Bowl, Footed,
  10 1/2 In. 350.00
Bowl, Plain,
  9 1/2 In. ..... 21.00 to 24.00
Bowl, Ribbed,
  9 1/2 In. ..... 23.00 to 42.00
Bowl, Salad,
  7 3/4 In. ..... 35.00 to 39.00
Bowl, Salad, Ribbed,
  7 3/4 In. 95.00

Butter 90.00
Butter, Cover . . . 50.00 to 75.00
Candlestick 300.00
Candlestick, Frosted,
  Pair 95.00
Candlestick,
  Pair 600.00
Candy Dish,
  Cover 59.00
Compote, 7 In. 35.00
Compote, Cover,
  7 In. . . . . 55.00 to 85.00
Cookie Jar,
  Cover . . . . 100.00 to 125.00
Creamer . . . . . . 25.00 to 32.00
Cup . . . . 26.00 to 35.00
Cup & Saucer . . 39.00 to 48.00
Flower Bowl 25.00
Flower Bowl, Crystal
  Frog . . . . 45.00 to 50.00
Grill Plate,
  10 1/2 In. . . . . 20.00 to 39.00
Plate, Dinner,
  10 1/2 In. . . . . 32.00 to 40.00
Plate, Luncheon,
  8 1/4 In. . . . . . 22.00 to 24.00
Plate, Salad,
  7 1/4 In. . . . . . 23.00 to 35.00
Plate, Solid Lace,
  13 In. 68.00
Platter,
  12 3/4 In. . . . . 38.00 to 60.00
Platter, 5 Sections,
  12 3/4 In. . . . . 29.00 to 45.00
Platter, Solid Lace,
  12 3/4 In. 85.00
Relish, 3 Sections,
  7 1/2 In. . . . . . 28.00 to 35.00
Relish, 3 Sections,
  10 1/2 In. . . . . 22.00 to 33.00
Relish, 3 Sections, Deep,
  7 1/2 In. . . . . . 85.00 to 95.00
Relish, 4 Sections,
  13 In. 70.00
Relish, 4 Sections, Solid
  Lace, 13 In. . . . 54.00 to 75.00
Saucer . . . . 13.00 to 18.00
Sherbet 165.00
Tumbler, 9 Oz.,
  4 1/2 In. . . . . . 22.00 to 35.00
Tumbler, Footed, 10 1/2 Oz.,
  5 In. . . . . . . 100.00 to 115.00
Vase,
  7 In. . . . . 1195.00 to 1300.00

OLD ENGLISH

Old English, or Threading, was made by the Indiana Glass Company, Dunkirk, Indiana, in the late 1920s and early 1930s. It was first made in Amber, Crystal, and Forest Green. Pink was a later color.

Amber
Candlestick, 4 In. 18.00

Crystal
Eggcup 8.00

Forest Green
Berry Bowl, 4 In. 24.00
Bowl, Fruit, Footed,
  9 In. 35.00
Candlestick, 4 In.,
  Pair . . . . 40.00 to 60.00
Tumbler, Footed,
  4 1/2 In. 28.00
Tumbler, Footed,
  5 1/2 In. . . . . . 35.00 to 44.00

Pink
Sherbet, Footed 20.00

OLD FLORENTINE
See Florentine No. 1

OLD QUILT

Old Quilt, or Checker-board, is an older pattern

first made by Westmore-land Glass Company, Grapeville, Pennsylvania, around 1910. In the 1940s, Westmoreland reintro-duced Old Quilt in Milk Glass. The pattern was made in limited editions of other colors, but the most commonly available pieces are in Milk Glass.

Milk Glass
Bowl, Fruit, 9 In. 25.00
Candy Box, Square,
  5 x 4 In. 59.00
Celery Dish, Footed 20.00
Compote, Cover 5.00
Goblet, Water, 5 1/2 In. . . 10.50
Pitcher, 8 1/2 In. 40.00
Pitcher, Small 45.00
Sugar, 4 In. 6.00
Sugar & Creamer, 4 In. . . 55.00
Sugar & Creamer,
  Large 10.50
Tray, 10 In. 31.00
Vase, 9 In. 39.00

OLD SANDWICH

Old Sandwich looks like the Pillar and Paneled Thumbprint patterns made in the mid-1800s. A. H. Heisey & Company, Newark, Ohio, introduced it in 1931 in Flamingo (pink), Moongleam (green), and Sahara (yellow). Some pieces in Cobalt, Tanger-ine (orange), and Zircon (light turquoise) can be found. Most items are marked with the Diamond H logo.

Cobalt
Mug, 18 Oz. 280.00

Flamingo
Sherbet, 2 3/4 In. 30.00
Tumbler, Whiskey,
   2 In. 140.00

Moongleam
Tumbler, Soda,
   10 Oz. . . . . . .80.00 to 103.00

Sahara
Ashtray, Individual 17.50
Candlestick, Pair 228.00
Pitcher, Ice Lip 81.00
Tumbler, Juice,
   5 Oz. . . . . 27.00 to 40.00

OPALESCENT HOBNAIL
See Moonstone

OPEN LACE
See Old Colony

OPEN ROSE
See Mayfair Open Rose

OPEN SCALLOP
See Old Colony

OPTIC DESIGN
See Raindrops

ORANGE BLOSSOM

Indiana Glass Company made Orange Blossom in

1957. The pattern is the same as Indiana Custard, but the Milk Glass items are called Orange Blossom.

Creamer 4.00
Sugar 5.00

ORCHID ETCH

A. H. Heisey & Company, Newark, Ohio, used the Orchid etching on several shapes of glass, including Waverly and Queen Anne. The pattern was made in Crystal from 1940 to 1957.

Bottle, Dressing,
   8 Oz. . . . . . . 145.00 to 200.00
Butter, Cover, 1/4 Lb. . . 110.00
Candlestick, 2-Light,
   Pair 130.00
Candlestick, 3-Light,
   7 1/4 In., Pair 150.00
Candy Dish, Footed 42.00
Compote 6.00
Cruet, Footed, Stopper,
   3 Oz. 200.00
Cup & Saucer 46.00
Decanter, 1 Pt. 203.00
Goblet, Wine, 3 Oz. 75.00
Oyster Cocktail,
   4 Oz., 3 7/8 In. 37.00
Plate, Dinner,
   10 3/4 In. 158.00
Relish, 4 Sections,
   Round, 9 In. 58.00
Sandwich Server, Center
   Handle, 12 In. 135.00
Sandwich Server,
   Waverly, 14 In. 80.00

Saucer, Champagne 25.00
Sherbet, 6 Oz., 6 In. 18.00
Sugar & Creamer,
   Individual 70.00
Torte Plate, 14 In. 37.00
Tumbler, Iced Tea,
   12 Oz. 61.00
Vase, Fan, Lariat,
   7 3/4 In. 91.00

OREGON GRAPE
See Grape

ORIENTAL POPPY
See Florentine No. 2

OVIDE

Hazel Atlas Glass Company made Ovide pattern from 1929 to the 1950s. Early pieces were made in Green; Black was introduced in 1932. By 1935, Platonite, an opaque white glass, was used with fired-on colors. Pieces were made with colored rims, overall fired-on colors, or decorations like birds, windmills, or Art Deco geometrics. Ovide is sometimes incorrectly called New Century.

Black
Candy Dish, Cover 50.00
Creamer 6.50
Cup 6.50
Cup & Saucer 11.00
Plate, Luncheon, 8 In. 6.00

Plate, Windmills,
Red Trim, 6 In. 6.00

Plate, Windmills,
Red Trim, 8 In. 14.00

Salt & Pepper,
Cloverleaf 28.00

Salt & Pepper, Floral 28.00

Sherbet, Windmills,
Red Trim 14.00

Green

Berry Bowl, 4 3/4 In. 6.00

Berry Bowl, Master,
8 In. 10.00

Creamer, Footed 6.00

Cup 5.00

Plate, Dinner,
9 In. 8.00

Salt & Pepper . . . 30.00 to 35.00

Saucer 3.00

Sherbet 3.00

Sugar 7.00

Sugar & Creamer 18.00

Platonite

Berry Bowl, Black Flowers,
4 3/4 In. . . . . . . 9.00 to 10.00

Berry Bowl, Fired-On
Gray, 4 3/4 In. 6.75

Bowl, Black Flowers,
7 In. 12.00

Bowl, Black Flowers,
9 In. 18.00

Bowl, Cereal, Black
Flowers, 5 1/2 In. 12.00

Bowl, Fired-On Yellow,
4 3/4 In. 6.00

Bowl Set, Black Flowers,
5, 6 & 7 In., 3 Piece . . . 45.00

Creamer, Blue Floral 9.00

Creamer, Fired-On
Chartreuse 5.50

Creamer, Fired-On
Yellow 5.00

Cup, Fired-On Yellow 5.00

Cup & Saucer, Black
Flowers 12.00

Cup & Saucer, Fired-On
Chartreuse 4.50

Cup & Saucer, Fired-On
Dark Green 4.50

Grease Jar, Cover, Black
Flowers 45.00

Mixing Bowl, Black Flowers,
9 In. 18.00

Pitcher, Black Flowers,
5 In. 30.00

Pitcher, Ribbed, Black
Flowers, 16 Oz. 35.00

Plate, Dinner, Fired-On
Chartreuse, 9 In. 4.50

Plate, Dinner, Fired-On
Dark Green, 9 In. 4.50

Plate, Dinner, Fired-On
Gray, 9 In. 4.50

Plate, Dinner, Fired-On
Dark Green, 9 In. 4.50

Plate, Dinner, Fired-On
Yellow, 9 In. 8.00

Plate, Dinner, Wide Red
Scroll, 9 In. 7.00

Plate, Fired-On Yellow,
7 In. 6.00

Plate, Luncheon, Black
Flowers, 8 1/2 In. 12.00

Plate, Sherbet, Black
Flowers, 6 In. 4.00

Salt & Pepper,
Black Flowers 25.00

Salt & Pepper,
Colored Rings 24.00

Salt & Pepper,
Fired-On Yellow 65.00

Saucer, Fired-On Yellow . . 3.00

Saucer, Green Ring 1.00

Sherbet, Black Flowers . . . 3.00

Sugar, Fired-On Yellow . . 5.00

Sugar & Creamer,
Black Flowers 18.00

Sugar & Creamer, Fired-On
Chartreuse . . . . . 8.00 to 12.00

Tumbler, Black
Flowers . . . . . . 15.00 to 18.00

OXFORD
See Chinex Classic

**Go to antique shows
and flea markets early;
there may be plenty of
glass left at the end of
the show, but the deal-
ers are tired and not as
eager to talk to the
customers.**

OYSTER & PEARL

Anchor Hocking Glass
Corporation, Lancaster,
Ohio, made only acces-
sory pieces in the Oyster
& Pearl pattern from 1938
to 1940. The first pieces
were Crystal or Pink.
Those with a white exte-
rior and fired-on pink or
green interior were made
later, as were Royal Ruby
pieces.

Crystal

Bowl, Fruit, 10 In. 20.00

Bowl, Handle, 5 1/2 In. . . . 5.00

Bowl, Heart Shape, Handle,
5 1/4 In. . . . . . . 8.00 to 10.00

Candleholder, 3 1/2 In.,
Pair . . . . 13.00 to 25.00

Sandwich
Server, 13 1/2 In. 20.00

Pink

Bowl, Deep,
Handles, 6 1/2 In. 20.00

Bowl, Handle,
5 1/2 In. 15.00

Bowl, Heart Shape, Handle,
5 1/4 In. . . . . . 12.00 to 19.00

Candleholder,
3 1/2 In. 18.00

Candleholder, 3 1/2 In.,
Pair 45.00

Relish, 2 Sections,
10 1/2 In. 18.00

Relish, 3 Sections,
11 1/2 In. 12.00

Royal Ruby

Bowl, Deep,
6 1/2 In. . . . . . 15.00 to 29.00

Bowl, Fruit,
10 1/2 In. . . . . 55.00 to 60.00

Bowl, Handle,
5 1/2 In. . . . . . 12.00 to 15.00

Bowl, Handle, Round,
5 In. 20.00

Candleholder, 3 1/2 In. . . 26.00
Candleholder, 3 1/2 In.,
 Pair . . . . 49.00 to 60.00

White
Bonbon, Fired-On Pink . . 12.00
Bowl, Heart Shape,
 Handle, Fired-On
 Pink, 5 1/4 In. 10.00

PANELED ASTER
See Madrid

PANELED CHERRY BLOSSOM
See Cherry Blossom

PANELED GRAPE

Crystal Paneled Grape with stained decorations was originally made by Jenkins Glass Company, Kokomo, Indiana, from 1903 to the 1930s. Westmoreland Glass Company, Grapeville, Pennsylvania, started making Paneled Grape in Milk Glass in the 1940s and continued until the factory closed in 1984. Some of Westmoreland's pieces have hand-painted swags, called Roses & Bows, or grapes. Westmoreland also made Paneled Grape in Crystal and other colors from the 1950s until 1984. Another company made a similar pattern, Panel Grape, in

various colors, but not Milk Glass, for distributor L. G. Wright. A reproduction canister was made by Summit Art Glass Company.

Milk Glass
Appetizer Set, Bowl,
 Plate, Ladle 57.00
Basket, Oval, Split
 Handle, 6 1/2 In. 25.00
Basket, Oval, Split Handle,
 Roses & Bows 50.00
Bottle, Oil, Stopper,
 2 Oz. 22.00
Bottle, Toilet, 5 Oz. 62.00
Bowl, 10 1/2 In. 125.00
Cake Stand, Skirted Edge,
 11 In. 95.00
Candlestick, 4 In., Pair . . 25.00
Candlestick, Roses & Bows,
 4 1/2 In., Pair 90.00
Candy Dish, Domed
 Cover, Footed, Roses
 & Bows 75.00
Cigarette Box, Cover, Roses
 & Bows, 4 x 6 In. 95.00
Compote, Cover 42.00
Compote, Cover,
 Roses & Bows, 7 In. . . 65.00
Creamer, 6 1/2 Oz. 16.00
Creamer, Individual 10.00
Cup & Saucer . . 22.00 to 23.00
Dish, Mayonnaise 30.00
Goblet, Water, 8 Oz. 18.00
Goblet, Wine, 2 Oz. 25.00
Honey, Cover, Low Foot,
 Roses & Bows, 5 In. . . . 65.00
Jardiniere, 4 In. 30.00

Never put your name on the mailbox. Do put the street number in reflecting numerals more than three inches high, in clear view. Make it easy for the police and fire departments to find your house.

Jardiniere, 5 In. 37.00
Jardiniere, 6 1/2 In. 45.00
Nappy 22.50
Nut Dish, Oval, Footed,
 6 1/2 In. 32.00
Pitcher, Footed, 1 Qt. 40.00
Planter, 5 x 9 In. 35.00
Plate, Luncheon,
 8 1/2 In. 24.00
Plate, Salad, 8 1/2 In. 24.00
Puff Box, 4 1/2 In. 32.00
Puff Box, Cover, Square,
 Roses & Bows, 4 In. . . . 65.00
Punch Cup . . . . . . 6.00 to 15.00
Punch Ladle 88.50
Salt & Pepper 20.00
Salt & Pepper, 4 1/2 In. . . 55.00
Sauceboat, Underplate . . . 60.00
Soap Dish 100.00
Sugar, No Lid 10.00
Sugar & Creamer 35.00
Vase, 9 1/2 In. 40.00
Vase, Hexagonal, Footed,
 Roses & Bows, 9 In. . . . 35.00
Vase, Ivy Ball, Footed . . . 50.00
Vase, Roses & Bows,
 6 1/2 In. 65.00
Vase, Roses & Bows,
 11 In. 40.00

PANSY & DORIC
See Doric & Pansy

PARROT
See Sylvan

PARTY LINE

Party Line was made by Paden City Glass Manufacturing Company, Paden City, West Virginia. It had many names, including Line 191, Tiered Semi

Optic, or Tiered Block. It is a durable pattern advertised in 1928 for home, restaurant, hotel, and soda fountain use. The dishes were made in Amber, Black, Blue, Cheri-Glo (pink), Crystal, Green, and Mulberry.

Cheri-Glo
Candlestick, 4 In., Pair . . 35.00
Tumbler, 5 1/2 In. 5.00

Green
Ice Bucket 45.00
Tumbler, Footed,
 6 7/8 In. 10.00

PATRICIAN

Federal Glass Company, Columbus, Ohio, made Patrician, sometimes called Hinge or Spoke, from 1933 to 1937. Full dinner sets were made in Golden Glo and Green, and smaller quantities in Crystal and Pink. Yellow pieces were produced later.

Crystal
Berry Bowl, Master,
 8 1/2 In. 42.00
Butter 90.00
Butter, Cover Only 30.00
Cookie Jar,
 Cover . . . . . . 79.00 to 150.00
Cookie Jar, Cover
 Only . . . . 40.00 to 44.00
Creamer . . . . . . 10.00 to 11.00
Cup . . . . 5.00 to 10.00
Cup & Saucer 17.00

Grill Plate, 10 1/2 In. 13.00
Plate, Dinner, 10 1/2 In. . . 13.00
Plate, Luncheon,
 9 In. 13.00
Salt & Pepper . . . 58.00 to 65.00
Saucer 5.00
Sherbet 13.00
Sugar & Creamer 18.00

Golden Glo
Berry Bowl,
 5 In. . . . . 9.00 to 14.50
Berry Bowl, Master,
 8 1/2 In. . . . . 38.00 to 53.00
Bowl, Cereal,
 6 In. . . . . 26.00 to 30.00
Bowl, Vegetable, Oval,
 10 In. . . . . 30.00 to 43.00
Butter, Cover . . 85.00 to 100.00
Butter, Cover
 Only . . . . 43.00 to 60.00
Cookie Jar,
 Cover . . . . . 85.00 to 110.00
Creamer . . . . 9.00 to 15.00
Cup . . . . 7.00 to 11.00
Cup & Saucer . . 14.00 to 22.00
Grill Plate,
 10 1/2 In. . . . . 12.50 to 15.00
Jam Dish,
 6 1/2 In. . . . . 25.00 to 45.00
Pitcher, Molded Handle, 75 Oz.,
 8 In. . . . . . . 110.00 to 125.00
Plate, Dinner,
 10 1/2 In. . . . . 5.00 to 15.00
Plate, Luncheon,
 9 In. . . . . 8.00 to 14.00
Plate, Salad,
 7 1/2 In. . . . . 15.00 to 18.00
Plate, Sherbet, 6 In. 10.00
Platter, Oval,
 11 1/2 In. . . . 24.00 to 40.00
Salt & Pepper . . . 55.00 to 65.00
Saltshaker . . . . . 25.00 to 29.00
Saucer . . . . 9.00 to 10.00
Sherbet . . . . . . 10.00 to 13.00
Soup, Cream . . . 16.00 to 22.00
Sugar . . . . 7.00 to 15.00
Sugar, Cover . . . 60.00 to 80.00
Tumbler, Footed, 8 Oz.,
 5 1/4 In. . . . . 50.00 to 65.00
Tumbler, Iced Tea, 14 Oz.,
 5 1/2 In. . . . . 48.00 to 49.00
Tumbler, Juice, 5 Oz.,
 4 In. 35.00

Tumbler, Water, 9 Oz.,
 4 1/2 In. . . . . . 20.00 to 32.50

Green
Berry Bowl, Master,
 8 1/2 In. 45.00
Bowl, Cereal, 6 In. 32.00
Bowl, Vegetable, Oval,
 10 In. . . . . 29.00 to 41.00
Butter,
 Cover . . . . 130.00 to 137.00
Butter, Cover Only 60.00
Creamer 12.00
Cup . . . . 10.00 to 13.00
Cup & Saucer . . 19.00 to 23.50
Jam Dish, 6 1/2 In. 45.00
Pitcher, Applied Handle,
 75 Oz., 8 1/4 In. 185.00
Pitcher, Molded Handle, 75 Oz.,
 8 In. . . . . . . 145.00 to 155.00
Plate, Luncheon,
 9 In. . . . . 12.50 to 16.00
Plate, Salad,
 7 1/2 In. . . . . 18.00 to 20.00
Plate, Sherbet,
 6 In. . . . . 8.00 to 12.00
Platter, Oval,
 11 1/2 In. 27.00
Salt & Pepper . . . 65.00 to 70.00
Saltshaker 40.00
Saucer . . . . 9.00 to 10.00
Sherbet . . . . 12.00 to 30.00
Sugar 10.00
Sugar & Creamer 24.00
Tumbler, Footed, 8 Oz.,
 5 1/2 In. 75.00
Tumbler, Footed, 12 1/2 Oz.,
 6 1/2 In. 115.00
Tumbler, Iced Tea, 14 Oz.,
 5 1/2 In. . . . . 50.00 to 65.00
Tumbler, Water, 9 Oz.,
 4 1/4 In. . . . . 30.00 to 32.00

Pink
Berry Bowl, Master,
 8 1/2 In. . . . . 35.00 to 39.00
Butter 90.00
Butter, Cover 235.00
Creamer 8.00
Cup 8.00
Cup & Saucer . . 22.00 to 28.50
Grill Plate,
 10 1/2 In. 11.00
Plate, Dinner,
 10 1/2 In. . . . . 45.00 to 65.00

Plate, Luncheon,
  9 In. 22.50
Salt & Pepper 115.00
Saucer . . . . 9.00 to 13.00
Sherbet 17.00
Sugar 12.00
Sugar, Cover 74.00
Tumbler, Iced Tea,
  14 Oz., 5 1/2 In. 46.00
Tumbler, Water, 9 Oz.,
  4 1/4 In. 25.00

PATRICK

Patrick pattern was made
by the Lancaster Glass
Company of Lancaster,
Ohio, about 1930. The
pattern was etched in
Rose or Topaz colored
glass.

Rose
Console, 11 In. 150.00
Plate, Luncheon, 8 In. . . . 55.00

Topaz
Cheese & Cracker Set . . 115.00
Cracker Plate, Indented,
  Handles 90.00
Dish, Mayonnaise, Footed,
  Spoon, 2 Piece 95.00

PEACH LUSTRE

Peach Lustre is both a pattern and a color name
used for Fire-King dinnerware made by Anchor
Hocking Glass Corpora-
tion from 1952 to 1963.
The pattern has a laurel
leaf design around the
edge of plates and bowls
and the side of cups. The

pieces are a lustrous
orange-yellow color. The
same pattern of laurel
leaves was made in 1953
in gray and is known as
Gray Laurel pattern.
Other related patterns are
listed in the Fire-King section in this book.

Bowl, Dessert,
  4 7/8 In. . . . . . . 2.00 to 4.00
Bowl, Vegetable,
  8 1/4 In. 10.00
Casserole, French, Cover . . 8.50
Casserole, French,
  No Cover 3.00
Creamer . . . . 3.00 to 4.00
Cup . . . . 1.00 to 3.00
Cup & Saucer . . . . 4.50 to 5.00
Mug 5.00
Plate, Dinner,
  9 1/8 In. . . . . . . 5.00 to 6.00
Saucer 1.00
Stand, For Bowl 7.00
Sugar, Cover 10.00
Sugar, No Cover 4.00
Sugar & Creamer 8.00
Vase, Horizontal Ribs,
  7 1/4 In. 12.00

PEACOCK & ROSE
See Peacock & Wild Rose

PEACOCK & WILD ROSE

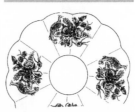

Line 300 was the name
used by Paden City Glass
Manufacturing Company,
Paden City, West Virginia,
for the pattern now called
Peacock & Wild Rose. It

was made in the 1930s of
Amber, Black, Cobalt
Blue, Crystal, Green, Light
Blue, Pink, and Red. A few
of the lists call this pattern
Peacock & Rose. A similar
pattern, Nora Bird, is
listed in its own section
in this book.

Amber
Cheese & Cracker Set . . 150.00
Black
Vase, 10 In. 325.00
Vase, 12 In. 295.00
Vase, Ivy, 5 1/4 In. 154.00
Crystal
Bowl, Footed, 9 In. 175.00
Console, 11 In. 65.00
Green
Bowl, Fruit, 8 1/2 In. . . . 300.00
Bowl, Oval, Footed,
  8 1/2 In. 285.00
Cake Plate, Footed,
  11 In. 95.00
Compote,
  6 1/4 In. . . . 165.00 to 175.00
Console, 14 In. 180.00
Dish, Mayonnaise,
  6 1/2 In. 59.00
Dish, Mayonnaise,
  Underplate, Ladle 250.00

❖

**Lock your doors. There
is a 12 percent chance
that your home will be
burglarized in the next
five years. In the next
fifteen years, the odds
are 33 percent; in thirty
years, 50 percent. And
that assumes there is no
increase in the rate of
burglaries nationwide.
Never leave the key
under the door mat.**

❖

Vase, Fan, 10 In. 375.00
Vase, Footed,
10 In. 250.00

Pink
Cake Plate 135.00
Cake Stand, Low
Foot 155.00
Compote, 6 1/4 In. 175.00
Sugar & Creamer 125.00
Vase, 10 In. 295.00
Vase, Fan, 8 1/4 In. 550.00

Red
Bowl, Footed,
9 1/2 In. 178.00

PEACOCK &
WILD ROSE
See also Crow's Foot

PEBBLE OPTIC
See Raindrops

PENNY LINE

Paden City Glass Manufac-
turing Company, Paden
City, West Virginia, made
Penny Line in Amber,
Cheri-glo, Crystal, Green,
Royal Blue, and Ruby. It
was No. 991 in the 1932
catalog.

Ruby
Mug & Saucer .. 13.00 to 24.00
Plate, Dinner,
12 In. .... 15.50 to 30.00
Plate, Luncheon,
8 In. 15.50
Sandwich Server, Center
Handle 30.00

Sherbet 8.00
Sugar & Creamer 16.00
Tumbler, Iced Tea,
12 Oz. 23.00

PETAL SWIRL
See Swirl

PETALWARE

Macbeth-Evans Glass
Company made Petalware
from 1930 to 1940. It was
first made in Crystal and
Pink. In 1932 the dinner-
ware was made in Monax,
and in 1933 in Cremax.
The pattern remained
popular, and in 1936 Co-
balt Blue and several other
variations were made.
Some pieces were hand-
painted with pastel bands
of ivory, green, and pink.
Some pieces were deco-
rated with gold or red
trim. Flower or fruit de-
signs in bright colors were
used on others. Bright
bands of fired-on blue,
green, red, and yellow
were used to decorate
some wares. Collectors
have given some of these
patterns their own names,
including Banded Petal-
ware, Daisy Petals, Dia-
mond Point, Petal, Shell,
and Vivid Bands.

Cobalt Blue
Mustard,
Underplate .... 9.00 to 13.00
Sherbet 30.00

Cremax
Berry Bowl, 9 In. 19.00
Bowl, Gold Trim, 8 In. .. 18.00
Cup .... 5.00 to 8.00
Cup, Red Trim 10.00
Cup & Saucer ... 5.00 to 14.00
Cup & Saucer, Gold Trim,
Flower 14.00
Cup & Saucer,
Pastel Bands 13.00
Plate, Dinner,
9 In. .... 9.00 to 16.00
Plate, Dinner, Gold Trim,
9 In. .... 9.00 to 11.00
Plate, Salad, 8 In. .. 8.00 to 9.00
Plate, Salad, Gold Trim,
8 In. 7.00
Plate, Salad, Pastel Bands,
8 In. .... 10.00 to 15.00
Plate, Salad, Red Trim,
8 In. 10.00
Plate, Sherbet,
6 In. .... 2.25 to 5.00
Plate, Sherbet,
Gold Trim, 6 In. 2.00
Platter, Oval, 13 In. 16.00
Salver, 11 In. 17.00
Salver, Gold Trim,
Flower, 11 In. 5.00
Saucer 5.00
Saucer, Pastel Bands 3.00
Sherbet, Gold Trim 12.00
Soup, Cream,
4 1/2 In. ..... 10.00 to 12.00
Sugar .... 8.00 to 10.00
Sugar, Gold Trim 11.00
Sugar & Creamer 22.00

Crystal
Creamer, Floral Rim 12.00
Cup, Floral Rim 10.00
Cup & Saucer 5.00
Cup & Saucer, Flower ... 14.00
Plate, 11 In. 4.50
Plate, Dinner, Pastel
Bands, 9 In. 16.00
Plate, Red Flower,
7 3/4 In. 11.00
Plate, Salad, 8 In. 2.50

Plate, Salad, Pastel
  Bands, 8 In. 15.00
Saucer 2.00
Saucer, Floral Rim 3.00
Saucer, Pastel Bands 6.00
Sugar, Floral Rim 10.00

Monax
Berry Bowl, Master,
  9 In. 18.00
Bowl, Cereal, 5 3/4 In. . . . 8.00
Bowl, Cereal, Red Trim,
  Floral, 5 3/4 In. 42.00
Creamer . . . . . . 10.00 to 12.00
Creamer, Gold
  Trim . . . . 6.00 to 7.00
Creamer, Red Flower 10.00
Creamer, Tall,
  Gold Trim 3.50
Cup 5.00
Cup, Floral Design 10.00
Cup, Red Trim Floral . . . 25.00
Cup & Saucer . . 10.00 to 13.00
Cup & Saucer,
  Floral Design 14.00
Cup & Saucer,
  Gold Trim 7.00
Cup & Saucer, Red Trim,
  Floral 13.00
Plate, Dinner,
  9 In. . . . . 10.00 to 16.00
Plate, Pastel Bands, 6 In. . . 7.00
Plate, Pastel Bands,
  8 In. 12.00
Plate, Salad, 8 In. 9.00
Plate, Salad, Gold Trim,
  8 In. . . . . 6.00 to 7.00
Plate, Salad, Red Floral,
  8 In. 10.00
Plate, Sherbet,
  6 In. . . . . 2.50 to 4.00
Plate, Sherbet, Red Flower,
  8 In. 10.00
Plate, Sherbet, Red Trim,
  Floral, 6 In. 22.00
Platter, Oval, 13 In. 21.00
Salver, 11 In. . . . 15.00 to 18.00
Salver, Pastel Bands,
  12 In. 25.00
Saucer . . . . 2.00 to 4.00
Sherbet, Footed,
  4 1/2 In. . . . . . . 8.00 to 20.00
Sherbet, Pastel Bands . . . 20.00
Soup, Cream 14.00

Soup, Cream,
  Underplate 12.00
Sugar . . . . 4.50 to 7.00
Sugar, Footed 10.00
Sugar,
  Gold Trim . . . . 10.00 to 12.00
Sugar, Red Floral 10.00
Sugar & Creamer 12.00

Monax Florette
Creamer 12.00
Cup & Saucer 15.00
Plate, Salad,
  8 In. . . . . 10.00 to. 12.00
Salver, 11 In. . . . 19.00 to 30.00
Saucer 6.00

Pink
Berry Bowl, Master,
  9 In. . . . . 25.00 to 35.00
Bowl, 10 7/8 In. 27.00
Bowl, Cereal,
  5 3/4 In. . . . . . 10.00 to 18.00
Bowl, Footed, 9 In. 25.00
Bowl, Gondola,
  17 1/2 In. 35.00
Bowl, Oval, Footed,
  Holiday, 10 1/2 In. 45.00
Bowl, Pheasant, 8 In. 55.00
Bowl, Wedding, 6 1/2 In.   22.00
Bowl, Wedding, 8 In. . . . 30.00
Compote, 6 In. 20.00
Creamer 15.00
Cup 6.00
Cup & Saucer . . . 8.50 to 15.00
Cup & Saucer,
  Pastel Bands 18.00
Honey Pot, Cover 75.00
Lazy Susan 245.00
Plate, Dinner,
  9 In. . . . . 13.00 to 20.00
Plate, Salad,
  8 In. . . . . 6.00 to 13.00
Plate, Sherbet,
  6 In. . . . . 6.00 to 8.00
Platter, Oval,
  13 In. . . . . 17.00 to 27.00
Powder Jar, Cover,
  4 3/4 In. 45.00
Punch Bowl Base 20.00
Punch Cup . . . . . 4.50 to 6.50
Relish, 3 Sections 40.00
Relish, Vineyard, 4 Sections,
  Square, 12 In. 40.00

Salver, 11 In. . . . 15.00 to 20.00
Saucer . . . . 1.50 to 5.00
Sherbet 16.00
Snack Set, 2 Piece 27.00
Soup, Cream,
  4 In. . . . . 13.00 to 21.00
Sugar . . . . 9.00 to 15.00
Sugar, Baltimore Pear . . . 15.00
Sugar, Footed 15.00
Sugar & Creamer 42.50
Tray, 5 Sections, Handle,
  15 3/4 In. 75.00
Tray, 6 Sections,
  16 1/2 In. 40.00
Tray, Venetian, 6 Sections,
  16 1/2 In. 20.00
Vase, 7 In. 35.00

Red
Cup & Saucer, Banded . . 37.00

PETTICOAT
See Ripple

PHILBE
See Fire-King

PIE CRUST
See Cremax

PILLAR FLUTE

Pillar Flute was made by
Imperial Glass Company,
Bellaire, Ohio, in Amber,
Blue, Crystal, Green, and a
pink called Rose Marie. It
was made about 1930.

Blue
Bowl, Cereal 25.00
Candleholder, 2-Light . . . 25.00
Creamer 17.00

VINTAGE COLOR
Sets the Mood

One of the many ways to enjoy collectibles is to use them. Assemble a set of your favorite dishes, or mix and match several sets, and use them at dinner parties. Arrange the pieces by color and you can't go wrong. Try using shades of green or an amber-to-yellow color combination. For a 1940s look, try Ruby, Royal Blue, or Forest Green. Pastel plastic dishes create the look of the 1950s, and Avocado Green and Harvest Gold bring back the 1960s.

GREEN

was one of the most popular colors for glass and pottery dinnerware. Glassware of the Depression era was made in various shades of light or medium green. Darker green was made later.

Block Optic is a geometric pattern inspired by the Art Deco style. This 5½-ounce sherbet sells for $6 to $12.

Sandwich-style patterns imitated pressed glass styles of the previous century. Indiana Glass Company made this 8¾-inch luncheon plate ($15).

Many Depression-era glass patterns have embossed floral motifs. The Princess cookie jar (right) is worth $55 to $75. The 12-inch Rosemary platter (below) sells for $22.

Solid-color dinnerware was common during the Depression. W. S. George Company made this medium green 9-inch Basketweave dinner plate.

Frankoma Pottery made this Lazy Bones sugar and creamer in Prairie Green in the 1950s. Value, $35.

Later, in the 1960s and 1970s, Avocado green became a popular color. It was used for kitchen appliances, carpeting, wall coverings, and matching glass, pottery, and Melmac dishes. These Mallo-Ware serving pieces were made by Mallory Plastics. Mallo-Ware items sell for $2 to $10.

PINK

dishes were almost as popular as green in the Depression era.

This 5½-inch Sierra cereal bowl ($16 to $23), Miss America relish with four sections ($25), and Sharon cup and saucer ($20 to $25) were made in the mid-1930s.

The Moderntone pattern was made in opaque white Platonite in the 1940s and early 1950s. Many items, like this cup and saucer, were coated with fired-on colors. Value, $5 to $6.

Harker Pottery Company used stencils to make designs with solid-color glazes on its Cameo Ware patterns. This Dainty Flower square salad plate was made in the 1940s. It's worth $15 to $25.

Collectors of 1950s dishes like to "think pink." International Molded Products made this Brookpark Modern Design–pattern cup ($2).

YELLOW AND AMBER

are related colors in glassware. Some yellow glass has a rich tint to it, like amber. Some amber glass is very light. Collectors usually use the color name given by the company.

The No. 612 pattern was made in yellow in the early 1930s. This 9-ounce footed tumbler is worth $30 to $36.

Later, the No. 620 creamer (left) ($9) and Normandie 9¼-inch luncheon plate (above) ($40 to $55) were made in amber.

The Ovide glass pattern was made in Platonite in the 1950s. This cup and saucer are coated with fired-on yellow. The set is worth $4.50.

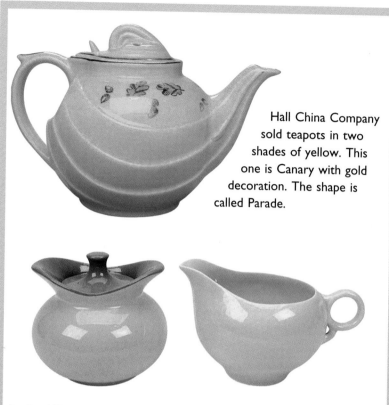

Hall China Company sold teapots in two shades of yellow. This one is Canary with gold decoration. The shape is called Parade.

In the 1950s, Universal Potteries, Inc., used the name Jonquil Yellow to describe the color of this Ballerina-pattern sugar and creamer. The cover is Dove Gray. Value for the set, $20.

Color names can be confusing. International Molded Products described this Brookpark Modern Design–pattern Melmac cream soup as Chartreuse, even though it is almost yellow.

WHITE OR IVORY

glass and pottery dinnerwares were usually decorated
with decals, stripes, or bands around the edges.

MacBeth-Evans Glass Company called the color of this Petalware
10½-inch dinner plate Cremax (left). Petalware was also made in
Monax, which is closer to white. The company also made Chinex
Classic, a more opaque ivory. This Chinex Classic dinner plate (right)
has a castle decal and a blue border. The plates are worth $10 to
$20 each.

Harker Pottery Company
used various decorations
on its Virginia shape. This
9¾-inch dinner plate has
the Deco Dahlia decal.

Hazel Atlas Glass Company made several patterns in Platonite. This Ripple cup and saucer (above) have a fired-on pink coating. The set is worth $5. The Ovide creamer (below) has red bands and sells for $9. These pieces were made in the 1950s.

Several glass patterns were available with iridescent finishes. You can mix and match pieces from different patterns to set your table.

This Peach Lustre creamer (top) ($3), Floragold covered sugar (bottom) ($16 to $23), and Iris 9-inch vase (right) ($20 to $35) were made in the 1930s. Don't put iridescent items in the dishwasher—the finish will come off.

CRYSTAL

Colored glassware is very popular among collectors, but almost every pattern had clear, colorless crystal pieces, too. Some patterns were made only in crystal.

The Moonstone pattern is recognizable by its opalescent hobnails. This 6-inch covered candy dish was made in the early 1940s and is worth $26.

Cambridge Glass Company made the Caprice pattern from about 1936 until the factory closed. Shown here: a 5-inch two-handle jelly dish with underplate, $40.

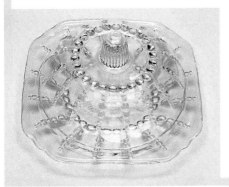

This Columbia-pattern covered butter was made mostly in crystal but is also found with a ruby-flashed cover. It sells for $19 to $25.

dishes, ranging from pale baby blue to deep turquoise,

were more common after the 1930s.

Jeannette Glass Company made the Swirl pattern in Ultramarine
from 1937 to 1938. The two-light candlestick sells for $22 to $30.

This turquoise cup
and saucer are from
the Metropolitan
dinnerware pattern
by Franciscan
Ceramics, Inc.

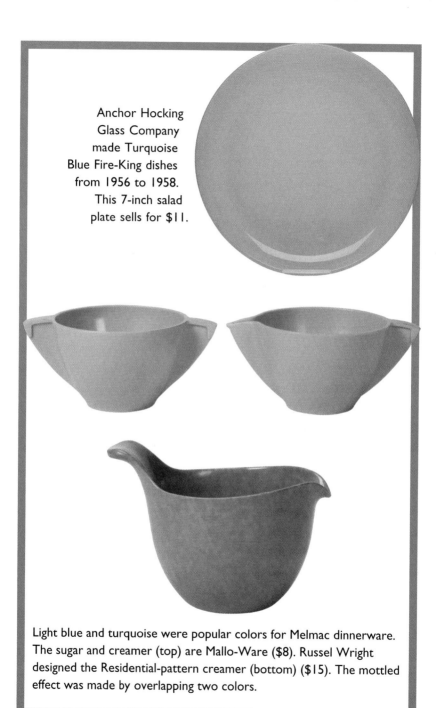

Anchor Hocking Glass Company made Turquoise Blue Fire-King dishes from 1956 to 1958. This 7-inch salad plate sells for $11.

Light blue and turquoise were popular colors for Melmac dinnerware. The sugar and creamer (top) are Mallo-Ware ($8). Russel Wright designed the Residential-pattern creamer (bottom) ($15). The mottled effect was made by overlapping two colors.

GEM TONES

are popular decorator colors. Fashion-minded
collectors can achieve a contemporary look by
mixing and matching some of the deeper
hues of vintage glassware.

Red glass, like
this Rock Crystal
saucer, can be
very hard to
find. This item
is worth $22.

Cobalt Blue is the most popular
color in the Moondrops pattern.
This 9-ounce tumbler sells for
about $20.

Hazel Atlas Glass Company made the Moderntone glass pattern in two deep colors, Cobalt Blue (top) and Amethyst (middle). The plate is worth $18 and the sugar is worth $10. The company also produced the Newport luncheon plate (bottom), worth $30.

Anchor Hocking Glass Company made this Sandwich-pattern glass bowl and saucer in Forest Green from 1956 to the 1960s. The 4⁵⁄₁₆-inch bowl was packed in Crystal Wedding oatmeal boxes as a giveaway. The pieces are worth $4 and $11, respectively.

Cup & Saucer 25.00
Relish, Oval, 8 In. 22.00
Tumbler, Flat 32.00
Vase, 6 In. 25.00

Green

Pitcher, 60 Oz. 45.00
Plate, Salad,
   8 In. . . . . 10.00 to 12.00
Tumbler, Whiskey 15.00

PINEAPPLE & FLORAL
See No. 618

PINWHEEL
See Sierra

PLANTATION

Plantation was made by
A. H. Heisey & Company,
Newark, Ohio, from 1948
to 1957. The stemware
has a faceted pineapple
stem, and other pieces
have embossed pineapple
borders. The pattern was
made in Crystal, some
with the Plantation Ivy
etching.

Butter, 1/4 Lb. 165.00
Creamer 35.00
Goblet, Claret,
   4 1/2 Oz. 70.00
Goblet, Water, 10 Oz. . . . 50.00
Oyster Cocktail, 4 Oz. . . . 36.00
Plate, Salad, 8 In. 32.00

POINSETTIA
See Floral

POPPY NO. 1
See Florentine No. 1

POPPY NO. 2
See Florentine No. 2

PORTIA

Portia was made by Cam-
bridge Glass Company
from 1932 until the early
1950s. It was made in
Amber, Crystal, Green,
Heatherbloom, and Yellow.

Crystal

Candlestick, 2-Light,
   Pair 75.00
Dish, Mayonnaise, 2 Sections,
   Underplate, 6 3/4 In. . . . 24.00
Goblet, Cocktail,
   3 Oz. 25.00
Sherry Set, Decanter, Goblets,
   4 Piece 206.00

PRETTY POLLY PARTY
DISHES
See Doric & Pansy

PRETZEL

Pretzel, also called No.
622 or Ribbon Candy, was
made by Indiana Glass

Company, Dunkirk, Indi-
ana, in the 1930s. Avocado,
Crystal, and Teal pieces
were made. Some repro-
ductions appeared in the
1970s in Amber and Blue.

Avocado

Pitcher, 39 Oz. 45.00

Crystal

Berry Bowl, Fruit Center,
   9 3/8 In. 20.00
Bowl, Stippled,
   7 1/2 In. 12.00
Celery Dish,
   10 1/4 In. 3.00
Creamer 6.00
Cup 5.00
Cup & Saucer . . . . 6.00 to 8.00
Dish, Olive, Leaf Shape,
   7 In. 5.00
Pickle, Handles,
   8 1/2 In. 5.50
Pitcher, 39 Oz. 450.00
Plate, 3 Sections, Square,
   7 1/4 In. . . . . . . 9.00 to 10.00
Plate, 8 3/8 In. 6.00
Plate, Bread & Butter,
   6 In. 3.00
Plate, Bread & Butter,
   Fruit Center, 6 In. 3.00
Plate, Dinner,
   9 3/8 In. 10.00
Plate, Dinner, Flower
   Center, 9 3/8 In. 13.00
Plate, Dinner, Fruit Center,
   9 3/8 In. . . . . 12.00 to 15.00
Plate, Fruit Center,
   6 In. 4.00
Plate, Salad,
   8 3/8 In. . . . . . . 6.00 to 8.00
Plate, Square, 2 Sections,
   7 1/4 In. 9.00
Plate, Tab Handle,
   6 In. . . . . 3.00 to 4.00
Relish, 3 Sections,
   7 In. 7.00
Snack Plate, Square,
   7 In. 8.00
Snack Set 15.00
Soup, Dish,
   7 1/2 In. . . . . 10.00 to 13.00
Sugar & Creamer . 9.00 to 10.00

PRIMO

Green and Mandarin Yellow are the two colors of Primo advertised in the 1932 U.S. Glass Company catalog.

Green
Cup 13.00
Grill Plate, 10 In. 12.00
Hostess Tray, Handles,
    10 1/2 In. 45.00
Plate, 5 3/4 In. 12.00
Plate, Salad, 7 1/2 In. 14.00
Saucer . . . . 3.00 to 4.00
Tumbler, Footed, 9 Oz.,
    5 3/4 In. . . . . . 19.00 to 22.00

Mandarin Yellow
Bowl, 4 1/2 In. 18.00
Creamer 16.00
Cup 12.00
Grill Plate, 10 In. 16.00
Plate, Salad, 7 1/2 In. 10.00
Tumbler, Footed, 9 Oz.,
    5 3/4 In. . . . . . 18.00 to 25.00

PRIMROSE

Primrose was a pattern made by Anchor Hocking Glass Corporation, Lancaster, Ohio, from 1960 to 1962. The white opaque glass was decorated with a red primrose. Other related patterns are listed in the Fire-King section in this book.

Bowl, Dessert,
    4 5/8 In. . . . . 3.00 to 4.00
Casserole, 1 Qt. 5.00
Creamer . . . . 3.00 to 5.00
Cup 1.50
Cup, Snack, 5 Oz. 3.50
Cup & Saucer . . . . 3.00 to 5.00
Custard Cup, 6 Oz. 4.00
Plate, Dinner, 9 1/8 In. . . . 3.50
Plate, Salad,
    7 3/8 In. . . . . . . 1.00 to 5.00
Platter, Oval, 12 In. 15.00
Saucer 1.00
Snack Set 7.00
Snack Tray, Rectangular,
    11 In. 5.00
Sugar . . . . 4.00 to 5.00
Sugar, No Cover 2.50
Sugar & Creamer, Cover . 15.00

PRIMUS
See Madrid

PRINCESS

Hocking Glass Company, Lancaster, Ohio, made the popular Princess pattern from 1931 to 1935. The first sets were made in Green or two shades of yellow, Apricot or Topaz, so if you are assembling a set, be careful of the color variations. Pink was added last. Blue pieces are found in the West. Some pieces have a frosted finish, some are decorated with hand-painted flowers. Green is sometimes trimmed with gold; other colors are sometimes trimmed with platinum. This pattern is also called Drape & Tassel, Lincoln Drape, or Tassel. Reproductions have been made.

Apricot
Cup . . . . 6.00 to 7.00
Grill Plate, 9 1/2 In. 7.00
Tumbler, Footed, 10 Oz.,
    5 1/4 In. . . . . 18.00 to 28.00

Green
Ashtray,
    4 1/2 In. . . . 75.00 to 100.00
Berry Bowl,
    4 1/2 In. . . . . 30.00 to 42.00
Bowl, Cereal,
    5 In. . . . . . . 35.00 to 50.00
Bowl, Hat Shape,
    9 1/2 In. . . . . 48.00 to 60.00
Bowl, Salad, Octagonal,
    9 In. . . . . 45.00 to 52.00
Bowl, Vegetable, Oval,
    10 In. . . . . . . 25.00 to 44.00
Butter, Cover,
    7 1/2 In. . . 105.00 to 125.00
Butter,
    No Cover . . . . 38.00 to 75.00
Cake Stand, Footed,
    10 In. . . . . . . 28.00 to 40.00
Candy Dish,
    Cover . . . . . . 59.00 to 85.00
Coaster . . . . 42.00 to 65.00
Cookie Jar,
    Cover . . . . . . 56.00 to 75.00
Cookie Jar, No Cover . . . 20.00
Cup . . . . 8.00 to 15.00
Cup & Saucer . . 18.00 to 27.00
Grill Plate,
    10 1/2 In. 14.00
Pitcher, 37 Oz.,
    6 In. 55.00
Pitcher, 60 Oz.,
    8 In. . . . . 55.00 to 75.00

Plate, Bread & Butter,
6 In. . . . . 10.00 to 11.00
Plate, Dinner,
9 1/2 In. . . . . . 18.00 to 32.00
Plate, Salad,
8 1/4 In. . . . . . 14.00 to 19.00
Plate, Sherbet,
5 1/2 In. . . . . . . 9.00 to 15.00
Platter, 12 In. . . . 27.00 to 40.00
Relish, Divided,
7 1/2 In. . . . . . 27.00 to 35.00
Salt & Pepper 64.00
Sandwich Server,
Handle, 10 1/4 In. 30.00
Saucer . . . . 8.00 to 10.00
Shaker, Spice, Pair 44.00
Sherbet, Footed 22.00
Sugar, Cover . . . 27.50 to 39.00
Sugar, No Cover 10.00
Sugar & Creamer 32.00
Tumbler, Footed, 10 Oz.,
5 1/4 In. . . . . . 32.00 to 35.00
Tumbler, Iced Tea, 13 Oz.,
5 1/4 In. . . . . . 30.00 to 50.00
Tumbler, Water, 9 Oz.,
4 In. . . . . 25.00 to 35.00
Vase, 8 In. . . . . . 35.00 to 60.00

Pink
Berry Bowl,
4 1/2 In. . . . . . 26.00 to 40.00
Bowl, Cereal,
5 In. . . . . 35.00 to 45.00
Bowl, Hat Shape,
9 In. . . . . 55.00 to 75.00
Bowl, Octagonal,
9 1/4 In. 70.00
Bowl, Vegetable, Oval,
10 In. 60.00
Butter, Cover 125.00
Cake Stand, Footed,
10 In. . . . . 32.00 to 50.00
Candy Dish,
Cover . . . . 75.00 to 80.00
Cup . . . . 9.00 to 15.00
Cup & Saucer . . 18.00 to 28.00
Grill Plate,
10 1/2 In. . . . . 15.00 to 16.00
Grill Plate, Handles,
9 1/2 In. 22.00
Pitcher, Juice, 37 Oz.,
6 In. . . . . 52.00 to 75.00
Pitcher, Water, 60 Oz.,
8 In. . . . . 58.00 to 85.00

Plate, Bread & Butter,
6 In. 13.00
Plate, Dinner,
9 1/2 In. . . . . . 24.00 to 32.00
Plate, Salad,
8 In. . . . . 15.00 to 28.00
Plate, Sherbet,
5 1/2 In. . . . . . 10.00 to 14.00
Platter, Oval,
12 In. . . . . 30.00 to 33.00
Relish, Divided,
7 1/2 In. 44.00
Salt & Pepper 62.00
Sandwich Server,
10 1/4 In. . . . . 31.00 to 33.00
Saucer 10.00
Sherbet . . . . 21.00 to 30.00
Sugar, Cover . . . 45.00 to 60.00
Sugar & Creamer 23.00
Tumbler, Footed, 12 1/2 Oz.,
6 1/2 In. . . . . 88.00 to 105.00
Tumbler, Iced Tea, 13 Oz.,
5 1/4 In. . . . . . 30.00 to 31.00
Tumbler, Juice, 5 Oz.,
3 In. 33.00
Tumbler, Water, 9 Oz.,
4 In. . . . . 25.00 to 33.00
Tumbler, Water, Footed, 10 Oz.,
5 1/2 In. . . . . . 28.00 to 34.00
Vase, 8 In. 62.00

Topaz
Bowl, Cereal, 5 In. 50.00
Bowl, Salad, Octagonal,
9 In. 165.00
Creamer 20.00
Creamer, Oval 14.00
Cup . . . . 7.00 to 10.00
Cup & Saucer . . 10.00 to 18.00
Grill Plate,
10 1/2 In. . . . . . 8.00 to 10.00
Plate, Dinner,
9 1/2 In. . . . . . 13.00 to 20.00
Plate, Salad,
8 In. . . . . 10.00 to 22.00
Plate, Sherbet,
5 1/2 In. . . . . . . 4.00 to 7.50
Relish, Plain,
7 1/2 In. 495.00
Salt & Pepper . . . 85.00 to 92.00
Saucer 3.00
Sugar 8.50
Sugar & Creamer,
Cover . . . . 40.00 to 55.00

Tumbler, Iced Tea, 13 Oz.,
5 1/4 In. . . . . . 26.00 to 38.00
Tumbler, Juice, 5 Oz.,
3 In. 32.00
Tumbler, Water, Footed,
9 Oz., 4 In. . . . 23.00 to 25.00
Tumbler, Water, Footed, 10 Oz.,
5 1/4 In. . . . . . 20.00 to 30.00

PRINCESS FEATHER

Westmoreland Glass
Company made Princess
Feather pattern from 1939
through 1948. It was originally made in Aqua, Crys-
tal, Green, and Pink. In the
1960s a reproduction ap-
peared in an amber shade
called Golden Sunset. The
pattern is sometimes
called Early American,
Flower, Oatmeal Lace, or
Scroll & Star. Reproduc-
tions have been made.

Crystal
Bowl, Dessert, 6 3/4 In. . . 10.00
Sherbet 8.00

Green
Pitcher, Large 35.00
Pitcher, Small 45.00

PRISMATIC LINE
See Queen Mary

PROVINCIAL
See Bubble

PYRAMID
See No. 610

PYREX

Pyrex Ovenware was introduced in 1915 by the Corning Glass Works of Corning, New York. The early heat-resistant cookware was made of clear glass. Pyrex Flameware was introduced in 1936 for stove-top cooking. In 1947, Corning started making opaque white Pyrex cookware and dinnerware. The outside of the dishes had printed decorations or were covered with fired-on colors, such as Dove Gray, Flamingo (red orange), Lime (chartreuse), Regency Green, and Turquoise Blue.

Flamingo Band
Bowl, Vegetable 12.00
Creamer 4.00
Cup & Saucer 4.00
Plate, Dinner,
    10 In. 9.00
Plate, Luncheon,
    8 In. 6.00

Lime Band
Plate, Dinner, 10 In. 10.00
Plate, Luncheon,
    8 In. 8.00

QUEEN MARY

Queen Mary, sometimes called Prismatic Line or Vertical Ribbed, was made by Anchor Hocking Glass Corporation from 1936 to 1943. It was first made in Pink, later in Crystal. Ashtrays were made in Forest Green and Royal Ruby in the 1950s.

Crystal
Ashtray, Oval,
    2 x 3 3/4 In. 4.00
Berry Bowl, 4 1/2 In. 4.00
Berry Bowl, 8 3/4 In. 16.00
Bowl, 7 In. 9.00
Bowl, Cereal,
    6 In. . . . . 7.00 to 9.00
Butter, Cover . . . 25.00 to 45.00
Candlestick, 2-Light, 4 1/2 In.,
    Pair . . . . 11.00 to 29.00
Candy Dish,
    Cover . . . . . . 20.00 to 25.00
Coaster, Round,
    3 1/2 In. . . . . . . 3.50 to 6.00
Creamer, Oval,
    5 1/2 In. . . . . . . 5.50 to 10.00
Cup 5.00
Cup, Large . . . . 3.00 to 6.50
Cup & Saucer 15.00
Cup & Saucer, Large 9.00
Plate, 6 In. . . . . . . 4.00 to 8.00
Plate, 6 5/8 In. . . . . 4.00 to 6.00
Plate, Dinner,
    9 3/4 In. . . . . . 18.00 to 25.00
Plate, Salad,
    8 3/4 In. 10.00
Plate, Sandwich,
    12 In. . . . . 10.00 to 18.00

Punch Set, Metal Rim On
    Bowl, 7 Pieces 200.00
Relish, 3 Sections,
    12 In. 12.00
Relish, 4 Sections,
    14 In. 20.00
Salt & Pepper . . . 19.00 to 30.00
Saltshaker 8.00
Saucer 4.50
Sherbet . . . . 6.00 to 15.00
Sugar, Oval . . . . . 5.00 to 10.00
Sugar & Creamer 12.00
Tumbler, Footed, 10 Oz.,
    5 In. . . . . 30.00 to 70.00

Forest Green
Ashtray, 3 1/2 In. . . 4.50 to 9.50

Pink
Berry Bowl,
    4 1/2 In. . . . . . . 5.00 to 11.00
Berry Bowl, 5 In. 9.00
Berry Bowl,
    8 3/4 In. 40.00
Bowl, Cereal,
    6 In. . . . . 23.00 to 32.00
Bowl, Handle, 4 In. 8.00
Bowl, Handles,
    5 1/2 In. . . . . . 10.00 to 18.00
Bowl, Rimmed, 6 In. 25.00
Bowl, Rimmed,
    7 1/2 In. 40.00
Butter, Cover 155.00
Candy Dish,
    Cover . . . . . 60.00 to 110.00
Creamer, Oval . . . 7.50 to 18.00
Cup, Large 12.00
Cup, Small . . . . . . 7.00 to 11.00
Cup & Saucer . . 12.00 to 18.00
Plate, Bread & Butter,
    6 1/2 In. . . . . . . 4.00 to 10.00
Plate, Dinner,
    9 1/2 In. . . . . . 57.00 to 65.00
Plate, Sandwich,
    12 In. . . . . 27.00 to 35.00
Plate, Sherbet, 6 In. 7.00
Punch Cup 7.00
Relish, 4 Sections,
    14 In. 45.00
Saucer 6.00
Sherbet, 6 In. 15.00
Sugar 8.00
Sugar &
    Creamer . . . . . 25.00 to 30.00

Tumbler, Footed, 10 Oz.,
5 In. . . . . 70.00 to 80.00
Tumbler, Juice, 5 Oz.,
3 1/2 In. . . . . 12.00 to 20.00

Royal Ruby
Ashtray, Round,
3 1/2 In. 4.50

RADIANCE

New Martinsville Glass
Company, New Mar-
tinsville, West Virginia,
made Radiance pattern,
Line No. 42, from 1936
to 1939. It was made in
Amber, Crystal, Emerald
Green, Ice Blue, Pink, and
Red. A few rare pieces
were made in Cobalt
Blue. A pattern by the
same name was made by
Cambridge.

Amber
Candlestick, 2-Light 39.00
Cheese Tray, 10 In. 35.00
Cup & Saucer 19.50
Goblet, Cordial, 1 Oz. . . . 27.00
Relish, 3 Sections, 8 In. . . 15.00
Tumbler, 9 Oz. 23.00

Cobalt Blue
Bonbon, Ruffled Edge, Metal
Footed, 6 In. 150.00
Celery Dish, 10 In. 150.00
Cup 25.00
Goblet, Cordial,
1 Oz. . . . . 45.00 to 50.00
Punch Cup 15.00
Vase, Crimped, 12 In. . . 275.00

Crystal
Butter, Chrome
Cover . . . . . . 20.00 to 38.00
Cake Salver 55.00
Candy Dish, 3 Sections,
Cover 40.00

Dish, Mayonnaise, Underplate,
3 Piece 32.00
Goblet, Cordial,
1 Oz. . . . . 13.00 to 25.00
Pitcher, 64 Oz. 125.00
Tumbler, 9 Oz. 16.00

Emerald Green
Vase, Flared, 10 In. 95.00

Ice Blue
Bowl, Flared, 12 In.. . . . . 75.00
Candlestick, 2-Light,
Pair . . . . 190.00 to 195.00
Cheese & Cracker Set,
11 In. 195.00
Punch Cup . . . . 12.00 to 15.00
Salt & Pepper 100.00

Pink
Salt & Pepper 195.00

Red
Butter 650.00
Candy Dish,
Cover . . . . . 75.00 to 145.00
Creamer 3.00
Cup & Saucer 24.00
Decanter, Silver
Overlay 250.00
Goblet, Cordial,
1 Oz. . . . . 30.00 to 65.00
Pitcher, 64 Oz. 1200.00
Relish, 3 Sections 45.00
Saucer 25.00
Sugar 30.00
Tumbler, 9 Oz. 42.00

RAINDROPS

Watch out for confusion
between Raindrops and
another pattern called
Pear Optic or Thumb-
print. The rounded, finger-
nail-shaped impressions of
the Raindrops pattern are
on the inside of the pieces;
the other pattern has

hexagonal depressions on
the outside. Federal Glass
Company made Crystal
and Green Raindrops lun-
cheon sets from 1929 to
1933.

Green
Berry Bowl, Round,
7 1/2 In. 35.00
Cup 6.00
Cup & Saucer . . . 7.50 to 13.00
Plate, Luncheon, 8 In. . . . 7.00
Plate, Sherbet, 6 In. 7.00
Saucer 3.00
Sugar, Cover 40.00
Tumbler, Whiskey,
1 Oz., 1 7/8 In. . . 7.00 to 9.00

RASPBERRY BAND
See Laurel

RESTAURANT WARE
See Fire-King

REX
See No. 610

RIBBED
See Manhattan

RIBBON

Black, Crystal, Green, and
Pink pieces were made in
Ribbon pattern in the
1930s. The pattern was
made by the Hazel Atlas
Glass Company.

Crystal
Salt & Pepper 25.00

Green
Berry Bowl, 8 In. 39.00

Candy Dish,
Cover . . . . . . 49.00 to 75.00
Creamer 15.00
Cup & Saucer 8.00
Plate, Luncheon,
8 In. . . . . 6.00 to 10.00
Plate, Sherbet,
6 1/4 In. . . . . . . 4.00 to 6.00
Salt & Pepper 31.00
Saucer 4.00
Sugar 15.00
Sugar, Footed 15.00
Sugar &
Creamer . . . . . 30.00 to 35.00
Tumbler, Footed,
10 Oz., 6 In. 33.00

RIBBON CANDY
See Pretzel

RIDGELEIGH

A. H. Heisey & Company, Newark, Ohio, made Ridgeleigh from 1935 to 1944. The pattern has narrow, prismlike vertical ribs and is similar to Anchor Hocking's Queen Mary and Fenton's Sheffield patterns. Many of the Heisey pieces are marked with the Diamond H logo. Items were made mostly in Crystal, although some pieces are available in Sahara (yellow) and Zircon (light turquoise).

Crystal
Bowl, 5 In. 15.00

Candlestick, 2 In. 16.00
Creamer 30.00
Creamer, Individual 20.00
Plate, Salad,
8 1/4 In. 15.00
Plate, Square, Salad,
8 In. 29.00
Sherbet, 6 Oz.,
5 In. 16.00
Sugar & Creamer,
Individual 9.50
Vase, 8 In. 81.00

RING

Hocking Glass Company made Ring from 1927 to 1933. The pattern, also known as Banded Rings, sometimes has colored rings added to the Crystal, Green, Mayfair Blue, Pink, or Red glass. The colored rings were made in various combinations of black, blue, orange, pink, platinum, red, and yellow. Platinum trim is on some pieces. Some solid red pieces also were made. The design is characterized by several sets of rings, each composed of four rings. Circle, a similar Hocking pattern, has only one group of rings.

Crystal
Cocktail Shaker 17.00
Cup, Platinum
Rim . . . . 6.00 to 9.50

Decanter, Multicolored Bands,
Straight Sides 40.00
Goblet, Platinum Rim, 9 Oz.,
7 1/4 In. . . . . . 10.00 to 15.00
Ice Bucket 24.00
Pitcher, 60 Oz.,
8 In. . . . . 15.00 to 18.00
Pitcher, 80 Oz.,
8 1/2 In. . . . . . 37.00 to 45.00
Plate, Luncheon, Platinum
Rim, 8 In. . . . . . . 3.00 to 5.00
Plate, Sherbet, Platinum
Rim, 6 1/4 In. 3.00
Salt & Pepper 20.00
Sandwich Server, Center Handle,
Platinum Rim 27.00
Sherbet, Footed,
4 3/4 In. 7.00
Sherbet, High,
4 3/4 In. . . . . . . 5.00 to 11.00
Sherbet, Low, Platinum
Rim 10.00
Sherbet, Multicolored Bands,
4 3/4 In. 12.00
Sugar, Platinum Rim 6.00
Tumbler, Flat, 5 Oz.,
3 1/2 In. . . . . . . 5.00 to 7.00
Tumbler, Flat, 10 Oz.,
4 3/4 In. . . . . . . 5.00 to 7.50
Tumbler, Footed, 5 Oz.,
3 1/2 In. 3.50
Tumbler, Footed, Iced
Tea, 6 1/2 In. 8.00
Tumbler, Gold Trim,
4 Oz., 3 In. 7.00
Tumbler, Iced Tea,
Footed, Platinum Rim,
6 1/2 In. 10.00
Tumbler, Platinum Rim, 10 Oz.,
4 3/4 In. . . . . . . 7.00 to 13.00
Tumbler, Whiskey,
Multicolored Bands,
1 1/2 Oz., 2 In. 15.00

Green
Berry Bowl, 5 In. . . 6.00 to 8.00
Berry Bowl, Master,
8 In. 15.00
Pitcher, 80 Oz.,
8 1/2 In. . . . . . 35.00 to 45.00
Plate, Off-Center Indent,
6 1/2 In. . . . . 5.00 to 7.00
Plate, Sherbet,
6 1/4 In. 2.00
Salt & Pepper 58.00

Sandwich Server, Center
Handle 28.00
Sherbet, Flat, 6 1/2 In. 12.00
Tumbler, 4 Oz., 3 In. 10.00
Tumbler, 5 Oz.,
3 1/2 In. . . . . . . 7.00 to 12.00
Tumbler, 10 Oz.,
4 3/4 In. 7.00

Pink
Plate, 3-Footed,
7 1/2 In. 19.00

Red
Plate, Luncheon, 8 In. . . . 19.50

RIPPLE

Ripple was made by Hazel Atlas Glass Company in the early 1950s. The dishes are Platonite, an almost-white glass, with fired-on pink and blue coatings. Collectors used to call the pattern Crinoline or Petticoat because the plates and bowls have ruffled edges.

Berry Bowl, Fired-On Pink,
5 In. 8.00
Cup & Saucer, Beaded Handle,
Fired-On Blue 5.50
Cup & Saucer, Fired-On Pink,
Plain Handle 5.00
Plate, Dinner, Pink Border,
9 In. 11.50
Sugar & Creamer, Beaded
Handle 15.00
Sugar & Creamer, Fired-On
Pink, Plain Handle 13.00

ROCK CRYSTAL

Rock Crystal, sometimes called Early American Rock Crystal, was made in many solid colors by McKee Glass Company. Amber, Blue-Green, Cobalt Blue, Crystal, Green, Pink, Red, and Yellow pieces were made in the 1920s and 1930s.

Amber
Bowl, 4 1/2 In. 23.00
Bowl, Salad, 10 1/4 In. . . 50.00
Compote, 7 In. 45.00
Goblet, Champagne,
6 Oz. 20.00
Goblet, Claret, 3 Oz. 50.00
Goblet, Water, 8 Oz. 26.00
Pitcher 295.00
Sandwich Server, Center
Handle, 10 3/4 In. 45.00
Tumbler, Footed,
5 3/4 In. 26.00
Vase, Footed, Gold Trim,
11 In. 150.00

Cobalt Blue
Candlestick, Frosted, Tall,
Pair 250.00

Crystal
Bowl, Center, Footed,
12 1/2 In. . . . . 75.00 to 98.00
Bowl, Round, Rolled
Edge, 13 In. 60.00
Bowl, Salad, Scalloped
Edge, 8 In. 60.00
Bowl, Scalloped Edge,
5 In. 15.00
Candelabra, 2-Light 20.00
Candy Dish, Cover, Footed,
9 1/4 In. . . . . . 75.00 to 85.00
Candy Dish, Flat 60.00

Creamer, Footed, 9 Oz. . . 20.00
Cruet, Oil, Flat, 6 Oz. . . 160.00
Cup . . . . 15.00 to 17.00
Cup & Saucer 28.00
Dish, Ice 32.00
Finger Bowl, 5 In. 15.00
Finger Bowl, Plain Edge,
5 In. 10.00
Goblet, Claret, 3 Oz. 20.00
Goblet, Cocktail,
3 1/2 Oz. . . . . . 10.00 to 17.00
Goblet, Cordial,
1 Oz. . . . . 15.00 to 25.00
Goblet, Water,
8 Oz. . . . . 18.00 to 22.00
Goblet, Wine,
2 Oz. . . . . 18.00 to 20.00
Parfait, 3 1/2 In. 28.00
Pickle, Oval, 7 In. 10.00
Pitcher, 48 Oz., 9 In. . . . 125.00
Plate, 7 1/2 In. 8.00
Plate, Scalloped Edge,
10 1/2 In. . . . . 50.00 to 60.00
Punch Bowl, 14 In. 350.00
Relish, 5 Sections,
12 1/2 In. . . . . 20.00 to 45.00
Relish, 6 Sections,
14 In. . . . . 38.00 to 43.00
Saucer 8.00
Sherbet,
3 1/2 In. . . . . . 10.00 to 16.00
Sugar, Cover, Footed 60.00
Sundae, Footed,
6 Oz. . . . . 10.00 to 12.00
Tumbler, 3 3/4 In. 16.00

Green
Goblet, Water, 8 Oz. 30.00
Vase, Footed, 11 In. 105.00

Pink
Bowl, Rolled Edge,
13 In. 60.00
Compote, 7 In. 20.00
Sandwich Server, Center
Handle, 10 3/4 In. 55.00

Red
Bowl, Scalloped Edge,
5 In. 55.00
Candy Dish, Cover,
Footed, 9 1/4 In. 100.00
Celery Dish, Oblong,
12 In. 85.00
Compote, 7 In. 95.00

Finger Bowl .... 42.00 to 45.00

Goblet, Cocktail,
3 1/2 In. ..... 40.00 to 65.00

Goblet, Cordial,
1 Oz. ...... 65.00 to 110.00

Goblet, Wine,
2 Oz. .... 42.00 to 45.00

Pitcher, No Cover 1200.00

Plate, Plain Edge,
7 1/2 In. 23.00

Plate, Scalloped Edge,
9 In. 60.00

Plate, Scalloped Edge,
10 1/2 In. 75.00

Saucer, Scalloped Edge .. 25.00

Sundae, 6 Oz. ... 30.00 to 42.00

Tumbler, Concave,
12 Oz. 69.00

Tumbler, Straight,
9 Oz. 54.00

Tumbler, Whiskey,
2 1/2 In. ..... 50.00 to 65.00

ROMANCE

Fostoria Glass Company, Moundsville, West Virginia, made items with the Romance etching from 1942 to 1986. The pattern is easily confused with June, another Fostoria pattern with an etching, because both etchings include a bow. The Romance etching is used on heavier blanks, and the border between the floral sprays is a different design. Romance pieces are always Crystal.

Candlestick,
5 1/2 In. 38.00

Cup 22.00

Goblet, Wine, 3 Oz.,
5 1/2 In. 35.00

Torte Plate, 14 In. 65.00

Tumbler, Water, Footed,
9 Oz., 5 1/2 In. 18.00

ROPE
See Colonial Fluted

ROSALIE

Rosalie etching was made by Cambridge Glass Company, Cambridge, Ohio, in the late 1920s and 1930s. Dishes were made in Amber, Bluebell, Carmen (red), Emerald, Heatherbloom, Peach-Blo, Topaz, and Willow Blue.

Carmen

Oyster Cocktail,
4 1/2 Oz. 95.00

Sherbet, 6 Oz.,
5 1/4 In. 95.00

Tumbler, 10 Oz.,
4 3/4 In. 125.00

Emerald

Candlestick, 4 In., Pair .. 80.00

Tumbler, Footed, 12 Oz.,
6 3/4 In. 43.00

ROSE CAMEO

Rose Cameo was made by the Belmont Tumbler Company, Bellaire, Ohio,

in 1933. It has been found only in Green and only in six different pieces, three of them bowls.

Berry Bowl,
4 1/2 In. ..... 16.00 to 19.00

Bowl, Cereal,
5 In. .... 23.00 to 25.00

Plate, Salad,
7 In. .... 11.00 to 15.00

Sherbet .... 13.00 to 15.00

Tumbler, Footed,
5 In. .... 23.00 to 25.00

ROSE ETCH

Rose Etch, also known as Heisey Rose, was made by A. H. Heisey & Company, Newark, Ohio, from 1949 to 1957. The etching was used on Crystal items, mostly from the Waverly and Queen Anne patterns. Most of the pieces are not marked.

Bonbon, Footed,
6 1/4 In. 41.00

Bowl, 5 1/2 In. 39.00

Candlestick, 3-Light,
7 1/2 In. 129.00

Cheese Dish, Cover, Lariat,
5 In. 87.00

Console, Dolphin-Footed,
11 In. 60.00

Goblet, Champagne,
6 Oz. 40.00

Goblet, Cordial,
1 Oz. 150.00

Pitcher, 73 Oz. 695.00

Plate, Salad, 7 In. 30.00

Plate, Salad, 8 In. 40.00
Relish, 3 Sections, Oval,
 11 In. 75.00
Salt & Pepper,
 4 1/8 In. 27.00
Sugar & Creamer,
 4 In. 61.00

ROSE LACE
See Royal Lace

ROSE POINT

Rose Point was made by the Cambridge Glass Company of Cambridge, Ohio, from 1936 to 1953. The elaborate pattern was made in Crystal and Crystal with gold trim. A few rare pieces were made in Red or Amber.

Crystal
Bowl, 11 In. 135.00
Bowl, 12 In. 95.00
Bowl, 4-Footed,
 11 In. 130.00
Bowl, Ruffled Edge, 4-Footed,
 13 In. 150.00
Bowl, Ruffled Edge, 4-Footed,
 Handles, Oval,
 12 1/2 In. 425.00
Butter, Cover 250.00
Candlestick, 4 In. 32.00
Candlestick, 6 In.,
 Pair 95.00
Candlestick, Bell Foot,
 5 In. 75.00
Cocktail Shaker,
 32 Oz. 325.00
Compote, 5 3/8 In. 100.00
Cruet, Oil,
 6 Oz. . . . . . . 145.00 to 275.00
Decanter, 14 Oz. 775.00
Decanter, 28 Oz. 595.00

Dish, Footed,
 7 1/2 x 12 1/2 In. 60.00
Goblet, Cocktail,
 3 Oz. . . . . 30.00 to 35.00
Goblet, Cordial, 1 Oz.,
 5 1/4 In. 95.00
Honey Dish, Cover 500.00
Ice Bucket, Metal Handle,
 Ice Tongs . . 225.00 to 235.00
Marmalade,
 Underplate 225.00
Pitcher, Ball,
 80 Oz. 350.00
Plate, Dinner,
 10 1/2 In. 225.00
Platter, 13 3/4 x 11 In. . . 175.00
Relish, 2 Sections 85.00
Relish, 5 Sections,
 12 In. 375.00
Sherbet, Tall 24.00
Tumbler, 12 Oz.,
 5 1/4 In. 185.00
Vase, 12 In. 275.00
Vase, Bud,
 10 In. . . . . . . 70.00 to 85.00

Gold Trim
Bowl, 4-Footed,
 12 In. 150.00
Candlestick, Pair 150.00
Relish, 3 Sections,
 6 1/2 In. 85.00

ROSEMARY

Rosemary, also called Cabbage Rose with Single Arch or Dutch Rose, was made by Federal Glass Company from 1935 to 1937. It was made in Amber, Green, Iridescent, and Pink. Pieces with bases, like creamers or cups, are sometimes con-

fused with Mayfair Federal because the molds used were those originally designed for the Mayfair pattern. The lower half of the Rosemary pieces are plain; the lower half of Mayfair Federal has a band of arches.

Amber
Berry Bowl,
 5 In. . . . . 6.75 to 7.00
Bowl, Vegetable, Oval,
 10 In. . . . . . . 16.00 to 18.00
Creamer . . . . 9.00 to 10.00
Cup & Saucer 13.00
Plate, Dinner,
 9 1/2 In. . . . . . . 9.00 to 11.00
Plate, Salad,
 6 3/4 In. . . . . . . 5.00 to 6.50
Platter, Oval,
 12 In. . . . . . . 15.00 to 19.00
Saucer . . . . 2.00 to 5.00
Soup, Cream . . . 14.00 to 20.00
Sugar . . . . 7.00 to 10.00
Tumbler, Water,
 9 Oz., 4 1/4 In. 30.00

Green
Sugar 14.00

Pink
Berry Bowl, 5 In. 14.00
Bowl, Vegetable, Oval,
 10 In. . . . . . . 40.00 to 45.00
Creamer 25.00
Cup & Saucer 25.00
Plate, Dinner,
 9 1/2 In. . . . . . 25.00 to 33.00
Plate, Salad,
 6 3/4 In. . . . . . 12.00 to 15.00
Platter, Oval,
 12 In. 40.00
Saucer 5.00
Soup, Cream 32.00
Tumbler, Flat, 9 Oz,
 4 1/4 In. . . . . . 60.00 to 65.00

ROSEMARY
See also Mayfair Federal

ROSES & BOWS
See Paneled Grape

ROULETTE

Hocking Glass Company made Roulette pattern from 1935 to 1939. Green luncheon and beverage sets were manufactured, as well as Pink beverage sets and some Crystal pieces. Collectors originally called the pattern Many Windows.

Green
Cup . . . . 4.00 to 8.00
Cup & Saucer . . . 8.00 to 12.50
Pitcher, 65 Oz., 8 In. 54.00
Plate, Luncheon,
  8 1/2 In. . . . . . . 5.00 to 10.00
Plate, Sherbet,
  6 In. . . . . 6.00 to 7.00
Sandwich Server,
  12 In. . . . . 16.00 to 27.50
Saucer 4.00
Sherbet . . . . 5.00 to 8.00
Tumbler, Iced Tea,
  Footed, 10 Oz.,
  5 1/2 In. . . . . . 30.00 to 39.00
Tumbler, Juice, 5 Oz.,
  3 1/4 In. 32.00
Tumbler, Water, 9 Oz.,
  4 1/2 In. . . . . . 22.00 to 33.00

Pink
Pitcher, 65 Oz.,
  8 In. . . . . 45.00 to 54.00
Tumbler, Iced Tea,
  12 Oz., 5 1/8 In. 35.00
Tumbler, Juice, 5 Oz.,
  3 1/4 In. 29.00
Tumbler, Water, 9 Oz.,
  4 1/8 In. . . . . 26.50 to 30.00
Tumbler, Whiskey,
  1 1/2 Oz. . . . . 14.00 to 16.00

ROUND ROBIN

Sometimes a pattern was advertised by a wholesaler, and the manufacturer remains unknown. One of these is Round Robin, sometimes called Accordion Pleats. It was pictured as a luncheon set in sales catalogs of the late 1920s and 1930s and offered in Crystal, Green, and Iridescent Marigold.

Green
Creamer . . . . . . 10.00 to 15.00
Cup 6.00
Plate, Sherbet,
  6 In. . . . . 3.00 to 4.00
Sherbet . . . . 9.00 to 10.00
Sugar 5.00

Iridescent Marigold
Sherbet . . . . 4.00 to 7.00

ROXANA

Hazel Atlas Glass Company made Roxana pattern in 1932. It was made in Crystal, White, and Yellow.

Yellow
Berry Bowl, 5 In. 16.00
Plate, Sherbet,
  6 In. . . . . 9.00 to 12.00
Sherbet . . . . 8.00 to 13.00
Tumbler, 9 Oz.,
  4 1/4 In. 19.00

ROYAL

Fostoria Glass Company, Moundsville, West Virginia, made items with Royal etching from 1925 to 1932. Dishes were made in Amber, Blue, Ebony, and Green.

Amber
Candleholder, 1-Light,
  Pair 45.00
Creamer, Footed, Large . . 30.00
Sugar, Footed, Large 30.00
Blue
Compote, 7 In. 65.00
Green
Goblet, Water, 9 Oz. 40.00
Sherbet 25.00

ROYAL LACE

Royal Lace was made from 1934 to 1941. The popular pattern by Hazel Atlas Glass Company was made in Cobalt Blue, Crystal, Green, and Pink, and in limited quantities in Amethyst. It is sometimes called Gladiola or Rose Lace. Reproductions have been made.

Amethyst
Toddy Jar, No Cover 50.00
Cobalt Blue
Berry Bowl,
  10 In. . . . . 40.00 to 88.00
Bowl, Straight Edge, 3-Footed,
  10 In. . . . . . . 95.00 to 125.00
Bowl, Vegetable, Oval,
  11 In. 90.00
Butter,
  Cover . . . . . 800.00 to 925.00

Butter, Cover
  Only ...... 225.00 to 245.00
Candlestick, Rolled Edge,
  Pair .... 250.00 to 280.00
Candlestick, Ruffled Edge,
  Pair 625.00
Cookie Jar,
  Cover ..... 395.00 to 450.00
Creamer 45.00
Creamer,
  Footed .... 58.00 to 65.00
Cup .... 25.00 to 55.00
Cup & Saucer .. 33.00 to 65.00
Grill Plate,
  9 7/8 In. ..... 45.00 to 50.00
Pitcher, 64 Oz., 8 In. ... 350.00
Pitcher, Ice Lip, 96 Oz.,
  8 1/2 In. ... 625.00 to 825.00
Pitcher, Straight Sides,
  48 Oz. ..... 110.00 to 225.00
Plate, Dinner,
  9 7/8 In. ..... 47.00 to 75.00
Plate, Luncheon,
  8 1/2 In. ..... 48.00 to 68.00
Plate, Sherbet,
  6 In. .... 13.00 to 24.00
Platter, Oval,
  13 In. .... 70.00 to 99.00
Salt &
  Pepper ..... 300.00 to 395.00
Saltshaker 30.00
Saucer .... 12.00 to 15.00
Sherbet,
  Footed .... 50.00 to 70.00
Sherbet, Metal
  Base .... 35.00 to 49.00
Soup, Cream .. 43.00 to 62.00
Sugar .... 22.00 to 50.00
Sugar, Cover 275.00
Sugar & Creamer 112.00
Toddy Set .... 285.00 to 315.00
Tumbler, 10 Oz.,
  4 7/8 In. ... 245.00 to 280.00
Tumbler, Iced Tea, 12 Oz.,
  5 3/8 In. ... 149.00 to 195.00
Tumbler, Juice, 5 Oz.,
  3 1/2 In. ..... 59.00 to 65.00
Tumbler, Water, 9 Oz.,
  4 1/8 In. ..... 45.00 to 60.00

Crystal

Bowl, Ruffled Edge, 3-Footed,
  10 In. .... 42.00 to 45.00
Butter, Cover .. 50.00 to 85.00

Cookie Jar,
  Cover .... 35.00 to 45.00
Creamer .... 12.00 to 17.00
Cup .... 9.00 to 10.00
Cup & Saucer 16.00
Grill Plate, 9 7/8 In. 15.00
Pitcher, Ice Lip, 96 Oz.,
  8 1/2 In. ..... 60.00 to 85.00
Plate, Dinner,
  9 7/8 In. ..... 16.00 to 25.00
Plate, Sherbet,
  6 In. .... 7.00 to 9.00
Salt & Pepper ... 45.00 to 65.00
Saucer 5.00
Sherbet .... 15.00 to 19.00
Soup, Cream ... 12.00 to 20.00
Sugar .... 10.00 to 25.00
Sugar, Cover ... 32.00 to 70.00
Sugar &
  Creamer ..... 24.00 to 39.00
Tumbler, Iced Tea,
  12 Oz., 5 3/8 In. 56.00
Tumbler, Juice,
  5 Oz., 3 1/2 In. 25.00
Tumbler, Water, 9 Oz.,
  4 1/8 In. ..... 11.00 to 20.00

Green

Berry Bowl, 5 In. 60.00
Bowl, Straight Edge,
  3-Footed, 10 In. 95.00
Cookie Jar ... 122.00 to 125.00
Creamer 25.00
Cup .... 20.00 to 30.00
Cup & Saucer .. 28.00 to 35.00
Grill Plate, 9 7/8 In. 29.00
Pitcher, 64 Oz., 8 In. ... 165.00
Plate, Dinner,
  9 7/8 In. ..... 36.00 to 41.00
Plate, Luncheon,
  8 1/2 In. 33.00
Plate, Sherbet,
  6 In. .... 8.00 to 15.00
Platter, Oval, 13 In. 48.00
Salt &
  Pepper ..... 120.00 to 175.00
Saltshaker .... 63.00 to 65.00
Saucer .... 10.00 to 15.00
Sherbet .... 28.00 to 36.00
Soup, Cream ... 35.00 to 36.00
Sugar .... 25.00 to 27.00
Sugar &
  Creamer ..... 45.00 to 90.00

Tumbler, 10 Oz.,
  4 7/8 In. ... 135.00 to 155.00
Tumbler, Juice, 5 Oz.,
  3 1/2 In. 42.00
Tumbler, Water, 9 Oz.,
  4 1/8 In. ..... 32.00 to 41.00

Pink

Berry Bowl,
  5 In. .... 22.00 to 35.00
Berry Bowl, Master,
  10 In. .... 25.00 to 70.00
Bowl, Rolled Edge, 3-Footed,
  10 In. ..... 110.00 to 225.00
Bowl, Ruffled Edge, 3-Footed,
  10 In. ...... 95.00 to 150.00
Bowl, Straight Edge, 3-Footed,
  10 In. .... 65.00 to 75.00
Bowl, Sugar 15.00
Butter, Cover 245.00
Butter, Cover Only 115.00
Candlestick, Rolled Edge,
  Pair .... 110.00 to 185.00
Candlestick, Ruffled Edge,
  Pair 225.00
Cookie Jar ..... 55.00 to 85.00
Creamer 25.00
Cup .... 11.00 to 25.00
Cup & Saucer .. 24.00 to 33.00
Nut Dish .... 645.00 to 700.00
Pitcher, 64 Oz.,
  8 In.. .... 145.00
Pitcher, 96 Oz.,
  8 1/2 In. ... 210.00 to 235.00
Pitcher, No Ice Lip,
  68 Oz., 8 In. 169.50
Pitcher, Straight Sides,
  48 Oz. ..... 110.00 to 175.00
Plate, Dinner,
  9 7/8 In. ..... 25.00 to 35.00
Plate, Luncheon,
  8 1/2 In. ..... 20.00 to 35.00
Plate, Sherbet,
  6 In. .... 8.00 to 12.00
Platter, Oval,
  13 In. .... 38.00 to 60.00
Salt & Pepper .. 70.00 to 125.00
Saltshaker 35.00
Sherbet 20.00
Soup, Cream ... 25.00 to 32.00
Sugar .... 20.00 to 22.00
Sugar & Creamer 30.00
Tumbler, Iced Tea,
  12 Oz., 5 3/8 In. 110.00

Tumbler, Juice, 5 Oz.,
3 1/2 In. 35.00

Tumbler, Water, 9 Oz.,
4 1/8 In. . . . . . 25.00 to 38.00

ROYAL RUBY

This pattern is identified by its bright red color. Many pieces have plain shapes. Anchor Hocking Glass Corporation made it from 1938 to 1967 and again from 1973 to 1977. The same shapes were made in Forest Green. These items are listed in this book under Forest Green. Reproduction tumblers were made in 1977 and 1978.

Apothecary Jar,
24 Oz. . . . . 18.50 to 22.00

Ashtray, Leaf,
4 1/2 In. . . . . 5.00 to 9.00

Berry Bowl,
4 1/2 In. . . . . . . 8.00 to 12.00

Berry Bowl, Master,
8 1/2 In. . . . . . 25.00 to 35.00

Bottle, 1 Qt. 55.00

Bowl, Cereal, 5 1/2 In. . . 10.00

Bowl, Coronation,
Handles, 4 1/2 In. 8.00

Bowl, Ruffled Edge,
6 1/4 In. 15.00

Bowl, Scallop, 5 1/4 In. . . 20.00

Bowl, Vegetable, Oval,
8 In. . . . . 35.00 to 48.00

Candle Cup, 2 5/8 In. 5.00

Candleholder, 3 1/2 In. . . 55.00

Candy Jar, Crystal, Ruby
Cover, 5 1/2 In. 20.00

Cocktail, Footed,
3 1/2 In. 10.00

Creamer 8.00

Creamer,
Footed . . . . . . 8.00 to 10.00

Cup 6.00

Cup, Punch 3.00

Cup, Round 6.00

Cup & Saucer . . . 8.00 to 10.00

Cup & Saucer,
Coupe 10.00

Goblet, Ball
Stem . . . . 10.00 to 15.00

Goblet, Cocktail,
Footed, 3 1/2 In. 12.00

Goblet, Cordial, Footed . . 13.00

Goblet, Water, 9 Oz. 11.00

Goblet, Wine,
2 1/2 Oz. . . . . . . 6.00 to 15.00

Marmalade, Crystal
Bottom, 5 1/8 In. 22.00

Nappy, Swirl,
6 1/2 In. 18.00

Pitcher, Ball,
3 Qt. . . . . 45.00 to 55.00

Pitcher, Flat, 64 Oz. 65.00

Pitcher, Tilt,
42 Oz. . . . . 30.00 to 59.50

Plate, Bread & Butter,
6 In. 8.00

Plate, Dinner,
9 1/8 In. . . . . . . 7.00 to 17.50

Plate, Luncheon,
8 3/8 In. . . . . . . 7.00 to 10.00

Plate, Salad,
7 3/4 In. . . . . . . 6.00 to 12.50

Plate, Sherbet,
6 1/4 In. 5.00

Puff Box, Red Top, Crystal
Bottom, 4 5/8 In. 28.00

Punch Bowl 35.00

Punch Bowl, Base,
10 Cups 125.00

Punch Bowl Stand 45.00

Punch Cup 3.50

Punch Set, 14 Piece 195.00

Saucer 2.50

Sherbet . . . . 8.00 to 10.50

Sherbet, Ball Stem,
6 1/2 Oz. . . . . . . 8.00 to 10.00

Sherbet, Flat 10.00

Sherbet, Footed,
Low 10.50

Sherbet, Straight Stem . . . 10.00

Soup, Dish,
7 1/2 In. . . . . . 12.00 to 20.00

Sugar 8.00

Sugar, Footed . . . . 7.00 to 10.00

Sugar &
Creamer . . . . . 15.00 to 18.00

Sugar & Creamer,
Footed 15.00

Tumbler, 5 Oz. 8.00

Tumbler, 9 Oz. . . . 6.50 to 10.00

Tumbler, Footed,
10 Oz. . . . . 7.00 to 10.00

Tumbler, Footed,
14 Oz. 14.00

Tumbler, High Point,
6 Oz. 15.00

Tumbler, High Point,
9 Oz. 15.00

Tumbler, Iced Tea,
13 Oz. 13.00

Tumbler, Iced Tea,
13 Oz., 4 Piece 40.00

Tumbler, Juice,
3 In. . . . . 5.00 to 9.00

Vase, 6 5/8 In. . . 10.00 to 15.00

Vase, 9 In. . . . . . 15.00 to 22.00

Vase, Ivy, 4 In. . . 6.00 to 12.00

RUSSIAN
See Holiday

S PATTERN

Macbeth-Evans Glass Company made S Pattern, or Stippled Rose Band, from 1930 to 1935. It was made before 1932 in Crystal, Pink, Topaz, and Crystal with gold, blue, or platinum trim. The 1934 listing mentions Green, Monax, and Red. Other pieces were made in Amber, Ritz Blue, Yellow, and Crystal with many colors of trim, including, amber, green, platinum, red, rose, silver, or white.

Amber

Cup 4.00

Plate, Dinner,
9 1/4 In. . . . . . . 7.00 to 9.00

Plate, Luncheon,
8 1/4 In. . . . . . . 4.00 to 5.00

Crystal

Bowl, Cereal, Amber
Band, 5 1/2 In. 9.50

Creamer, Thick 6.00

Creamer, Thin 6.00

Cup, Platinum Rim,
Thick 4.00

Cup, Thin 3.00

Cup & Saucer . . . . 5.00 to 6.00

Cup & Saucer, Platinum
Rim 6.00

Cup & Saucer, Platinum
Rim, Thick 7.00

Plate, 8 In. 4.50

Plate, Luncheon,
8 1/4 In. . . . . . . 4.00 to 8.00

Plate, Luncheon, Amber
Band, 8 1/4 In. 6.50

Plate, Luncheon, Platinum
Rim, 8 1/4 In. 5.00

Plate, Sherbet, Amber
Band, 6 In. 3.00

Saucer 2.50

Saucer, Amber Band 3.00

Sugar, Platinum Rim,
Thick 4.00

Sugar, Thick 6.00

Sugar, Thin 6.00

Sugar & Creamer 12.00

Tumbler, 10 Oz.,
4 3/4 In. . . . . . . 9.00 to 13.00

Tumbler, Juice, Amber Band,
5 Oz., 3 1/2 In. 8.50

Tumbler, Water, Platinum Rim,
9 Oz., 4 In. . . . 11.00 to 12.00

Monax

Plate, Sherbet, 6 In. 8.00

Yellow

Cake Plate, 13 In. 75.00

Cup 4.50

Plate, Luncheon,
8 1/4 In. . . . . . . 4.00 to 6.00

Saucer 3.00

SAIL BOAT
See White Ship

SAILING SHIP
See White Ship

SANDWICH ANCHOR HOCKING

Many glass companies used the name Sandwich for one of their patterns. The three most popular patterns were made by Anchor Hocking Glass Corporation, Indiana Glass Company, and Duncan & Miller Glass Company. The Anchor Hocking Sandwich pattern was made from 1939 to 1964 and can be distinguished by the three lines around the edge of each flower petal. It was made in Royal Ruby in 1938 and 1939; and in Pink from 1938 to 1940. Crystal was made from 1939 to 1966 and again from 1977 to 1993; Forest Green and White (opaque) date from 1956 to the 1960s; Desert Gold from 1961 to 1964. A reproduction line was introduced in 1977 by another company in Amber, Blue, Crystal, and Red.

Amber

Bowl, Cereal, 6 3/4 In. . . 17.00

Bowl, Smooth Edge,
4 7/8 In. 4.00

Cookie Jar, Cover 38.00

Cup . . . . 5.00 to 8.00

Cup & Saucer . . . . 7.00 to 8.00

Plate, Dinner, 9 In. 9.00

Sandwich Server,
12 In. 26.00

Saucer 3.00

Crystal

Berry Bowl,
4 7/8 In. . . . . . . 5.00 to 6.00

Bowl, 4 5/16 In. 5.00

Bowl, Cereal, 6 3/4 In. . . 49.00

Bowl, Cereal, Scalloped,
6 3/4 In. 9.50

Bowl, Dessert, Scalloped,
4 7/8 In. . . . . . 17.00 to 20.00

Bowl, Oval,
8 1/4 In. . . . . . . 6.00 to 10.00

Bowl, Salad, 9 In. 23.00

Bowl, Scalloped,
5 1/4 In. . . . . . . 7.50 to 8.00

Bowl, Scalloped,
6 1/2 In. . . . . . 7.00 to 11.00

Bowl, Scalloped,
7 5/8 In. 14.00

Bowl, Scalloped,
8 1/4 In. . . . . . 8.00 to 18.00

Bowl, Scalloped, Deep,
6 1/2 In. . . . . . 7.00 to 12.00

Bowl, Vegetable, Oval . . . 7.00

Butter 25.00

Butter, Cover . . . 40.00 to 48.00

Cookie Jar,
Cover . . . . . . 34.00 to 45.00

Creamer . . . . 5.00 to 8.00

Cup . . . . 3.00 to 7.00

Cup, Coffee 3.00

Cup & Saucer . . . . 4.00 to 10.00

Custard Cup . . . . . 3.00 to 5.00

Custard Cup, Scalloped,
5 Oz. . . . . 12.00 to 14.00

Custard Cup,
Underplate . . . 16.00 to 25.00

Pitcher, Ice Lip,
1/2 Gal. . . . . . . 75.00 to 85.00

Plate, Dessert,
7 In. . . . . 10.00 to 11.00

Plate, Dinner,
9 In. . . . . 15.00 to 20.00

Plate, Luncheon,
    8 In. . . . . 4.00 to 7.00
Punch Bowl, 4 Qt.,
    9 3/4 In. . . . . 20.00 to 30.00
Punch Bowl,
    Stand . . . . 47.00 to 70.00
Punch Bowl Set,
    9 3/4 In., 16 Piece 55.00
Punch Bowl Stand 30.00
Punch Cup . . . . . . 2.00 to 4.00
Sandwich Server, 12 In. . . 35.00
Saucer . . . . 2.00 to 4.00
Sherbet, Footed . . 7.00 to 10.00
Snack Plate, Indent for Punch
    Cup, 9 In. . . . . . . 5.00 to 8.00
Sugar . . . . 6.00 to 10.00
Sugar, Cover . . . 17.00 to 28.00
Sugar & Creamer,
    Open . . . . 12.00 to 30.00
Tumbler, Footed,
    9 Oz. . . . . 28.00 to 32.00
Tumbler, Juice, 3 Oz.,
    3 3/8 In. . . . . . 18.00 to 23.00
Tumbler, Juice, 5 Oz.,
    3 9/16 In. . . . . . . 4.00 to 7.00
Tumbler, Water,
    9 Oz. . . . . 8.00 to 10.00

Desert Gold
Bowl, 4 7/8 In. 4.00
Bowl, Salad, 9 In. 33.00
Cookie Jar, Cover 38.00
Cup 4.00
Cup & Saucer 5.00
Plate, Dinner,
    9 In. . . . . 7.00 to 10.00
Sandwich Server,
    12 In. . . . . . . 15.00 to 17.00
Saucer 3.00

Forest Green
Bowl, Dessert,
    Crimped, 5 In. 4.00
Bowl, Scalloped,
    8 1/4 In. 125.00
Bowl, Scalloped, Deep,
    6 1/2 In. 85.00
Creamer . . . . . . 30.00 to 35.00
Cup 22.00
Cup & Saucer 50.00
Custard Cup 3.00
Pitcher, Juice, 6 In. 210.00
Plate, Dinner,
    9 In. . . . . . . 135.00 to 145.00
Saucer 22.00

Sugar . . . . 30.00 to 50.00
Sugar & Creamer 65.00
Tumbler, 12 Oz. 300.00
Tumbler, Juice, 3 Oz.,
    3 3/8 In. . . . . 4.00 to 7.00

Pink
Bowl, 4 7/8 In. 7.00

Royal Ruby
Bowl, 5 1/4 In. 35.00
Bowl, Cereal, Scalloped,
    6 3/4 In. 38.00
Bowl, Scalloped,
    5 1/4 In. . . . . . 22.00 to 35.00
Sherbet, Footed 8.00
Tumbler, Footed, 12 Oz.,
    4 7/8 In. . . . . . 10.00 to 12.00

White
Cup, Gold Trim 3.50
Punch Bowl, 4 Qt. 30.00
Punch Bowl Stand 30.00
Punch Cup 4.00

SANDWICH DUNCAN & MILLER

Duncan & Miller Sandwich is easy to recognize. It has long been said the pattern was designed by Mr. Heisey's son-in-law and that he added the diamond and H mark used by Heisey as part of the border design. New research suggests this is not true and that the so-called diamond and H mark is really a mold flaw. The plates in this series have ground bot-

toms. The star in the center of the plate does not go to the edge of the circle. Duncan & Miller Glass Company, Washington, Pennsylvania, named its pattern No. 41 Early American Sandwich Glass in 1925. The glass was made in Amber, Cobalt Blue, Crystal, Green, Pink, and Red. The pattern remained in production until 1955, when some of the molds were bought by other companies. Lancaster Colony made pieces in Amberina, Blue, and Green in the 1970s. Tiffin made Milk Glass pieces. Reproductions have been made.

Crystal
Cake Plate, Footed,
    12 In. 75.00
Candlestick, 4 In. 14.00
Dish, Ice Cream, 5 Oz.,
    4 1/2 In. 9.00
Epergne, Fruit & Flower,
    Footed, 14 In. 250.00
Goblet, 9 Oz.,
    6 In. . . . . 14.00 to 19.00
Goblet, Cocktail,
    3 Oz., 4 1/4 In. 6.50
Pitcher, 64 Oz., 8 In. . . . 125.00
Relish, 2 Sections,
    Handle, 6 In. 16.00
Sugar & Creamer 18.00

Green
Bowl, Grapefruit,
    Rimmed 14.00
Plate, 7 In. 8.00

❖

Mayonnaise can be used to remove old masking tape, stickers, or labels from glass or china.

❖

SANDWICH INDIANA

Another Sandwich pattern was made by the Indiana Glass Company, Dunkirk, Indiana, from the 1920s through the 1980s. It can be distinguished by the single line around the flower petals. The colors changed through the years. Amber was made from the late 1920s to the 1980s, Crystal from the late 1920s to the 1990s, Light Green and Pink from the 1920s to the 1930s, Red from 1933 to the 1970s, Teal Blue from the 1950s to the 1980s, Opaque White in the 1950s, and Smoky Blue in 1976 and 1977. The scroll design varies with the size of the plate. Tiara Home Products sold Sandwich in Red (1969), Amber (1970), and Crystal (1978), and in Amber, Chantilly Green, and Crystal in the 1980s. Tiara also sold a few pieces from redesigned molds. A Teal Blue butter dish was also made. Reproductions have been made.

Amber

Ashtray, Club
Shape . . . . 3.00 to 4.00
Ashtray, Heart Shape 3.00

Ashtray, Spade Shape 4.00
Butter, Cover, Domed . . . 55.00
Cup 4.00
Goblet, Wine, Footed,
4 Oz., 3 In. 5.00
Goblet, 9 Oz. 13.00
Salt & Pepper 18.00
Saucer 3.00
Sherbet, Footed,
3 1/4 In. . . . . 5.00 to 6.00
Tumbler, Iced Tea,
Footed, 12 Oz. 10.00

Crystal

Ashtray, Diamond Shape . . 3.50
Bowl, 6 In. 6.00
Candlestick, 3 1/2 In.,
Pair 20.00
Celery Dish 16.00
Cup . . . . 3.00 to 4.00
Plate, Sherbet, 6 In. 3.00
Sandwich Server, 13 In. . . 23.00
Saucer 3.00
Sherbet, Footed,
3 1/4 In. . . . . 5.00 to 9.00
Snack Plate, Oval, Indent For
Cup, 8 In. . . . . . 6.00 to 12.00
Sugar . . . . 5.00 to 8.00
Sugar, Diamond Shape . . . 8.50
Sugar & Creamer,
Tray, Diamond
Shape . . . . 13.00 to 16.00

Light Green

Ashtray, Club Shape 8.50
Plate, Dinner,
10 1/2 In. . . . . 20.00 to 25.00
Saucer, 4 1/2 In. 5.50
Tumbler, Cocktail, Footed,
3 Oz., 3 1/2 In. 5.50

Red

Tumbler, Water, Footed,
8 Oz. 45.00

Teal Blue

Ashtray, Spade Shape 6.00
Snack Plate, Oval, Indent For
Cup, 8 In. . . . . . 9.00 to 10.00

SAWTOOTH
See English Hobnail

SAXON
See Coronation

SCROLL & STAR
See Princess Feather

SEVENTEEN HUNDRED
LINE
See 1700 Line

SHAMROCK
See Cloverleaf

SHARON

Sharon, or Cabbage Rose, was made by the Federal Glass Company from 1935 to 1939. The pattern was made in Amber, Crystal, Green, and Pink. A cheese dish was reproduced in 1976 in Amber, Blue, Dark Green, Light Green, and Pink. Other items have been reproduced in various colors.

Amber

Berry Bowl,
5 In. . . . . 7.00 to 10.00
Berry Bowl, Master,
8 1/2 In. . . . . . . 6.00 to 10.00
Bowl, Cereal,
6 In. . . . . 22.00 to 23.00
Bowl, Fruit,
10 1/2 In. . . . . 21.00 to 28.00
Bowl, Vegetable, Oval,
9 1/2 In. . . . . . 16.00 to 38.00
Butter, Cover, Round,
7 1/2 In. . . . . . 45.00 to 56.00
Butter, Cover Only 15.00
Butter, No
Cover . . . . 20.00 to 24.00

Cake Plate, Footed,
  11 1/2 In. . . . . 25.00 to 28.00
Candy Dish,
  Cover . . . . 40.00 to 50.00
Cheese Dish, Cover 195.00
Creamer . . . . 14.00 to 15.00
Cup . . . . 5.00 to 12.00
Cup & Saucer . . 10.00 to 18.00
Jam Dish, 7 1/2 In. 40.00
Pitcher, Ice Lip,
  80 Oz. . . . . . 135.00 to 165.00
Plate, Bread & Butter,
  6 In. . . . . 4.00 to 6.00
Plate, Dinner,
  9 1/2 In. . . . . . . 6.00 to 15.00
Plate, Salad,
  7 1/2 In. . . . . . 15.00 to 17.00
Platter, Oval,
  12 1/2 In. . . . . 10.00 to 22.50
Salt & Pepper . . . 38.00 to 45.00
Saltshaker 20.00
Saucer . . . . 6.00 to 13.00
Sherbet . . . . 9.00 to 15.00
Soup, Cream . . . 25.00 to 32.00
Soup, Dish,
  7 3/4 In. . . . . . 40.00 to 58.00
Sugar . . . . 9.00 to 20.00
Sugar, Cover . . . 25.00 to 45.00
Sugar &
  Creamer . . . . . 22.00 to 40.00
Tumbler, Thin, 9 Oz.,
  4 1/8 In. . . . . 27.00 to 32.00
Tumbler, Iced Tea, Footed,
  15 Oz., 6 1/2 In. 138.00
Tumbler, Thick, 9 Oz.,
  4 1/8 In. . . . . . 30.00 to 35.00
Tumbler, Thick, 12 Oz.,
  5 1/4 In. 65.00
Tumbler, Thin, 12 Oz.,
  5 1/4 In. . . . . . 55.00 to 60.00

Crystal

Cake Plate, Footed,
  11 1/2 In. . . . . . 8.00 to 12.00
Tumbler, Footed, 15 Oz.,
  6 1/2 In. 27.00

Green

Berry Bowl,
  5 In. . . . . 18.00 to 25.00
Berry Bowl, Master,
  8 1/2 In. . . . . . 35.00 to 41.00
Bowl, Cereal,
  6 In. . . . . 23.00 to 30.00
Bowl, Fruit,
  10 1/2 In. . . . . 45.00 to 50.00

Bowl, Vegetable, Oval,
  9 1/2 In. . . . . . 28.00 to 45.00
Butter, Cover . . . 85.00 to 92.00
Butter, Cover Only 45.00
Candy Jar,
  Cover Only 100.00
Creamer . . . . 20.00 to 28.00
Cup . . . . 10.00 to 20.00
Cup & Saucer . . 32.00 to 38.00
Pitcher, Ice Lip,
  80 Oz. 500.00
Plate, Bread & Butter,
  6 In. . . . . 8.00 to 9.00
Plate, Dinner,
  9 1/2 In. . . . . . 22.00 to 30.00
Plate, Salad,
  7 1/2 In. 24.00
Platter, Oval,
  12 1/2 In. . . . . 29.00 to 42.00
Salt & Pepper 75.00
Saltshaker 40.00
Saucer 12.00
Sherbet . . . . 35.00 to 40.00
Soup, Cream . . . 45.00 to 60.00
Sugar, Cover . . . 30.00 to 50.00
Sugar & Creamer,
  Cover 89.00
Tumbler, Iced Tea, Thick,
  15 Oz., 5 1/4 In. 140.00
Tumbler, Iced Tea, Thin,
  15 Oz., 5 1/4 In. 175.00
Tumbler, Thick, 9 Oz.,
  4 1/8 In. 145.00
Tumbler, Thick, 12 Oz.,
  5 1/4 In. 150.00

Pink

Berry Bowl,
  5 In. . . . . 11.00 to 17.50
Berry Bowl, Master,
  8 1/2 In. . . . . . 30.00 to 40.00
Bowl, Cereal,
  6 In. . . . . 23.00 to 32.00
Bowl, Fruit,
  10 1/2 In. . . . . 39.00 to 65.00
Bowl, Vegetable, Oval,
  9 1/2 In. . . . . . 28.00 to 43.00
Butter, Cover . . . 37.00 to 65.00
Butter, Cover
  Only . . . . 25.00 to 35.00
Cake Plate, 3-Footed,
  11 1/2 In. . . . . 44.00 to 55.00
Candy Jar,
  Cover . . . . 50.00 to 65.00

Candy Jar, Cover
  Only 40.00
Creamer . . . . 16.00 to 30.00
Creamer,
  Footed . . . . . . 17.00 to 20.00
Cup . . . . 13.00 to 15.00
Cup & Saucer . . 23.00 to 31.00
Jam Jar 250.00
Pitcher, Ice Lip,
  80 Oz. 170.00
Pitcher, Ice Lip,
  9 In. 190.00
Plate, Bread & Butter,
  6 In. . . . . 8.00 to 14.00
Plate, Dinner,
  9 1/2 In. . . . . . 17.00 to 26.50
Plate, Salad,
  7 1/2 In. . . . . . 23.00 to 35.00
Platter, Oval,
  12 1/2 In. . . . . 28.00 to 40.00
Salt & Pepper . . . 50.00 to 65.00
Saltshaker 31.00
Saucer . . . . 10.00 to 14.00
Sherbet . . . . 12.00 to 22.50
Soup, Cream,
  5 In. . . . . 35.00 to 60.00
Soup, Dish,
  7 3/4 In. . . . . . 52.00 to 65.00
Sugar . . . . 14.00 to 25.00
Sugar, Cover 55.00
Sugar & Creamer 34.00
Sugar & Creamer,
  Cover . . . . 59.00 to 85.00
Tumbler, Iced Tea,
  Footed, 15 Oz.,
  6 1/2 In. . . . . . 55.00 to 65.00
Tumbler, Iced Tea, Thick,
  15 Oz., 5 1/4 In. 165.00
Tumbler, Iced Tea, Thin,
  15 Oz., 5 1/2 In. 50.00

❖

**When you open your
windows in warm
weather, watch out for
blowing curtains. They
may hit glass or china
displayed nearby and
cause damage.**

❖

Tumbler, Thick, 9 Oz.,
    4 1/8 In. . . . . . 38.00 to 65.00
Tumbler, Thick, 12 Oz.,
    5 1/4 In. 155.00
Tumbler, Thin, 9 Oz.,
    4 1/8 In. . . . . . 25.00 to 45.00
Tumbler, Thin, 12 Oz.,
    5 1/4 In. . . . . . 50.00 to 60.00

SHEAF OF WHEAT

Anchor Hocking Glass Corporation, Lancaster, Ohio, made two wheat patterns. Sheaf of Wheat has an embossed wheat design. It was made from 1957 to 1959 in Crystal and Jade-ite. The other pattern, Wheat, is opaque white with a color decal and is listed in its own section in this book.

Crystal
Berry Bowl, 4 1/2 In. 9.00
Bowl, Dessert,
    4 1/2 In. . . . . . . 8.00 to 9.00
Cup & Saucer . . . 9.00 to 10.00
Plate, Dinner, 9 In. 35.00
Tumbler, Juice, 6 Oz. . . . 15.00
Tumbler, Water, 9 Oz. . . . 21.00

Jade-ite
Cup 70.00

SHEFFIELD
See Chinex Classic

SHELL

Shell is a Fire-King dinner-ware pattern made by Anchor Hocking Glass Corporation, Lancaster, Ohio, from 1965 to 1976. It is similar to Swirl, but the edges of Shell items are noticeably scalloped. Dishes were labeled Golden Shell (white with gold trim), Jade-ite Shell, and Lustre Shell (peach lustre). Plain white and iridized white pieces can be found, too. Some collectors use the name Shell for Petalware, which is listed in its own section in this book.

Jade-ite
Bowl, Cereal,
    6 3/8 In. 21.00
Bowl, Dessert,
    4 3/4 In. 25.00
Cup, After Dinner 10.00
Cup & Saucer,
    After Dinner 15.00
Plate, Salad, 7 1/4 In. 25.00

Peach Lustre
Cup 10.00
Cup, After Dinner 10.00
Cup & Saucer,
    After Dinner 20.00

White
Creamer 3.00
Cup & Saucer 3.00
Plate, Dinner,
    10 In. . . . . 4.00 to 7.00
Plate, Salad,
    7 1/4 In. 3.00
Saucer, After Dinner 8.00
Sugar, Cover 8.00

White With Gold
Bowl, 4 3/4 In. . . . . 2.00 to 3.00
Bowl, Cereal,
    6 3/8 In. 11.00
Bowl, Dessert,
    4 3/4 In. 3.50
Bowl, Vegetable, Round,
    8 1/2 In. . . . . . . 5.00 to 9.00
Creamer 3.50
Cup, Short 2.00
Plate, Dinner, 10 In. 6.00
Platter, 9 1/2 x 13 In. 10.00
Platter, 16 x 11 1/2 In. . . . 20.00
Soup, Dish,
    7 5/8 In. . . . . . . 4.00 to 12.00
Sugar 2.00

SHELL
See also Petalware

SHIPS
See White Ship

SHIRLEY TEMPLE

Shirley Temple is not really a pattern, but the dishes with the white enamel decoration picturing Shirley have become popular with collectors. The most famous were made as giveaways with cereal from 1934 to 1942. Several companies, including Hazel Atlas Glass Company and U.S. Glass, made the glassware. Sugars and creamers, bowls, plates, and mugs were made. The milk pitcher and mug have been reproduced since 1982 and the bowl has been reproduced since 1986. Other items with the Shirley Temple decal include a Fostoria Mayfair Green sugar bowl and teacup, a White mug, and an $8\frac{7}{8}$-inch Modern-tone Cobalt Blue plate. In

1972 Libbey Glass Company made tumblers in six sizes.

Cobalt Blue

Mug, Child's,
3 3/4 In. ..... 59.00 to 60.00
Pitcher, Milk ... 45.00 to 60.00

SIERRA

Sierra, or Pinwheel, was made by Jeannette Glass Company from 1931 to 1933. It is found in Green, Pink, and Ultramarine.

Green

Bowl, Cereal,
5 1/2 In. ..... 16.00 to 25.00
Butter, Cover ... 69.00 to 90.00
Cup 16.00
Salt & Pepper 50.00
Sugar 28.00
Sugar, Cover, 3 In. 60.00

Pink

Berry Bowl, Master,
8 1/2 In. 40.00
Bowl, Cereal,
5 1/2 In. ..... 16.00 to 23.00
Bowl, Vegetable,
Oval, 9 1/4 In. 115.00
Butter, Cover 63.00
Butter, Cover Only 30.00
Creamer 28.00
Cup .... 13.00 to 16.00
Cup & Saucer .. 13.00 to 28.00
Pitcher, 32 Oz.,
6 1/2 In. 165.00
Plate, Dinner,
9 In. .... 20.00 to 33.00
Platter, Oval,
11 In. ...... 50.00 to 57.00
Salt & Pepper ... 50.00 to 60.00

Sandwich Tray, Handles,
10 1/4 In. .... 23.00 to 35.00
Saucer .... 8.00 to 10.00
Sugar, Cover ... 22.00 to 50.00
Sugar & Creamer,
Cover 165.00

SKOL

Skol is a Swedish-modern pattern made in the late 1950s and 1960s by Hazel Atlas, then a division of Continental Can Company, Clarksburg, West Virginia. Some collectors call the pattern Dots because of the embossed circles on the outside of the pieces. Items were made in Avocado, Capri Blue, Crystal, and Harvest Gold.

Capri Blue

Bowl, 4 7/8 In. 7.00
Cup .... 5.50 to 6.00
Cup & Saucer .... 5.00 to 9.00
Saucer 2.00
Sherbet, 3 In. 8.00
Tumbler, 3 5/8 In. . 6.00 to 7.00

Crystal

Cup 5.00
Cup & Saucer 7.00
Sherbet, 3 In. 5.00
Tumbler, 2 3/4 In. 5.00
Tumbler, 3 5/8 In. . 6.00 to 7.00
Tumbler, 5 In. 8.00

SMOCKING
See Windsor

SNOWFLAKE
See Doric

When you move, stuff glasses and cups with crumpled paper, then wrap in bubble wrap.

SORENO

Soreno was made by Anchor Hocking Glass Corporation, Lancaster, Ohio, from 1966 to 1970. The pattern has textured horizontal ribs and was made mostly in Avocado and Honey Gold, although pieces in Aquamarine, Aurora (iridescent crystal), Lustre (various colors), and Mardi-Gras can be found. Other related patterns are listed in the Fire-King section in this book.

Aquamarine

Tumbler, On The Rocks,
9 Oz. 6.00

Avocado

Bowl, 4 Qt., 11 3/8 In. 8.00
Plate, Dinner, 10 In. 4.00
Tumbler, Water,
12 Oz., 5 In. 3.00

Honey Gold

Ashtray, 4 1/4 In. 2.50
Ashtray, Round, 8 In. 5.00
Tumbler, Juice, 6 Oz. 3.00

SPHINX
See Centaur

SPIRAL

It is easy to confuse Spiral, a Hocking Glass Company pattern, with Twisted

Optic, made by Imperial Glass Company. Ask to be shown examples of each, because even a picture will not be much help. Looking from the top to the base, Twisted Optic spirals right to left; Spiral twists left to right. There are a few pieces that are exceptions. Spiral pattern beverage and luncheon sets were manufactured from 1928 to 1930 in Crystal, Green, and Pink. It is also sometimes called Spiral Optic or Swirled Big Rib.

Green

Butter Or Ice Tub	28.00 to 30.00
Candy Dish, Cover	32.00
Cup	8.00
Dish, Preserve, Cover	32.00 to 35.00
Plate, Luncheon, 8 In.	4.00 to 7.00
Plate, Sherbet, 6 In.	3.00 to 6.00
Platter, 12 In.	35.00
Salt & Pepper	40.00
Sandwich Server, Center Handle	22.00
Saucer	4.00
Sherbet	6.00
Tumbler, Flat, 9 Oz.	11.00

Pink

Sherbet, Footed	6.00

SPIRAL FLUTES
See Swirl Duncan & Miller

SPIRAL OPTIC
See Spiral

SPOKE
See Patrician

❖

Install locks on all garage doors and windows.

❖

SPORTSMAN SERIES

Hazel Atlas Glass Company made this unusual pattern in the 1940s. It was made in Amethyst, Cobalt Blue, or Crystal with fired-on decoration. Although the name of the series was Sportsman, designs included not only golf, sailboats, hunting, and angelfish, but a few odd choices like windmills. We list White Ship and Windmill separately, although they are sometimes considered part of this pattern.

Cobalt Blue

Cocktail Mixer, Stirrer	25.00
Cocktail Shaker & Tumbler Set, Fox Hunt, 11 Piece	220.00
Pitcher, 8 1/2 In.	35.00
Tumbler, Bird Dog, 4 5/8 In.	25.00
Tumbler, Bromo-Seltzer, 4 5/8 In.	20.00
Tumbler, Couple Dancing, 4 5/8 In.	25.00
Tumbler, Dancing Sailor, 4 7/8 In.	12.00
Tumbler, Dutch Girl, Tulips, 4 5/8 In.	20.00
Tumbler, Fish, 4 5/8 In.	14.00
Tumbler, Hunt Scene, 4 5/8 In.	10.00
Tumbler, Old Mother Goose, 4 5/8 In.	30.00
Tumbler, Skiers, 4 7/8 In.	12.00

Crystal

Ice Bowl, Small	28.00
Tumbler, Iced Tea, 10 1/2 Oz., 4 7/8 In.	15.00
Tumbler, Juice, 3 3/4 In.	12.00 to 15.00

SPUN

Spun was made by Imperial Glass Company, Bellaire, Ohio, in 1935, in Aqua, Cobalt Blue, Crystal, Fired-On Orange, Red, and pastel colors.

Aqua

Pitcher, Water	75.00

Cobalt Blue

Tumbler, 5 In.	18.00

SQUARE
See Charm

STAR

Federal Glass Company, Columbus, Ohio, made the Star pattern in the 1950s. All of the pieces have a central star motif and were made in Amber and Crystal. The tumblers, creamer, and sugar have star-shaped bases.

Amber

Bowl, Dessert,
4 5/8 In. 5.00
Creamer 8.50
Plate, Dinner,
9 3/8 In. 8.00
Plate, Salad, 6 1/4 In. 4.00
Saucer 4.00
Sugar 7.50
Tumbler, Water, 9 Oz.,
3 7/8 In. 7.50

Crystal

Bowl, Vegetable,
8 3/8 In. 9.00
Pitcher, 36 Oz.,
5 3/4 In. 9.00
Sugar 4.00
Tumbler, Juice, 4 1/2 Oz.,
3 3/8 In. . . . . . . 4.00 to 5.00
Tumbler, Whiskey, 1 1/2 Oz.,
2 1/4 In. 3.00

STARLIGHT

Starlight was made by the Hazel Atlas Company of Wheeling, West Virginia, from 1938 to 1940. Full table settings were made of Cobalt Blue, Crystal, Pink, and White. The pattern is pressed, not etched.

Crystal

Bowl, Fruit, Handles 7.00

Bowl, Salad, 11 1/2 In. . . 28.00
Creamer 7.00
Cup 6.00
Cup & Saucer . . . 7.00 to 10.00
Plate, Dinner,
9 1/2 In. . . . . . . 8.00 to 18.00
Relish 10.00
Salt & Pepper 25.00
Sugar . . . . 5.00 to 6.00

STARS & STRIPES

Stars & Stripes is a clear glass pattern made about 1942 by Anchor Hocking Glass Corporation. The pieces have appropriate wartime patriotic designs of stars, stripes, and eagles.

Plate, 8 In. . . . . . 10.00 to 20.00
Sherbet 15.00
Tumbler, 10 Oz., 5 In. . . . 35.00

STIPPLED ROSE BAND
See S Pattern

STRAWBERRY

Strawberry and Cherry-Berry are similar patterns.

The U.S. Glass Company made luncheon sets with strawberry decoration in the early 1930s. Green and Pink were the most commonly used colors, although Crystal and Iridescent Marigold pieces were also made.

Green

Berry Bowl, 4 In. 12.00
Butter,
Cover . . . . . 165.00 to 220.00
Plate, Sherbet, 6 In. 12.00
Sherbet, Footed 11.00

Pink

Berry Bowl,
4 In. . . . . 12.00 to 14.00
Compote,
5 3/4 In. . . . . . 25.00 to 28.00
Pitcher, Water,
7 3/4 In. 225.00
Plate, Salad, 7 1/2 In. 20.00

STRAWBERRY
See also Cherry-Berry

SUN RAY

Sun Ray has embossed panels of vertical ribs that fan out like rays of the sun. Fostoria Glass Company, Moundsville, West Virginia, made the pattern in mainly Crystal from 1935 to 1944. Pieces in Blue, Green, Red, and Yellow have been seen, too.

Crystal

Relish, 2 Sections 16.00
Sherbet, 5 1/2 Oz.,
 3 1/2 In. 9.00

SUNBURST

Crystal dinner sets were made in Sunburst pattern from 1938 to 1941 by Jeannette Glass Company, Jeannette, Pennsylvania.

Berry Bowl, 4 3/4 In. 5.00
Berry Bowl, Master,
 8 1/2 In. 12.00
Bowl, 11 In. .... 25.00 to 29.00
Candlestick, 2-Light,
 Pair 40.00
Cup 10.00
Cup & Saucer ... 8.00 to 14.00
Plate, 5 1/2 In. 11.00
Plate, Dinner,
 9 1/4 In. ..... 14.00 to 24.00
Relish, Oval, 2 Sections,
 8 In. 24.00
Sandwich Server,
 11 3/4 In. .... 12.00 to 27.00
Sugar 9.00

SUNFLOWER

Sunflower was made by Jeannette Glass Company, Jeannette, Pennsylvania, in the late 1920s and early 1930s. It is most commonly found in Pink and two shades of Green. The darker green was used for cake plates given as a premium in sacks of flour. Small quantities of Delphite pieces also were made.

Green

Ashtray, Round,
 5 In. 19.00
Cake Plate, 3-Footed,
 10 In. ...... 12.00 to 35.00
Plate, Dinner, 9 In. 22.00
Sugar 22.00

Pink

Ashtray, Round,
 5 In. .... 10.00 to 15.00
Cake Plate, 3-Footed,
 10 In. .... 8.00 to 25.00
Creamer 22.00
Cup & Saucer 22.00
Plate, Dinner,
 9 In. .... 17.00 to 22.00
Saucer 10.00
Tumbler, Footed, 8 Oz.,
 4 3/4 In. ..... 27.00 to 35.00

SWANKYSWIGS

In October 1933, Kraft Cheese Company began to market cheese spreads in decorated, reusable glass tumblers. The tumbler was made in a 5-ounce size with a smooth beverage lip and a permanent color decoration. The designs were tested and changed as public demand indicated. Hazel Atlas Glass Company made the glasses, which were decorated by hand by a crew of about 280 girls, working in shifts around the clock. In 1937 a silk-screen process was developed, and the Tulip design was made by this new, faster method. The glasses were made thinner and lighter in weight. The decorated Swankyswigs were discontinued from 1941 to 1946, the war years. They were made again from 1947 through 1958. Since then, plain glasses have been used, although a few specially decorated Swankyswigs were produced.

Antique No. 1

Brown, 3 1/2 In. 5.00

Band No. 2

Red & Black, 3 3/8 In. 4.00
Red & Black, 4 3/4 In. 4.00
Red & Black, 5 In. 10.00

Band No. 3

Blue & White,
 3 3/8 In. 4.00

Daisy

Red, White, Green,
 3 3/4 In. 4.00
Red, White, Green,
 4 1/2 In. ..... 15.00 to 20.00

Forget-Me-Not

Blue, 3 1/2 In. 3.00

Kiddie Kup

Green & Yellow,
 Little Jack Horner,
 Frosted, 4 1/2 In. 15.00
Green & Yellow, Miss Muffett,
 Frosted, 4 1/2 In. 15.00
Red, Bicycle, Children, Animals,
 Plastic Lid, 4 1/2 In. ... 10.00

Posy Cornflower No. 1

Light Blue, 3 1/2 In. 5.00

Posy Cornflower No. 2

Black, 3 1/2 In. 4.00
Blue, 3 1/2 In. 4.00
Dark Blue, 3 1/2 In. 4.00

Light Blue,
3 1/2 In. . . . . . . 4.00 to 5.00

Red, 3 1/2 In. 4.00

Posy Jonquil

Yellow, 3 1/2 In. 5.00

Posy Tulip, No. 1

Blue, 3 1/2 In. 4.00

Green, 3 1/2 In. 4.00

Red, 3 1/2 In. 4.00

Red/Green, No Pot,
4 1/2 In. . . . . . 12.00 to 17.00

Posy Violet

Purple, 3 1/2 In. 6.00

Sailboat No. 1

Blue, 3 1/2 In. 10.00

Green, 3 1/2 In. 12.00

SWEET PEAR
See Avocado

SWIRL

Swirl, sometimes called
Double Swirl or Petal
Swirl, was made by Jean-
nette Glass Company in
1937 and 1938. Ultrama-
rine, in a variety of shades,
was the most commonly
used color, but Amber,
Delphite, Ice Blue, and
Pink were also used. Some
pieces have a smooth
edge, while others have a
flower-petal rim.

Amber

Bowl, Cereal, 5 1/4 In. . . 13.00

Candy Dish, 3-Footed . . . 16.00

Creamer, Flat 3.50

Sugar & Creamer 25.00

Delphite

Bowl, Cereal,
5 1/4 In. . . . . . 14.00 to 16.00

Bowl, Salad, 9 In. 30.00

Creamer, Footed 13.00

Sugar, Flat 13.00

Sugar & Creamer, Flat . . . 27.00

Pink

Berry Bowl . . . . 12.00 to 16.00

Bowl, Cereal,
5 1/2 In. . . . . . 13.00 to 14.00

Bowl, Cereal, Smooth
Edge, 5 1/4 In. 17.00

Butter 45.00

Butter,
Cover . . . . . 235.00 to 375.00

Candlestick, Pair 120.00

Candy Dish,
Cover . . . . . 50.00 to 105.00

Candy Dish, Open,
3-Footed . . . . 10.00 to 16.00

Coaster,
3 1/4 In. . . . . . 11.00 to 18.00

Cup . . . . 11.00 to 12.00

Plate, 7 In. 5.00

Plate, Dinner,
9 1/4 In. . . . . . 13.00 to 17.00

Plate, Sherbet,
6 1/2 In. 8.00

Sandwich Server,
12 1/2 In. . . . . 20.00 to 25.00

Sherbet, Low,
Footed . . . . . . 17.00 to 23.00

Soup, Dish, Lug 54.00

Tumbler, 9 Oz.,
4 5/8 In. . . . . . 22.00 to 26.00

Vase, Ruffled Edge, Footed,
6 1/2 In. . . . . . 24.00 to 35.00

Ultramarine

Berry Bowl,
5 1/4 In. . . . . . 14.00 to 27.00

Bowl, Cereal, 5 1/4 In. . . 18.00

Bowl, Footed, Closed Handles,
10 In. . . . . 30.00 to 40.00

Bowl, Salad,
9 In. . . . . 25.00 to 34.00

Candlestick,
2-Light . . . . . . 22.00 to 30.00

Candlestick,
Pair . . . . 31.00 to 55.00

Candy Dish,
3-Footed . . . . . 15.00 to 20.00

Candy Dish,
Cover . . . . . 175.00 to 190.00

Console, Footed,
10 1/2 In. 25.00

Creamer,
Footed . . . . 10.00 to 20.00

Cup . . . . 12.00 to 19.00

Cup & Saucer . . 19.00 to 23.00

Plate, Dinner,
9 1/4 In. 22.00

Plate, Luncheon,
7 1/4 In. . . . . . . 7.00 to 16.00

Plate, Salad, 9 In. 15.00

Plate, Salad, Ruffled Edge,
9 In. 30.00

Plate, Sherbet,
6 1/2 In. . . . . . . 6.00 to 10.00

Salt & Pepper . . . 45.00 to 50.00

Sandwich Server,
12 1/2 In. . . . . 38.00 to 45.00

Saucer . . . . 4.00 to 8.00

Sherbet . . . . 21.00 to 30.00

Soup, Dish,
Lug . . . . 48.00 to 65.00

Sugar, Footed . . . 15.00 to 16.00

Sugar & Creamer,
Footed . . . . 32.00 to 37.00

Tumbler, 13 Oz.,
5 1/8 In. . . . 180.00 to 185.00

Tumbler, Footed,
9 Oz. . . . . 35.00 to 55.00

Vase, Footed,
8 1/2 In. . . . . . 26.00 to 37.00

SWIRL DUNCAN & MILLER

Duncan & Miller Glass
Company, Washington,
Pennsylvania, made a Swirl
pattern, too, sometimes
called Spiral Flutes. It was
made of Amber, Crystal,
and Green glass in 1924,
and Pink in 1926. A few
pieces have been reported

with gold trim and in Blue
or Vaseline-colored glass.

Amber
Compote, 4 3/8 In. 15.00
Plate, Salad, 7 1/2 In. 4.00
Tumbler, Cocktail, Footed,
2 1/2 Oz., 3 3/8 In. 7.00

Crystal
Bowl, 8 In. 18.00

Pink
Bowl, Bouillon,
3 3/4 In. 15.00
Pie Plate, 6 In. . . . 4.00 to 5.00

SWIRL FIRE-KING

Swirl Fire-King is named
for its wide swirled bor-
der. It was made from
1949 to 1962 in Azure-ite
(opaque blue-white),
Golden Anniversary (22K
gold on Ivory), Ivory, Jade-
ite, Pink, Rose-ite, Sunrise
(red trim), and White
(Anchorwhite) with or
without Lustre or pastel
trim. Other related pat-
terns are listed in the Fire-
King section in this book.

Amber
Casserole 5.00

Azure-ite
Plate, Dinner,
9 1/8 In. 12.00
Plate, Salad, 7 3/8 In. 8.00
Saucer, 5 3/4 In. 4.00

Golden Anniversary
Bowl, 4 3/4 In. 2.00
Bowl, 8 In. 6.00
Bowl, Dessert,
4 7/8 In. 4.00
Creamer . . . . 3.00 to 5.00

Cup 3.00
Cup & Saucer 2.00
Plate, 7 1/2 In. 2.00
Plate, Dinner,
9 1/8 In. . . . . . . 3.00 to 6.00
Platter, Oval 10.00
Saucer, 5 3/4 In. 2.00
Soup, Dish 7.00
Sugar 5.00
Sugar, Open 3.00

Ivory
Cup 3.00
Cup & Saucer . . . 4.00 to 12.00
Mixing Bowl,
8 In. . . . . 9.00 to 15.00
Plate, Dinner,
9 1/8 In. . . . . . 9.00 to 14.00
Plate, Salad,
7 3/4 In. 14.00
Platter, Oval,
9 x 12 In. 29.00
Saucer, 5 3/4 In. . . . 1.00 to 4.00
Soup, Dish,
7 5/8 In. . . . . . 12.00 to 20.00

Jade-ite
Mixing Bowl Set,
4 Piece 220.00
Mixing Bowl Set,
5 Piece 375.00

Lustre Trim
Cup & Saucer 10.00
Cup & Saucer,
After Dinner 15.00
Plate, Salad, 7 3/8 In. . . . 10.00

Pink
Bowl, Fruit, 4 7/8 In. 10.00
Creamer 15.00
Cup 7.00
Cup & Saucer 8.00
Plate, Dinner,
9 1/8 In. . . . . 10.00 to 15.00
Plate, Salad,
7 3/8 In. . . . . . 7.00 to 15.00
Saucer, 5 3/4 In. 4.00
Serving Dish,
11 In. 19.00
Soup, Dish 14.00
Soup, Flat Rim,
7 5/8 In. 20.00
Sugar 10.00
Sugar, Cover 25.00

White
Mixing Bowl, 7 In. 9.00
Mixing Bowl,
8 In. . . . . 9.00 to 11.00
Mixing Bowl, 9 In. 16.00

SWIRLED BIG RIB
See Spiral

SWIRLED
SHARP RIB
See Diana

SYLVAN

Sylvan is often called Parrot or Three Parrot be-
cause of the center pattern
on the plates. It was made
by Federal Glass Company
in 1931 and 1932 in
Amber, Blue, Crystal, and
Green. The molds were
later used for the Madrid
pattern.

Amber
Berry Bowl, 5 In. 22.00
Bread & Butter, 6 In. 35.00
Cup & Saucer 80.00
Grill Plate, 10 1/2 In. 32.00
Jam Dish, 7 In. 35.00
Plate, Bread & Butter,
6 In. 25.00
Plate, Dinner, 9 In. 49.00
Plate, Salad, 7 1/2 In. 25.00
Plate, Sherbet, 5 3/4 In. . . 15.00
Saucer 18.00
Sherbet, Cone,
Footed . . . . 27.00 to 35.00

Green
Berry Bowl,
5 In. . . . . 30.00 to 45.00
Bowl, Vegetable,
Oval, 10 In. . . . 61.00 to 75.00

Butter 65.00
Butter,
    Cover ..... 400.00 to 475.00
Creamer .... 50.00 to 65.00
Cup 49.00
Cup & Saucer .. 40.00 to 80.00
Grill Plate, Round,
    10 1/2 In. .... 30.00 to 60.00
Hot Plate, Pointed Edge,
    5 In. 975.00
Pitcher, 80 Oz.,
    8 1/2 In. 6800.00
Plate, Dinner,
    9 In. .... 59.00 to 65.00
Plate, Salad,
    7 1/2 In. ..... 38.00 to 50.00
Platter, Oval,
    11 1/4 In. .... 55.00 to 70.00
Salt &
    Pepper ..... 225.00 to 350.00
Saucer .... 16.00 to 35.00
Sherbet, 4 1/2 In. 1400.00
Sherbet, Cone 35.00
Soup, Dish,
    7 In. .... 60.00 to 65.00
Sugar, 3 3/4 In. 35.00
Sugar Cover 210.00
Sugar,
    Cover Only . 210.00 to 275.00
Tumbler, 4 1/4 In. 325.00
Tumbler, Flat, 12 Oz.,
    5 1/2 In. 395.00
Tumbler, Footed, 10 Oz.,
    4 1/4 In. 225.00
Tumbler, Footed, 12 Oz.,
    5 3/4 In. 375.00

If the metal top on your saltshaker won't unscrew, try this: Turn the saltshaker upside down in a small bowl of white vinegar. Let it soak for about 12 hours. The cap should then be loose. Rub soap on the inside of the cap to keep it from sticking again.

TALLY HO

Tally Ho was made by Cambridge Glass Company, Cambridge, Ohio, beginning around 1932. The pressed pattern was produced plain in several colors, including Amber, Carmen, Crystal, and Royal Blue, and used as a blank for several etchings, including Elaine, Rose Point, and Valencia.

Amber
Ice Bucket 76.00

Carmen
Tumbler, 4 In. 9.00
Tumbler, Footed, 5 Oz. .. 26.00

Crystal
Bowl, Shallow, 2 Handles,
    10 1/4 In. 44.00

TASSEL
See Princess

TEA ROOM

The very Art Deco design of Tea Room has made it popular with collectors; it is even called Moderne Art by some. The Indiana

Glass Company, Dunkirk, Indiana, made it from 1926 to 1931. Dinner sets were made of Amber, Crystal, Green, and Pink glass.

Amber
Sugar &
    Creamer ... 180.00 to 300.00

Crystal
Bowl, Banana Split,
    7 1/2 In. ..... 45.00 to 95.00
Celery Dish, 8 1/2 In. ... 15.00
Creamer, Footed,
    4 1/2 In. 15.00
Creamer, Round,
    3 3/4 In. 25.00
Saltshaker 28.00
Sherbet, Low 12.00
Sherbet, Tall, 4 1/2 In. ... 30.00
Sugar & Creamer,
    Tray 110.00
Tumbler, Malted Milk, Footed,
    12 Oz. .... 45.00 to 50.00
Vase, Ruffled Edge,
    9 1/2 In. ..... 12.00 to 50.00
Vase, Ruffled Edge,
    11 In. ..... 130.00 to 245.00

Green
Bowl, Salad, Round,
    8 3/4 In. ... 110.00 to 150.00
Candlestick,
    Pair .... 100.00 to 195.00
Celery Dish,
    8 1/4 In. 35.00
Creamer, 4 In. 25.00
Cup & Saucer 150.00
Finger Bowl 115.00
Goblet, 9 Oz. 85.00
Ice Bucket .... 75.00 to 100.00
Mustard, Cover 100.00
Parfait, Green 55.00
Pitcher, 64 Oz. 200.00
Relish,
    2 Sections .... 30.00 to 40.00
Salt & Pepper 135.00
Saltshaker ..... 38.00 to 40.00
Sandwich Server,
    Center Handle,
    10 1/2 In. .. 195.00 to 210.00
Sugar, Round,
    4 In. .... 15.00 to 30.00
Sugar & Creamer 95.00

Sugar & Creamer,
Berry Set, Center
Handle ...... 60.00 to 65.00
Sugar & Creamer,
Tray .... 75.00 to 95.00
Tumbler, Footed, 6 Oz.,
5 In. .... 30.00 to 50.00
Tumbler, Footed,
8 Oz. .... 38.00 to 55.00
Tumbler, Footed,
9 Oz. 45.00
Tumbler, Malted Milk,
12 Oz. 55.00
Vase, Ruffled Edge,
6 1/2 In. 150.00
Vase, 11 In. .. 200.00 to 275.00

Pink
Bowl, Banana Split,
7 1/2 In. 215.00
Bowl, Salad, Deep 130.00
Bowl, Vegetable, Oval,
9 1/2 In. .... 75.00 to 110.00
Candlestick, Pair 90.00
Celery Dish 50.00
Finger Bowl .... 79.00 to 90.00
Ice Bucket .... 75.00 to 135.00
Mustard, Cover 100.00
Parfait .... 55.00 to 145.00
Pitcher ...... 95.00 to 210.00
Plate, Sherbet,
6 1/2 In. 42.00
Relish,
2 Sections .... 35.00 to 40.00
Salt & Pepper .. 65.00 to 135.00
Sandwich Server, Center
Handle, 10 1/2 In. 160.00
Sherbet, Low ... 28.00 to 50.00
Sherbet, Tall ... 50.00 to 70.00
Sugar & Creamer,
Round .... 55.00 to 60.00
Sugar & Creamer, Tray, Center
Handle, Berry Set 95.00
Tray, Center
Handle .... 145.00 to 155.00
Tray, For Sugar &
Creamer ..... 55.00 to 60.00
Tumbler, 6 Oz.,
4 3/4 In. ..... 35.00 to 60.00
Tumbler,
11 Oz. .... 45.00 to 65.00
Tumbler, Flat, 8 Oz. ... 215.00
Tumbler, Footed,
8 Oz. 38.00
Vase, 11 In. .. 180.00 to 200.00

Vase, Ruffled Edge,
6 1/2 In. .... 85.00 to 120.00

TEAR DROP
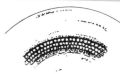

Tear Drop, a pattern available in full dinnerware sets, was made by Duncan & Miller Glass Company, Washington, Pennsylvania, from 1934 to 1955. It was made only in Crystal.

Butter, Metal
Cover ...... 20.00 to 24.00
Candlestick, 4 In. 10.00
Cruet, Stopper,
4 1/4 In. 20.00
Cup & Saucer 7.00
Goblet, Claret 18.00
Goblet, Wine, 3 Oz.,
4 3/4 In. 18.00
Marmalade,
Cover ...... 35.00 to 40.00
Plate, 6 In. 4.00
Plate, Luncheon,
8 1/2 In. 7.00
Plate, Salad, 7 1/2 In. 5.00
Relish, 2 Sections 15.00
Relish, 2 Sections,
Round 8.00
Relish, 5 Sections,
Scalloped, 12 In. 32.00
Sherbet, 5 Oz., 2 1/2 In. ... 6.00
Sugar & Creamer 16.00

❖

Some disciplined collectors have a rule: Only add a new piece to the collection if you can get rid of a less desirable old one. Most of us just keep adding.

❖

Tumbler, Juice, Footed,
5 Oz., 3 1/2 In. 12.00

TERRACE

Terrace was made by Duncan & Miller Glass Company, Washington, Pennsylvania, in 1955 in Amber, Blue, Crystal, and Ruby.

Blue
Dish, Lemon, 2 Handles,
Underplate, 6 In. 27.00
Crystal
Bowl, Low, 9 In. 20.00
Relish, 2 Sections,
5 3/4 In. 12.50
Relish, 4 Sections,
12 In. 23.00
Ruby
Bowl, 2 Handles, 6 In. ... 56.00

THISTLE

Thistle pattern was made by Macbeth-Evans Glass Company from 1929 to 1930. The pattern pictures large thistles primarily on Pink pieces, but Crystal, Green, and Yellow dishes also were made. Reproductions have been made.

Crystal
Plate, Luncheon, 8 In. ... 10.00

Green

Bowl, Fruit,
   10 1/4 In. 410.00
Cup 38.00
Cup & Saucer 36.00
Plate, Luncheon,
   8 In. . . . . 18.00 to 24.00
Saucer 12.00

Pink

Bowl, 5 1/2 In. 60.00
Cake Plate, 13 In. 300.00
Cup 35.00
Cup & Saucer . . 39.00 to 49.00
Grill Plate,
   10 1/4 In. 45.00
Plate, Luncheon,
   8 In. . . . . 24.00 to 27.00

THREADING
See Old English

THREE BANDS

Three Bands is the collector-given name for a pattern by Anchor Hocking Glass Company, Lancaster, Ohio. The dishes have three slightly scalloped bands embossed around the edge or top. Pieces were made in Burgundy, Ivory, Jade-ite, and Peach Lustre from 1952 to 1956. Other related patterns are listed in the Fire-King section in this book.

Ivory

Bowl, Dessert 20.00
Cup & Saucer 4.00

THREE PARROT
See Sylvan

TIERED BLOCK
See Party Line

TIERED OCTAGON
See Octagon

❖

When you move, wrap dishes in bubble wrap and pack on edge. If you have no bubble wrap, put each dish in a plastic bag to keep it clean, then wrap in newspaper and pack on edge. Put about three inches of crumpled paper on the bottom of the carton.

❖

TIERED SEMI OPTIC
See Party Line

TROJAN

The Fostoria Glass Company made Trojan. The etched glass dishes were made in Rose from 1929 to 1935, Topaz from 1929 to 1938, and Gold Tint from 1938 to 1944. It also was made in Green. Crystal bases were used on some pieces from 1931 to 1944.

Topaz

Creamer, Footed 20.00
Goblet, Cocktail, 3 Oz.,
   5 1/4 In. 30.00
Plate, Bread & Butter,
   6 In. . . . . 5.00 to 9.00
Plate, Salad, 7 1/2 In. 8.00
Relish, 8 1/2 In. 20.00

Sherbet, Low,
   4 1/4 In. 16.00
Soup, Cream, Footed 22.00
Tumbler, 5 Oz. 25.00
Tumbler, Footed,
   2 1/2 Oz. . . . . . 65.00 to 85.00
Tumbler, Footed,
   12 Oz. 30.00

TULIP

Tulip pattern pictures the side of a tulip in a very stylized border. It was made by the Dell Glass Company of Millville, New Jersey, during the 1930s. Amber, Amethyst, Blue, Crystal, and Green pieces were made. Fire-King made mixing bowls with tulip decals. Fire-King is listed in its own section in this book.

Amethyst

Cup 22.00

Blue

Creamer 25.00
Cup 14.00
Cup & Saucer 24.00
Ice Tub, 4 3/4 In. Wide,
   2 5/8 In. Deep 95.00
Plate, Bread & Butter,
   6 In. . . . . 7.00 to 10.00
Plate, Salad, 7 1/4 In. 17.00
Saucer 9.00

Green

Creamer 20.00
Cup 15.00
Cup & Saucer 23.00

Plate, Bread & Butter,
6 In. 9.00

Plate, Dinner,
10 In. 34.00

Plate, Salad,
7 1/4 In. 15.00

Saucer 5.00

Sherbet . . . . 20.00 to 25.00

TURQUOISE BLUE

Turquoise Blue, one of the patterns made by Anchor Hocking Glass Corporation, is a plain pattern named for its color. Mixing bowls were made in 1-pt., 1-qt., 2-qt., and 3-qt. sizes. It was made from 1956 to 1958. Other related patterns are listed in the Fire-King section in this book.

Berry Bowl,
4 1/2 In. . . . . . . 6.00 to 8.00

Bowl, Cereal, 5 In. 18.00

Bowl, Cereal, Footed,
10 Oz., 4 7/8 In. 15.00

Bowl, Vegetable, 8 In. . . . 22.00

Creamer . . . . 8.00 to 10.00

Cup 4.00

Cup & Saucer . . . 5.00 to 12.00

Mixing Bowl, Splash Proof,
6 3/4 In. 20.00

Mixing Bowl, Splash Proof,
8 1/2 In. 25.00

Mug, Coffee,
8 Oz. . . . . 10.00 to 16.00

Plate, Bread & Butter,
6 1/8 In. . . . . . 20.00 to 25.00

Plate, Dinner,
9 In. . . . . 7.00 to 9.00

Plate, Dinner,
10 In. . . . . . . 28.00 to 38.00

Plate, Salad,
7 In. . . . . . . 11.00 to 12.00

Relish, 3 Sections,
22K Gold Trim 15.00

Saucer 2.00

Soup, Dish,
6 5/8 In. . . . . 25.00 to 30.00

Sugar 10.00

TWIST

Twist is one of the most popular patterns by A. H. Heisey & Company, Newark, Ohio. The Art Deco–style pattern includes square, stepped feet and lightning bolt handles. Pieces were made from 1928 to 1937 in Flamingo (pink), Marigold (deep yellow), Moongleam (green), and Sahara (light yellow). Most pieces are marked with the Diamond H logo.

Flamingo

Bowl, 8 In. 50.00

Ice Bucket 52.00

Moongleam

Plate, Cheese,
2 Handles 15.00

Sahara

Pickle, 7 In. 25.00

Relish, 10 In. 35.00

Vase, Nasturtium, 8 In. . . 98.00

❖

In snowy weather, make tracks both going in and out of your door. Just one set of tracks leaving the house is an invitation to an intruder. Or perhaps walk out of the house backwards.

❖

TWISTED OPTIC

Twisted Optic, or Line No. 313, is the pattern sometimes confused with Spiral. Be sure to look at the information about that pattern. Imperial Glass Company of Bellaire, Ohio, made Twisted Optic luncheon sets from 1927 to 1930 in Amber, Blue, Canary Yellow, two shades of Green, and Pink.

Amber

Compote, Ladle 30.00

Sugar 7.00

Vase, Handles, Rolled
Rim, 7 1/2 In. 35.00

Blue

Candlestick, 3 1/2 In.,
Pair 55.00

Juice Set, Pitcher, 2 7/8-In.
Tumblers, 9 Piece 45.00

Water Set, Pitcher, 5-In.
Tumblers, 7 Piece 50.00

Green

Creamer 3.00

Cup 4.00

Dish, Mayonnaise 20.00

Plate, Luncheon,
8 In. . . . . 2.00 to 9.00

Plate, Salad, 7 In. 3.00

Pink

Bowl, Ruffled Edge 18.00

Bowl, Salad, Round,
7 In. 17.00

Coaster 12.00

Cup 5.00

Cup & Saucer 6.00

Plate, Luncheon,
8 In. . . . . 2.00 to 9.00

U.S. OCTAGON
See Octagon

VERNON
See No. 616

VERSAILLES

Versailles by Fostoria
Glass Company was made
in many colors during the
years of its production,
1928 to 1944. Azure Blue,
Green, and Rose were
made from 1928 to 1944,
Topaz from 1929 to 1938,
and Gold Tint from 1938
to 1944. Crystal bases
were used with colored
glass from 1931 to 1944.

Azure Blue
Bowl, 6 In. 45.00
Bowl, Handle, 6 In. 35.00
Compote, 7 In. 150.00
Oyster Cocktail 50.00
Pitcher 850.00
Sauceboat, Under-
plate . . . . . 925.00 to 1250.00
Sherbet, 4 1/4 In. 32.00
Tumbler, 9 Oz.,
5 1/4 In. 55.00
Tumbler, Iced Tea, Footed,
12 Oz., 6 In. 60.00
Underplate, For Soup,
Cream 25.00

Topaz
Baker, Oval, 9 In. 55.00
Berry Bowl, 5 In. 23.00

Bowl, Centerpiece, Scroll,
10 In. . . . . . . 45.00 to 58.00
Candlestick, Scroll, 5 In.,
Pair . . . . 70.00 to 90.00
Console, 12 In. 75.00
Cup & Saucer 23.00
Finger Bowl,
Underplate 60.00
Goblet, Wine, 3 Oz.,
5 1/2 In. 50.00
Pitcher 350.00
Plate, Dinner, 9 1/2 In. . . 40.00
Plate, Salad, 7 1/2 In. 7.00
Saltshaker 43.00
Soup, Dish 65.00
Underplate, For Finger
Bowl 15.00
Vase, Flip, 8 In. 350.00

VERTICAL RIBBED
See Queen Mary

VESPER

Vesper was made by the
Fostoria Glass Company
of Ohio and West Virginia
from 1926 to 1934. Din-
ner sets were made in
Amber, Blue, and Green.

Amber
Bowl, 5 1/2 In. 12.00
Plate, Bread & Butter,
6 In. 5.50

Blue
Plate, Dinner,
10 1/2 In. 155.00

Green
Bowl, Cereal, 6 1/2 In. . . 27.00
Finger Bowl,
Underplate . . . 38.00 to 40.00

VICTORY

The Diamond Glass-Ware
Company, Indiana, Penn-
sylvania, made Victory pattern from 1929 to 1932. It
is known in Amber, Black,
Cobalt Blue, Green, and
Pink. A few pieces have
gold trim.

Amber
Sugar 16.00

Cobalt Blue
Bowl, Cereal,
6 1/2 In. 50.00
Candlestick, Pair 125.00
Cup 30.00
Cup & Saucer . . 37.00 to 50.00
Goblet, Water, 7 Oz.,
5 In. . . . . 75.00 to 90.00
Gravy Boat,
Underplate 350.00
Plate, Bread & Butter,
6 In. 16.00
Plate, Dinner, 9 In. 55.00
Plate, Luncheon,
8 In. . . . . 25.00 to 28.00
Sandwich Server, Center
Handle 80.00
Sandwich Server,
Gold Trim 75.00
Saucer 10.00
Soup, Dish 65.00

Green
Bowl, 12 1/2 In. 44.00
Bowl, Vegetable, Oval,
9 In. 39.00
Cup & Saucer 13.00
Plate, Bread & Butter,
5 3/4 In. 9.00
Plate, Dinner, 9 In. 25.00
Plate, Luncheon,
7 3/4 In. 5.50
Sandwich Server,
Center Handle 40.00
Saucer 4.00

Soup, Dish,
8 1/2 In. 19.00
Sugar, Footed 15.00

Pink
Cup 10.00
Cup & Saucer . . 15.00 to 18.00
Gravy 50.00
Plate, Cracker 20.00
Plate, Dinner, 9 In. 25.00
Sandwich Server, Center
Handle 30.00
Soup, Dish, 12 1/2 In. . . . 35.00

VITROCK

Vitrock is both a kitchenware and a dinnerware
pattern. It has a raised
flowered rim and is often
called Floral Rim or
Flower Rim by collectors.
It was made by Hocking
Glass Company from 1934
to 1937 and resembles
embossed china. It was
made in White, sometimes
with fired-on colors, in
solid Red or Green, and
with decal-decorated
centers.

White
Berry Bowl, 4 In. 5.25
Bowl, Cereal,
7 1/2 In. 10.00
Bowl, Cereal, Fired-On
Red, 7 1/2 In. 75.00
Bowl, Cereal, Tulips,
7 1/2 In. . . . . 25.00 to 35.00
Bowl, Fruit, 6 In. 5.00
Bowl, Vegetable, Tulips,
9 1/2 In. 35.00

Canister, Coffee, Dark,
40 Oz. 300.00
Canister, Metal Cover,
Red Circle Flowers 56.00
Canister, Sugar, Dark,
40 Oz. 300.00
Cup 8.00
Cup & Saucer . . . . 8.00 to 9.00
Flour Shaker, Cover, Red
Circle 33.00
Grease Jar, Lid, Tulips . . . 40.00
Grease Jar, Red
Flowers 48.00
Pepper Shaker, Cover, Red,
Green Tulips . . 28.00 to 34.00
Plate, Salad, 7 1/4 In. 3.00
Platter, 11 1/2 In. 38.00
Saucer 3.00
Shaker, Cover, Red
Circle 30.00
Soup, Cream,
5 1/2 In. . . . . 12.00 to 17.00
Sugar & Creamer 5.00
Vase, Tab Handles,
7 3/4 In. . . . . 18.00 to 25.00

VIVID BANDS
See Petalware

WAFFLE
See Waterford

WATERFORD

Waterford, or Waffle, pattern was made by Anchor
Hocking Glass Corpora-
tion from 1938 to 1944.
Crystal and Pink are the
most common colors; Yel-
low and White were used

less extensively. Some of
the Opaque White pieces
also have fired-on pink and
green. In the 1950s some
Forest Green pieces were
made.

Crystal
Berry Bowl,
4 3/4 In. . . . . . . 4.00 to 8.00
Berry Bowl,
8 1/4 In. . . . . . 8.00 to 20.00
Bowl, Cereal,
5 1/2 In. 30.00
Butter 5.00
Butter, Cover . . . 25.00 to 30.00
Cake Plate, Handles,
10 1/4 In. . . . 10.00 to 14.00
Coaster, 4 In. . . . . . 3.00 to 5.00
Creamer 5.00
Creamer, Oval 7.00
Cup 7.00
Cup & Saucer 11.00
Goblet,
5 1/4 In. . . . . 10.00 to 17.00
Goblet, Miss America Style,
5 1/2 In. . . . . 32.00 to 35.00
Pitcher, Juice, Tilted,
42 Oz. 25.00
Plate, Dinner,
9 5/8 In. . . . . . 8.00 to 14.00
Plate, Salad,
7 1/8 In. . . . . . . 6.00 to 8.00
Plate, Sherbet,
6 In. . . . . 4.00 to 6.00
Relish, 5 Sections,
13 3/4 In. . . . . 16.00 to 25.00
Salt & Pepper 9.00
Salt & Pepper, Red Plastic
Cover . . . . 11.00 to 13.00
Salt & Pepper, Tall 16.00
Sandwich Server,
13 3/4 In. . . . . 8.00 to 20.00
Saucer . . . . 2.00 to 4.00
Sherbet, Footed . . . 4.00 to 6.00
Sherbet, Footed, Scalloped
Base . . . . 10.00 to 13.00
Sugar, Cover . . . . 6.00 to 18.00
Sugar, Cover,
Oval . . . . 8.00 to 12.00
Sugar, No Cover . . 5.00 to 7.00
Sugar & Creamer, Miss
America Style,
Cover . . . . 20.00 to 25.00

❖

Never leave ladders leaning on the building or piled up near the house. Chain and lock the ladders so the casual burglar can't use them. Trim your trees to make access to the roof more difficult.

❖

Tumbler, Water, Footed, 10 Oz.,
4 7/8 In. . . . . . 10.00 to 15.00

Forest Green
Ashtray 8.00

Pink
Berry Bowl,
4 3/4 In. . . . . . 16.00 to 24.00
Berry Bowl,
8 1/4 In. 27.00
Butter 25.00
Cake Plate, Handles,
10 1/4 In. . . . . 20.00 to 22.00
Cup & Saucer . . 20.00 to 21.00
Plate, Dinner,
9 5/8 In. 25.00
Sandwich Server,
13 3/4 In. . . . . 30.00 to 32.00
Saucer 5.00
Sherbet . . . . 15.00 to 18.00
Tumbler, Footed, 10 Oz.,
4 7/8 In. . . . . . 24.00 to 31.00

WAVERLY

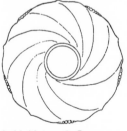

A. H. Heisey & Company, Newark, Ohio, made the Waverly pattern, originally

called Oceanic, from 1940 to 1957. The items were made in Crystal and sold plain or with Heisey's popular Orchid and Rose etchings.

Bowl, 4 Sections, 9 In. . . 95.00
Bowl, Round, Footed,
6 1/2 In. 25.00
Cake Stand 25.00
Cup 12.00
Sugar & Creamer 13.50

WEDDING BAND
See Moderntone

WESTMORELAND SANDWICH
See Princess Feather

WEXFORD

Wexord is an imitation cut glass pattern made by Anchor Hocking Glass Corporation, Lancaster, Ohio, from 1967 to 1998. Pieces were made in Crystal, Green, Pewter Mist, and with fired-on decorations. Other related patterns are listed in the Fire-King section in this book.

Crystal
Ashtray, 8 1/2 In. 6.00
Bowl, Footed, Center
Piece, 8 In. 12.00
Bowl, Fruit, Footed,
10 In. 12.00

Bowl, Salad, 5 1/4 In. 3.50
Bowl, Serving, Scalloped,
14 In. 10.00
Candy Dish, Cover,
Footed, 6 3/4 In. 12.00
Creamer, 8 Oz. 3.00
Cruet, Stopper, 5 1/2 Oz. . . 3.50
Goblet, Water, Footed,
9 1/2 Oz. 3.00
Jar, Storage, Cover,
58 Oz. 5.00
Pitcher, Water,
64 Oz. . . . . 8.00 to 18.00
Punch Bowl, 11 Qt. 10.00
Punch Bowl Set, Stand,
18 Pieces 55.00
Punch Cup, 7 Oz. 2.00
Relish, 3 Sections,
8 1/2 In. 4.00
Sherbet, Footed,
7 Oz. 2.00
Sugar, Cover,
8 Oz. 3.00
Sugar & Creamer . . 3.50 to 6.00
Tumbler, Iced Tea,
16 Oz. 3.50
Vase, Bud, 9 In. 3.00
Vase, Footed, 10 1/2 In. . . 13.00

WHEAT

Wheat glass was made by Anchor Hocking Glass Corporation from 1962 to 1966. It is part of the Fire-King Ovenware line. It is a white opaque glass decorated with a natural-looking spray of wheat. A few pieces were given added decoration. Anchor Hocking also made transparent glassware with an embossed wheat design. Sheaf of Wheat is listed in its own section in this book. Other companies made glassware with Wheat designs, but only the Anchor Hocking glass is listed here.

Bowl, 4 5/8 In. 3.00
Bowl, Vegetable,
  8 1/4 In. 12.00
Cake Pan, Square,
  8 In. . . . . 6.00 to 10.00
Casserole, 1 Qt. 6.00
Casserole, Cover,
  1 1/2 Quart . . . . 8.00 to 15.00
Casserole, Knob Cover,
  1 Pt. 9.00
Creamer 4.00
Cup & Saucer . . . . 3.50 to 6.00
Custard Cup,
  6 Oz. . . . . 3.00 to 4.00
Plate, Dinner,
  10 In. . . . . 4.50 to 7.00
Platter,
  9 x 12 In. . . . . 12.00 to 13.00
Snack Set, Tray & Cup,
  2 Piece 4.50
Soup, Dish . . . . 5.00 to 8.00
Sugar 3.50
Tumbler, Juice,
  5 Oz. . . . . 6.00 to 15.00

WHIRLY-TWIRLY

Anchor Hocking Glass Corporation made Whirly-Twirly pattern in the 1940s. It was Forest Green or Royal Ruby.

Forest Green
Pitcher, 3 Qt. 38.00
Tumbler, 5 Oz.,
  3 1/2 In. . . . . . . 4.00 to 5.00

Tumbler, 9 Oz., 4 In. 6.00

Royal Ruby
Tumbler, 5 Oz.,
  3 1/2 In. . . . . . . 7.00 to 9.00
Tumbler, 9 Oz.,
  4 In. . . . . 9.00 to 10.00
Tumbler, 12 Oz.,
  5 In. 11.00

WHITE SAIL
See White Ship

WHITE SHIP

White Ship, also called Sail Boat, Sailing Ship, or White Sail, is really part of the Sportsman series made by Hazel Atlas Glass Company in 1938. The ships are enamel decorations on Amethyst, Cobalt Blue, or Crystal. The enamel decorations are sometimes in color.

Cobalt Blue
Ice Bowl 35.00
Pitcher, Ice Lip, 86 Oz.,
  9 1/4 In. . . . . 65.00 to 70.00
Pitcher & Tumbler Set,
  Ice Lip, 86 Oz.,
  6 Tumblers, 9 Oz. 125.00
Plate, Dinner, 9 In. 65.00
Plate, Salad, 8 In. 55.00
Tumbler, Iced Tea,
  10 1/2 Oz., 4 7/8 In. . . . 15.00
Tumbler, Juice, 5 Oz.,
  3 1/2 In. 17.00
Tumbler, Old Fashioned, 8 Oz.,
  3 1/2 In. . . . . 16.00 to 24.00
Tumbler, Roly Poly,
  6 Oz. 15.00

Tumbler, Water, 9 Oz.,
  3 3/4 In. . . . . 12.00 to 14.00

WILDFLOWER
See No. 618

WILDROSE
See Dogwood

WILDROSE WITH APPLE
  BLOSSOM
See Flower Garden with
  Butterflies

WINDMILL

Windmill, or Dutch, is a part of the Sportsman series made by Hazel Atlas Glass Company in 1938. It pictures a landscape with a windmill. The windmills are enamel decorations on Cobalt Blue, Crystal, or Amethyst glass.

Cobalt Blue
Cocktail Shaker,
  Stirrer . . . . . . 25.00 to 58.00
Ice Bowl, Small 28.00
Tumbler, Heavy
  Bottom, 4 Oz. 28.00
Tumbler, Water,
  4 1/2 In. 13.00

Outdoor lights help prevent crime, but install them high enough so that they are difficult to unscrew.

Crystal

Tumbler, Roly Poly,
6 Oz. . . . . 7.00 to 10.00

WINDSOR

Windsor pattern, also called Diamond, Smocking, or Windsor Diamond, was made by Jeannette Glass Company, Jeannette, Pennsylvania, from 1936 to 1946. The pattern is most easily found in Crystal, Green, and Pink, although pieces were made in Amberina, Delphite, Ice Blue, and Red.

Crystal

Ashtray 9.00
Berry Bowl,
4 3/4 In. . . . . 3.00 to 5.00
Bowl, 7 3/8 In. 15.00
Bowl, 8 1/4 In. . . . 9.00 to 15.00
Bowl, Boat Shape,
11 3/4 x 7 In. 30.00
Bowl, Cereal,
5 1/2 In. 11.00
Bowl, Pointed Edge,
5 In. 10.00
Bowl, Pointed Edge,
8 In. 10.00
Butter, Cover . . . 25.00 to 30.00
Candlestick,
3 In. . . . . 8.00 to 12.50
Candlestick, 3 In.,
Pair . . . . 18.00 to 29.00
Chop Plate, 13 5/8 In. . . . 20.00
Creamer . . . . 4.00 to 8.00
Cup . . . . 3.00 to 5.00
Cup & Saucer . . . 4.00 to 10.00

Pitcher, 16 Oz.,
4 1/2 In. . . . . . 20.00 to 27.50
Pitcher, 52 Oz.,
6 3/4 In. . . . . . 12.00 to 30.00
Plate, Dinner,
9 In. . . . . 7.00 to 18.00
Plate, Salad,
7 In. 16.00
Powder Box,
Cover . . . . 8.50 to 15.00
Punch Bowl, Pointed
Edge, 10 1/2 In. 40.00
Relish, 2 Sections,
11 1/2 In. 10.00
Relish, 3 Sections,
11 1/2 In. 15.00
Relish, Oval, Scalloped
Edge, 11 1/2 In. 15.00
Salt & Pepper 9.00
Saltshaker 9.00
Sandwich Server,
10 1/4 In. . . . . . 6.00 to 18.00
Soup, Cream,
5 In. . . . . 5.00 to 6.00
Sugar, Cover . . . 10.00 to 12.00
Sugar, Cover Only 5.00
Sugar &
Creamer . . . . . . 9.50 to 14.00
Tumbler, 5 Oz.,
3 1/4 In. . . . . . . 8.00 to 12.00
Tumbler, Footed,
7 1/4 In. 19.00
Tumbler, Footed,
9 Oz., 4 In. 9.00
Tumbler, Footed,
11 Oz., 5 In. . . . 9.00 to 11.50

Delphite

Ashtray 52.00

Green

Ashtray 45.00
Berry Bowl,
4 3/4 In. . . . . . 10.00 to 12.00
Bowl, Boat Shape,
7 x 11 3/4 In. . 40.00 to 55.00
Bowl, Cereal . . . 25.00 to 28.00
Bowl, Vegetable, Oval,
9 1/2 In. . . . . . 33.00 to 38.00
Butter, Cover . . . 90.00 to 98.00
Cake Plate, Footed,
10 3/4 In. . . . . 33.00 to 40.00
Chop Plate,
13 5/8 In. . . . . 38.00 to 55.00
Coaster . . . . 22.00 to 24.00

Creamer . . . . . . 12.00 to 18.00
Cup 12.00
Cup & Saucer . . 18.00 to 22.00
Pitcher, 52 Oz.,
6 3/4 In. 68.00
Plate, Dinner,
9 In. . . . . 25.00 to 28.00
Plate, Salad,
7 In. . . . . 19.00 to 30.00
Plate, Sherbet, 6 In. 8.00
Platter, Oval,
11 1/2 In. . . . . 22.00 to 43.00
Salt & Pepper . . . 37.00 to 55.00
Saltshaker 25.00
Sandwich Server,
Handles, 10 In. 27.00
Saucer 8.00
Sherbet 12.00
Soup, Cream 30.00
Sugar, Cover 33.00
Sugar, No Cover 15.00
Tray, 2 Handles,
4 1/8 x 9 In. 45.00
Tray, 2 Handles, Square,
4 In. . . . . 15.00 to 26.00
Tumbler, 9 Oz.,
4 In. . . . . 28.00 to 30.00
Tumbler, 12 Oz.,
5 In. . . . . 50.00 to 52.00
Tumbler, Juice, 5 Oz.,
3 1/4 In. . . . . . 36.00 to 37.00

Ice Blue

Candlestick, Shell, Footed,
2 1/2 In., Pair 165.00
Cup 55.00
Plate, 9 In. 55.00

Pink

Ashtray,
5 3/4 In. . . . . . 31.00 to 55.00
Berry Bowl,
4 3/4 In. . . . . . . 9.00 to 12.50
Berry Bowl, Master,
8 1/2 In. . . . . . 16.00 to 30.00
Berry Bowl, Pointed Edge,
4 3/4 In. . . . . . 25.00 to 43.00
Bowl, 3-Footed,
7 1/8 In. 37.00
Bowl, Boat Shape,
7 x 11 3/4 In. . 28.00 to 50.00
Bowl, Cereal,
5 3/8 In. . . . . . 20.00 to 37.00
Bowl, Fruit,
12 1/2 In. . . 120.00 to 135.00

Bowl, Handles,
    8 In. . . . . 25.00 to 35.00

Bowl, Handles,
    9 1/2 In. 30.00

Bowl, Pointed Edge,
    5 In. . . . . 39.00 to 40.00

Bowl, Pointed Edge,
    8 In. . . . . 65.00 to 105.00

Butter, Cover . . . 48.00 to 68.00

Cake Plate, Footed,
    10 3/4 In. 27.00

Chop Plate,
    13 5/8 In. . . . . 33.00 to 50.00

Chop Plate, 19 In. 35.00

Compote, 6 In. 15.00

Console,
    12 1/2 In. . . 105.00 to 135.00

Creamer . . . . 11.00 to 16.00

Cup . . . . 10.00 to 12.00

Cup & Saucer . . 15.00 to 19.00

Pitcher, 16 Oz.,
    4 1/2 In. 300.00

Pitcher, 52 Oz.,
    6 3/4 In. . . . . . 24.00 to 50.00

Plate, Dinner,
    9 In. . . . . 18.00 to 28.50

Plate, Salad,
    7 In. . . . . 15.00 to 24.00

Plate, Sherbet,
    6 In. . . . . 5.00 to 6.00

Platter, Oval,
    11 1/2 In. . . . . 20.00 to 30.00

Relish, 3 Sections,
    Oval 350.00

Salt & Pepper . . . 36.00 to 50.00

Saltshaker 20.00

Sandwich Server, Handles,
    10 1/4 In. . . . . 15.00 to 28.00

Saucer . . . . 2.50 to 6.00

Sherbet . . . . 11.00 to 16.00

Soup, Cream . . . 23.00 to 38.00

Sugar, Cover . . . 28.00 to 40.00

Sugar, Cover,
    Holiday . . . . 125.00 to 165.00

Sugar, Cover,
    Ruffled Edge 30.00

Sugar, Open . . . . 10.00 to 16.00

Sugar & Creamer,
    Cover . . . . 35.00 to 49.00

Tray, 2 Sections,
    8 3/4 x 8 3/4 In. 210.00

Tray, 8 1/2 x 9 3/4 In. . . 265.00

Tray, Handles,
    4 1/8 x 9 In. 45.00

Tray, Handles,
    8 1/2 x 9 3/4 In. 45.00

Tumbler, 11 Oz.,
    4 5/8 In. . . . . . 17.00 to 23.00

Tumbler, Iced Tea,
    12 Oz., 5 In. . . 24.00 to 40.00

Tumbler, Juice, 5 Oz.,
    3 1/4 In. . . . . 25.00 to 39.00

Tumbler, Water, 9 Oz.,
    4 In. . . . . 15.00 to 24.00

WINDSOR DIAMOND
See Windsor

WINGED MEDALLION
See Madrid

X DESIGN

X Design was a Hazel
Atlas Glass Company pat-
tern made from 1928 to
1932. The name indicates
that the pattern has rows
of X's in grids. It was
made in Crystal, Green,
and Pink. Only a table set
was made.

Green
Salt & Pepper 6.00

Tumbler, 5 1/4 In. 12.00

Pink
Saltshaker 6.00

DEPRESSION GLASS

Clubs and Publications

CLUBS

Akro Agate Collectors Club, *Clarksburg Crow* (newsletter), 10 Bailey St., Clarksburg, WV 26301-2524.
Web site: www.akroagate.com

Fenton Art Glass Collectors of America, Inc., *Butterfly Net* (newsletter), P.O. Box 384, Williamstown, WV 26187.
Web site: www.collectoronline.com/club-FAGCA.html

Fostoria Glass Collectors, Inc., *Glass Works* (newsletter), P.O. Box 1625, Orange, CA 92856.
Web site: www.fostoriacollectors.org

Fostoria Glass Society of America, Inc., *Facets of Fostoria* (newsletter), P.O. Box 826, Moundsville, WV 26041.
Web site: www.fostoriaglass.org

Heisey Collectors of America, *Heisey News* (newsletter), 169 W. Church St., Newark, OH 43055.
Web site: www.heiseymuseum.org

Michiana Association of Candlewick Collectors, *The Spyglass* (newsletter), 17370 Battles Rd., South Bend, IN 46614.

National Cambridge Collectors, Inc., *Cambridge Crystal Ball* (newsletter), P.O. Box 416, Cambridge, OH 43725-0416.
Web site: www.cambridgeglass.org

National Depression Glass Association, *News & Views* (newsletter), P.O. Box 8264, Wichita, KS 67208-0264.
Web site: www.glassshow.com/NDGA

National Duncan Glass Society, *National Duncan Glass Society Journal* (newsletter), P.O. Box 965, Washington, PA 15301.
Web site: www.duncan-glass.com

National Fenton Glass Society, *Fenton Flyer* (newsletter), P.O. Box 4008, Marietta, OH 45750.

Web site: www.axces.com/nfgs

National Imperial Glass Collectors Society, *Glasszette* (newsletter), P.O. Box 534, Bellaire, OH 43906.

Web site: www.imperialglass.org

National Milk Glass Collectors Society, *Opaque News* (newsletter), 500 Union Cemetery Rd., Greensburg, PA 15601.

Web site: www.nmgcs.org

National Westmoreland Glass Collectors Club, *The Towne Crier* (newsletter), P.O. Box 100, Grapeville, PA 15634.

Web site: www.glassshow.com/Clubs/NWGCC/west.html

Tiffin Glass Collectors Club, *Tiffin Glassmasters* (newsletter), P.O. Box 554, Tiffin, OH 44883.

Web site: www.tiffinglass.org

Westmoreland Glass Society, Inc., *Westmoreland Glass Society, Inc.* (newsletter), P.O. Box 2883, Iowa City, IA 52240-2883.

Web site: www.glassshow.com/Clubs/wgis/wgis.html

PUBLICATIONS

Candlewick Collector (newsletter), 17609 Falling Water Rd., Strongsville, OH 44136.

The Daze (newspaper), Box 58, Clio, MI 48420.

Fire-King News (newsletter), P.O. Box 473, Addison, AL 35540.

Glass & More (newsletter), P.O. Box 923, Gardendale, AL 35071.

Web site: glassandmore.com

Glass Messenger (newsletter), 700 Elizabeth St., Williamstown, WV 26187. Web site: www.fentonartglass.com (published by the Fenton Art Glass Company).

Snack Set Searchers (newsletter), P.O. Box 908, Hallock, MN 56728.

DEPRESSION GLASS

References

Bickenheuser, Fred. *Tiffin Glassmasters.* 3 volumes. Privately printed, 1979–1985 (Glassmasters Publications, P.O. Box 524, Grove City, OH 43123).

Bredehoft, Tom and Neila. *Fifty Years of Collectible Glass, 1920–1970: Tableware, Kitchenware, Barware, and Water Sets,* Volume 1. Iola, Wisconsin: Krause, 2000.

————. *Fifty Years of Collectible Glass, 1920–1970: Stemware, Decorations, Decorative Accessories,* Volume 2. Iola, Wisconsin: Krause, 2000.

————. *Collector's Encyclopedia of Heisey Glass, 1925–1938.* Paducah, Kentucky: Collector Books, 1986, revised prices 1999.

Brown, O. O. *Paden City Glass Manufacturing Company, Paden City, W. Va.: Catalogue Reprints from the 1920s.* Marietta, Ohio: Antique Publications, 2000.

Chase, Mark, and Michael Kelly. *Collectible Drinking Glasses.* Paducah, Kentucky: Collector Books, 1996, price update 1999.

Clements, Monica Lynn, and Patricia Rosser Clements. *Pocket Guide to Pink Depression Era Glass.* Atglen, Pennsylvania: Schiffer Publishing Ltd., 2000.

————. *An Unauthorized Guide to Fire-King Glasswares.* Atglen, Pennsylvania: Schiffer Publishing Ltd., 1999.

Florence, Gene. *Anchor Hocking's Fire-King and More.* 1st–2nd editions. Paducah, Kentucky: Collector Books, 1998–2000.

————. *Collectible Glassware from the '40s, '50s, '60s: An Illustrated Value Guide.* 1st–5th editions. Paducah, Kentucky: Collector Books, 1992–2000.

————. *Collector's Encyclopedia of Akro Agate.* Revised edition. Paducah, Kentucky: Collector Books, 1975, revised prices 1992.

————. *Collector's Encyclopedia of Depression Glass.* 1st–14th editions. Paducah, Kentucky: Collector Books, 1982–2000.

————. *Elegant Glassware of the Depression Era.* 1st–9th editions. Paducah, Kentucky: Collector Books, 1983–2001.

————. *Kitchen Glassware of the Depression Years*. 1st–5th editions. Paducah, Kentucky: Collector Books, 1981–1995.

————. *Very Rare Glassware of the Depression Years*. 1st–6th editions. Paducah, Kentucky: Collector Books, 1988–1999.

Grisel, Ruth Ann. *Westmoreland Glass: Our Children's Heirlooms*. Privately printed, 1993 (FSJ Publishing Co., P.O. Box 122, Iowa City, IA 52244).

Hardy, Roger and Claudia. *The Complete Line of the Akro Agate Co.* Privately printed, 1992 (10 Bailey St., Clarksburg, WV 26301–2524).

Heacock, William. *Fenton Glass: The First Twenty-five Years*. Marietta, Ohio: Antique Publications, 1978.

————. *Fenton Glass: The Second Twenty-five Years*. Marietta, Ohio: Antique Publications, 1980.

————. *Fenton Glass: The Third Twenty-five Years*. Marietta, Ohio: Antique Publications, 1989.

Hopper, Philip. *Forest Green Glass*. Atglen, Pennsylvania: Schiffer Publishing Ltd., 2000.

————. *More Royal Ruby*. Atglen, Pennsylvania: Schiffer Publishing Ltd., 1999.

————. *Royal Ruby*. Atglen, Pennsylvania: Schiffer Publishing Ltd., 1999.

Keller, Joe, and David Ross. *Jadite*. Atglen, Pennsylvania: Schiffer Publishing Ltd., 1998.

Kerr, Ann. *Fostoria: An Identification and Value Guide of Pressed, Blown & Hand Molded Shapes*. Paducah, Kentucky: Collector Books, 1994.

Kilgo, Garry and Dale, and Jerry and Gail Watkins. *A Collector's Guide to Anchor Hocking Fire-King Glassware*. 2nd edition. Privately printed, 1997 (K & W Collectibles, P.O. Box 473, Addison, AL 35540).

Kovar, Lorraine. *Westmoreland Glass, 1888–1940*. Volume 3. Marietta, Ohio: Antique Publications, 1997.

————. *Westmoreland Glass, 1950–1984*. Volumes 1 and 2. Marietta, Ohio: Antique Publications, 1991.

Kovel, Ralph and Terry. ***Kovels' Antiques & Collectibles Price List.*** **New York: Three Rivers Press, annual.**

Krause, Gail. *The Encyclopedia of Duncan*. Hicksville, New York: Exposition Press, Inc., 1976.

Long, Milbra, and Emily Seate. *Fostoria, Useful and Ornamental: The Crystal for America*. Paducah, Kentucky: Collector Books, 2000.

————. *Fostoria Tableware: The Crystal for America, 1924–1943*. Paducah, Kentucky: Collector Books, 1999.

————. *Fostoria Tableware: The Crystal for America, 1944–1986*. Paducah, Kentucky: Collector Books, 2000.

Luckey, Carl F., with Mary Burris. *Identification & Value Guide to Depression Era Glassware.* 3rd edition. Iola, Wisconsin: Books Americana/Krause, 1994.

Mauzy, Barbara. *Pyrex: The Unauthorized Collector's Guide.* Atglen, Pennsylvania: Schiffer Publishing Ltd., 2000.

Mauzy, Barbara and Jim. *Mauzy's Comprehensive Handbook of Depression Glass Prices.* 2nd edition. Atglen, Pennsylvania: Schiffer Publishing Ltd., 2000.

McGrain, Patrick, editor. *Fostoria: The Popular Years.* Privately printed, 1982 (P.O. Box 219, Frederick, MD 21701).

Measell, James, and Berry Wiggins. *Great American Glass of the Roaring 20s & Depression Era.* Marietta, Ohio: Antique Publications, 1998.

———. *Great American Glass of the Roaring 20s & Depression Era.* Book 2. Marietta, Ohio: Antique Publications, 2000.

Measell, James, editor. *Imperial Glass Encyclopedia: A–Cane.* Volume 1. Marietta, Ohio: Antique Publications, 1999.

———. *Imperial Glass Encyclopedia: Cape Cod–L.* Volume 2. Marietta, Ohio: Antique Publications, 1999.

———. *Imperial Glass Encyclopedia: M–Z.* Volume 3. Marietta, Ohio: Antique Publications, 1999.

———. *New Martinsville Glass, 1900–1944.* Marietta, Ohio: Antique Publications, 1994.

Miller, C. L. *Depression Era Dime Store Glass.* Atglen, Pennsylvania: Schiffer Publishing Ltd., 1999.

National Cambridge Collectors, Inc. *Colors in Cambridge Glass.* Paducah, Kentucky: Collector Books, 1984.

———. *Etchings by Cambridge.* Volume 1. Privately printed, 1997 (Brookville Publishing, P.O. Box 3, Brookville, Ohio 45309–0003).

Newbound, Betty and Bill. *Collector's Encyclopedia of Milk Glass Identification & Values.* Paducah, Kentucky: Collector Books, 1995.

Page, Bob, and Dale Frederiksen. *Tiffin Is Forever.* Privately printed, 1994 (Page-Frederiksen Publishing Company, Replacements, Ltd., PO Box 26029, Greensboro, NC 27420).

———. *Crystal Stemware Identification Guide.* Privately printed, 1997 (Page-Frederiksen Publishing Company, Replacements, Ltd., PO Box 26029, Greensboro, NC 27420).

Piña, Leslie, and Jerry Gallagher. *Tiffin Glass, 1914–1940.* Atglen, Pennsylvania: Schiffer Publishing, Ltd., 1996.

Piña, Leslie, and Paula Ockner. *Depression Era Art Deco Glass.* Atglen, Pennsylvania: Schiffer Publishing Ltd., 1999.

Piña, Leslie. *Depression Era Glass by Duncan.* Atglen, Pennsylvania: Schiffer Publishing Ltd., 1999.

————. *Fostoria American Line 2056.* Atglen, Pennsylvania: Schiffer Publishing Ltd., 1999.

————. *Fostoria Designer George Sakier, with Values.* Atglen, Pennsylvania: Schiffer Publishing Ltd., 1996.

————. *Fostoria: Serving the American Table 1887–1986, with Price Guide.* Atglen, Pennsylvania: Schiffer Publishing Ltd., 1995.

Ream, Louise, et al. *Encyclopedia of Heisey Glassware: Etchings and Carvings.* 2nd edition. Privately printed, 1994 (Heisey Collectors of America, 160 W. Church St., Newark, OH 43255).

Riggs, Sherry, and Paula Pendergrass. *20th Century Glass Candle Holders.* Atglen, Pennsylvania: Schiffer Publishing Ltd., 1999.

Rogove, Susan Tobier, and Marcia Buan Steinhauer. *Pyrex by Corning.* Marietta, Ohio: Antique Publications, 1993.

Schroy, Ellen T. *Warman's Depression Glass.* 2nd edition. Iola, Wisconsin: Krause, 2000.

Scott, Virginia R. *The Collector's Guide to Imperial Candlewick.* Privately printed, 1990 (275 Milledge Terr., Athens, GA 30606).

Smith, Bill and Phyllis. *Cambridge Glass 1927–1929.* Privately printed, 1986 (4003 Old Columbus Rd., Springfield, OH 45502).

Stout, Sandra McPhee. *The Complete Book of McKee Glass.* North Kansas City, Missouri: Trojan Press, 1972.

Venable, Charles, et al. *China & Glass in America, 1880–1980: From Tabletop to TV Tray.* Dallas, Texas: Dallas Museum of Art, 2000.

Walk, John. *The Big Book of Fenton Glass: 1940–1970.* 2nd edition. Atglen, Pennsylvania: Schiffer Publishing Ltd., 1999.

Washburn, Kent G. *Price Survey.* 4th edition. Privately printed, 1994 (8048 Midcrown, Suite 26, San Antonio, TX 78218–2334).

Weatherman, Hazel Marie. *Colored Glassware of the Depression Era I.* Privately printed, 1970 (Weatherman Glassbooks, P.O. Box 280, Ozark, MO 65721).

————. *Colored Glassware of the Depression Era 2.* Privately printed, 1974 (Weatherman Glassbooks, P.O. Box 280, Ozark, MO 65721).

————. *Decorated Tumbler.* Privately printed, 1978 (Weatherman Glassbooks, P.O. Box 280, Ozark, MO 65721).

————. *Fostoria: Its First Fifty Years.* Privately printed, 1972 (Weatherman Glassbooks, P.O. Box 280, Ozark, MO 65721).

Whitmyer, Margaret and Kenn. *Bedroom & Bathroom Glassware of the Depression Years.* Paducah, Kentucky: Collector Books, 1990.

Wilson, Chas West. *Westmoreland Glass Identification & Value Guide.* Paducah, Kentucky: Collector Books, 1996.

Yeske, Doris. *Depression Glass: A Collector's Guide.* 3rd edition. Atglen, Pennsylvania: Schiffer Publishing Ltd., 1999.

DEPRESSION GLASS

Factories

FACTORY	LOCATION	DATES
A. H. Heisey & Company	Newark, Ohio	1896–1957
Akro Agate Company	Clarksburg, West Virginia	1914–1951
Bartlett-Collins	Sapulpa, Oklahoma	1914–present
Belmont Tumbler Company	Bellaire, Ohio	1915– 1938
Cambridge Glass Company	Cambridge, Ohio	1901–1954; 1955–1958
Central Glass Works	Wheeling, West Virginia	1863–1939
Consolidated Lamp & Glass Company	Coraopolis, Pennsylvania	1893– 1933; 1936–1964
Co-Operative Flint Glass Company	Beaver Falls, Pennsylvania	1879–1937
Dell Glass Company	Millville, New Jersey	1930s
Diamond Glass-Ware Company	Indiana, Pennsylvania	1904–1931
Dunbar Flint Glass Corporation/Dunbar Glass Corporation	Dunbar, West Virginia	1913–1953
Duncan & Miller Glass Company	Washington, Pennsylvania	1893–1955
Federal Glass Company	Columbus, Ohio	1900–1980
Fenton Art Glass Company	Williamstown, West Virginia	1906–present
Fostoria Glass Company	Fostoria, Ohio; Moundsville, West Virginia	1887–1986
Hazel Atlas Glass Company/ Hazel Ware (division of Continental Can Company)	Washington, Pennsylvania; Zanesville, Ohio; Clarksburg, West Virginia; Wheeling, West Virginia	1902–1956; 1956–1964
Hocking Glass Company/ Anchor Hocking Glass Corporation/Anchor Hocking Corporation	Lancaster, Ohio	1905–present; (Anchor Glass Corporation, 1937–1969; Anchor Hocking Corporation, 1969–present)
Imperial Glass Company	Bellaire, Ohio	1904–1984
Indiana Glass Company	Dunkirk, Indiana	1907–present

FACTORY	LOCATION	DATES
Jeannette Glass Company	Jeannette, Pennsylvania	1898–present
Jenkins Glass Company	Kokomo, Indiana; Arcadia, Indiana	1900–1932
L. E. Smith Glass Company	Mt. Pleasant, Pennsylvania	1907–present
Lancaster Glass Company	Lancaster, Ohio	1908–1937
Libbey Glass Company	Toledo, Ohio	1892–present
Liberty Works	Egg Harbor, New Jersey	1903–c.1932
Louie Glass Company	Weston, West Virginia	1926–1995
Macbeth-Evans Glass Company	Indiana (several factories); Toledo, Ohio; Charleroi, Pennsylvania; Corning, New York	1899–1936; acquired by Corning
McKee Glass Company	Jeannette, Pennsylvania	1850–1961; acquired by Jeannette Glass Company
Morgantown Glass Works	Morgantown, West Virginia	1900–1972
New Martinsville Glass Manufacturing Company	New Martinsville, West Virginia	1900–1944; acquired by Viking Glass Company
Paden City Glass Manufacturing Company	Paden City, West Virginia	1916–1951
Seneca Glass Company	Fostoria, Ohio; Morgantown, West Virginia	1891–1983
Silex (division of Macbeth-Evans)	Corning, New York	1929–1955; sold to Corning Glass Works
Standard Glass Manufacturing Company (became subsidiary of Hocking/Anchor Hocking in 1940)	Lancaster, Ohio	1924–c.1984
Tiffin Glass Company (Factory R of United States Glass Company)	Tiffin, Ohio	1892–1963
U.S. Glass Company	Pennsylvania (several factories); Tiffin, Ohio; Gas City, Indiana; West Virginia	1891–1963
Viking Glass Company/ Dalzell-Viking Glass Company	New Martinsville, West Virginia	1944–1998 (changed name 1987)
Westmoreland Glass Company	Grapeville, Pennsylvania	1889–1985

CERAMIC DINNERWARE

DINNERWARE

Introduction

This year we changed the format of the dinnerware section of this book to make it more helpful and easier to use. Dinnerware and their prices are listed alphabetically by manufacturer and then by pattern name. (Exceptions to this are the patterns Autumn Leaf and Willow, which are listed by pattern name because they were made by several manufacturers.) Under the manufacturer's name is a paragraph giving the history of the company. The patterns listed with each manufacturer's name include a sentence or two describing color variations, the years of manufacture, and sometimes the designer's name. Following each pattern name is a list of dinnerware pieces and their prices. Pictures of patterns and marks of patterns and factories are also included. At the back of the book, there is an index of the ceramic dinnerware patterns listed in this book. Use this as a cross-reference to help you find patterns and prices under the maker's name. Although hundreds of patterns are included in this list, many patterns were not seen at sales this year and are not included in the price section.

Some companies have changed their names during the years of dinnerware production. In both the main price listing and in the References, we use the company name or trademark name most closely associated with the dishes. For example, Gladding, McBean & Company became Franciscan Ceramics Inc. and eventually was purchased by the Waterford Wedgwood Group. We use the name Franciscan, which has been in use most of the time the dinnerware was made—no matter what the maker's name actually was at the time.

This book has changed to reflect the collecting trends of the twenty-first century. The inexpensive dinnerware sets made in America are the main focus of this section of *Kovels' Depression Glass and Dinnerware Price List*. Also included are sets made in other countries but sold in quantity in America. Azalea pattern, made in Japan, and Liberty Blue, made in England, are two of these entries. Prices listed are for the most popular everyday sets being collected today. Formal dinnerwares made by firms like Lenox or Royal Worcester are not included.

Because dishes were made by so many manufacturers, problems can arise with variations in vocabulary. Most sugar bowls made for these dinnerware sets had covers. Today many have lost their original covers and are sold as open sugars. We do not include the word *open* in the description, but we do indicate if there is a cover. A gravy boat with an underplate is a gravy boat with the plate that it rests on. Sometimes the underplate is permanently attached to the gravy boat. A mayonnaise bowl may also have an underplate.

A lug soup is a bowl with a flat handle called a lug. Other soup bowls may have pierced handles or no handles. We list a pickle dish as a pickle and also list a pickle tray. The tray is flat. A snack set is a cup and a matching plate with an off-center indentation for the cup. An after-dinner coffee cup is larger than a demitasse but smaller than a coffee cup. A few mixing bowls have covers, which are very rare. We list the bowls with and without the covers. Sometimes a cover is listed alone. A French baker or fluted baker is a bowl with straight sides. A covered butter dish is listed as "butter, cover." If it is just the cover to a butter dish (and some are listed because they are expensive), the listing says "butter, cover only."

Sometimes collectors use different words to describe the same dish. An oatmeal bowl and a cereal bowl are both names for a bowl about 6 inches in diameter. A berry bowl and a fruit bowl may also be the same size, and a plate about 6 inches in diameter can be called a dessert plate, bread plate, or sherbet plate. If possible, we list these dishes by the name the manufacturer used.

Dealers often use a term like "30s" or "36s" to indicate the size of a dish. When the dinnerware was made, it was packed in barrels. The terms 30s or 36s refer to the number of pieces that fit in a barrel. The larger the number, the smaller the size of the piece. If that is the common way the piece is described today, we have included it in the listing. The height of a pitcher or jug is one indication of size; the number of liquid ounces it holds is also important. We have tried to list both. Wherever possible, we have used both the name of the piece and the size, so the listing is "plate, dinner, 10 in." Although most dinner plates are 10 inches in diameter, a few are smaller and we have listed the actual size in each case.

The terms "kitchenware" and "dinnerware" are used in the original sense. A dinnerware set includes all the pieces that might have been used on a dinner table, including dishes, bowls, platters, tumblers, cups, pitchers, and serving bowls. A kitchenware set has bowls and storage dishes of the type used in a kitchen and does not include dinner plates or cups. Kitchenware includes rolling pins, pie servers, and other kitchen utensils. A few kitchenware bowls are listed, but other pieces are not. Several manufacturers used the term "fine china" to differentiate their informal pottery lines from their more formal china pieces. The term "fine china" is used in this book only if that is what it was called by the factory.

Colors often were given romantic names and, whenever possible, we have used these original factory names. Some colors, such as Camellia (rose), Cadet (light blue), Indian Red (orange), or Dresden (deep blue), are explained in the paragraph descriptions.

It is important to remember that descriptions of any line of dinnerware may include many different names—a manufacturer's name, a trademark name, a pattern name (describing the decorations applied to a dish), and sometimes a shape name (describing the shape of the dish). For example, Taverne is a pattern; Laurel is the shape of the dish decorated with that pattern; and Taylor, Smith & Taylor is the name of the company that made the dinnerware. Sometimes a name refers to both a pattern and a shape; if it does, we explain how the name is used in this book.

Pieces of American dinnerware are constantly being discovered in attics, basements, garage sales, flea markets, Internet sales, and antiques shops. The publications that offer replacement dishes through the mail use descriptions that often include both pattern and shape names. Learn to recognize the shapes and shape names that were used by each maker. Authors of other books about dinnerware have sometimes arbitrarily named patterns. These names may differ in different books, yet describe the same pattern. We have tried to cross-reference these pattern names so you can locate them in any of the books.

We have included a bibliography of books on dinnerware at the end of the main section. The books are listed by manufacturer name unless they are general books on dinnerware or marks. Some dishes are marked with only the pattern name; others are marked with only the company's name; still others are not marked at all. Some of the books we list are filled with photographs that can help you identify your dishes.

Prices listed in this book are actual prices asked by dealers at shows, shops, on the Internet, and through national advertising. They are not the prices you would pay at a garage sale or church bazaar (that's where you might find bargains). Prices from matching services were not included because these are higher still. As is true in any type of shopping, you often pay a little extra for immediate availability and expert knowledge. The only reason one pattern has more prices listed than another is because more prices were available for those patterns. It is probably also an indication of the popularity of the pattern. Prices are not estimates. If a high and low are given, we have recorded several sales. There is a regional variation in the prices, especially for the solid-colored wares. In general, these pieces are high-priced in the East and West, lower in the middle of the country.

There have been a few reissues of dinnerware. Harlequin was put back into production in 1979 for Woolworth's, the sole distributor. Complete dinner sets were made in the original colors, except that the salmon is a deeper color than the original. The sugar bowls were made with closed handles. Fiesta was reissued by Homer Laughlin China Company in 1986. The original molds and marks were used. The new Fiesta has a china body that shrinks a little more than the semivitreous clay body used before. This means that most new pieces are slightly smaller than old ones. But dinner plates, soup bowls, and cereal bowls were made slightly larger to accommodate modern tastes. New molds were made for these pieces. New dinner plates are $10\frac{1}{2}$ inches in diameter. The new dishes were first made in cobalt blue (darker than the original), black, white, apricot, and rose. Other colors have been added. A few of the pieces have been slightly redesigned since 1986, with variations in handles and bases. A special line was made with added cartoon decorations. A Fiesta look-alike has been made by Franciscan since 1978 under the name Kaleidoscope, and a similar line called Cantinaware has been sold by

Target stores. We have tried to indicate in the paragraphs in the price section if any reproductions of a pattern have been made.

This book is a report of prices for pieces offered for sale during the past year. Most of the patterns included in earlier books are found here because collectors still buy these patterns. Many newly popular patterns are also included.

Depression glass and prices for these pieces can be found in the first half of this book. Melmac and other plastic dinnerware are found after this section.

Particular patterns can be found by using either the Depression Glass or Dinnerware main listings. Depression Glass begins on page 7 and Dinnerware on page 139.

AUTUMN LEAF

Autumn Leaf pattern china was made for the Jewel Tea Company beginning in 1933. Hall China Company, East Liverpool, Ohio; Crooksville China Company, Crooksville, Ohio; Harker Potteries, Chester, West Virginia; and Paden City Pottery, Paden City, West Virginia, made dishes with this design. Autumn Leaf has remained popular and was made by Hall China Company until 1978. Some special pieces in the Autumn Leaf pattern are still being made.

Baker, Fort Pitt, Oval,
  Individual, 12 Oz. ... 225.00
Baker, French,
  4 1/2 In. 50.00
Bean Pot, Handle 950.00
Bowl, Fruit,
  5 1/2 In. ...... 7.00 to 13.00
Bowl, Sunshine No. 3,
  6 In. 22.00
Bowl, Sunshine No. 4,
  7 1/2 In. 27.00
Bowl, Vegetable,
  Oval .... 30.00 to 46.00
Bowl, Vegetable, Oval,
  2 Sections,
  10 1/2 In. 125.00

Bowl, Vegetable, Oval,
  Cover, 10 1/2 In. 65.00
Bowl, Vegetable, Round,
  9 In. .... 30.00 to 70.00
Casserole, 7 1/4 In. 22.50
Casserole, Cover 65.00
Coffeepot ...... 50.00 to 95.00
Coffeepot, Jewel
  Tea Co............. 325.00
Cookie Jar, Zeisel 290.00
Creamer 30.00
Cup 10.00
Cup & Saucer 16.00
Cup & Saucer,
  St. Denis 60.00
Drip Jar 40.00
Gravy Boat, Underplate .. 65.00
Jug, Ball,
  No. 3 .... 35.00 to 60.00
Mug, Irish Coffee 110.00
Pie Plate, 3 Piece 50.00
Pitcher, Milk,
  5 3/4 In. ..... 25.00 to 47.00
Plate, Bread & Butter,
  6 In. .... 8.00 to 13.00
Plate, Breakfast, 9 In. ... 11.00
Plate, Dinner,
  10 In. ...... 16.00 to 30.00
Plate, Salad,
  7 1/4 In. ...... 8.00 to 16.00
Salt & Pepper, Casper,
  Ruffled Base 35.00
Saucer .... 3.00 to 11.00
Soup, Cream 36.00
Soup, Dish, 8 1/2 In. 18.00
Stack Set 175.00
Sugar, Cover,
  Ruffled Edge .. 32.00 to 45.00
Sugar & Creamer,
  Cover .... 25.00 to 70.00
Teapot, Aladdin 35.00
Warmer, Oval 245.00

❖

Use denture cleaning tablets to remove a stain from a ceramic teapot. Follow the directions for use with false teeth.

❖

BAUER

John Andrew Bauer, who had worked in Paducah, Kentucky, moved to California in 1909 for his health. The Bauer pottery made flowerpots, stoneware, and art pottery. In 1923 it became the J. A. Bauer Company. The company closed in 1962. Dinnerware was first made in 1930. The solid bright color ware called "Plain Ware," popular for "casual dining," was the first American dinnerware of this type, years before Fiesta ware.

MONTEREY is a solid-color pottery line made from 1936 to the early 1940s. The plate borders are a series of separated rings. The pottery sold full dinnerware sets with matching serving pieces. Colors in the set are mix-and-match. Colors include Burgundy, California Orange-Red, Canary Yellow, Green, Ivory, Monterey Blue, Red-Brown, Turquoise Blue, and White. Other colors, including Chartreuse, have been reported.

Canary Yellow

Bowl, Fruit	5.00
Cup	4.00
Cup & Saucer	7.00
Plate, Bread & Butter, 6 In.	5.00
Salt & Pepper	18.00

Green

Cup	4.00
Cup & Saucer	7.00
Plate, Bread & Butter, 6 In.	5.00
Plate, Dinner, 10 In.	8.00

Turquoise Blue

Bowl, Fruit	5.00
Cup & Saucer	7.00
Plate, Dinner, 10 In.	8.00
Platter, Oval, 11 In.	14.00
Saltshaker	10.00
Saucer	3.00

RING, sometimes called Beehive, is a solid-color pottery line made from c.1933 to 1962. Mix-and-match sets were made in Black, Burgundy, Chinese Yellow, Delph Blue, Ivory, Jade Green, Orange Red, and Royal Blue. Later, Light Brown and White were used. Papaya was used from 1941 to 1945. Other colors reported by collectors are Chartreuse, Gray, Light Green, Orange, Pale Blue, Pink, Red Brown, Spruce, and Turquoise. Early dishes had faint rings, but from 1936 to 1946 the rings were more distinct.

Burgundy

Bowl, Vegetable, Oval, 10 In.	120.00
Chop Plate, 12 1/2 In.	128.00
Cup, Coffee	8.00
Plate, Salad, 7 1/2 In.	38.00

Chinese Yellow

Bowl, Fruit, 5 In.	10.00
Bowl, Vegetable, Oval, 8 In.	41.00
Creamer	33.00
Custard Cup	14.50
Mixing Bowl, No. 24	21.00

Mixing Bowl, No. 36	25.00
Pitcher, 2 Qt.	95.00
Plate, Dinner, 9 In.	31.00
Plate, Dinner, 10 1/2 In.	75.00 to 85.00
Plate, Salad, 7 1/2 In.	11.00 to 35.00
Platter, 9 1/4 In.	32.00
Platter, 12 In.	50.00

Jade Green

Baking Dish, Individual, 4 In.	78.00
Cup & Saucer	23.00
Goblet, 4 1/2 In.	62.00
Jardiniere, No. 10, 12 1/2 x 11 1/2 In.	207.00
Punch Cup, 2 3/4 In.	36.00
Tumbler, 6 Oz., 3 1/2 In.	19.00
Vase, 5 1/2 In.	327.00

Orange Red

Bowl, No. 5, 5 3/4 In.	8.00
Bowl, Serving, Salad, Low, 9 In.	66.00
Butter, Cover	128.00
Goblet, 4 1/2 In.	30.00
Mixing Bowl, No. 18	24.00
Mixing Bowl, No. 24	32.00
Mixing Bowl, No. 36	19.50
Pitcher, 2 Qt.	134.00
Pitcher, 7 In.	55.00
Plate, Salad, 8 In.	29.00
Punch Bowl, 14 1/4 x 7 1/2 In.	504.00

Pale Blue

Plate, Salad, 7 1/2 In.	21.00

Royal Blue

Bowl, Fruit, 5 In.	36.00
Bowl, Salad, Low, 9 In.	195.00
Bowl, Vegetable, 10 In.	67.00
Cup, Coffee	21.00
Plate, Dinner, 9 1/4 In.	26.00
Plate, Salad, 7 1/2 In.	21.00
Saltshaker, Barrel	90.00
Sugar, Cover, 3 In.	44.00
Tumbler, Handle, 12 Oz.	58.00
Vase, 8 In.	47.00

Turquoise

Cup, Coffee	11.00
Vase, Cylinder, 1930s, 10 In.	125.00

BLUE RIDGE

Blue Ridge is a mark used by Southern Potteries, Inc. Collectors use this name to refer to all of the dinnerwares made by Southern Potteries, which worked in Erwin, Tennessee, from 1917 to 1957. Dishes were decorated with decals from 1917 to 1938. Then the factory changed to hand-painted decoration. The pottery made hundreds of different patterns. Because all of the later designs were decorated by hand, there were many variations.

BLUEBELL BOUQUET, a 1948 pattern, was made with two different color combinations. It has large red flowers, tulips, and small bluebells with either yellow or green leaves.

Bowl, Vegetable, 9 In.	20.00
Creamer	15.00
Cup & Saucer	15.00 to 18.00
Plate, Dessert, 7 In.	8.00

Plate, Dinner,
  10 1/2 In. . . . . 22.00. to 23.00
Platter, 11 1/2 In. 35.00
Platter, 13 In. 35.00
Sugar, Cover 23.00

BOUNTIFUL is a pattern picturing red, blue, and yellow fruit.
Bowl, Cereal,
  6 In. 24.00
Plate, Bread & Butter,
  6 In. 14.00
Plate, Salad, 8 In. 18.00

CARNIVAL is a name used by several companies, including Homer Laughlin and Stangl. The Blue Ridge pattern is decorated with red, blue, and yellow irislike flowers and green leaves.

Cup & Saucer 18.00
Plate, Bread & Butter,
  6 In.. . . . . 7.00
Plate, Dinner, 9 3/8 In. . . 23.00

CRAB APPLE is one of the most popular dinnerware patterns made by the pottery. It is decorated with hand-painted clusters of red apples and green leaves. There is a thin red spatter border. The pattern was used after 1930 and discontinued only when the factory closed in 1957.

Bowl, Vegetable,
  9 1/4 In. 11.00
Cake Lifter,
  9 1/4 In. 61.00
Gravy Boat 23.00
Plate, Dessert, 6 In. 8.50

Platter, 11 1/2 In. 11.50
Relish, 5 x 9 In. 39.00

EASTER PARADE has pastel decorations. Outlines of flowers and leaves are colored inside with pale yellow, pink, and blue. Light green leaves complete the decoration.

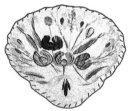

Celery Dish, Leaf Shape . 55.00
Sugar, Footed 58.00

FRUIT FANTASY was introduced in 1944. It is decorated with purple grapes, yellow pears, and red cherries. It has a sponged edge.
Bowl, Salad 85.00
Shaker, Footed 62.00

HARVESTIME is a 1950s pattern that has 3 stalks of wheat tied with a bow as a center decoration.
Bowl, Vegetable,
  Round 14.00
Pitcher 35.00
Soup, Dish 12.00

PLANTATION IVY is a 1951 pattern. It has a stylized hand-painted design or an ivy vine in green and yellow on a modern white dinnerware shape.
Berry Bowl, 5 1/2 In. 8.00
Bowl, Vegetable,
  8 7/8 In. 20.00
Creamer 15.00
Cup & Saucer 15.00
Plate, 6 1/2 In. 4.50
Plate, Dinner,
  9 1/2 In. 15.00

ROOSTERS of many sorts were used as decorations on Southern Potteries pieces. The Rooster crowing from the fence top with a sun and a barn in the distance is a pattern called Cock o' the Morn. Another pattern was known as Cock o' the Walk. Most other patterns picturing the bird are called Rooster by collectors, although Rooster was a giftware line and the dinnerware, on the Clinchfield shape, was known as Game Cock. These pieces have a rooster center and a series of red three-line designs as the border. This pattern pictures a red rooster standing on a sketchy line that looks like a cloud.

Egg Plate, 9 In. 74.00
Plate, Dinner, 9 1/2 In. . . 51.00

ROSE MARIE is a flower pattern offered in 1944 that features pink and orange petaled flowers, yellow tulips, and green leaves. It has a border design of three dots and a dash repeated around the edge.
Salt & Pepper, Footed . . . 90.00
Sugar & Creamer,
  Footed 140.00

◆❖◆

**Rub salt inside old tea
and coffee cups to
remove stains.**

◆❖◆

◆

Remove traces of gum, adhesive tape, and other stick tape by rubbing the glue with lemon juice.

◆

ROSE OF SHARON is an over-all pattern of small flowers. There are pink flowers, blue flowers, and dark and light green leaves.

Salt & Pepper, Footed . . . 35.00
Sugar & Creamer,
    Footed 140.00

STANHOME IVY is one of many ivy-decorated patterns. It was made on the Skyline shape after 1952. It has ivy leaves, clusters of red berries, and brown vines.

Cup & Saucer 5.00
Platter, Oval,
    14 x 12 In. 11.00
Sauce Bowl, 5 1/4 In. 4.00

WINNIE pattern from the 1950s features a flower with five red petals and a yellow center. There are also red buds and green leaves. It is on the Skyline shape.

Plate, Dinner, 9 1/2 In. . . . 7.50
Plate, Dinner, Skyline
    Style, 10 1/4 In. 9.00

COORS

The Coors Porcelain Company of Golden, Colorado, was owned by the Coors Brewing Company. Dishes were made from the turn of the century. Coors stopped making nonessential wares at the start of World War II. After the war, the pottery made ovenware, teapots, vases, and a general line of pottery, but no dinner-ware—except for special orders. The company is still in business making industrial porcelain.

ROSEBUD, the most popular pattern made by the Coors Porcelain Company, was produced from 1934 to 1942. It is a solid-color pattern with a styl-ized flower and leaves on the edge of the plates or sides of the cups. It was made in Blue, Green (sometimes called tur-quoise), Ivory, Maroon, Orange, and Yellow

Blue
Jug, Refrigerator,
    Stopper 158.00
Plate, 7 In. 15.00
Green
Bowl, Pudding, 7 Pt. 37.00
Casserole, Cover,
    7 1/2 In. . . . . . 53.00 to 76.00
Plate, Dinner, 9 In. 29.00
Maroon
Bowl, Pudding, 2 Pt. 28.00
Cake Plate, 11 In. 51.00
Cup, 3 1/2 x 2 1/2 In. 20.00
Custard Cup 17.00
Saltshaker 31.00
Orange
Casserole 18.00
Plate, 7 In. 15.50
Plate, Dessert, 6 1/2 In. . . 16.00
Yellow
Casserole, Cover,
    7 In. . . . . 61.00 to 65.00
Creamer, 2 3/4 x 3 In. . . . 56.00

CROOKSVILLE

Crooksville China Company worked in Crooksville, Ohio, from 1902 to 1959. The company made pottery baking dishes, teapots, cookie jars, and other kitchenwares. Semiporcelain and pottery dinnerwares were also made.

IVA-LURE is easy to identify because the mark *Iva-lure* by Crooksville is on the bottom of each piece. Iva-lure is the shape; it was decorated with many different decals.

Iva-lure by CROOKSVILLE U.S.A D.R

Bowl, Fruit, Slightly Square Shape, Floral Design, 5 1/2 In.	5.00
Plate, Bread & Butter, 6 In.	4.00 to 5.00
Saucer	4.00
Serving Plate, Gold Trim, Handle, Marked, 8 3/4 x 9 In.	35.00

SILHOUETTE looks just like its name. The 1930s pattern shows a black silhouette of two people eating at a table and a dog begging for food in front of the table. The pieces have platinum trim. The pattern is similar to Taverne by Hall, but Taverne has no dog. Matching metal pieces and glassware were made.

Bowl, 6 In.	10.00
Candy Dish, 6 3/4 x 4 3/4 In.	22.00 to 36.00
Cookie Jar	300.00
Gravy Boat	67.00
Mug	74.00
Pie Baker, 10 In.	13.00
Platter, 9 1/2 In.	12.00
Teapot	23.00

E. M. KNOWLES

J. K. U.S.A

Edwin M. Knowles China Company was founded in Chester, West Virginia, in 1900. The offices were located in nearby East Liverpool, Ohio. In 1913, a new factory was built in Newell, West Virginia. The company closed in 1963. The name was purchased by another company and has appeared on plates since 1977.

GRASS is a pattern designed by Russel Wright. It was made from 1957 to 1962. The gray dinnerware has a few abstract lines of gold and dark gray strewn across the pieces. It is one of the few pieces by Wright that is not just a solid color.

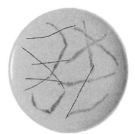

Bowl, 12 1/4 In.	19.50
Cup & Saucer	20.50
Plate, Bread & Butter, 6 1/4 In.	12.50
Plate, Dinner, 10 In.	16.50
Plate, Salad, 8 1/4 In.	15.00
Platter, 16 In.	74.00

QUEEN ANNE'S LACE was made from 1955 to 1962. It is one of many Russel Wright designs. It has an abstract decal design on white dinnerware.

Bowl, Fruit, Footed	13.00
Plate, Bread & Butter, 6 In.	7.00
Plate, Dinner, 10 1/4 In.	15.00

WHEAT is a 1954 pattern with a simple design of wheat stalks.

Bowl, Fruit 11.00
Plate, Bread & Butter,
  6 In. 10.00
Plate, Luncheon,
  7 1/2 In. 13.00
Platter, Medium 35.00

WILLIAMSBURG is a flower-decorated pattern made from 1961 to 1963.

Creamer 12.00
Cup 6.00
Plate, Bread & Butter,
  6 In. 7.00
Plate, Dinner, 10 In. 15.00
Platter, Small 25.00
Saucer 5.00
Sugar, Cover 25.00

ENOCH WEDGWOOD

Enoch Wedgwood Ltd. is an English factory established in Tunstall, Staffordshire, in 1860. It was called Wedgwood & Co. until 1965. The company is now part of the Waterford Wedgwood Group.

A & P, Grand Union, and other grocery chains offered Liberty Blue dishes to tie in with the 1776–1976 bicentennial celebration of America's independence. They were made by Enoch Wedgwood Company of England in the tradition of the nineteenth-century Staffordshire historical blue china. The dishes have a floral wreath border and central transfer designs of scenes from American history. They were sold beginning in April 1977. There was a different center design on each plate. Dishes are marked *Liberty Blue* on the back.

Berry Bowl, 8 3/4 In. 55.00
Bowl, Oval, 9 In. 50.00
Butter Chip 16.00
Creamer 30.00
Cup 3.00
Cup & Saucer .... 7.00 to 8.00
Plate, Bread & Butter,
  6 In. 3.00
Plate, Dinner,
  10 In. .... 7.00 to 15.00
Sugar, Cover 45.00

EVA ZEISEL

Eva Zeisel designed dishes for many potteries. These dishes are listed by factory, including Hall (Hall-craft line) and Red Wing (Town and Country).

FRANCISCAN

Franciscan is a trademark that appears on pottery. Gladding, McBean and Company started in Lincoln, California, in 1875. The company acquired Tropico Potteries, Inc., of Glendale, California, in 1923. The firm made sewer pipes, floor tiles, dinnerwares, and art pottery with a variety of trademarks. By 1934, all dinnerware and art pottery was made in Glendale. They made china and cream-color, decorated earthenware. The name used in advertisements and marks was changed from Franciscan Pottery to Franciscan Ware in 1936. In the 1960s, a line of dishes was made in Japan for Franciscan. In 1962, Gladding, McBean and Company merged with Lock Joint Pipe Company to become Interpace. The California pottery plant was sold by Interpace to Wedgwood Limited of England, which renamed it Franciscan Ceramics Inc. All production moved to England.

AMAPOLA is set with an orange-yellow background and an overall pattern of flowers in related brown and yellow colors. It has a border.

Bowl, Vegetable, Round,
  Open, 9 1/2 In. 40.00
Plate, Dinner, 10 3/4 In. . . 12.00

ANTIGUA is a pattern in the Whitestone line. It has a wide broken band in yellow and brown tones as a border. Each piece of the band has geometric designs. It was made in Japan in the 1960s.

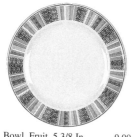

Bowl, Fruit, 5 3/8 In. 9.00
Cup . . . . 6.00 to 8.00
Cup & Saucer . . 10.00 to 14.00
Plate, Bread & Butter,
  6 In. 8.00
Plate, Dinner,
  10 3/8 In. 22.00
Plate, Salad, 8 1/4 In. 8.00
Relish, 10 1/2 In. 34.00
Saucer 10.00
Sugar 14.00

ANTIQUE GREEN is a plain shape with a greenish border and a narrow band inside the border. It was introduced in 1966.

Cup 42.00
Cup & Saucer . . 32.00 to 45.00
Plate, Bread & Butter,
  6 1/4 In. 19.00

APPLE pattern dishes were introduced in 1940 and are still being made by Waterford Wedgwood USA. It is a cream-color ware with a raised border of red apples, green leaves, and brown stems. The dishes made in the United States from 1940 to 1984 are lighter in color than those made in England from 1984 to the present.

Ashtray, 9 In. 72.00
Ashtray,
  4 1/2 In. . . . . . 23.00 to 30.00
Berry Bowl, 5 1/2 In. 18.00
Bowl, Cereal,
  6 In. . . . . 10.00 to 22.00
Bowl, Cereal, Oatmeal,
  5 1/2 In. 25.00
Bowl, Fruit,
  5 1/4 In. . . . . . . 9.00 to 18.00
Bowl, Salad,
  10 In. . . . . 118.00 to 149.00

Bowl, Vegetable, Oval, Divided,
  10 7/8 In. . . . . 45.00 to 79.00
Bowl, Vegetable, Round,
  8 3/8 In. 33.00
Bowl, Vegetable, Round,
  9 In. . . . . 30.00 to 55.00
Butter 20.00
Butter, Cover, Finial 29.00
Butter, Cover,
  No Finial 65.00
Candlestick, 2 5/8 In. 80.00
Candlestick, 2 5/8 In.,
  Pair . . . . 145.00 to 175.00
Casserole, Cover,
  1 1/2 Qt. . . . . 95.00 to 110.00
Celery Dish, 10 In. 40.00
Chop Plate,
  14 In. . . . . . 150.00 to 195.00
Cookie Jar, Cover 325.00
Creamer . . . . 14.00 to 27.00
Cup 7.00
Cup & Saucer . . . 9.00 to 23.00
Cup & Saucer, After Dinner,
  2 1/2 In. . . . . . 60.00 to 63.00
Cup & Saucer, Jumbo,
  3 1/4 In. 76.00
Dish, Baked Apple 250.00
Gravy Boat, Attached
  Underplate . . . 25.00 to 45.00
Mixing Bowl, 8 In. 185.00
Mug, 7 Oz., 2 3/4 In. 37.00
Mug, 10 Oz.,
  4 1/4 In. . . . 125.00 to 149.00
Pitcher, Milk, 6 1/4 In. . . 95.00
Pitcher, Syrup, 6 1/4 In. . . 83.00
Plate, Bread & Butter,
  6 3/8 In. . . . . . . 5.00 to 10.00
Plate, Dinner,
  10 5/8 In. . . . . 15.00 to 28.00
Plate, Luncheon,
  9 5/8 In. . . . . . 11.00 to 23.00
Plate, Salad,
  8 In. . . . . 10.00 to 22.00
Platter,
  12 5/8 In. . . . . 36.00 to 50.00
Platter, 14 In. . . . 45.00 to 75.00
Platter,
  19 1/4 In. . . 225.00 to 345.00
Relish, 3 Sections,
  10 3/8 In. . . . . 70.00 to 89.00
Salt & Pepper,
  2 1/4 In. . . . . . 20.00 to 44.00
Salt & Pepper,
  6 1/4 In. 83.00

146

Salt & Pepper Mill, Wooden
Base, 5 1/2 In. 225.00
Saucer .... 3.00 to 10.00
Soup, Cream 34.00
Soup, Dish, 8 1/2 In. 28.00
Spoon Rest 12.00
Steak Plate, Oval Coupe,
11 In. 120.00
Sugar, Cover 35.00
Sugar, No Cover 33.00
Tumbler, Water, 10 Oz.,
5 1/4 In. 43.00

ARCADIA was introduced in
1941. It was part of the Merced
line of fine china. The decoration was an inner band of stylized leaves in one of four
different colors: blue, gold,
green, and maroon. Each piece
has a narrow gold edge.

Blue
Plate, Dinner,
10 1/2 In. 62.00
Gold
Chop Plate, 13 3/8 In. ... 70.00
Cup & Saucer 48.00
Plate, Bread & Butter,
6 3/8 In. 19.00
Plate, Salad, 8 3/8 In. 25.00
Platter, Oval, 16 In. 90.00
Saucer 13.00
Green
Cup 22.00
Cup & Saucer .. 28.00 to 48.00
Gravy Boat, Attached
Underplate 185.00
Plate, Bread & Butter,
6 3/8 In. 19.00
Plate, Dinner, 10 1/2 In. .. 62.00
Plate, Salad, 8 3/8 In. 27.00

Saucer 13.00
Teapot, Cover 85.00
Maroon
Plate, Salad, 8 3/8 In. 15.00
Saucer 6.00

AUTUMN pattern, of course, is
decorated with leaves. Oak
leaves of blue, yellow, and
brown are scattered near the
edges of plates or on the sides
of bowls. It was introduced in
1955.

Bowl, Fruit, 5 1/8 In. 16.00
Bowl, Vegetable,
7 1/2 In. 16.00
Bowl, Vegetable, Divided,
13 3/4 In. 20.00
Butter 8.00
Creamer .... 10.00 to 36.00
Cup 10.00
Cup & Saucer 20.00
Gravy Boat, Attached
Underplate 22.00
Plate, Bread & Butter,
6 1/2 In. .... 5.00 to 9.00
Sugar, Cover 10.00

BEVERLY pattern has a wreath
border between thin gold lines.
It was introduced in 1942.
Cup & Saucer 30.00
Plate, Dinner, 10 1/2 In. .. 30.00
Plate, Salad, 8 3/8 In. 17.00
Salt & Pepper 75.00

BLUE FANCY is a pattern on a
modern white fine china shape.
It has a narrow border of blue
geometric designs of hearts and
scrolls. It is part of the White-

stone line that was made in
Japan in the 1960s.

Plate, Bread & Butter,
6 In. 3.00
Plate, Dinner, 10 3/8 In. ... 10.00

BOUQUET is decorated with a
hand-painted floral spray of
white, amber, and blue. It was
made from 1980 to 1984.

Bowl, Cereal,
6 In. .... 12.00 to 22.00
Bowl, Fruit,
5 1/4 In. 10.00
Creamer .... 16.00 to 21.00
Cup & Saucer .. 17.00 to 23.00
Plate, Salad, 8 In. 14.00
Platter, 13 In. 42.00
Sugar, Cover ... 19.00 to 26.00

**When packing a piece of
pottery for shipping,
look at the shape. If it
has a hollow space
larger than one inch
across, fill the space
with sponge foam or
bubble wrap.**

CAFE ROYAL was introduced about 1980. It is made from the same molds as Desert Rose, but is decorated in shades of brown.

Bowl, Cereal,
  6 In. . . . . 12.00 to 14.00
Bowl, Vegetable,
  Divided, 11 In. 40.00
Bowl, Vegetable,
  Round, 9 In. 40.00
Creamer 21.00
Cup 18.00
Cup & Saucer . . 16.00 to 20.00
Ginger Jar 295.00
Plate, Dinner, 10 3/4 In. . . 23.00
Plate, Luncheon,
  9 1/2 In. 15.00
Plate, Salad,
  8 In. . . . . 11.00 to 12.00
Platter, 14 1/4 In. 48.00
Saucer 6.00
Sugar, Cover 26.00
Tea Canister 195.00
Tile, 6 In. 22.00

CANTATA has a center design of blue and purple flowers and green leaves. There is a narrow green border. The pattern was made in Japan from 1965 to 1969.

Bowl, Fruit, 5 In. 7.00
Cup 12.00
Plate, Dinner, 10 3/8 In. . . 13.00
Soup, Dish, 6 In. 12.00

CANTON is a fine china pattern introduced in 1950. The pattern was decorated with abstract flowers of gray and black.

Creamer . . . . . . 17.00 to 28.00
Cup & Saucer 16.00
Plate, Bread & Butter,
  6 3/8 In. 12.00
Soup, Cream 16.00
Sugar, Cover . . . 32.00 to 95.00

CARMEL, introduced in 1952, is part of the Encanto line of fine china that has a plain rimless plate. The center design is a pink and platinum tulip plant. There is a platinum edge. Some early dishes may not have the edge trim.

Bowl, Vegetable, Oval,
  9 In. 109.00
Cup & Saucer . . 38.00 to 40.00
Plate, Bread & Butter,
  6 3/8 In. 10.00
Plate, Dinner,
  10 1/2 In. 49.00

Plate, Salad, 8 In. 23.00
Saucer 11.00

CHANTILLY is a fine china pattern that has a border design of yellow, orange, and brown roses.

Bowl, Cereal, 6 3/8 In. . . 12.00
Bowl, Fruit, 5 3/8 In. 12.00
Cup 12.00

CHEROKEE ROSE came in three variations: wide gold band, thin gold band, and wide green band. The center design is a bunch of pink roses and green leaves. The first patterns were introduced in 1941, the wide gold band in 1942.

Green Band
Cup & Saucer 24.00
Plate, Bread & Butter,
  6 3/8 In. 12.00
Plate, Dinner,
  10 1/2 In. . . . . 14.00 to 15.00
Plate, Luncheon,
  9 In. 24.00
Salt & Pepper 32.00
Saucer 12.00
Soup, Cream,
  Saucer . . . . . . 12.00 to 28.00

❖

To remove coffee stains, try wiping the cup with a damp cloth and baking soda.

❖

CLOUD NINE is a plain white, undecorated plate. It is part of the Whitestone line made in Japan from 1960 to 1969.

Creamer 22.00
Cup 5.00
Cup & Saucer 19.00
Pitcher, Water, 8 In. 40.00
Plate, Bread & Butter,
　6 In. . . . . 9.00 to 10.00
Plate, Dinner, 10 3/8 In. . . 4.00
Saucer 2.00
Sugar, Cover 21.00

CONCH is one of many patterns picturing sea creatures in Franciscan's Sculptures line. The sand-color or white plate is decorated with an embossed picture of a conch. It was introduced in 1977.

Sand
Plate, Luncheon, Sea
　Sculptures, 9 1/8 In. . . . 12.00

White
Plate, Dinner, Sea
　Sculptures, 10 3/4 In. . . 25.00
Plate, Luncheon, Sea
　Sculptures, 9 1/8 In. . . . 18.00

CONCORD is a 1941 pattern. The dishes have a wide gray-green band on the rim and a ring of grapevines near the center. Cups and bowls are gray-green on the outside.

Cup & Saucer 35.00
Plate, Dinner, 10 1/2 In. . . 32.00
Sugar, Cover 75.00

CORONADO is a solid-color line with a swirl border. It was made in Apple Green, Celestial Ivory, Chartreuse, Coral, Gray, Maroon, Turquoise, and Yellow. Most colors were made in two different finishes, glossy and matte. It was made from 1934 to 1954.

Celestial Ivory
Bowl, Cereal, 6 1/2 In. . . 12.00
Bowl, Vegetable, Round,
　7 1/2 In. 22.00
Chop Plate,
　12 In. . . . . 25.00 to 30.00
Coffeepot, Cover,
　After Dinner 95.00
Creamer 20.00
Cup & Saucer . . . 8.00 to 22.00
Cup & Saucer,
　After Dinner 45.00
Custard, Flanged Rim,
　Marked 2.00
Gravy Boat, Attached
　Underplate . . . 28.00 to 35.00
Plate, Bread & Butter,
　6 1/2 In. . . . . . . 6.00 to 10.00
Plate, Dessert, 6 1/4 In. . . . 3.00
Plate, Dinner, 10 3/8 In. . . 20.00
Plate, Luncheon,
　9 1/2 In. . . . . . 15.00 to 18.00
Plate, Salad,
　8 In. . . . . 9.00 to 14.00
Platter, Oval,
　12 In. 35.00

Relish, 9 1/2 In. 20.00
Salt & Pepper 22.00
Saucer . . . . 6.00 to 7.00
Sugar, Cover . . . 20.00 to 35.00
Teapot 60.00
Vase, 5 1/2 In. 175.00

Coral
Bowl, Vegetable, 8 In. . . . 15.00
Chop Plate,
　12 In. . . . . 25.00 to 35.00
Creamer 20.00
Cup & Saucer . . 12.00 to 14.00
Gravy Boat, Attached
　Underplate 35.00
Pitcher, Water, 7 In. 75.00
Plate, Bread & Butter,
　6 1/4 In. . . . . . . 5.00 to 8.00
Plate, Dessert, 7 1/2 In. . . 10.00
Plate, Dinner,
　10 1/2 In. . . . . 12.00 to 15.00
Plate, Luncheon,
　9 1/4 In. . . . . . 10.00 to 15.00
Plate, Salad, 8 In. 8.00
Relish, 9 1/4 In. 20.00
Soup, Cream, Saucer 35.00
Soup, Dish 20.00
Sugar, Cover . . . 16.00 to 20.00
Teapot 60.00

Gray
Cup & Saucer 18.00

Maroon
Cup & Saucer 15.00
Gravy Boat, Attached
　Underplate 24.00
Plate, Bread & Butter,
　6 1/2 In. 8.00
Plate, Luncheon, 9 In. . . . 16.00

Turquoise
Ashtray 13.00
Bowl, Cereal, 6 1/4 In. . . 13.00
Bowl, Fruit,
　6 In. . . . . 10.00 to 12.00
Bowl, Vegetable,
　7 1/2 In. . . . . . 15.00 to 22.00
Butter, Cover 40.00
Chop Plate, 11 3/4 In. . . . 35.00
Creamer . . . . . . 12.00 to 20.00
Cup & Saucer . . 12.00 to 14.00
Gravy Boat, Attached
　Underplate . . . 30.00 to 40.00
Nut Cup, Footed 25.00

Plate, Bread & Butter,
6 1/2 In. . . . . . . 5.00 to 9.00
Plate, Dessert,
7 1/2 In. . . . . . . 7.00 to 9.00
Plate, Dinner,
10 1/2 In. . . . . 18.00 to 25.00
Plate, Luncheon,
9 1/2 In. . . . . . 12.00 to 18.00
Plate, Salad,
8 1/2 In. . . . . . . 8.00 to 12.00
Platter, Oval,
13 In. . . . . 30.00 to 45.00
Relish,
9 1/4 In. . . . . . 20.00 to 30.00
Salt 12.00
Salt & Pepper 25.00
Sherbet, 5 In. 15.00
Soup, Cream, Saucer 35.00
Sugar, Cover . . . 18.00 to 20.00
Sugar, Open 15.00
Teapot . . . . 45.00 to 95.00

Yellow

Bowl, Cereal, 6 1/2 In. . . . 9.00
Coffeepot, Cover,
After Dinner 99.00
Gravy Boat, Attached
Underplate 32.00
Pepper 10.00
Plate, Bread & Butter,
6 1/4 In. . . . . . . 5.00 to 9.00
Plate, Dessert, 8 In. 8.00
Plate, Luncheon, 9 In. . . . 12.00
Salt & Pepper 20.00
Sherbet, Footed 18.00
Soup, Cream, Saucer 35.00
Sugar, Cover 18.00

COUNTRY CRAFT was made
from 1962 to 1989. The line
was made to look "hand
thrown" and has slight ringed
grooves in the surface. The only
decoration is a colored rim. It
was made in five colors,
Almond Cream, Blue, Peach,
Raspberry, and Russet (brown).

Almond Cream

Saucer 2.00

Peach

Plate, Dinner, 10 7/8 In. . . 3.00

Russet

Bowl, Cereal, 6 3/8 In. . . 22.00

Creamer 42.00
Cup 21.00
Cup & Saucer 30.00
Plate, Salad, 8 3/8 In. 14.00

CREOLE pattern is brown with
a darker brown rim. It was first
offered in 1973.

Bowl, Cereal, 7 1/8 In. . . 22.00
Bowl, Vegetable, Round,
9 1/2 In. . . . . . 22.00 to 56.00
Creamer 18.00
Cup 21.00
Cup & Saucer 15.00
Gravy Boat 24.00
Plate, Dinner,
10 3/4 In. . . . 12.00 to 14.00
Plate, Salad,
8 3/4 In. . . . . . 12.00 to 14.00
Platter, Oval, 12 In. 62.00
Platter, Oval, 14 In. 25.00
Salt & Pepper 16.00
Soup, Dish 12.00
Sugar, Cover 22.00

CRINOLINE pattern has a border of pink flowers and ribbons.
It is a fine china pattern introduced in 1942. Another pattern
was given the same name in
1973. It has yellow flowers.

Bowl, Vegetable, Oval,
9 In. 55.00
Cup & Saucer . . 28.00 to 39.00
Plate, Bread & Butter,
6 3/8 In. 12.00
Plate, Dinner,
10 1/2 In. . . . 25.00 to 30.00
Soup, Cream, Saucer 30.00

CYPRESS pattern has white
cypress leaves on a plain gray
background. It is part of the
Flair dinnerware line that was
introduced in 1962.

Plate, Bread & Butter,
6 1/2 In. 10.00
Plate, Salad, 8 1/4 In. 14.00

DAFFODIL is part of the Greenhouse line, a mix-and-match
line that includes Blue Bell,
Poppy, and Sweet Pea. It has an
off-center design of yellow daf-
fodils and green leaves with an
art nouveau influence. It was
introduced in 1975.

Bowl, Cereal, 7 1/4 In. . . 14.00
Plate, Dinner, 10 3/4 In. . . 18.00
Plate, Salad,
8 In. . . . . 13.00 to 15.00
Saucer 10.00

DAISY pattern has a rimless plate with clusters of blue and yellow flowers and gray-green leaves.

Bowl, Vegetable, Divided,
　13 3/4 In. 79.00
Bowl, Vegetable, Round,
　7 1/2 In. 34.00
Bowl, Vegetable, Round,
　9 3/8 In. 53.00
Butter, Cover 65.00
Candy Dish 38.00
Creamer 42.00
Cup & Saucer 23.00
Gravy Boat, Attached
　Underplate 94.00
Mug 16.00
Plate, Bread & Butter,
　6 1/2 In. 10.00
Platter, Medium,
　13 3/4 In. 93.00
Relish 45.00
Saucer 6.00
Sugar, Cover 53.00

DAISY WREATH has a rim decorated with yellow daisies, smaller rust-color flowers, and scattered green-brown leaves. It was introduced in 1975.

Bowl, Cereal, 7 1/4 In. . . 10.00
Bowl, Fruit, 5 3/4 In. 8.00
Plate, Dinner, 10 3/4 In. . . 14.00
Plate, Salad, 8 In. 10.00
Sugar, Cover 13.00

DAWN is a plain gray pattern of fine china made with or without a narrow platinum border. It was introduced in 1950.

Cup . . . . 18.00 to 30.00
Plate, Dinner, 10 1/2 In. . . 28.00

DEL MAR is decorated with a ring of abstract shapes in blue and gray-green. It was made from 1959 to 1969, and is part of the Family-Discovery line of fine china. Another pattern named Del Mar, not included here, was made in 1937. It is decorated with white sailboats and seagulls on a blue ground.

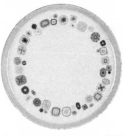

Cup 20.00
Gravy Boat, Attached
　Underplate 94.00
Sugar, Cover 18.00

DEL MONTE has a gold twisted rope design on the inner rim and gold trim on the outer

edge of the plates. Bowls have the gold twisted rope design around the center of the outside. The rope design is inside the cups. It was part of the Merced line, the first fine china line made by Gladding, McBean in 1942.

Creamer 76.00
Cup & Saucer, After
　Dinner 34.00
Gravy Boat, Attached
　Underplate 174.00
Soup, Dish 32.00
Sugar, Cover 103.00

DEL RIO has a pale gray rim with a decoration of a band of stylized white daisylike flowers and thin leaves. The decoration is added as a ring around the center of the outside of pieces like sugars, creamers, and bowls. It is part of the fine china line that was introduced in 1956.

Bowl, Fruit, 6 1/4 In. 42.00
Saucer 14.00

DESERT ROSE is one of the most popular patterns of earthenware ever sold in America. It was introduced in 1942 and is still being made. The pieces are decorated with large pink five-petal roses with yellow centers. Groupings of three leaves are added to the rose branch. Pieces made today in England are decorated with paler pink and grayer green. Some pieces were made in Portugal and Germany. Matching glasses and tablecloths, clocks, and other items have been made.

Ashtray,
  3 1/2 In. . . . . . 20.00 to 25.00
Ashtray, Cigarette Rest . . 65.00
Baker, Microwave,
  8 3/4 x 9 1/2 In. 215.00
Baker, Microwave,
  9 x 13 1/2 In. 285.00
Berry Bowl, 5 In. 10.00
Bowl, Cereal,
  6 In. . . . . 12.00 to 16.00
Bowl, Cereal, Footed,
  5 1/2 In. 32.00
Bowl, Fruit,
  5 1/4 In. . . . . . 6.00 to 18.00
Bowl, Salad,
  10 1/2 In. 125.00
Bowl, Vegetable, Divided,
  10 7/8 In. . . . 45.00 to 79.00
Bowl, Vegetable, Round,
  8 In. . . . . 24.00 to 38.00
Bowl, Vegetable, Round,
  9 In. . . . . 30.00 to 42.00
Butter, 1/4 Lb. 43.00
Butter, Cover 45.00
Candleholder, Pair 125.00
Casserole 30.00
Celery Dish 85.00
Chop Plate, 12 In. 65.00

Cigarette Box 135.00
Coffeepot 155.00
Compote, 4 x 8 In. 100.00
Creamer . . . . . . 18.00 to 24.00
Cup . . . . 7.00 to 12.00
Cup & Saucer . . . 6.00 to 20.00
Cup & Saucer, After
  Dinner . . . . . . 50.00 to 65.00
Dinner Bell, No Clapper,
  Small 100.00
Dish, Heart Shape, 5 3/4 x
  5 1/2 In. . . . 125.00 to 145.00
Eggcup . . . . 23.00 to 26.00
Ginger Jar, Cover 255.00
Goblet, Water, 6 1/2 In. . . 25.00
Gravy Boat 94.00
Gravy Boat, Attached
  Underplate . . . 30.00 to 40.00
Grill Plate, 11 1/2 In. 22.00
Mixing Bowl,
  6 In. . . . . . . 125.00 to 175.00
Mug, 12 Oz.,
  4 1/2 In. . . . . . 38.00 to 42.00
Napkin Ring 53.00
Pepper Shaker 10.00
Pitcher, Milk, Qt.,
  6 1/4 In. . . . . 75.00 to 105.00
Pitcher, Syrup, Pt.,
  6 1/8 In. . . . . . 75.00 to 92.00
Pitcher, Water, 2 1/2 Qt.,
  8 3/4 In. . . . 125.00 to 148.00
Plate, Bread & Butter,
  6 1/2 In. . . . . . . 5.00 to 8.00
Plate, Child's,
  8 7/8 In. 65.00
Plate, Dinner,
  10 1/2 In. . . . . 15.00 to 25.00
Plate, Luncheon,
  9 1/2 In. . . . . . 15.00 to 22.00
Plate, Salad,
  8 In. . . . . 7.50 to 18.00
Plate, Steak, Coupe,
  Oval, 11 In. 35.00
Platter,
  12 3/4 In. . . . 25.00 to 35.00
Platter, 14 In. . . . 45.00 to 47.00
Platter, 19 In. 295.00
Relish,
  3 Sections . . . . 65.00 to 85.00
Salt & Pepper,
  2 1/4 In. . . . . . 25.00 to 48.00
Salt & Pepper,
  6 In. 80.00

Salt & Pepper Mill,
  Chrome 425.00
Saltshaker 26.00
Saucer 6.00
Snack Plate, Microwave,
  Square, 8 1/4 In. 245.00
Soup, Dish, 8 1/2 In. 16.00
Sugar, Cover . . . 20.00 to 53.00
Sugar, No Cover 37.00
Sugar & Creamer 70.00
Teapot, Cover . . 65.00 to 85.00
Toast Cover 225.00
Tumbler, Juice, 6 Oz.,
  3 1/4 In. 47.00

DUET was introduced in 1956. It was a modern shape called Eclipse that was also used for the popular Starburst pattern. It is decorated with two sprigs of a pink flower with gray leaves.

Cup . . . . 5.00 to 18.00
Cup & Saucer 12.00
Plate, Bread & Butter,
  6 1/2 In. . . . . . . 4.00 to 7.00
Plate, Dinner,
  10 3/4 In. . . . . 7.00 to 15.00
Plate, Luncheon,
  9 1/2 In. 20.00
Plate, Salad, 8 In. 15.00
Saucer 3.00

EARTH BORN was introduced in 1978. It is plain white with a narrow brown rim trim.
Cup & Saucer 15.00
Plate, Dinner, 10 3/4 In. . . 13.00
Plate, Salad, 8 3/4 In. 10.00

EL DORADO was one of ten patterns made on the Madeira shape. It was introduced in

1966. Pieces have a sculpted relief floral pattern with a yellow rim or exterior.

Creamer 30.00
Cup & Saucer . . 10.00 to 23.00
Plate, Dinner, 10 1/2 In. . . 30.00
Plate, Salad, 8 1/2 In. 14.00
Platter, Oval, 11 3/4 In. . . 69.00
Soup, Dish 23.00
Sugar, Cover 40.00

EL PATIO was made from 1934 to 1956. The solid-color ware was made in more than twenty colors. In 1939, they introduced Apple Green, Deep Yellow, Flame Orange, Gloss White, Golden Glow, Light Yellow, Mexican Blue, and Redwood. By 1948 Bright Green, Maroon, and Satin Gray were added. Soon after, Bright Yellow Gloss, Chartreuse Satin, Coral Gloss, Coral Satin, Glacial Blue Gloss, Ivory Satin, and Turquoise Satin were added.

Apple Green
Saucer 5.00
Coral Satin
Bowl, Cereal, 5 1/2 In. . . 15.00
Bowl, Vegetable, Oval,
9 In. 30.00
Creamer 13.00
Cup 13.00

Plate, Bread & Butter,
6 1/4 In. 5.00
Plate, Luncheon,
9 1/4 In. 15.00
Flame Orange
Bowl, Fruit, 5 1/4 In. 8.00
Plate, Bread & Butter,
6 1/2 In. 7.00
Golden Glow
Saucer 5.00
Redwood
Cup 13.00
Satin Gray
Bowl, Cereal,
Flared, 6 In. 15.00
Bowl, Fruit, 5 1/4 In. 13.00
Creamer 13.00
Cup 13.00
Plate, Bread & Butter,
6 1/4 In. 5.00
Plate, Luncheon,
9 1/4 In. 15.00
Plate, Salad, 8 1/4 In. 13.00
Platter, Oval, 11 1/2 In. . . 30.00
Turquoise Satin
Bowl, Fruit, 5 1/4 In. 13.00
Cup 13.00
Cup & Saucer 18.00
Plate, Bread & Butter,
6 1/4 In. 5.00
Plate, Luncheon,
9 1/4 In. 15.00
Sugar, Cover 18.00

EMERALD ISLE was introduced in 1965. It is decorated in grays, brown, and black with an abstract center design of black lines in a fan shape.

Plate, Bread & Butter,
6 1/8 In. . . . . . . 6.00 to 12.00

Do not use any type of tape on porcelain or pottery that has over-glazed decorations. Gilding and enamels may pull off when the tape is removed. Antiques shops often tape a lid to a bowl; when you buy, ask the dealer to remove the tape to be sure no damage has been done.

Plate, Salad, 8 3/4 In. 8.00

FAN SHELL is one of the patterns in the Sculptures line introduced in 1977. A raised design is featured on a sand-color or white plate.

Plate, Dinner, Sea
Sculptures, 10 3/4 In. . . 25.00
Plate, Luncheon, Sea
Sculptures,
9 1/8 In. . . . . . 12.00 to 30.00

FERN DELL was introduced in 1957. It is part of the Flair line. The design includes fern leaves in gray and tan and pale blue-gray.

Cup & Saucer 23.00
Saucer 6.00

FLORAL is part of the Madeira line of earthenware. It was introduced in 1971. The six-petal flowers are purple, orange, and yellow with leaves in varying shades of green. There is a chartreuse-gray inner border line. A related pattern called Floral was made in England. It has a similar decoration but fewer flowers. These pieces are marked *Made in England.*

Bowl, Cereal, 6 1/4 In.   . . 10.00
Bowl, Vegetable, Round   . 55.00
Creamer . . . . . . 17.00 to 36.00
Cup & Saucer 21.00
Gravy Boat, Underplate,
    Lid . . . . 20.00 to 28.00
Plate, Dinner,
    10 1/2 In. . . . . 10.00 to 15.00
Plate, Salad, 8 1/2 In. 12.00
Platter, Oval, 11 3/4 In. . . 57.00
Platter, Oval, 13 1/2 In. . . 30.00
Saucer 5.00
Soup, Dish 21.00
Sugar, Cover 20.00

FREMONT is part of the fine china line made by Gladding, McBean in 1942. It has a white body with a stylized tree in green and brown in the center and a gold line inner border.

Bowl, Fruit, 6 1/4 In. 37.00
Bowl, Vegetable, Oval,
    9 In. 124.00
Coffeepot, Cover 95.00
Creamer 35.00
Cup & Saucer 45.00
Cup & Saucer, After
    Dinner 15.00
Gravy Boat 185.00
Plate, Bread & Butter,
    6 3/8 In. 18.00
Plate, Dinner,
    10 1/2 In. . . . . 38.00 to 59.00
Plate, Salad,
    8 3/8 In. . . . . . 25.00 to 32.00
Platter, Oval, 16 In. 219.00
Saucer 6.00
Sugar, Cover 60.00
Teapot, Cover 120.00

FRENCH FLORAL plates are covered with an overall design of small blue flower heads joined by thin white lines. The bowls, cups, and other rounded pieces are plain with a blue trim line. It was discontinued in 1979.

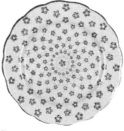

Cup 23.00
Plate, Salad, 8 In. 16.00
Soup, Dish 23.00

FRESH FRUIT looks like hand-painted earthenware. It was first made in 1980, continued in production in England in 1984, and discontinued in 1988. Pieces are decorated with large designs of branches holding fruit. The plates have several fruits with leaves as a border.

Bowl, Cereal,
    6 In. . . . . 22.00 to 24.00
Cup 21.00
Cup & Saucer 23.00
Mug, 7 Oz. 35.00
Napkin Ring 35.00
Sugar, Cover 50.00

FRUIT was made from 1963 to 1984. It is decorated with large center drawings of varied fruits. It has a colored border. Another pattern with small fruit as a border was made in the 1940s, but that pattern is not listed here.

Bowl, 9 In. 60.00
Bowl, Cereal,
    6 In. 24.00
Bowl, Vegetable, Round,
    Open 28.00
Butter, Cover 75.00
Casserole, Cover, Small
    Fruit, 1 1/2 Qt. 200.00
Cup & Saucer 26.00
Plate, Bread & Butter,
    6 1/2 In. 10.00
Plate, Dinner,
    10 1/2 In. 35.00
Plate, Salad,
    8 1/2 In. 25.00
Saucer 4.00

GABRIELLE was made from about 1969 to 1978. The fine china pattern has a lacy band of orange-yellow and gray-green.

Cup & Saucer 39.00
Plate, Bread & Butter,
  6 1/4 In. . . . . . 8.00 to 15.00
Plate, Dinner,
  10 1/2 In. 50.00
Plate, Salad,
  8 1/4 In. 22.00

GLENFIELD is a contemporary-looking fine china dinnerware that features wheat stalks and a platinum rim. It was introduced about 1961.

Cup & Saucer 23.00
Sugar, Cover 48.00

GOLD BAND can refer to one of two patterns of fine china by the same name. The 1950s version has a plain shape without a rim. The 1949 pieces, sometimes called Gold Band 301, were made in the Merced line and have a wide rim. Both were trimmed with a narrow gold line at the edge.

Cup 40.00
Cup & Saucer 45.00
Plate, Dinner, 10 1/2 In. . . 58.00
Plate, Salad, 8 3/8 In. 25.00

HACIENDA GOLD is part of the Hacienda line introduced about 1962. It was still being made in 1974. The pattern has a center design of an orange-yellow (called gold) circle with a variety of geometric loops and bands. It also has a narrow orange-yellow band just inside the edge. It is on a body that has tiny grooves, giving it a hand-thrown look.

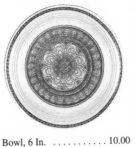

Bowl, 6 In. 10.00
Bowl, 8 In. 15.00
Bowl, Vegetable, Divided,
  11 In. . . . . . . 22.00 to 43.00
Bowl, Vegetable, Round,
  8 In. 33.00
Butter 10.00
Butter, Cover . . . 18.00 to 39.00
Creamer . . . . 15.00 to 19.00
Cup & Saucer . . . 7.00 to 15.00
Gravy Boat,
  Underplate . . . 20.00 to 50.00
Pitcher . . . . 20.00 to 24.00

Plate, Bread & Butter,
  6 3/4 In. 8.00
Plate, Dinner,
  10 7/8 In. . . . . 9.00 to 13.00
Plate, Salad,
  8 3/8 In. . . . . 10.00 to 11.00
Platter, Medium,
  13 3/4 In. . . . 22.00 to 59.00
Salt & Pepper . . . 12.00 to 29.00
Saucer 4.00
Sugar, Cover . . . 20.00 to 29.00

HACIENDA GREEN is the same as Hacienda Gold except the decorations are green. The interior of the cups and some other pieces in both patterns are glazed in the appropriate color.

Bowl, Cereal, 6 3/8 In. . . 15.00
Bowl, Fruit, 5 1/4 In. 20.00
Bowl, Vegetable, Divided,
  11 In. 69.00
Bowl, Vegetable, Round,
  Open 45.00
Butter, Cover . . . 12.00 to 48.00
Casserole, 2 Handles 48.00
Coffeepot 25.00
Creamer . . . . 18.00 to 27.00
Cup & Saucer 22.00
Gravy Boat, Attached
  Underplate 69.00
Pitcher, Water, 8 In. 38.00
Plate, Bread & Butter,
  6 3/4 In. . . . . . . 4.00 to 10.00
Plate, Dinner,
  10 7/8 In. . . . . 10.00 to 24.00
Plate, Luncheon,
  9 3/4 In. 19.00
Plate, Salad,
  8 3/8 In. . . . . . . 8.00 to 12.00
Platter,
  13 3/4 In. . . . . 30.00 to 65.00
Salt & Pepper . . . 19.00 to 40.00
Saucer . . . . 4.00 to 8.00
Soup, Dish . . . . . . 7.00 to 18.00
Sugar, Cover . . . 28.00 to 48.00
Sugar & Creamer 60.00
Teapot, Cover 65.00

HAPPY TALK is a white earthenware that looks like china. It was made about 1959 and made in Japan. The decoration is a scattered gray flower head with six thin petals, scattered pink three-petal flower heads, and a few thin lines suggesting stems. It was discontinued about 1963.

Bowl, Cereal, 6 In. 8.00
Bowl, Vegetable, Round,
    Open, 8 In. 30.00
Plate, Bread & Butter,
    6 In. 8.00
Plate, Dinner,
    10 3/8 In. 20.00
Saucer 10.00

HAWAII was part of the White-stone line made from 1967 to about 1969. The design includes rectangular blocks filled with vertical palm leaves in a row. It is orange, yellow, and brown.

Bowl, Fruit, 5 In. 10.00
Bowl, Vegetable, 8 In. . . . 26.00
Cup & Saucer 12.00
Plate, Bread & Butter,
    6 In. 8.00
Plate, Dinner, 10 3/8 In. . . 14.00
Plate, Salad, 8 1/4 In. 10.00
Saucer 4.00
Sugar, Cover 16.00

HERITAGE pattern has a peas-antlike inspiration. The black designs on a white body seem to be modern adaptations of colorful Pennsylvania Dutch decorations. It was made from 1960 to 1969.

Bowl, Fruit, 5 In. 15.00
Bowl, Vegetable, Divided,
    10 7/8 In. 35.00
Bowl, Vegetable, Oval,
    8 1/4 In. 63.00
Coffeepot 98.00
Creamer . . . . . . 14.00 to 15.00
Cup 12.00
Cup & Saucer . . 15.00 to 22.00
Pitcher, 8 1/4 In. 24.00
Plate, Bread & Butter,
    6 1/8 In. . . . . . 8.00 to 10.00
Plate, Dinner, 10 1/8 In. . . 17.00
Plate, Salad,
    8 3/4 In. . . . . 10.00 to 12.00

◆

Several types of glue are needed to repair broken pottery and porcelain. Commercial glues found in a local hardware store are often satisfac-tory. Read the labels. Some types work only with pieces that are porous, others only with pieces that are not porous. Instant glue is difficult to use if the break is complicated.

◆

Platter, 13 In. . . . 22.00 to 40.00
Platter, 14 3/4 In. 50.00
Salt & Pepper . . . 12.00 to 22.00
Saucer 6.00
Soup, Dish 18.00
Sugar, Cover 25.00

HUNTINGTON is a plain fine china pattern with platinum bands as the only decoration. It was first made in 1948.

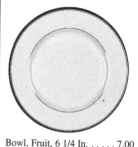

Bowl, Fruit, 6 1/4 In. 7.00
Cup & Saucer . . 25.00 to 45.00
Plate, Dinner,
    10 1/2 In. . . . 25.00 to 55.00
Plate, Salad, 8 3/8 In. 13.00
Saucer 5.00

HUNTINGTON ROSE is part of the fine china line. It was intro-duced in 1955. It has a single pink rose with gray leaves in the center of a platinum-trimmed plate or on the side of bowls and cups.

Bowl, Vegetable, Oval . . 135.00
Creamer 70.00
Platter, 12 1/2 In. 145.00
Soup, Dish, Rimmed 65.00
Sugar, Cover 105.00

INDIAN SUMMER was made from 1958 to 1969. It is a pattern of scattered maple leaves in the fall colors of orange, yellow, brown, and gray-green.

Bowl, Cereal, 6 1/4 In. . . . 3.00
Bowl, Fruit, 5 In. 3.00
Creamer 12.00
Gravy Boat, Attached
    Underplate 25.00
Plate, Bread & Butter,
    6 1/8 In. 4.00
Plate, Dinner,
    10 1/8 In. . . . . 12.00 to 13.00
Plate, Salad, 8 3/8 In. 7.00
Platter, 13 In. 24.00
Saltshaker 5.00
Saucer 4.00

IVY resembles the famous Wedgwood Ivy pattern made in the eighteenth century. It has a hand-painted band of ivory leaves as a border. It was made from about 1948 to 1983.

Bowl, Fruit,
    5 1/4 In. . . . . . 15.00 to 24.00
Bowl, Salad, 11 1/4 In. . . 20.00
Bowl, Vegetable, Round,
    8 In. . . . . 45.00 to 79.00
Butter, Cover . . . 50.00 to 65.00

◆

Silver and gold trim will wash off dishes in time. Do not unload any dishes with metallic trim until they have completely cooled.

◆

Casserole, Cover,
    Handles 95.00
Creamer . . . . 30.00 to 35.00
Cup 16.00
Cup & Saucer . . 19.00 to 38.00
Gravy Boat, Attached
    Underplate 65.00
Pickle 23.00
Plate, Bread & Butter,
    6 1/4 In. . . . . . . 7.00 to 12.00
Plate, Dinner,
    10 1/2 In. . . . . 25.00 to 45.00
Plate, Luncheon,
    9 1/2 In. 18.00
Plate, Salad, 8 1/2 In. 25.00
Platter, Oval,
    11 1/4 In. . . . . 40.00 to 45.00
Saucer 6.00
Snack Set, TV, Divided,
    Mug, Oblong 175.00
Soup, Dish 62.00
Sugar, Cover 67.00
Tumbler, 5 1/8 In. 65.00

JAMOCA is a casual dining pattern typical of its day. It was introduced in 1973. The dark brown background and orange geometric border and center design made it one of the most popular patterns of the 1970s.

Bowl, Cereal,
    7 1/8 In. . . . . . 12.00 to 18.00
Bowl, Fruit, 5 1/2 In. 16.00
Bowl, Vegetable, Oval,
    9 1/2 In. 15.00
Creamer 36.00
Goblet, Water, 6 1/2 In. . . 16.00
Plate, Bread & Butter,
    6 3/4 In. 9.00
Plate, Dinner,
    10 3/4 In. . . . . 12.00 to 14.00
Plate, Salad,
    8 3/4 In. . . . . . 10.00 to 12.00
Platter, Oval, 12 In. 57.00
Platter, Oval, 14 In. 81.00
Salt & Pepper 38.00
Saucer . . . . 5.00 to 9.00
Soup, Dish 13.00

LARKSPUR was introduced in 1958. The decoration is a band of leaf and flowerlike shapes in pink, blue, and browns.

Plate, Bread & Butter,
    6 1/2 In. 6.00
Plate, Dinner, 10 1/2 In. . . 14.00
Saltshaker 10.00
Saucer 5.00

LATTICE is a pattern in the Wicker Weave line made about 1978 to 1981. It has an embossed latticelike design on the plate rim and the sides of other pieces. Lattice is a light cream color.

Plate, Salad, 8 In. 16.00
Saucer 12.00

LORRAINE was made in Green or Maroon. It is part of the fine china line made by Gladding,

McBean in 1946. It has an overall design of a single color of line drawings of stylized flowers, leaves, and fanciful shapes.

Green

Bowl, Fruit,
  6 1/4 In. . . . . . 35.00 to 39.00
Creamer 42.00
Cup & Saucer 75.00
Gravy Boat, Attached
  Underplate 150.00
Plate, Bread & Butter,
  6 3/8 In. 25.00
Plate, Dinner,
  10 1/2 In. 50.00
Plate, Salad,
  8 3/8 In. . . . . . 24.00 to 35.00
Saucer . . . . 10.00 to 40.00
Soup, Dish, 8 1/4 In. 45.00

Maroon

Plate, Bread & Butter,
  6 3/8 In. 19.00

LUCERNE is a white body with two-tone gray scroll-like decorations as a band. It was part of the first Franciscan designs made in Japan starting in 1959.

Plate, Bread & Butter,
  6 3/8 In. . . . . . . 9.00 to 10.00
Plate, Salad, 8 1/8 In. 14.00

MADEIRA is the name of both a shape and a pattern of earthenware dishes. The pattern is dark brown with an overall center design of pale yellow lines forming flowers and scrolls. It was introduced in 1967.

Bowl, Vegetable,
  7 1/8 In. 25.00
Bowl, Vegetable, Divided,
  11 1/8 In. 20.00
Bowl, Vegetable, Round,
  9 In. 41.00
Bowl, Vegetable, Round,
  7 In. . . . . 25.00 to 35.00
Butter, Cover . . . 25.00 to 53.00
Candleholder,
  6 1/8 In. . . . . . 27.00 to 55.00
Casserole,
  Cover Only 15.00
Chip & Dip Set,
  2 Piece 75.00
Coffeepot . . . . . . 39.00 to 85.00
Creamer . . . . . . 20.00 to 22.00
Cup 10.00
Cup & Saucer . . 12.00 to 16.00
Gravy Boat 74.00
Jelly Server 25.00
Plate, Bread & Butter,
  6 3/4 In. . . . . 6.00 to 9.00
Plate, Dinner,
  10 1/2 In. . . . . 12.00 to 18.00
Plate, Salad,
  8 1/2 In. . . . . . . 8.00 to 12.00
Platter,
  11 3/4 In. 57.00
Platter,
  13 1/2 In. . . . . 20.00 to 21.00
Salt & Pepper . . 18.00 to 43.00
Saucer . . . . 3.00 to 5.00
Soup, Dish 10.00
Sugar, Cover . . . 10.00 to 30.00

MANDARIN is an English-made pattern from the 1970s. The colorful floral border and center design of red, blue, and gray-green is reminiscent of nineteenth-century English designs.

Plate, Dinner,
  9 7/8 In. 25.00
Platter, 12 1/4 In. 69.00
Platter, 14 1/4 In. 35.00
Saucer . . . . 6.00 to 10.00

MARIPOSA is part of the fine china line made by Gladding, McBean in 1949. It is decorated with a bouquet of realistic flowers in natural colors.

Bowl, Fruit, 6 1/4 In. 54.00
Bowl, Vegetable, 9 In. . . 195.00
Cup & Saucer . . 68.00 to 94.00
Cup & Saucer, After
  Dinner 69.00
Plate, Bread & Butter,
  6 3/8 In. . . . . . 26.00 to 38.00
Plate, Dinner,
  10 1/2 In. . . . . 62.00 to 81.00
Plate, Salad,
  8 3/8 In. . . . . . 36.00 to 48.00
Salt & Pepper . . 98.00 to 124.00
Saucer . . . . 17.00 to 62.00
Teapot, No Cover 184.00

MAYPOLE is decorated with large stylized yellow and pink flowers with green leaves that fill the center of the plate. There is a chartreuse and yellow band near the edge. It was made after 1974.

Bowl, Cereal, 7 1/8 In.	. . 15.00
Cup & Saucer	. . . . 25.00
Plate, Dinner, 10 3/4 In.	. . . 25.00
Plate, Salad, 8 3/4 In.	. . . . 14.00
Soup, Dish	. . . . 15.00

MAYTIME, part of the same line as Indian Summer, was introduced in 1960. It is decorated with a few pale pink and blue 16-petal flowers.

Creamer	. . . . 15.00
Cup & Saucer	. . . . 10.00
Plate, Bread & Butter, 6 1/8 In.	. . . . 8.00
Plate, Dinner, 10 1/8 In.	. . . 16.00
Platter, Medium, 13 In.	. . 25.00

MEADOW ROSE was made in 1977. It is a variation of the Desert Rose pattern, but the flowers are yellow instead of pink.

Cup	. . . . 12.00
Cup & Saucer	. . 16.00 to 21.00
Plate, Dinner, 10 5/8 In.	. . 22.00
Saucer	. . . . 5.00
Sugar, Cover	. . . . 48.00
Teapot	. . . . 195.00

MELROSE, a fine china pattern, has trailing pink roses and gray-green leaves on the dishes. It was made in the 1960s.

Creamer	. . . . 48.00
Sugar, Cover	. . . . 61.00

MERRY-GO-ROUND is another pattern in the Whitestone line, like Hawaii, Antigua, Cantata, and Happy Talk. It was an earthenware made in Japan after 1959. The pattern does not look like a carousel or merry-go-round; it has pink and light green circles and lines as a border.

Bowl, Fruit, 5 In.	. . . . 7.00
Bowl, Vegetable, Round, Open, 8 In.	. . . 34.00 to 35.00
Creamer	. . . . . . 23.00 to 36.00
Cup & Saucer	. . 10.00 to 16.00
Gravy Boat	. . . . 30.00

Plate, Bread & Butter, 6 In.	. . . . 7.00 to 8.00
Plate, Dinner, 10 3/8 In.	. . . . 16.00 to 17.00
Platter, 13 1/4 In.	. . . . 36.00
Relish, 2 Sections, 10 1/2 In.	. . . . 39.00
Salt & Pepper	. . . . 10.00
Saucer	. . . . 5.00
Sugar, Cover	. . . 10.00 to 30.00

MIDNIGHT MIST was made from 1966 to 1976. It is an elegant fine china pattern with a dark blue (almost black) band.

Creamer	. . . . . 180.00 to 217.00
Cup	. . . . 109.00
Cup & Saucer	. . 51.00 to 121.00
Plate, Bread & Butter, 6 1/4 In.	. . . . 73.00
Plate, Dinner, 10 1/2 In.	. . . . 101.00
Plate, Salad, 8 1/4 In.	. . . . 100.00
Saucer	. . . . 40.00
Teapot	. . . . 257.00
Underplate, For Gravy Boat	. . . . 187.00

MONACO is the same shape as Midnight Mist, but has a gold band for decoration. It was introduced in 1968.

Cup & Saucer	. . . . 51.00
Plate, Bread & Butter, 6 1/4 In.	. . . . 21.00
Saucer	. . . . 14.00

MONTECITO ware was made in Celadon, Coral, Eggplant, Gray, Satin Ivory, Turquoise, and Yellow. It was produced from 1937 until 1942. A totally different pattern named Montecito was introduced after 1957 by the company but is not listed here.

Bowl, Fruit, 6 1/4 In.	. . . . 12.00
Cup & Saucer	. . . . 24.00
Plate, Bread & Butter, 6 3/8 In.	. . . . 12.00
Plate, Salad, 8 1/4 In.	. . . . . 16.00

MOON GLOW is part of the 7000 line of fine china that includes Midnight Mist and Monaco. The design for Moon Glow is a plain platinum band. It was issued from 1966 to 1976.

Cup & Saucer 56.00
Saucer 12.00

MOONDANCE is decorated with what looks like a spiral of ink blots in gray to dark blue. There is also a dark blue band. The fine china pattern was first made in 1972.

Bowl, Fruit, 5 1/4 In. 19.00
Bowl, Vegetable, Oval,
   Open 17.00
Cup & Saucer 23.00
Plate, Dinner,
   10 1/2 In. 30.00
Plate, Salad, 8 1/2 In. 14.00

MOUNTAIN LAUREL has a simple design of gold laurel leaves. It is part of the fine china line introduced by Gladding, McBean in 1941.

Bowl, Cereal, 6 In. 28.00
Bowl, Fruit, 5 3/8 In. 14.00
Creamer . . . . . . 24.00 to 65.00
Cup & Saucer 32.00
Plate, Bread & Butter,
   6 3/8 In. . . . . . 16.00 to 19.00
Plate, Dinner,
   10 1/2 In. 28.00
Plate, Luncheon,
   9 In. 22.00
Platter, 12 1/2 In. 65.00
Sugar, No Cover 74.00

NEWPORT, a fine china pattern, was made from 1959 to 1961. It has a border design of groups of three leaves in blue and brown.

Creamer 20.00
Cup 13.00
Cup & Saucer 16.00
Plate, Bread & Butter,
   6 3/8 In. 7.00
Plate, Dinner, 10 3/8 In. . . 16.00
Plate, Salad, 8 1/8 In. 10.00

NUT TREE is part of the same line as Moondance. It was made in shades of brown with a center design that looks a little like a snowflake. It was made in 1970.

Bowl, Cereal, 7 In. 3.00
Bowl, Vegetable, Round . 36.00
Butter, Cover 38.00
Coffeepot 45.00
Creamer . . . . 8.00 to 19.00
Cup & Saucer . . 16.00 to 25.00
Gravy Boat, Underplate . . 38.00
Plate, Bread & Butter,
   6 3/4 In. . . . . 8.00 to 9.00
Plate, Dinner,
   10 1/2 In. . . . . 21.00 to 23.00
Plate, Salad,
   8 1/2 In. . . . . . 3.00 to 12.00
Platter, Oval,
   11 3/4 In. 38.00
Platter, Oval,
   13 1/2 In. 13.00
Salt & Pepper 26.00
Saucer 5.00

OASIS is part of the popular Eclipse line, modern shapes designed in 1955. The pattern is a series of lines, rectangles, and asterisks in blue and black.

Bowl, Vegetable, Divided,
   8 1/4 In. 45.00
Casserole, Cover 65.00
Eggcup 45.00
Plate, Bread & Butter,
   6 1/2 In. 12.00
Soup, Dish 17.00
Tumbler, Juice 45.00

Wash tea and coffee cups as soon as possible to avoid stains.

OCTOBER is a hand-painted line picturing fall-color maple-like leaves. It was introduced in 1977.

Baker, Microwave, Rectangular,
   13 3/4 In. 145.00
Baker, Microwave, Square,
   9 5/8 In. 120.00
Bowl, Cereal,
   7 In. . . . . 12.00 to 19.00
Bowl, Fruit,
   5 1/2 In. . . . . . 15.00 to 23.00
Bowl, Vegetable, Round,
   8 In. . . . . 93.00 to 96.00
Butter 45.00
Butter, Cover 119.00
Creamer . . . . . . 18.00 to 44.00
Cup 20.00
Cup & Saucer . . 10.00 to 24.00
Gravy Boat, Attached
   Underplate 132.00
Mug 82.00
Pitcher, 48 Oz.,
   6 1/2 In. 305.00
Plate, Bread & Butter,
   6 3/8 In. 25.00
Plate, Dinner,
   10 5/8 In. . . . . 25.00 to 67.00
Plate, Salad,
   8 In. . . . . 10.00 to 19.00
Platter, Oval,
   14 In. . . . . . . 70.00 to 100.00
Salt & Pepper . . . 34.00 to 61.00
Saltshaker 36.00
Saucer . . . . 5.00 to 10.00

Soup, Dish 14.00
Sugar, Cover . . . 42.00 to 45.00
Sugar & Creamer,
   Cover 80.00
Teapot 153.00

OLYMPIC is decorated with realistic violets and leaves. It was introduced in 1950.

Ashtray 49.00
Bowl, Fruit, 4 3/4 In. 37.00
Bowl, Vegetable, Oval,
   9 In. 112.00
Creamer 90.00
Cup & Saucer 45.00
Plate, Bread & Butter,
   6 3/8 In. 18.00
Plate, Dinner, 10 1/2 In. . . 59.00
Platter, 12 In. 160.00
Platter, 16 In. 219.00
Sugar, Cover 108.00
Sugar, No Cover 74.00

PALOMAR, part of the fine china line, was made in many colors, including Cameo Pink, Gray, Jade, Jasper, Robin's Egg Blue, and Yellow. Each color has either platinum or gold trim. It was introduced in 1948.

Cameo Pink
Cup & Saucer 34.00
Plate, Bread & Butter,
   6 3/8 In. 15.00
Plate, Dinner, 10 1/2 In. . . 27.00
Plate, Salad, 8 3/8 In. 15.00

Gray
Plate, Dinner, 10 1/2 In. . . 50.00
Plate, Salad, 8 3/8 In. 22.00

Jade
Bowl, Fruit, 5 3/8 In. 30.00
Cup 34.00
Plate, Bread & Butter,
   6 3/8 In. 15.00
Plate, Dinner, 10 1/2 In. . . 50.00
Plate, Salad,
   8 3/8 In. . . . . . 22.00 to 35.00

PEBBLE BEACH was first made in 1969. It was decorated with blobs that formed flowers and a border in earth tones. Sev-

eral different color combinations were used.

Bowl, Fruit, 5 1/4 In 9.00
Bowl, Vegetable, Round,
   Open . . . . 20.00 to 29.00
Creamer . . . . . . 12.00 to 19.00
Cup 10.00
Cup & Saucer . . . 9.00 to 16.00
Mug 12.00
Plate, Bread & Butter,
   6 3/4 In. . . . . . . 8.00 to 10.00
Plate, Dinner,
   10 1/2 In. . . . . 13.00 to 26.00
Plate, Salad,
   8 1/2 In. . . . . . . 7.00 to 12.00
Platter, Oval, 11 3/4 In. . . 25.00
Salt & Pepper 19.00
Saucer 5.00
Soup, Dish . . . . . 11.00 to 21.00
Sugar 10.00
Sugar, Cover . . . 18.00 to 21.00

PICKWICK was introduced in 1965. It was one of the patterns made in Japan. The design is orange-and-yellow fruit and leaves in a wide band around the edge of the plates and bowls.

Bowl, Cereal, 6 In. 19.00
Bowl, Vegetable, 8 In. . . . 55.00
Creamer 36.00
Cup & Saucer . . . 6.00 to 21.00
Pitcher, Water, 8 In. 50.00
Plate, Bread & Butter,
   6 In. . . . . 6.00 to 10.00
Plate, Dinner,
   10 3/8 In. . . . . 18.00 to 26.00
Saucer 3.00
Sugar, Cover 23.00

PICNIC is a shape and a pattern name. The pattern, introduced in 1973, has yellow and green flower heads in a cluster in the center of the plate. There are yellow and green flowers and bands around the edge. Cups and bowls have the band on the outside.

Bowl, Cereal,
   7 1/8 In. . . . . . 10.00 to 12.00

Bowl, Vegetable,
   9 1/2 In. . . . . . 25.00 to 32.00
Cup & Saucer . . 15.00 to 18.00
Mug 65.00
Pitcher, 32 Oz.,
   7 1/8 In. 65.00
Plate, Bread & Butter,
   6 3/4 In. 8.00
Plate, Dinner,
   10 3/4 In. . . . 14.00 to 26.00
Plate, Salad,
   8 3/4 In. . . . . . 10.00 to 12.00
Platter, Oval, 14 In. 30.00
Salt & Pepper 22.00
Saucer . . . . 5.00 to 12.00
Soup, Dish, Rimmed 18.00

PINK-A-DILLY is decorated with sprigs of pink roses with green leaves. It is one of the Japanese-made designs introduced in 1959. It remained in production until about 1969.

Creamer 10.00
Cup & Saucer . . 15.00 to 18.00
Plate, Bread & Butter,
   6 In. 8.00
Plate, Dinner,
   10 3/8 In. . . . . 15.00 to 18.00
Saucer 4.00

PLATINA is a plain white dinnerware with a swirled or fluted border on plates or on the body of cups and bowls. It has a platinum edge. The design was made in 1959.

Cup & Saucer 54.00
Plate, Dinner, 10 3/4 In. . . 70.00
Saucer 13.00
Soup, Dish 55.00

PLATINUM BAND is a plain white fine china dinnerware with a platinum edge. It was introduced in 1949.

Creamer . . . . . . 40.00 to 45.00
Cup & Saucer . . 15.00 to 33.00
Gravy Boat 65.00
Plate, Bread & Butter,
   6 3/8 In. . . . . . 10.00 to 22.00
Plate, Dinner,
   10 1/2 In. . . . . 34.00 to 42.00

Plate, Salad,
8 In. . . . . 22.00 to 24.00
Platter, 16 In. 65.00
Saucer 7.00
Sugar, Cover 60.00

POPPY is part of the Greenhouse line, a mix-and-match line that includes Daffodil, Sweet Pea, and Blue Bell. All have similar off-center designs of flowers. Poppy has sprigs of yellow or red flowers, poppies, and leaves. It was introduced in 1975 and discontinued in 1978.

Bowl, Cereal, 7 1/4 In. . . 18.00
Bowl, Dessert, 4 In. 25.00
Butter 100.00
Cup & Saucer 25.00
Plate, Dinner, 10 3/4 In. . . 35.00

RADIANCE was introduced in 1958. It has a border of green and yellow stalks of flowers.

Cup & Saucer 12.00
Gravy Boat, Attached
Underplate 24.00
Plate, Salad,
8 3/8 In. 16.00
Relish, 2 Sections,
10 3/8 In. 24.00
Soup, Dish, 6 1/4 In. . . . 12.00

REFLECTIONS is a 1982 pattern with a hand-thrown look. The solid-color ware came in Black, Blue, Burgundy, Jade, Lilac, Peach, Sand, Silver Gray, Smoke Gray, and White. Production stopped in the United States in 1984. There was also an English-made pattern called

Reflections made in the 1970s. It has earth-tone blobs filling the center and bands of brown and yellow as a border. It is not listed here.

Blue
Cup & Saucer 20.00
Burgundy
Cup & Saucer 13.00
Plate, Dinner, 10 7/8 In. . . 14.00
Lilac
Plate, Bread & Butter,
6 3/4 In. 10.00
Plate, Dinner, 10 7/8 In. . . 14.00
Peach
Cup 8.00
Cup & Saucer 18.00
Sand
Cup & Saucer 13.00
Silver Gray
Cup 12.00
Plate, Bread & Butter,
6 3/4 In. 10.00
Plate, Dinner, 10 7/8 In. . . 30.00
Smoke Gray
Cup & Saucer 14.00
Plate, Dinner, 10 7/8 In. . . 14.00
Plate, Salad, 8 3/8 In. . . . 12.00
White
Plate, Dinner, 10 7/8 In. . . 14.00

REGENCY has a stylized sheaf of wheat as the center design and platinum trim. It was introduced in 1953.

Bowl, Sugar, Cover 38.00
Creamer 27.00

RENAISSANCE patterns were made on the Del Rey shape by 1957. Renaissance Grey and Renaissance Gold appeared in 1957. Renaissance Platinum was introduced in 1966. Royal Renaissance (blue) was introduced in 1971. Each had a wide, colored border with a lacy design. Renaissance Gold was expensive because the border was actually finished with gold.

Gold
Cup & Saucer 54.00
Plate, Dinner, 10 5/8 In. . . 69.00
Plate, Salad, 8 1/2 In. 31.00
Grey
Bowl, Vegetable, Oval,
9 In. 115.00
Cup & Saucer . . 45.00 to 61.00
Gravy Boat, Attached
Underplate 180.00
Plate, Bread & Butter,
6 3/8 In. . . . . . 16.00 to 19.00
Plate, Dinner,
10 5/8 In. . . . . 44.00 to 61.00
Plate, Salad,
8 1/2 In. . . . . . 27.00 to 48.00
Platter,
15 1/2 In. . . 175.00 to 189.00
Saucer . . . . 12.00 to 13.00
Platinum
Plate, Bread & Butter,
6 3/8 In. 25.00
Plate, Dinner, 10 5/8 In. . . 59.00
Saucer 16.00

ROSETTE is a 1980s pattern decorated with a band of pink and white flowers.

Bowl, Cereal, 6 In. 22.00
Bowl, Vegetable, Round,
8 1/4 In. 63.00
Cup & Saucer 23.00
Plate, Dinner, 10 1/2 In. . . 30.00
Platter, Oval, 13 In. 69.00
Saucer 6.00

ROSSMORE has a small center pattern of pink and light green leafy shapes in a circle. It is a fine china pattern first offered for sale in 1945.

Bowl, Vegetable, Oval . . 112.00

Creamer . . . . . . 30.00 to 72.00
Pepper Shaker 40.00
Plate, Bread & Butter,
  6 3/8 In. . . . . . 15.00 to 22.00
Plate, Dinner,
  10 1/2 In. . . . . 34.00 to 50.00
Plate, Salad,
  8 3/8 In. . . . . . 24.00 to 29.00
Salt & Pepper 22.00
Saucer . . . . 10.00 to 34.00
Soup, Dish 25.00
Sugar, Cover 38.00

SAND DOLLAR is one of many fine china patterns picturing sea creatures that are part of the Sculptures line. The sand-color or white plate is decorated with an embossed picture of a sand dollar. It was introduced in 1977.

Sand
Plate, Dinner, Sea
  Sculptures, 10 3/4 In. . . 26.00
Plate, Luncheon, Sea
  Sculptures, 9 1/8 In. . . . 12.00

White
Plate, Dinner, Sea Sculptures,
  10 3/4 In. . . . 32.00 to 35.00
Plate, Luncheon, Sea Sculptures,
  9 1/8 In. 30.00

SANDALWOOD is a plain solid-color plate in pale tan, the color of sandalwood. It has platinum trim. It was introduced in 1952.
Cup 34.00
Cup & Saucer 15.00
Plate, Bread & Butter,
  6 3/8 In. 15.00
Plate, Dinner,
  10 1/2 In. . . . 28.00 to 50.00

SIERRA SAND was made from 1963 to 1984. The line was made to look hand thrown and has slight ringed grooves in the surface. The only decoration is a series of brown and tan bands at the edge.
Cup 10.00
Cup & Saucer . . 15.00 to 18.00
Plate, Bread & Butter,
  6 3/4 In. . . . . . 8.00 to 10.00
Plate, Dinner,
  10 7/8 In. . . . . 12.00 to 15.00
Plate, Luncheon,
  9 3/4 In. 8.00
Platter, Oval, 11 1/2 In. . . 25.00
Saucer 5.00

SILKSTONE was introduced in 1982. The stoneware dishes are white with a ridged border.
Creamer 20.00
Sugar, Cover 30.00

SILVER LINING, a fine china pattern, was made from 1971 to 1976. The only trim is a thin line forming a simple geometric border.
Plate, Bread & Butter,
  6 1/4 In. . . . . . 12.00 to 14.00
Plate, Dinner, 10 1/2 In. . . 46.00
Plate, Salad, 8 1/4 In. 20.00

SILVER PINE is a simple bluish gray fine china pattern with a decoration of black clusters of pine needle–like lines. It was introduced in 1955.

Cup 20.00
Cup & Saucer 38.00

Plate, Bread & Butter,
  6 3/8 In. . . . . . 13.00 to 18.00
Plate, Dinner, 10 1/2 In. . . 34.00
Plate, Salad,
  8 In. . . . . 18.00 to 28.00
Platter, 12 In. . . 75.00 to 105.00
Platter, 16 In. 80.00

SIMPLICITY is white ware with plain platinum trim. It is part of a porcelain line introduced in 1961.
Bowl, Fruit, 4 5/8 In. 15.00
Bowl, Vegetable, Oval,
  Open 45.00
Creamer 25.00
Cup & Saucer 20.00
Gravy Boat, Attached
  Underplate 60.00
Plate, Bread & Butter,
  6 1/4 In. 12.00
Plate, Dinner,
  10 1/2 In. . . . 20.00 to 25.00
Plate, Salad,
  8 1/2 In. . . . . 16.00 to 20.00
Platter, 12 1/2 In. 55.00
Platter, 15 In. 50.00
Soup, Dish, 6 In. 18.00

SNOW PINE is part of the same line as Simplicity, but it has a pale decoration of clusters of pine branches and three pinecones.
Creamer 25.00
Cup & Saucer 27.00
Soup, Dish 18.00

SPICE is an earthenware design introduced in 1961. It is a pale beige pattern with tan trim and decorations. Plates and some pitchers have a treelike decoration inspired by Pennsylvania Dutch designs. Cups and serving pieces are glazed solid black on the outside.
Bowl, Cereal, 7 3/8 In. . . . 16.00
Bowl, Fruit, 5 1/8 In. 14.00
Bowl, Salad, 11 In. 20.00
Bowl, Sugar, Cover 35.00
Bowl, Vegetable 45.00

Bread Tray, 18 In. 50.00
Creamer 30.00
Cup & Saucer 16.00
Plate, Bread & Butter,
6 1/2 In. . . . . . 3.00 to 10.00
Plate, Dinner,
10 1/2 In. . . . . . 6.00 to 16.00
Plate, Luncheon,
9 1/4 In. . . . . . 4.00 to 14.00
Plate, Salad, 8 1/4 In. 16.00
Platter, 16 1/2 In. 15.00

SPRING SONG is decorated with sprigs of pink and blue leaves and a suggestion of Queen Anne's Lace. It is a 1959 pattern.

Cup 8.00
Plate, Bread & Butter,
6 1/8 In. 4.00

STARBURST, one of the most popular patterns with today's collectors, was made from 1954 to 1985. It is decorated with futuristic starlike forms in turquoise blue and yellow. The dish shapes were also very modern.

Bowl, Fruit, 5 In. 14.00
Bowl, Vegetable, Oval,
8 3/8 In. 25.00
Chop Plate,
13 1/4 In. 65.00
Cup 10.00
Cup & Saucer . . 15.00 to 19.00
Gravy Boat, Attached
Underplate 69.00
Gravy Boat, Attached
Underplate,
Ladle . . . . . . 72.00 to 75.00
Mug, 7 Oz., 3 In. 95.00

Mug, 12 Oz., 5 In. 65.00
Plate, Bread & Butter,
6 1/2 In. . . . . . . 7.00 to 15.00
Plate, Dinner,
10 3/4 In. . . . . 12.00 to 15.00
Plate, Salad, 8 In. 20.00
Platter, Oval, 15 In. 55.00
Salt & Pepper 55.00
Saucer . . . . 5.00 to 6.00
Snack Plate, Cup Well . . . 95.00

SUNDANCE is the same as the Moondance pattern, except it is decorated in yellow and orange tones. It was made in 1972.

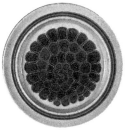

Bowl, Vegetable, Round, Open,
8 7/8 In. . . . . . 26.00 to 35.00
Creamer . . . . . . 12.00 to 25.00
Cup & Saucer . . 15.00 to 17.00
Plate, Bread & Butter,
6 3/4 In. 7.00
Plate, Dinner,
10 1/2 In. . . . . 17.00 to 20.00
Plate, Salad,
8 1/2 In. . . . . . . 8.00 to 14.00
Platter, Oval,
11 3/4 In. . . . . 25.00 to 40.00
Platter, Oval,
13 1/2 In. . . . . 25.00 to 42.00
Saucer 4.00
Soup, Dish . . . . 12.00 to 23.00
Sugar 27.00
Sugar, Cover 30.00

TAHITI was introduced in 1965. Plates are decorated in shades of brown and tan. The center is lighter than the very dark brown band. There is a row of white dots separating the colors. It came in several different combinations of browns.

Bowl, Vegetable, Oval,
8 1/4 In. 55.00
Butter, Cover 53.00
Creamer 36.00
Cup & Saucer 17.00
Pepper Shaker 23.00
Plate, Bread & Butter,
6 1/8 In. . . . . . . 8.00 to 9.00
Platter, 13 In. 57.00
Saucer 7.00
Sugar, Cover 48.00

TALISMAN has platinum trim and a very pale stylized border of flowers. The fine china pattern, made in Japan, was introduced in 1961.

Bowl, Fruit, 4 5/8 In. 20.00
Plate, Bread & Butter,
6 3/8 In. 12.00

TARA is a traditional china line, white with platinum trim and a narrow border of gray leaves and flowers. It was made in 1959 in Japan. It remained in production only a short time, perhaps just two years.

Bowl, Vegetable, Oval,
9 In. 20.00
Creamer 15.00
Cup & Saucer 12.00
Gravy Boat 25.00
Plate, Bread & Butter,
6 3/8 In. 4.00
Plate, Dinner,
10 3/8 In. 11.00
Plate, Salad, 8 1/8 In. 8.00
Platter, 12 3/4 In. 20.00
Saucer 3.00
Sugar, Cover 25.00

TEAK is solid black with solid white interiors for bowls and cups. The china pattern was introduced in 1952.

Bowl, Fruit,
4 3/4 In. 34.00
Cup 37.00
Cup & Saucer 42.00
Soup, Dish 42.00
Sugar, Cover 95.00

TERRA COTTA has a border of rust, brown, and terra-cotta leaves. It was introduced in 1965.

Cup & Saucer	18.00
Pitcher, 8 1/4 In.	38.00
Plate, Bread & Butter, 6 1/8 In.	8.00
Plate, Dinner, 10 1/8 In.	18.00
Plate, Salad, 8 3/8 In.	14.00
Platter, 14 3/4 In.	38.00
Sugar, Cover	32.00

TIEMPO appeared in stores in 1950. The solid-color pattern has square plates and matching serving pieces. The set came in mix-and-match colors. It was made in Copper, Coral (tan), Hot Chocolate, Leaf (green-black), Mustard, Salt (white), Sprout (lime green), and Stone (gray).

Hot Chocolate

Bowl, Fruit, 4 1/2 In.	13.00
Chop Plate, 12 3/4 In.	38.00
Coaster, 3 In.	15.00
Pitcher, Water, 8 3/4 In.	75.00
Plate, Bread & Butter, 6 In.	8.00
Plate, Dinner, 9 3/4 In.	20.00
Teapot	75.00
Tumbler, 5 In.	25.00

Leaf

Bowl, Fruit, 4 1/2 In.	13.00
Cup & Saucer	15.00
Plate, Bread & Butter, 6 In.	8.00
Plate, Dinner, 9 3/4 In.	20.00
Sugar, Cover	23.00

Mustard

Cup	30.00

Sprout

Bowl, Fruit, 4 1/2 In.	13.00
Bowl, Vegetable, Divided, 11 In.	28.00
Coaster, 3 In.	15.00
Creamer	18.00
Cup & Saucer	15.00
Gravy Boat, Handle	40.00
Plate, Bread & Butter, 6 In.	8.00
Plate, Dinner, 9 3/4 In.	20.00
Platter, 13 In.	30.00
Relish, 9 1/4 x 5 In.	20.00
Sugar, Cover	23.00
Tumbler, 5 In.	25.00

Stone

Creamer	23.00
Cup & Saucer	20.00

TOFFEE is decorated with brown, orange, yellow, and rust-color dots forming flowers, and several border lines. It has the handmade look popular when it was made in 1975. Production stopped in the United States in 1984.

Bowl, Cereal, 6 3/8 In.	12.00
Bowl, Vegetable, Oval, Open	30.00
Creamer	20.00
Cup & Saucer	15.00
Gravy Boat, Attached Underplate	30.00
Plate, Dinner, 10 7/8 In.	15.00
Plate, Salad, 8 3/8 In.	10.00
Platter, Oval, 13 3/4 In.	28.00
Sugar, Cover	30.00

TRIANON was introduced in 1959. It is decorated with single pale blue and tan maple leaves scattered on the rim.

Cup & Saucer	29.00 to 30.00
Plate, Bread & Butter, 6 3/8 In.	13.00 to 16.00
Plate, Dinner, 10 3/8 In.	34.00
Plate, Salad, 8 1/8 In.	17.00 to 26.00

Saucer	8.00

TRIO is a modern-looking fine china pattern decorated with abstract leaves and dried flowers scattered on the pieces. It was made from 1954 through 1958.

Coffeepot	85.00
Creamer	36.00
Plate, Bread & Butter, 6 In.	7.00
Plate, Dinner, 10 In.	23.00
Saucer	5.00
Sugar, Cover	40.00

TULIP TIME was one of the handmade-looking patterns made from 1962 until 1984. The center design is a Pennsylvania Dutch tulip in turquoise and tan. There is a matching rim.

Bowl, Cereal, 6 3/8 In.	19.00
Bowl, Fruit, 5 1/4 In.	16.00
Bowl, Salad, 11 In.	10.00
Bowl, Vegetable, Divided, 11 In.	30.00
Butter, Cover	20.00
Creamer	12.00 to 32.00
Cup & Saucer	17.00 to 20.00
Gravy Boat, Attached Underplate	24.00
Pitcher, Milk, Qt., 6 In.	35.00
Plate, Bread & Butter, 6 3/4 In.	7.00 to 8.00
Plate, Dinner, 10 7/8 In.	15.00 to 23.00
Plate, Luncheon, 9 3/4 In.	18.00
Plate, Salad, 8 3/8 In.	12.00

Platter, Oval, 13 3/4 In. . . . 81.00
Salt & Pepper 43.00

TWICE NICE is decorated with a pair of leaves, one tan, one brown. It was introduced in 1959.

Creamer 14.00
Gravy Boat, Attached
    Underplate 14.00

WESTWOOD is a white pattern of china with a thin gray inner line, a sprig of three thin leaves, and some golden-yellow berries. It was introduced in 1942.

Bowl, Fruit, 6 1/4 In. 32.00
Cup & Saucer, After
    Dinner 28.00
Plate, Dinner,
    10 5/8 In. . . . . 18.00 to 28.00
Platter, 12 1/2 In. 151.00
Soup, Cream 41.00

WHEAT line was introduced in 1951 but lasted only until 1956. It is a solid-color ware with a raised design of a sheaf of wheat. It came in Harvest Brown, Summer Tan, and Winter Green.

Harvest Brown
Ashtray 20.00
Bread Tray, 15 1/4 In. . . . 70.00
Candleholder 45.00
Plate, Dinner, 10 1/2 In. . . 20.00
Plate, Salad, 8 1/2 In. 13.00
Platter, 15 1/2 In. 90.00
Spoon Rest 14.00
Summer Tan
Creamer 40.00

Winter Green
Cup & Saucer 12.00
Plate, Salad, 8 1/2 In. 12.00

WILDFLOWER is a colorful pattern with a border of wildflowers that spill into the center of the plate. It is made in eight different color combinations. The hand-painted pattern started in 1942.

Bowl, Vegetable, Cover . 895.00
Tumbler, 10 Oz.,
    5 1/4 In. 175.00

WINTER BOUQUET has a stylized center design of dried stalks of twigs and wheat heads drawn in black. It was made with or without platinum trim. The china pattern was introduced in 1954.

Bowl, Vegetable, Oval,
    9 In. 91.00
Cup & Saucer 39.00
Plate, Dinner, 10 1/2 In. . . 50.00
Plate, Salad, 8 In. 22.00

FRANKOMA

John Frank established the ceramics department at the University of Oklahoma in Norman, Oklahoma, in 1927. In 1933 he started his own Frank Potteries. He used light-color clay found nearby in Ada to make his pottery. In 1934 the company name was changed to Frankoma

Potteries. The operation moved to Sapulpa, Oklahoma, in 1938 and the name became Frankoma Pottery. Red clay was found near the pottery in 1953, and by 1954 all of the pieces were made of red, not light-color, clay. The company is still working. Collectors prize the early pieces made of the light Ada clay, so these pieces cost twice as much as newer red clay pieces.

MAYAN-AZTEC pattern was introduced in 1948. It was made in Desert Gold, Prairie Green, White Sand, and Woodland Moss and has a Mayan geometric border. The names were simplified, and on the 1994 price list, the pattern, called Aztec, was available in Gold, Green, and White.

Desert Gold
Bowl, 6 3/4 x
    13 x 1 5/8 In. 12.00
Creamer 23.00
Platter, Oval,
    17 3/4 x 10 1/2 In. 55.00
Salt & Pepper 28.00
Sugar, Cover, 4 In. 16.00

❖

Be sure trash cans, sheds, and cars are not close to the house. A burglar can use them to climb up to a second-story window.

❖

Prairie Green
Butter Dish, Cover 25.00
Woodland Moss
Tray, 9 In. 35.00

PLAINSMAN was originally named Oklahoma. The pattern started in 1948 and is still being made. It is available in Autumn Yellow, Black, Brown Satin, Desert Gold, Flame, Peach Glow, Prairie Green, Robin's Egg Blue, White Sand, and Woodland Moss. The 1994 catalog offered 22 pieces of Plainsman with the simplified color names of Brown, Country Blue, Gold, Green, Forest, and Navy.

Desert Gold
Cup 9.95
Mug, 16 Oz. 9.95
Sugar 8.95
Prairie Green
Ashtray, 6 3/4 x 4 1/2 In. . . 8.00
Cup & Saucer 15.00
Pitcher, 9 1/2 In. 46.00
Plate, Dinner, 10 In. 3.00
Plate, Salad, 7 In. 10.00
Platter, 13 In. 14.95
Woodland Moss
Bowl, 7 1/2 x 2 3/4 In. . . . 18.50
Bowl, Cereal, 14 Oz.,
   5 1/2 In. 12.95
Plate, Dinner, 10 1/2 In. . . 14.95
Plate, Luncheon, 9 In. 9.95
Teapot, 12 Cup, 7 In. 41.00
Tumbler, Juice, 6 Oz. 8.95

WAGON WHEEL was made from 1941 to 1983. A few pieces are still being made. Many of the pieces in this pattern are shaped like wagon wheels. Most pieces were made in Desert Gold and Prairie Green. A few were made in other colors.

Desert Gold
Bowl, Vegetable, Ada
   Clay, 8 In. 10.50
Casserole, Handles,
   No. 94V, Ada Clay 25.00
Pitcher 13.00
Plate, Dinner,
   10 In. 15.50
Salt & Pepper 15.00
Prairie Green
Creamer, 4 In. 22.00
Cup & Saucer 10.50
Pitcher, 7 x 5 1/4 In. 25.00
Plate, Dinner, 10 In. 15.50
Sugar, No. 510, Individual,
   Ada Clay, 2 1/2 In. 10.00
Teapot, Ada Clay,
   2 Cup 6.00

HALL

Hall China Company started in East Liverpool, Ohio, in 1903. The firm made many types of wares. Collectors search for the Hall teapots made from the 1920s to the 1950s. They are listed in this section. Some pieces listed here are identified by the shape name *Pert*. The dinnerwares of the same period, especially Autumn Leaf pattern, are also popular. The Hall China Company is still working. Autumn Leaf pattern dishes are listed in their own category in this book.

BLUE BOUQUET is a pattern made for the Standard Coffee of New Orleans, Louisiana. The coffee company gave Blue Bouquet pattern dinnerware and kitchenware as premiums from the early 1950s to the early 1960s. Although it was made in Ohio, it is most easily found in the South. The pattern is very plain with a thin blue border interrupted by roses. Blue Ridge also made a pattern called Blue Bouquet.

Bowl, Vegetable, Round,
   9 1/4 In. 30.00
Cruet 15.00
Eggcup, Double 65.00
Pepper, Handle 30.00
Saltshaker, Handle 30.00
Spoon 135.00
Sugar, Cover 30.00

CAMEO ROSE has gray and white decal decorations and gold trim. It was not made by the cameo process used for Cameo Shellware and other designs. Reproductions using the Cameo Rose decoration have been made since 1997. These, unlike the originals, are marked *Limited Edition*.

Bowl, Vegetable, Cover . . 95.00
Bowl, Vegetable, Oval,
   10 1/2 In. 30.00
Creamer 13.00
Cup 10.00

Plate, 7 1/4 In. 9.00
Plate, 8 In. 10.00
Platter, Oval, 11 1/2 In. . . 25.00
Platter, Oval, 13 1/4 In. . . 45.00
Platter, Oval, 15 1/2 In. . . 85.00
Sugar, Cover 20.00

CHINESE RED is a color used by Hall China Company. This bright red was used on many shapes of dishes. The few listed here are not included in the more recognizable sets.

Jug, Ball, No. 3 . . . . 17.50
Jug, Pert, 6 1/2 In. 26.00
Drip Jar, Pert, Cover 40.00
Salt & Pepper, 4 In. 12.50
Sugar, Pert 19.00

CROCUS was made in the 1930s. The decal-decorated dinnerware was sometimes called Holland. The design was a border of oddly shaped crocuses in black, lavender, red, green, and pink. Most pieces have platinum trim. Reproductions using the Crocus decoration have been made since 1993. These, unlike the originals, are marked *Limited Edition*. Other firms, including Stangl Pottery and Blue Ridge, had very different-looking dinnerwares called Crocus.

Bowl, Vegetable, Round,
    9 1/4 In. 30.00
Leftover, Cover, Square,
    7 x 3 1/2 In. 125.00
Plate, Salad, 8 1/4 In. 11.00
Tureen, Soup 425.00

HEATHER ROSE is a decal-decorated Hall Pottery pattern. Both dinnerware and utility ware pieces were made with this decoration. It pictures a realistic-looking pale pinkish purple rose on a stem with many leaves.

Coffeepot 62.00
Casserole, Cover, Flare
    Ware 25.00
Gravy, 8 1/2 In. 10.00
Jug, 6 Cups 13.00
Plate, 9 1/2 In. 12.50
Platter, Handles, 11 In. . . 22.25
Sugar, Cover, 4 1/2 In. . . 15.50

POPPY, sometimes called Orange Poppy by collectors, was made from 1933 through the 1950s. The decals picture realistic groups of orange poppies with a few leaves. Reproductions using the Poppy decoration but called Orange Poppy have been made. These, unlike the originals, are marked *Limited Edition*. Another Hall pattern called Red Poppy has bright red stylized flowers with black leaves and trim. Poppy is a name used by at least five companies.

Baker, French Flute 35.00
Bean Pot,
    Handle . . . . 145.00 to 150.00
Bowl, 9 In. 20.00
Bowl, 10 In. 85.00
Coffeepot, S-Cover 100.00
Cup & Saucer 20.00
Gravy Boat,
    No Underplate 90.00
Jar, Pretzel,
    7 In. . . . . . 125.00 to 170.00
Jug, Ball 150.00
Plate, Dinner, 10 In. 33.00
Salt & Pepper, Handles . . 30.00

RED POPPY has bright red flowers and black leaves. The pattern, made in East Liverpool, Ohio, from 1930 through 1950,

was a premium item for Grand Union Tea Company. Matching metal pieces, such as wastebaskets and breadboxes, were made, and glass tumblers are known. Reproductions using the Red Poppy decoration have been made since 1993. These, unlike the originals, are marked *Limited Edition*.

Grease Jar, Cover 15.00
Mixing Bowl, Large 35.00
Plate, Luncheon,
    9 In. 10.00

ROSE PARADE has a solid Cadet Blue body with contrasting white knobs and handles. A rose decal was added to the white spaces. Sometimes the flower is pink, sometimes blue. The pattern was made from 1941 through the 1950s. Serving pieces, not dinnerware sets, were made.

HALL'S
SUPERIOR
QUALITY
KITCHENWARE

MADE IN
U. S. A.
Rose Parade

Casserole 65.00
Saltshaker . . . . . 20.00 to 35.00
Shaker, Pepper 35.00

ROSE WHITE, first made in 1941, is similar to Rose Parade. The same shapes were used, but the pieces are all white with a slightly different rose-decal decoration. There is platinum trim on many pieces.

Bean Pot, 7 1/2 In. 120.00
Salt & Pepper,
    4 1/2 In. 24.00
Sugar & Creamer 22.50

ROYAL ROSE is a Hall China Company pattern that can confuse you. It is Cadet Blue with Hi-white handles and knobs. The floral decal is the one used on Rose White. Pieces have platinum trim. The shapes are different from those used for Rose Parade.

Pepper, Handle 16.00
Saltshaker 30.00

SPRINGTIME has an arrangement of pink flowers as the decoration.

Bowl, Fruit,
    5 1/2 In. 5.00
Bowl, Oval 19.00

Cake Plate 17.00
Plate, 6 In. 4.00
Plate, 7 In. . . . . . 7.00 to 15.00
Plate, 9 In. 10.00
Sugar & Creamer,
    Cover 35.00

TAVERNE serving pieces were made by the Hall China Company in the 1930s. Matching dinnerware was made by Taylor, Smith & Taylor of Chester, West Virginia. A rolling pin was made by Harker Pottery Company. The silhouetted figures eating at a table are very similar to those seen on the pattern Silhouette, but there is no dog in this decal. In some of the literature, Taverne is called Silhouette.

Coaster 40.00
Cookie Jar, 7 In. 395.00
Gravy Boat 16.00
Mug 65.00
Pie Server 30.00
Pitcher, 5 3/4 In. 30.00
Salt & Pepper 70.00

TEAPOTS of all sizes and shapes were made by the Hall China Company of East Liverpool, Ohio, starting in the 1920s. Each pot has a special design name such as Airflow or Boston. Each shape could be made in one of several colors, often with names like Cadet (light blue), Camellia (rose), Canary (yellow), Dresden (deep blue), Delphinium (medium purple-blue), Green Lustre (dark green), Indian Red (orange), Mahogany (dark brown), and Marine (dark purple-blue). An infuser is an optional piece that was usually sold separately. It held the tea leaves while the water was poured through them. Coffeepots were also made by Hall. Reproduction teapots have been made since 1992. These,

unlike the originals, are marked *Limited Edition.*

Automobile
Delphinium 750.00
Boston
Orange Poppy 295.00
Donut
Chinese Red,
    7 3/4 x 9 1/2 In. 355.00
Melody
Orange Poppy 350.00
New York
Cobalt, 2 Cup 55.00
Pert
Chinese Red, 6 Cup 39.00
Rose White, 3 Cup 45.00
Streamline
Chinese Red . . . 75.00 to 175.00

TOMORROW'S CLASSIC was designed by Eva Zeisel for the Hall China Company's Hallcraft line in 1952. It remained popular until the 1960s. The solid white dinnerware, sometimes decorated with decals, is marked with her name.

HALLCRAFT

Bowl, Fantasy, Oval,
   14 1/2 In. 56.00
Bowl, Vegetable, Fantasy,
   9 3/4 In. 31.00
Bowl, Vegetable, Square,
   8 3/4 In. 18.50
Candleholder, Fantasy . . . 27.00
Coffeepot, Fantasy,
   9 In. 75.00
Cruet, Bouquet 15.50
Cup & Saucer, Fantasy . . 15.50
Gravy Boat . . . . 16.00 to 20.50
Gravy Boat, Harlequin . . . 25.00
Plate, Dinner, Fantasy,
   11 In. 15.00
Platter, Fantasy, 15 In. . . 41.00
Sugar & Creamer,
   Fantasy 31.00
Teapot, Fantasy,
   6 x 5 1/2 In. . 50.00 to 122.00

HARKER

Harker Pottery Company
was incorporated in 1890
in East Liverpool, Ohio.
The plant was moved in
1931 to Chester, West
Virginia. It closed in 1972.
The pottery made a popu-
lar line of dinnerware, including intaglio or engobe
pieces that were usually
marked *Cameo ware*.

CHESTERTON was a pattern
produced from 1945 to 1965.
The pieces have a gadroon border that was left white. Pieces
were then decorated with a
solid color. Hollow ware has
white interiors. Chesterton was
made in Avocado, Celadon,
Charcoal, Chocolate Brown,
Coral Golden Harvest, Lime,
Pink Cocoa, Pumpkin, Silver-
Gray, Teal, Wedgwood Blue,
White, Yellow, and perhaps
other colors. Teal pieces are
called Corinthian.

Avocado
Platter, Oval,
   11 3/4 x 8 1/2 In. 16.00
Silver-Gray
Creamer 15.00
Cup & Saucer 11.00
Gravy Boat,
   Underplate 38.00
Plate, Bread & Butter,
   6 1/4 In. . . . . 4.00 to 7.00
Plate, Dinner,
   10 In. . . . . 9.00 to 12.00
Plate, Luncheon,
   9 In. 16.00
Platter, 13 In. . . . 20.00 to 22.00
Sugar, Cover 25.00

CORINTHIAN is the teal green
version of the gadroon edge
shape often marked *Royal Gadroon*. It was made in 1947.

Teal
Cake Plate 20.00
Platter, Small 25.00
Salt & Pepper 20.00
Sugar, Cover 18.00

PERSIAN KEY is an intaglio
pattern that has a border of
squares and circles on a celadon
background. It was made about
1966.

Cup & Saucer 12.00
Plate, Dinner, 10 In. 12.00
Platter, Small 20.00
Soup, Dish 9.00

SPRINGTIME is an intaglio
pattern with white flowers and
grass on a pink background. It
was made about 1959.
Plate, Dinner, 10 In. 16.00
Platter, Small 33.00

❖

When you give your keys to a parking attendant remove your house keys.

❖

WHITE CLOVER is an intaglio dinnerware that was designed by Russel Wright for Harker Pottery Company. It has the very sleek modern shapes inspired by his other design, American Modern, but a sprig of clover decoration was added. It was made in four colors: Charcoal, Coral Sand, Golden Spice, and Meadow Green. The dinnerware was advertised as ovenproof, chip-resistant, and detergent-resistant. The pattern was discontinued in 1955.

Coral Sand

Platter, 11 In. 20.00

Meadow Green

Cup & Saucer 15.00
Plate, Bread & Butter,
  6 In. 5.00
Plate, Dinner, 10 In. 15.00

Harmony House was a mark used on dinnerware sold by Sears, Roebuck & Company. Harmony House dishes were made by various factories, including

Hall, Harker, Homer Laughlin, Laurel Pottery, Salem China, and Universal, from 1940 until the early 1970s. Later pieces were made in Japan. The Cattail (Cat-tail) pattern is listed in this book under Universal Potteries, Inc.

MODERNE is a plain modern dinnerware with a narrow trim.

Bowl, Fruit 10.00
Bowl, Vegetable, Oval . . . 23.00
Creamer 18.00
Cup & Saucer 15.00
Plate, Bread & Butter,
  6 In. 8.00
Plate, Dinner, 10 In. 15.00
Platter, Medium 33.00
Soup, Dish 15.00
Sugar, Cover 25.00

MOUNT VERNON was made by Hall China for Sears. The pattern has a blue sprig border, a center design of blue sprigs encircling a pink rose, and gold trim. It was offered for sale from 1941 to 1959.

Plate, Dinner, 10 In. 20.00
Plate, Salad, 8 In. 18.00

ORIENT is a pattern featuring branches in an Asian-inspired design.

Bowl, Cereal, 4 1/2 In. . . 10.00
Creamer 10.00
Cup & Saucer 12.00
Gravy Boat,
  Underplate 18.00
Plate, Dinner, 10 In. 14.00
Plate, Salad, 7 1/2 In. 8.00
Soup, Dish, 7 1/2 In. 10.00
Sugar, 4 1/2 In. 12.00

PETITE ROSE has a scalloped dark rose border and clusters of roses.

Cup 12.00
Plate, Salad,
  7 1/2 In. 8.00

PLATINUM GARLAND is a fine china design made in Japan. It has a border of platinum stalks of grass with seed heads.

Creamer 15.00
Sugar, Cover 25.00

ROSEBUD is a china pattern on a modern rimless shape. It has a center of a rosebud with scattered gray leaves. It was made in Japan.

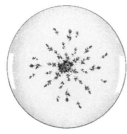

Cup 10.00
Plate, Dinner, 10 In. 15.00

SHERATON is a fine china pattern made in Japan. It is blue-gray and white with white roses, green leaves, and platinum trim.

Bowl, Fruit 11.00
Plate, Dinner, 10 In. 16.00

SUNNY GLADE is a flower-decorated pattern.

Creamer 16.00
Cup & Saucer 15.00
Plate, Bread & Butter,
  6 In. 4.00
Plate, Salad, 7 1/2 In. 8.00

TANGERINE is decorated with a decal of tangerines.

Coffeepot, 10 In. 35.00
Creamer 4.00

VINTAGE dinnerware was made in solid colors with white

handles and interiors. It was made in Japan.

Cup & Saucer 10.00
Cup & Saucer, After
  Dinner 35.00

HOMER LAUGHLIN

Homer Laughlin started in 1896 as the Homer Laughlin China Company in East Liverpool, Ohio. It was the continuation of an earlier pottery called Laughlin Brothers. In 1905 the company built a second plant in Newell, West Virginia. Both potteries worked until 1929, when the East Liverpool factory closed. Homer Laughlin is still working in West Virginia.

AMBERSTONE is made on the Fiesta shapes. Fiesta, the popular dinnerware pattern, is made in bright solid colors. In 1967 a new pattern, Amberstone, was created. Pieces were glazed a rich brown and some have black machine-stamped underglaze patterns. Some pieces were used for supermarket promotions with the backstamp *Genuine Sheffield.* Full sets of dishes were made.

Sheffield ⚜ ™
AMBERSTONE
MADE IN U.S.A.

Bowl, Fruit 7.00
Coffeepot 28.00
Cup & Saucer 8.00
Marmalade 55.00
Pitcher, Water, Disc 50.00
Plate, Bread & Butter,
  6 In. 4.00
Plate, Dinner,
  10 In. . . . . 7.00 to 8.00
Sugar & Creamer 22.00

APPLE BLOSSOM was made from 1935 to 1955. It has a flowered border and gold trim. Crooksville China Company of Crooksville, Ohio, made a pink-flowered pattern called Apple Blossom that is not listed here.

Bowl, Fruit 12.00
Bowl, Vegetable, Cover . . 85.00
Cup & Saucer 24.00
Plate, Bread & Butter,
  6 In. 10.00
Platter, Medium 45.00

CAVALIER shape, designed by Don Schreckengost, was made from the 1950s to the 1970s. It was decorated in many ways, including solid color combinations and decals.

Cavalier
EGGSHELL
HOMER LAUGHLIN
U.S.A.

Bowl, Cereal, 6 1/2 In. . . 10.00
Creamer . . . . . . 15.00 to 20.00
Cup 8.00
Cup, Berkshire 7.00
Cup & Saucer . . 13.00 to 25.00
Plate, Dinner,
  10 In. . . . . . . 15.00 to 25.00
Platter, Burgundy Border,
  11 3/4 In. 18.00

Platter, Burgundy Border,
13 1/2 In. 22.00

Platter, Turkey, Gray
Border, 15 In. 35.00

Platter, Turkey, Teal Border,
15 In. . . . . 35.00 to 55.00

Sugar, Cover 25.00

CONCHITA is one of the Mexican-inspired designs that became the rage for dinnerwares in the late 1930s. Several were made by Homer Laughlin China Company. Conchita dinnerware is a decal-decorated ware made on the Century shape, Swing shape, and others. The decoration pictures three pots of cacti in one corner. On large flat pieces like plates, there is also a group of hanging gourds and peppers. Pieces have a thin red border trim. Conchita decals were also used on kitchenwares made on Kitchen Kraft shapes.

Bowl, Fruit, Swing
Shape 16.00

Cup & Saucer, Swing
Shape 22.00

Plate, Swing Shape, 6 In. . . 9.00

Plate, Swing Shape,
10 In. 44.00

Soup, Dish, Swing
Shape 35.00

CRINOLINE has a floral decal center, gray border, and platinum trim. It was made on the Cavalier shape.

Bowl, Gray, Fruit,
Lily-Of-The-Valley 3.50

Plate, Salad, Gray, Lily-
Of-The-Valley, 8 In. 8.00

Platter, Gray, Lily-Of-The-
Valley, 11 1/2 In. 17.00

Platter, Gray, Lily-Of-The-
Valley, 13 1/2 In. 19.00

Teapot, Lily-Of-
The-Valley 39.00

DAISY, or Hawaiian 12-point Daisy, is a Fiesta Casual pattern. It was first made in 1962 and discontinued in 1968. Daisy pattern, on the familiar Fiesta shape, has a turquoise rim and turquoise and brown daisies in the center. Patterns named Daisy were also made by Red Wing, Stangl, and Taylor, Smith & Taylor. They are not listed here.

Cup & Saucer 88.00
Plate, 8 1/4 In. 7.00

DOGWOOD pattern is a decal-decorated line of dinnerware made in the 1960s. The edges are gold, and the decoration features realistic pink and white sprays of dogwood.

Bowl, Cereal 12.00
Soup, Dish 9.00
Soup, Dish, Rimmed 30.00

EGGSHELL shapes were introduced in 1937. Many pieces are marked with the word *eggshell* and the name of the shape: Georgian, Nautilus, Swing, or Theme. Each shape could have many different decorations. Eggshell Georgian was made from 1937 to the 1960s. Dishes were decorated with many different decal decorations with wide, colored bands, or with floral sprigs with narrow bands.

Bowl, Vegetable, Cover . . 30.00
Creamer 5.00
Cup 4.00
Cup & Saucer 12.00
Plate, Bread & Butter,
6 In. 4.00
Plate, Dinner, 10 In. 9.00
Plate, Salad, 8 In. 5.00
Platter, 15 1/2 In. 25.00
Platter, Buddah,
13 1/2 In. 25.00
Platter, Oval, 12 In. 20.00
Sauceboat, Cashmere
Underplate 15.00
Soup, Dish 9.00

EGGSHELL NAUTILUS is a shape that was made from 1937 to the 1950s. The nautilus shell motif can be seen in the handles. The shape was decorated in many different ways, and some of the decal decorations have special pattern names. See also Nantucket.

Berry Bowl, 5 1/4 In. 10.00
Creamer 18.00
Plate, Cardinal, Square,
8 In. 7.00
Plate, Cashmere, 10 In. . . . 9.00
Plate, Luncheon,
8 1/4 In. 13.00
Platter, 11 In. 70.00
Sugar, Cover 25.00
Sugar & Creamer 29.00

EGGSHELL SWING is a shape made in the 1950s. It was decorated with wide stripes in pastels, floral designs, and decals picturing Asian or Mexican figures.

Cup, Greenbriar Decal 9.00

Eggcup, Red Beauty 27.00

Platter, With Abstract Vase & Floral Decal, 13 In. 24.00

Soup, Dish, With Abstract Vase & Floral Decal, 8 In. 16.00

EGGSHELL THEME was made from 1939 to the 1990s. It has an embossed border of fruit with a center that is plain or has a decal design.

Bowl, Fruit 12.00

Cup & Saucer 15.00

Cup & Saucer, After Dinner 25.00

Plate, Dinner, 10 In. 12.00

Plate, Square, 8 In. 11.00

Platter, 10 In. 22.00

Sugar & Creamer, Cover . 28.00

EPICURE was introduced in 1955. It is a solid-color, sculptured pattern decorated in Charcoal Gray, Dawn Pink, Snow White, or Turquoise Blue.

Charcoal Gray

Casserole, Cover, Individual 125.00

Pepper Shaker 12.00

Saucer 5.00

Dawn Pink

Creamer 20.00

Pepper Shaker 12.00

Plate, 6 1/2 In. 8.00

Salt & Pepper . . . 25.00 to 28.00

Saltshaker 12.00

Saucer 5.00

Sugar, Cover 30.00

Turquoise Blue

Creamer 20.00

Plate, 6 1/2 In. 8.00

FIESTA ware was introduced in 1936. It was designed by Frederick Hurten Rhead. The line was redesigned in 1969, withdrawn in 1973, and reissued in 1986. The design is characterized by a band of concentric circles, beginning at the rim. The complete Fiesta line in 1937 had 54 different pieces. Rarities include the covered onion bowl, the green disk water jug, the 10-inch cake plate, and the syrup pitcher. Cups had full-circle handles until 1969, when partial-circle handles were made. The original Fiesta colors were Dark Blue, Fiesta Red, Light Green, Old Ivory, and Yellow. Later, Chartreuse, Forest Green, Gray, Medium Green, Rose, and Turquoise were added. From 1970 to 1972 the redesigned Fiesta Ironstone was made only in Antique Gold, Mango Red, and Turf Green. Homer Laughlin reissued Fiesta in 1986 using new colors but the original marks and molds. The new colors were Apricot, Black, Cobalt Blue, Rose (pink), and White. Other colors and the years they were introduced are Turquoise, 1988; Yellow, 1988; Periwinkle Blue, 1989; Sea Mist Green, 1991; Lilac, 1993; Persimmon, 1995; Chartreuse, 1997; Sapphire, 1997; Pearl Gray, 1999; Juniper (dark green), 2000; and Cinnabar, 2001. Most Fiesta ware was marked with the incised word *Fiesta*. Some pieces were hand-stamped before glazing. The word *genuine* was added to the mark in the 1940s. The Fiesta shape was also made with decal decorations, but these are not considered Fiesta by collectors; instead, they are collected by the pattern names. There is also a Fiesta Kitchen Kraft line, a group of kitchenware pieces made in the early 1940s in Blue, Green, Red, or Yellow. These were bake-and-serve wares. Glassware and linens were made to match the Fiesta colors.

Chartreuse

Ashtray . . . . . . 80.00 to 94.00

Bowl, Dessert, 6 In. 88.00

Bowl, Fruit, 4 3/4 In. . . . . 25.00 to 35.00

Bowl, Fruit, 5 1/2 In. . . . . 28.00 to 50.00

Chop Plate, 15 In. 61.00

Coffeepot 485.00

Cup & Saucer 48.00

Cup & Saucer, After
Dinner 525.00

Eggcup 143.00

Mug, Tom & Jerry 77.00

Nappy, 8 1/2 In. 60.00

Pitcher, Juice, Disk,
30 Oz. 85.00

Pitcher, Water, Disk,
2 Qt. 165.00

Plate, Bread & Butter,
7 In. 13.00

Plate, Compartment,
10 1/2 In. 85.00

Plate, Dessert, 6 In. 8.00

Plate, Dinner, 10 In. 47.00

Plate, Luncheon, 9 In. ... 20.00

Platter, Oval,
12 In. 58.00

Saltshaker 24.00

Saucer, After Dinner ... 225.00

Soup, Cream 95.00

Sugar & Creamer 83.00

Cobalt Blue

Ashtray 66.00

Bowl, Fruit,
4 3/4 In. 33.00

Candleholder, Bulb,
Pair 165.00

Candleholder, Pyramid,
Pair 358.00

Carafe 220.00

Casserole 154.00

Coffeepot 350.00

Cup 35.00

Cup & Saucer 38.00

Cup & Saucer, After
Dinner 10.00

Jug, 2 Pt. 77.00

Mixing Bowl, No. 5,
9 In. 143.00

Mug 50.00

Plate, Deep, 8 In. 66.00

Plate, Dessert, 6 In. 7.00

Plate, Dinner, 10 In. 40.00

Platter, Oval, 12 In. 28.00

Saltshaker 53.00

Saucer .... 13.00 to 20.00

Teapot, Medium,
6 Cup ..... 125.00 to 143.00

Dark Blue

Bowl, Fruit, 11 3/4 In. .. 275.00

Bowl, Salad, Footed .. 248.00

Carafe 495.00

Chop Plate, 13 In. 44.00

Coffeepot, After
Dinner 625.00

Compote, 12 In. 132.00

Creamer, Stick Handle ... 44.00

Cup 35.00

Cup & Saucer .. 43.00 to 77.00

Cup & Saucer, After
Dinner 50.00

Eggcup 88.00

Marmalade,
Cover .... 248.00 to 395.00

Mixing Bowl, No. 1,
5 In. 231.00

Mixing Bowl, No. 7,
11 In. 303.00

Mug 72.00

Nappy, 9 1/2 In. 44.00

Pitcher, Water, Disk,
2 Qt. .... 143.00 to 185.00

Platter, Oval, 12 In. 44.00

Relish, Multicolored
Sections 303.00

Sauceboat ..... 66.00 to 75.00

Soup, Cream 110.00

Soup, Onion,
Cover .... 523.00 to 925.00

Syrup 275.00

Tray, Figure 8 .... 88.00

Tumbler, Juice,
5 Oz. ..... 40.00 to 50.00

Tumbler, Water,
10 Oz. .... 77.00 to 95.00

Vase, 8 In. 468.00

Fiesta Red

Ashtray 61.00

Bowl, Dessert, 6 In. 77.00

Bowl, Fruit,
4 3/4 In. ..... 33.00 to 66.00

Bowl, Fruit, 5 1/2 In. 38.00

Bowl, Fruit, 11 3/4 In. .. 330.00

Bowl, Salad, Footed ... 650.00

Bowl, Salad, Individual,
7 1/2 In. 83.00

Candleholder, Bulb,
Pair 132.00

Candleholder, Pyramid,
Pair 358.00

Carafe ...... 193.00 to 475.00

Chop Plate, 13 In. 45.00

Chop Plate,
15 In. ..... 50.00 to 75.00

Coffeepot .... 138.00 to 395.00

Compote, Footed, Low,
12 In. ..... 121.00 to 165.00

Creamer, Individual 220.00

Creamer, Stick
Handle ...... 85.00 to 88.00

Cup & Saucer .. 38.00 to 50.00

Cup & Saucer, After
Dinner ..... 110.00 to 176.00

Eggcup 143.00

Grill Plate, 12 In. 95.00

Marmalade 358.00

Mixing Bowl, No. 1,
5 In. 231.00

Mixing Bowl, No. 2,
6 In. 176.00

Mixing Bowl, No. 4,
8 In. ..... 121.00 to 155.00

Mug, Tom & Jerry 72.00

Mustard 275.00

Nappy,
8 1/2 In. ..... 37.00 to 60.00

Pitcher, Juice, Disk,
30 Oz. ..... 468.00 to 650.00

Pitcher, Water, Disk,
2 Qt. 110.00

Plate, Bread & Butter,
7 In. 9.00

Plate, Deep, 8 In. 55.00

Plate, Dinner,
10 In. .... 40.00 to 66.00

Plate, Luncheon, 9 In. ... 18.00

Platter, Oval, 12 In. 50.00

Salt & Pepper 35.00

Saltshaker 83.00

Sauceboat ..... 65.00 to 77.00

Soup, Cream 55.00

Soup, Onion,
Cover ..... 385.00 to 950.00

Sugar & Creamer 77.00

Syrup 330.00

Teapot, Large, 8 Cup ... 187.00

Teapot, Medium, 6 Cup .. 99.00

Tray, Relish, Red Inserts 400.00

Tumbler, Juice,
5 Oz. .... 40.00 to 94.00

Tumbler, Water, 10 Oz. .. 72.00

Vase, 10 In. 660.00

Vase, Bud, 6 1/2 In. 99.00

Forest Green

Ashtray 61.00
Bowl, Fruit,
   4 3/4 In. . . . . . 25.00 to 35.00
Casserole, Cover 410.00
Coffeepot . . . . 695.00 to 795.00
Cup & Saucer . . 44.00 to 47.00
Grill Plate, 10 1/2 In. . . . 125.00
Mug, Tom &
   Jerry . . . . 90.00 to 95.00
Nappy, 8 1/2 In. 55.00
Pitcher, Jug, 2 Pt. 215.00
Pitcher, Water, Disk,
   2 Qt. . . . . . . 143.00 to 340.00
Plate, Deep, 8 In. 83.00
Plate, Dessert, 6 In. 13.00
Plate, Dinner,
   10 In. . . . . 40.00 to 55.00
Plate, Luncheon, 9 In. . . . 53.00
Platter, Oval, 12 In. 50.00
Salt & Pepper 61.00
Sauceboat 90.00
Saucer, After Dinner . . . 225.00
Soup, Cream . . 70.00 to 116.00
Sugar & Creamer 83.00
Teapot, Medium,
   6 Cup 395.00

Gray

Ashtray 80.00
Bowl, Fruit,
   4 3/4 In. . . . . . 35.00 to 77.00
Casserole 176.00
Casserole, Cover 375.00
Chop Plate, 13 In. 55.00
Cup & Saucer . . 45.00 to 83.00
Cup & Saucer, After
   Dinner . . . . . . 248.00 to 750.00
Eggcup . . . . . . 121.00 to 195.00
Mug, Tom & Jerry 95.00
Pitcher, Juice, Disk,
   30 Oz. 245.00
Plate, Deep, 8 In. 55.00
Plate, Dessert, 6 In. 53.00
Saucer, After Dinner . . . 225.00
Soup, Cream 99.00
Sugar & Creamer 83.00
Teapot, Medium,
   6 Cup 395.00
Tumbler, Juice,
   5 Oz. 143.00

Light Green

Ashtray 44.00
Bowl, Fruit, 4 3/4 In. 95.00
Bowl, Salad, Footed . . . 475.00
Cake Plate 880.00
Candleholder, Bulb,
   Pair 99.00
Carafe 295.00
Casserole, Cover 150.00
Chop Plate,
   13 In. . . . . 35.00 to 38.00
Chop Plate,
   15 In. . . . . 39.00 to 48.00
Coffeepot . . . . 176.00 to 250.00
Compote, Footed, Low,
   12 In. . . . . . 132.00 to 165.00
Creamer, Stick Handle . . . 39.00
Cup & Saucer . . 27.00 to 34.00
Cup & Saucer, After
   Dinner 85.00
Marmalade 220.00
Mixing Bowl, No. 1,
   5 In. . . . . . . 165.00 to 230.00
Mixing Bowl, No. 2,
   6 In. 77.00
Mixing Bowl, No. 3,
   7 In. 225.00
Mixing Bowl, No. 4,
   8 In. 195.00
Mixing Bowl, No. 5,
   9 In. 225.00
Mixing Bowl, No. 7,
   11 In. 475.00
Mug 56.00
Mustard 204.00
Pitcher, Juice, Disk,
   30 Oz. 225.00
Pitcher, Water, Disk,
   2 Qt. 99.00
Plate, Bread & Butter,
   7 In. . . . . 8.00 to 9.00
Plate, Deep,
   8 In. . . . . 35.00 to 40.00
Plate, Dessert,
   6 In. . . . . 5.00 to 9.00
Plate, Dinner,
   10 In. . . . . . . 20.00 to 28.00
Plate, Luncheon,
   9 In. . . . . . . 11.00 to 12.00
Platter, Oval,
   12 In. . . . . . . 33.00 to 65.00
Saltshaker 31.00
Sauceboat 45.00

Soup, Cream 105.00
Soup, Onion,
   Cover . . . . . 413.00 to 750.00
Sugar & Creamer 55.00
Syrup 303.00
Teapot, Large, 8 Cup . . . 176.00
Tray, Utility 77.00
Tumbler, Juice,
   5 Oz. . . . . 33.00 to 45.00
Tumbler, Water,
   10 Oz. 65.00
Vase, 8 In. 468.00
Vase, 10 In. 523.00
Vase, 12 In. 743.00
Vase, Bud, 6 1/2 In. 88.00

Medium Green

Ashtray 220.00
Bowl, Dessert, 6 In. 550.00
Bowl, Fruit, 4 3/4 In. . . . 850.00
Bowl, Fruit, 5 1/2 In. . . . 121.00
Bowl, Salad, Individual . . 99.00
Chop Plate, 15 In. 650.00
Creamer 88.00
Cup & Saucer . . 65.00 to 127.00
Mug . . . . 100.00 to 150.00
Nappy,
   8 1/2 In. . . . 105.00 to 195.00
Pitcher, Water, Disk,
   2 Qt. 2100.00
Plate, Bread & Butter,
   7 In. 30.00
Plate, Deep, 8 In. 110.00
Plate, Dessert, 6 In. 138.00
Plate, Dinner,
   10 In. . . . . . . 187.00 to 209.00
Plate, Luncheon,
   9 In. . . . . 50.00 to 99.00
Platter, Oval, 12 In. 165.00
Salt & Pepper 264.00
Sauceboat 165.00
Sugar 143.00
Teapot, Large, 8 Cup . . 2500.00
Teapot, Medium,
   6 Cup 1485.00

Old Ivory

Ashtray 61.00
Bowl, Fruit, 4 3/4 In. 35.00
Bowl, Fruit, 5 1/2 In. 77.00
Bowl, Fruit, 11 3/4 In. . . 248.00
Candleholder, Pyramid,
   Pair 303.00

Candlestick, Bulb, Pair . . 75.00
Carafe . . . . . 198.00 to 525.00
Chop Plate, 13 In. 50.00
Chop Plate, 15 In. 70.00
Coffeepot 110.00
Compote, Footed, Low,
  12 In. 198.00
Compote, Sweet 66.00
Creamer, Stick Handle . . . 35.00
Cup & Saucer 44.00
Eggcup 53.00
Marmalade 248.00
Mixing Bowl, No. 1,
  5 In. . . . . . . 175.00 to 350.00
Mustard 253.00
Pitcher, Water, Disk,
  2 Qt. . . . . 94.00 to 175.00
Plate, Deep,
  8 In. . . . . 55.00 to 56.00
Plate, Dessert, 6 In. 5.00
Plate, Dinner,
  10 In. . . . . 40.00 to 79.00
Relish, Multicolored
  Sections 220.00
Saltshaker 66.00
Sauceboat . . . . . . 61.00 to 75.00
Saucer 20.00
Soup, Cream 60.00
Soup, Onion,
  Cover . . . . 400.00 to 895.00
Teapot, Medium,
  6 Cup 175.00
Tumbler, Juice, 5 Oz. . . . 50.00
Tumbler, Water, 10 Oz. . . 75.00
Vase, 8 In. . . . 440.00 to 895.00
Vase, 12 In. 660.00
Vase, Bud, 6 1/2 In. 99.00

Rose

Bowl, Fruit,
  4 3/4 In. . . . . . 35.00 to 58.00
Bowl, Fruit,
  5 1/2 In. . . . . . 40.00 to 55.00
Casserole, Cover 375.00
Chop Plate, 15 In. 118.00
Coffeepot 850.00
Cup & Saucer 48.00
Mug . . . . 65.00 to 85.00
Nappy,
  8 1/2 In. . . . . . 36.00 to 55.00
Pitcher, Jug, 2 Pt. 83.00
Pitcher, Water, Disk,
  2 Qt. . . . . . . 245.00 to 275.00

Plate, Bread & Butter,
  7 In. 14.00
Plate, Dessert, 6 In. 53.00
Plate, Dinner, 10 In. 58.00
Plate, Luncheon,
  9 In. . . . . 20.00 to 33.00
Platter, Oval,
  12 In. . . . . 39.00 to 58.00
Saltshaker 121.00
Sauceboat . . . . . . 66.00 to 82.00
Saucer, After Dinner . . . 175.00
Sugar, Cover 54.00
Sugar & Creamer 94.00
Teapot, Medium,
  6 Cup . . . . . 350.00 to 395.00
Tumbler, Juice, 5 Oz. . . . 55.00

Turquoise

Ashtray 44.00
Bowl, Fruit, 4 3/4 In. 22.00
Bowl, Fruit, 5 1/2 In. 23.00
Bowl, Salad, Footed . . . 231.00
Carafe . . . . . . 248.00 to 375.00
Casserole . . . . 135.00 to 138.00
Chop Plate,
  13 In. . . . . 35.00 to 39.00
Coffeepot, After
  Dinner 440.00
Cup & Saucer . . 27.00 to 34.00
Cup & Saucer, After
  Dinner . . . . . . 65.00 to 121.00
Eggcup 50.00
Mixing Bowl, No. 1,
  5 In. 385.00
Mixing Bowl, No. 3,
  7 In. 99.00
Mixing Bowl, No. 6,
  10 In. 350.00
Mug . . . . 55.00 to 83.00
Mug, Tom & Jerry 55.00
Mustard . . . . . 110.00 to 154.00
Nappy,
  8 1/2 In. . . . . . 22.00 to 25.00
Nappy, 9 1/2 In. 39.00
Pitcher, Jug, 2 Pt. 55.00
Pitcher, Water, Disk,
  2 Qt. . . . . 77.00 to 125.00
Plate, Bread & Butter,
  7 In. . . . . 5.00 to 10.00
Plate, Deep, 8 In. 35.00
Plate, Dessert,
  6 In. . . . . 5.00 to 8.00
Plate, Dinner,
  10 In. . . . . 30.00 to 89.00

When restoring antiques or houses, take color pictures before and after for records of colors used, exact placement of decorative details, and insurance claims.

Plate, Luncheon,
  9 In. 59.00
Platter, Oval,
  12 In. . . . . 22.00 to 38.00
Relish, 5 Multicolored
  Sections . . . 275.00 to 300.00
Saltshaker 11.00
Sauceboat . . . . . . 45.00 to 55.00
Saucer 15.00
Soup, Cream 165.00
Soup, Onion, Cover . . . 7500.00
Sugar & Creamer 55.00
Teapot, Large, 8 Cup . . . 143.00
Teapot, Medium, 6 Cup . . 94.00
Tray, for Sugar & Creamer,
  Figure 8 . . . . . 20.00 to 99.00
Tray, Utility . . . . 40.00 to 94.00
Tumbler, Juice, 5 Oz. . . . 45.00
Tumbler, Water, 10 Oz. . . 58.00
Vase, 8 In. . . . 413.00 to 975.00

Yellow

Bowl, Dessert, 6 In. 25.00
Bowl, Fruit, 4 3/4 In. 18.00
Bowl, Fruit,
  5 1/2 In. . . . . . 23.00 to 77.00
Bowl, Fruit, 11 3/4 In. . . 193.00
Bowl, Salad,
  Footed . . . . . 193.00 to 470.00
Candleholder, Bulb,
  Pair . . . . 85.00 to 138.00
Candleholder, Pyramid,
  Pair 220.00
Carafe 220.00
Casserole 143.00
Casserole, French 495.00
Chop Plate, 13 In. 38.00
Chop Plate,
  15 In. . . . . 44.00 to 48.00
Coffeepot 55.00

Coffeepot, After
   Dinner 303.00
Compote, Footed, Low,
   12 In. 121.00
Creamer, Individual 72.00
Creamer, Stick Handle . . . 39.00
Cup & Saucer . . 20.00 to 34.00
Cup & Saucer, After
   Dinner . . . . . . 65.00 to 110.00
Marmalade 220.00
Mixing Bowl, No. 1,
   5 In. 325.00
Mixing Bowl, No. 2,
   6 In. . . . . . . 66.00 to 140.00
Mixing Bowl, No. 4,
   8 In. 145.00
Mixing Bowl, No. 5,
   9 In. 121.00
Mixing Bowl, No. 6,
   10 In. 121.00
Mug 41.00
Mug, Tom & Jerry 110.00
Mustard 198.00
Nappy, 8 1/2 In. 40.00
Pitcher, Juice, Disk,
   30 Oz. 39.00
Pitcher, Water, Disk,
   2 Qt. 100.00
Plate, Bread & Butter,
   7 In. . . . . 5.00 to 8.00
Plate, Deep,
   8 In. . . . . 35.00 to 42.00
Plate, Dessert, 6 In. 5.00
Plate, Dinner,
   10 In. . . . . . . 22.00 to 32.00
Plate, Luncheon,
   9 In. . . . . 11.00 to 12.00
Platter, Oval, 12 In. 33.00
Relish 248.00
Sauceboat . . . . . . 45.00 to 55.00
Soup, Onion, Cover 358.00
Sugar,
   Individual . . 94.00 to 135.00
Sugar & Creamer 66.00
Syrup 275.00
Teapot, Medium, 6 Cup . . 99.00
Tray, Utility 47.00
Tumbler, Juice,
   5 Oz. . . . . 40.00 to 45.00
Vase, 8 In. 468.00
Vase, 10 In. 633.00
Vase, 12 In. 770.00
Vase, Bud, 6 1/2 In. 55.00

FIESTA KITCHEN KRAFT was a bake-and-serve line made in the early 1940s. It was made in Blue, Green, Red, Yellow, and other colors.

Green
Cake Plate, 11 In. 65.00
Casserole, Individual,
   No Cover 88.00
Jar, Cover, Medium 193.00
Mixing Bowl, 6 In. 61.00
Pie Plate, 9 In. 22.00
Salt & Pepper 66.00

Red
Cake Plate, 9 In. 41.00
Saltshaker 75.00

Spruce Green
Platter, 13 In. 413.00

Yellow
Cake Plate,
   11 In. . . . . . . 33.00 to 35.00
Casserole, 8 1/2 In. 120.00
Casserole, Individual 83.00
Mixing Bowl,
   10 In. 55.00
Pie Plate, 10 In. 45.00
Platter, 13 In. 39.00
Salt & Pepper 55.00

HACIENDA is a Mexican-inspired pattern introduced in 1938. The dinnerware was made on the Century shape. The decal shows a bench, cactus, and a portion of the side of a Mexican home. Most pieces have red trim at the handles and edge. After 1936, Franciscan also

made a dinnerware pattern called Hacienda.

Gravy Boat 30.00
Plate, 6 In. 11.00
Saucer 9.00

HARLEQUIN, a solid-color dinnerware, was less expensive than Fiesta. It was made from 1938 to 1964 and sold unmarked in Woolworth stores. The rings molded into the plate are at the edge of the plate well, and the rim is plain. Dishes were made in Chartreuse, Coral, Forest Green, Gray, Green (spruce green), Maroon (sometimes called red), Mauve Blue, Medium Green, Rose, Tangerine (red), Turquoise, and Yellow.

Chartreuse
Casserole, Cover 240.00
Casserole, No Cover . . . 100.00
Cup 10.00
Plate, Dessert, 6 In. 5.00
Sugar & Creamer, After
   Dinner 435.00

Forest Green
Bowl, Oatmeal, 36s 26.00
Platter, 11 In. 30.00

Gray
Bowl, Oatmeal, 36s 26.00
Bowl, Salad, Individual,
   7 1/2 In. 40.00
Creamer 85.00
Cup & Saucer 15.00
Pitcher, Ball,
   22 Oz. 175.00
Plate, Luncheon,
   9 In. . . . . 14.00 to 19.00

Sugar, Cover 30.00
Teapot ...... 185.00 to 225.00

Green

Ashtray, Saucer 75.00
Bowl, Plate, Dessert,
    6 In. 3.00
Bowl, Salad, Individual,
    7 1/2 In. 42.00
Casserole, Cover 195.00
Cup 11.00
Cup & Saucer 15.00
Nut Dish ..... 25.00 to 110.00
Pitcher, Ball,
    22 Oz. ..... 105.00 to 135.00
Plate, Luncheon, 9 In. ... 14.00

Maroon

Casserole, Cover 195.00
Marmalade, Cover 220.00
Nappy, 9 In. 28.00
Nut Dish 25.00
Plate, Dessert, 6 In. 3.00
Teapot, Cover 150.00
Tumbler 62.00

Mauve Blue

Casserole,
    Cover .... 85.00 to 95.00
Cup & Saucer, After
    Dinner 100.00
Nut Dish 25.00
Plate, Deep, 8 In. 30.00
Sugar, Cover 25.00
Teapot 95.00
Tumbler 53.00

Medium Green

Bowl, Fruit, 5 1/2 In. 30.00
Creamer 15.00
Plate, Bread & Butter,
    7 In. 45.00
Plate, Deep, 8 In. 125.00
Plate, Dinner, 10 In. 125.00

Rose

Bowl, 36s 40.00
Bowl, Fruit, 5 1/2 In. 11.00
Bowl, Oatmeal,
    36s .... 12.00 to 26.00
Bowl, Salad, Individual,
    7 1/4 In. ..... 18.00 to 20.00
Casserole, Cover 160.00
Creamer,
    Novelty ...... 28.00 to 45.00

Cup & Saucer .. 12.00 to 15.00
Cup & Saucer, After
    Dinner 140.00
Nut Dish 95.00
Pitcher, Ball 75.00
Pitcher, Water,
    Service ..... 70.00 to 80.00
Plate, Deep, 8 In. 30.00
Plate, Dinner, 10 In. 36.00
Plate, Luncheon, 9 In. ... 14.00
Saltshaker 11.00
Soup, Cream 20.00
Teapot ..... 100.00 to 195.00
Tumbler .... 53.00 to 85.00

Tangerine

Plate, Dinner, 10 In. 25.00
Sugar, Cover 35.00
Teapot 95.00

Turquoise

Ashtray, Regular 60.00
Bowl, Fruit, 5 1/2 In. 7.00
Bowl, Salad, Individual,
    7 1/2 In. 20.00
Creamer 12.00
Cup 5.00
Cup & Saucer ... 6.00 to 11.00
Plate, Luncheon, 9 In. ... 10.00
Plate, Salad, 7 In. 3.00
Platter, Oval, 13 In. 25.00

Yellow

Bowl, 36s 40.00
Bowl, Deep, 5 1/2 In. ... 26.00
Bowl, Fruit, 5 1/2 In. 7.00
Bowl, Oatmeal, 36s 9.00
Bowl, Serving, 8 1/2 In. .. 26.00
Casserole, Cover 85.00
Creamer, Novelty 45.00
Cup & Saucer ... 8.00 to 11.00
Marmalade 485.00
Nut Dish 25.00
Pitcher, Ball, 22 Oz. 60.00
Pitcher, Juice 75.00
Relish 95.00
Saucer, After Dinner 13.00
Tumbler, Pair 47.00

JUBILEE is a 1948 dinnerware shape. The dinnerware called Jubilee is a solid-color line. The colors are Celadon Green,

Cream Beige, Mist Gray, and Shell Pink. Jubilee was colored in different ways to produce dinnerware patterns with other names. Jubilee was revived in 1977 and 1978.

Celadon Green

Teapot 42.00

Cream Beige

Teapot 49.00
Tumbler, Juice 138.00

Mist Gray

Mixing Bowl, Large ... 290.00
Plate, Luncheon, 9 In. ... 15.00

Shell Pink

Calendar Plate, 1953,
    10 In. 15.00
Plate, Dinner, 10 In. 19.00
Plate, Luncheon, 9 In. ... 17.00
Sauceboat 18.00
Tumbler, Juice 138.00

KITCHEN KRAFT oven-to-table pieces were introduced in the early 1930s. The pieces were made in plain solid colors or with decals. They were usually marked *Kitchen Kraft, OvenServe.*

Brown

Baker, 5 1/2 In. 8.00

Chinese Willow Decal

Casserole, Cover, 8 In. .. 48.00

Columbine Decal

Bowl, 8 1/2 In. 49.00
Casserole, Cover 72.00

Pink

Ramekin, Handle 10.00

Pumpkin

Baker, Oval, 6 1/2 In. . . . 11.00
Bowl, 4 1/2 In. 7.00
Bowl, Fruit, 5 1/2 In. 10.00
Custard Cup, 3 1/2 In. 8.00
Custard, Deep,
    3 1/2 In. . . . . . . 6.00 to 7.00
Plate, Bread & Butter,
    6 5/8 In. 7.00
Platter, 11 1/2 In. 24.00
Ramekin, Handle 8.00

Star Decal

Casserole, Underplate,
    8 1/2 In. 59.00

Tulip Decal

Pie Plate, 9 1/2 In. 32.00

Yellow

Plate, Luncheon, 9 In. . . . 13.00

MARIGOLD is a scalloped-edge shape made in 1934. Some pieces are plain, some have decal decorations, and some have hand painting on the raised decorations that are part of the plate. Marigold glaze is a pale yellow.

Bowl, Deep, 5 In. 22.00
Bowl, Fruit 4.00
Bowl, Vegetable, Oval,
    9 In. 17.00
Casserole, Cover 47.00
Creamer 19.00
Platter, 11 In. 22.00
Platter, 15 In. 69.00

MAX-I-CANA was made in the 1930s. The design includes a Mexican man and some cactus pots. The dinnerware was made on either Fiesta or Yellowstone shape.

Cup, Yellowstone
    Shape 15.00
Plate, Yellowstone
    Shape, 9 In. 24.00

MEXICANA was the first of the Mexican-inspired patterns that became popular as dinnerware in the 1930s. This decal-decorated set, designed by Frederick

Hurten Rhead, was first offered in 1938. The design shows a collection of orange and yellow pots with a few cacti. The edge of the dish well is rimmed with red or, occasionally, yellow, green, or blue. Almost all of the pieces are Century line, a popular Homer Laughlin dinnerware shape.

Bowl, Fruit, 5 In. 11.00
Bowl, Vegetable,
    8 1/2 In. 34.00
Cup & Saucer 24.00
Gravy Boat 50.00
Plate, Dessert, 6 In. 10.00
Plate, Bread & Butter,
    7 In. 17.00
Soup, Dish 25.00

MEXICANA KITCHEN KRAFT is the kitchenware that matched Mexicana dinnerware. Both were made with the same decorations. Mixing bowls, casseroles, pie plates, pie servers, cake plates, and other pieces were made in this pattern.

Baker, Red Trim, Oval,
    11 In. 28.00
Cake Plate, 10 1/2 In. . . . 69.00
Cake Server 125.00
Casserole, Cover, Blue Trim,
    8 1/2 In. 140.00
Casserole, Underplate,
    Red Trim, 8 1/2 In. 48.00

NANTUCKET is a pattern that appeared in the 1953 Montgomery Ward's catalog. It has a border of stylized pink and blue flowers and gray leaves.

Casserole, Cover 42.00
Cup, Eggshell Nautilus
    Shape 5.00
Sauceboat, Eggshell Nautilus
    Shape 18.00
Soup, Dish, Eggshell Nautilus
    Shape 9.00

NAUTILUS
See Eggshell Nautilus

PRISCILLA is a decal-decorated ware with pale pink roses and sprigs of flowers.

Bowl, Fruit, 5 In. . 4.50 to 9.00
Bowl, Vegetable, Oval,
    In. 25.00
Bowl, Vegetable, Round,
    8 In. 25.00
Creamer 20.00
Cup & Saucer . . . 8.00 to 10.00
Gravy Boat, Underplate . . 30.00
Mixing Bowl,
    10 In. . . . . . . 45.00 to 48.00
Pie Plate, 9 1/2 In. 26.00
Plate, Bread & Butter,
    6 In. 9.00
Plate, Dinner,
    9 In. . . . . 9.00 to 18.00
Plate, Luncheon, 8 In. . . . 16.00
Soup, Dish, 8 In. 15.00
Sugar, Cover . . . 14.00 to 25.00

REPUBLIC was made in the early 1900s and lasted to the 1940s. It is a shape with an embossed scalloped edge decorated in many different ways.

Plate, 18 K Gold Trim,
    6 In. 4.00
Plate, 18 K Gold Trim,
    10 In. 10.00
Platter, Fish Decal,
    15 In. 90.00

RHYTHM is a solid-color dinnerware made by Homer Laughlin China Company from about 1951 to 1958. It is a pattern with simple, modern shapes. The dishes were made in many of the Harlequin colors, including Chartreuse, Forest Green,

Gray, Maroon, Turquoise, and Yellow. Other companies also made patterns named Rhythm but they are not listed here.

Chartreuse
Mixing Bowl, 10 In. 61.00
Snack Plate 30.00

Forest Green
Creamer 9.00
Cup & Saucer 12.00
Gravy Boat 12.00
Mixing Bowl, 6 In. 135.00
Mixing Bowl, 10 In. . . . 165.00

Gray
Cup 8.00
Plate, Bread & Butter,
6 In. 5.00
Plate, Dinner, 9 In. 9.00
Plate, Salad, 7 1/4 In. . . . 7.00
Salt & Pepper, Pair 18.00
Soup, Coupe, 8 1/4 In. . . . 12.00

Maroon
Cup & Saucer 15.00

Turquoise
Plate, Dinner, 10 In. 6.00
Spoon Rest 176.00

Yellow
Creamer 12.00
Cup & Saucer 15.00
Mixing Bowl, 8 In. 145.00
Plate, Salad, 7 In. 13.00
Snack Plate 30.00
Soup, Dish, 8 In. 15.00

RHYTHM ROSE was made from the mid-1940s to the mid-1950s. The pattern features a center rose decal.

Cake Plate, 11 In. 35.00
Creamer 20.00
Mixing, Bowl, Large 47.00
Sauceboat 19.00

RIVIERA, a solid-color ware, was made from 1938 to 1950. It was unmarked and sold exclusively by the Murphy Company. Plates and cup handles are squared. Colors are Ivory, Light Green, Mauve Blue, Red, Yellow, and, rarely, Dark Blue.

Dark Blue
Plate, 7 In. 75.00

Ivory
Cup & Saucer, After
Dinner 115.00
Plate, Deep, 8 In. 45.00
Plate, Luncheon, 9 In. . . . 15.00
Tumbler, Handle 175.00

Light Green
Plate, Dessert, 6 In. 8.00
Sugar, Cover 25.00
Teapot 185.00

Mauve Blue
Casserole,
Cover . . . . . . 61.00 to 110.00
Cup 7.00
Saucer 7.00
Sugar 6.00
Tumbler, Handle 60.00

Red
Bowl, Fruit, 5 1/2 In. 8.00
Butter, Cover, 1/2 Lb. . . 110.00
Butter, Cover, 1/4 Lb. . . . 85.00
Plate, Luncheon, 9 In. . . . 18.00
Syrup, Cover 95.00
Tumbler, Juice 85.00

Yellow
Butter, Cover, 1/2 Lb. . . . 66.00
Casserole, Cover 101.00

Cup 7.00
Pitcher, Juice 195.00
Platter, 11 1/2 In. 20.00
Saucer 7.00
Tumbler, Handle 50.00

SERENADE was made from 1939 to the 1940s. It was made in plain colors: Blue, Green, Pink, or Yellow.

Blue
Creamer 10.50
Saucer 4.00

Green
Casserole, Cover 160.00

Pink
Cup & Saucer 15.00

Yellow
Chop Plate, 13 In. 7.25

SKYTONE is both a pattern and a shape. The pattern made by Homer Laughlin is plain and light-blue colored. If the dishes have decals, the pieces are known by the name of the decal.

Bowl, Vegetable, Round,
7 1/2 In. 10.00
Coffeepot 60.00
Cup & Saucer 6.50
Cup & Saucer, After
Dinner 29.00
Gravy Boat, Attached
Underplate 16.00
Plate, Dinner,
10 In. 10.00

Plate, Salad,
7 1/2 In. 7.00

Teapot, 7 1/2 In. 45.00

SWING
See Eggshell Swing

THEME
See Eggshell Theme

VIRGINIA ROSE is the name of a shape of dishes made from 1933 to the 1970s. The shapes are decorated with a variety of decal decorations. The dishes with a design of a spray of roses and green leaves is the pattern most often called Virginia Rose by collectors. If no decal name is mentioned here, it is the Virginia Rose decal design.

Bowl, Deep,
5 In. . . . . 30.00 to 36.00

Bowl, Fruit,
5 1/2 In. . . . . . 7.00 to 12.00

Bowl, Fruit, Blue
Dresden, 5 1/2 In. 6.00

Bowl, Fruit, Bouquet,
5 1/2 In. 4.00

Bowl, Fruit, Meadow
Goldenrod, 5 1/2 In. 5.00

Bowl, Fruit, Spring Song,
5 1/2 In. 3.50

Bowl, Moss Rose,
9 In. 18.00

Bowl, Oatmeal, 6 In. 19.00

Bowl, Oatmeal, Bouquet,
6 In. 13.00

Bowl, Oatmeal, Moss
Rose, 6 In. 18.00

Bowl, Oatmeal, Spring
Song, 6 In. 12.00

Bowl, Spring Song,
8 1/2 In. 22.00

Bowl, Spring Song,
9 1/2 In. 30.00

Bowl, Sugar, Cover,
Louise 22.00

Bowl, Vegetable, Medieval
Rose 65.00

Bowl, Vegetable, Oval,
8 In. . . . . 30.00 to 39.00

Bowl, Vegetable, Oval,
10 In. 28.00

Bowl, Vegetable, Oval,
Bouquet, 10 In. 20.00

Bowl, Vegetable, Oval,
Golden Rose II, 9 In. . . 17.00

Bowl, Vegetable, Oval, Meadow
Goldenrod, 9 In. 21.00

Cake Plate, Spring Wreath,
10 3/4 In. 32.00

Casserole, Cover,
8 In. . . . . 55.00 to 112.00

Casserole, Cover,
Helene, 8 1/2 In. 58.00

Casserole, Cover,
Round Sides 98.00

Creamer, Golden Rose . . . 16.00

Creamer, Marsh Bouquet . 15.00

Creamer, Meadow
Goldenrod . . . . 13.00 to 17.00

Creamer, Patrician 15.00

Cup, Bouquet . . . . 8.00 to 12.00

Cup, Golden Rose 8.00

Cup, Meadow Goldenrod . . 8.00

Cup & Saucer,
Blue Dresden 22.00

Cup & Saucer, Garden
Theme, Gold Trim 14.00

Cup & Saucer,
Golden Rose II 10.00

Cup & Saucer,
Spring Song 9.00

Gravy Boat . . . . 20.00 to 29.00

Gravy Boat,
Silver Scrolls 21.00

Gravy Boat, Underplate,
Garden Ring 22.00

Gravy Boat, Underplate,
Silver Scrolls 39.00

Mixing Bowl, 8 In. 57.00

Mixing Bowl, Spring
Wreath, 6 In. 35.00

Pie Plate,
9 1/2 In. . . . . 39.00 to 48.00

Pie Plate, 10 1/2 In. 55.00

Pie Plate, Armand,
9 1/2 In. 35.00

Plate, Bread & Butter,
Bouquet, 7 In. 6.50

Plate, Bread & Butter, Marigold
Springtime, 7 In. 7.00

Plate, Bread & Butter,
Moss Rose, 7 In. . 7.50 to 8.00

Plate, Dessert, 6 In. 7.00

Plate, Dessert, Gold Rim,
Marked 1949, 6 1/2 In. . 10.00

Plate, Dessert, Marigold
Springtime, 6 In. 5.00

Plate, Dessert, Meadow
Goldenrod, 6 In. 6.00

Plate, Dessert, Patrician,
6 In. 5.00

Plate, Dessert, Spring Song,
6 In. 5.00

Plate, Dinner, 10 In. 35.00

Plate, Dinner, Bouquet,
10 In. 20.00

Plate, Dinner, Gold Rim,
Marked 1949, 10 In. . . . 12.00

Plate, Dinner, Golden Rose II,
10 In. 21.00

Plate, Dinner, Meadow
Goldenrod, 10 In. 23.00

Plate, Dinner, Nosegay,
10 In. 22.00

Plate, Luncheon,
9 In. . . . . 7.00 to 10.00

Plate, Luncheon, Marigold
Springtime, 9 In. 8.00

Plate, Luncheon,
Nosegay, 9 In. 13.00

Plate, Luncheon, Spring Song,
9 In. 7.00

Plate, Salad,
8 In. . . . . 17.00 to 18.00

Plate, Salad, Bouquet,
8 In. 22.00

Plate, Salad, Garden Ring,
8 In. 15.00

Platter, 10 1/2 In. 38.00

Platter, 11 1/2 In. 25.00
Platter, 13 In. 29.00
Platter, Blue Dresden,
   13 1/2 . . . . 22.00
Platter, Bouquet,
   11 1/2 In. 23.00
Platter, Bouquet, 13 In. . . 29.00
Platter, Double Gold Bank,
   13 In. 32.00
Platter, Garden Ring,
   15 1/2 In. 35.00
Platter, Gold Trim, Garden
   Theme, 11 1/2 In. 29.00
Platter, Golden Rose,
   12 1/2 In. 36.00
Platter, Golden Rose II,
   13 In. 24.00
Platter, Marigold Springtime,
   13 In. 24.00
Platter, Marsh Bouquet,
   11 1/2 In. 27.00
Platter, Meadow Goldenrod,
   13 In. 23.00
Platter, Patrician,
   15 1/2 In. 42.00
Platter, Red Beauty 32.00
Platter, Spring Promise,
   11 1/2 In. 23.00
Sauceboat, Underplate,
   Patrician 39.00
Saucer 10.00
Saucer, Meadow
   Goldenrod 3.00
Soup, Dish . . . . . 18.00 to 20.00
Soup, Dish, Coupe 24.00
Soup, Dish, Coupe,
   Golden Rose II 19.00
Soup, Dish, Spring
   Wreath 15.00
Sugar, Cover . . . 17.00 to 23.00
Sugar, Cover,
   Golden Rose 21.00
Sugar, Cover,
   Marsh Bouquet 23.00
Sugar, Cover, Patrician . . 19.00
Sugar Cover, Marigold
   Springtime 11.00

WELLS is a shape that was
made from about 1930 to 1935.
Some pieces were marked with
special marks that included the
word *Wells*. The Wells Art
Glaze pieces are solid-color

Matte Green, Peach, Rust, or
Vellum (ivory). Other pieces on
the Wells shape are ivory with
decals. Cups have unusual
"wing" handles; lids have spiral
handles.

Matte Green
Sauceboat,
   Art Glaze 32.00

Rust
Cup, Art Glaze 20.00
Cup & Saucer,
   Art Glaze . . . . 26.00 to 30.00
Jug, Cover, Art Glaze,
   9 In. 140.00
Plate, Art Glaze, 7 In. . . . 19.00
Plate, Art Glaze, 9 In. . . . 23.00
Platter, Art Glaze,
   15 1/2 In. 85.00

Vellum
Bowl, 8 1/2 In. 24.00
Bowl, Oatmeal, 36s 25.00
Bowl, Oval, 9 In. 24.00
Butter, Cover, Red Beauty
   Decal, Round 295.00
Cake Plate,
   Floral Decal 42.00
Casserole, Cover 57.00
Cup & Saucer 16.00
Cup & Saucer, Pink
   Floral Decal 14.00
Gravy Boat,
   Underplate 42.00
Plate, Dessert, 6 In. 7.00
Plate, Salad, 8 In. 14.00
Platter, 11 3/4 In. 26.00
Platter, Pink Clover,
   11 1/2 In. 28.00
Soup, Cream, Underplate,
   Red Beauty Decal 60.00
Sugar, Cover 24.00

HULL

Hull pottery was made in
Crooksville, Ohio, from
1905. Addis E. Hull bought
the Acme Pottery Com-
pany and started making
ceramic wares. In 1917,
A. E. Hull Pottery began
making art pottery as well
as commercial wares. For
a short time, 1921 to
1929, the firm also sold
pottery imported from
Europe. The dinnerwares
of the 1940s (including the
Little Red Riding Hood
line), the high gloss art-
wares of the 1950s, and
the matte wares of the
1940s are all popular with
collectors. The firm offi-
cially closed in March
1986.

LITTLE RED RIDING HOOD
is one of the easiest patterns of
American dinnerware to recognize. Three-dimensional figures
of the little girl with the red
hood have been adapted into
saltshakers, teapots, and other
pieces. The pattern was made
from 1943 to 1957.

Canister,
   Cereal . . . . . 900.00 to 995.00
Canister,
   Salt . . . . . . 900.00 to 1050.00

Have a window or a peephole in every outside door.

Cookie Jar ... 310.00 to 495.00
Mug, Child's 1800.00
Salt &
　Pepper ...... 95.00 to 105.00
Sugar & Creamer 375.00
Teapot 395.00

IROQUOIS

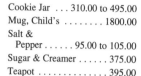

Iroquois China Company was founded in 1905 in Syracuse, New York. The company made mostly hotel china until 1946, when it introduced Russel Wright's Casual pattern. By the 1960s, production was limited to a few patterns, and in 1969 the factory closed.

BLUE DIAMONDS is a pattern of three diamonds on a modern shape. It is part of the Informal line designed by Ben Seibel.
Cup 9.00
Bowl, Fruit 11.00
Bowl, Vegetable, Oval ... 35.00
Plate, Salad 14.00
Soup, Dish 21.00

CASUAL is a dinnerware designed by Russel Wright in 1946. It was a modern solid-color high-fired china that was guaranteed not to chip. The original colors were Ice Blue, Lemon Yellow, and Sugar White. Added later were Aqua, Avocado Yellow, Brick Red, Cantaloupe, Charcoal, Lettuce Green, Nutmeg, Oyster, Parsley, Pink Sherbet, and Ripe Apricot.

Avocado Yellow
Bowl, Fruit, 5 1/2 In. 12.00
Creamer 15.00
Cup & Saucer 10.00
Plate, Bread & Butter,
　6 1/2 In. 5.00

Cantaloupe
Cup 20.00

Charcoal
Platter, Oval, 14 In. 50.00
Saucer 12.00
Sugar, Stacking 18.00

Ice Blue
Creamer 20.00
Cup & Saucer 16.00
Sugar, Cover 30.00

Lemon Yellow
Bowl, Cereal, 5 In. 11.00
Bowl, Fruit, Round,
　5 3/4 In. 13.00
Creamer 12.00
Cup & Saucer 20.00
Plate, Bread & Butter,
　6 In. .... 4.50 to 6.00
Plate, Dinner, 10 In. 11.00

Lettuce Green
Cup & Saucer 8.00
Plate, Bread & Butter,
　6 In. .... 4.00 to 8.00
Plate, Dinner, 10 In. 5.00
Soup, Dish 42.00
Sugar, Cover,
　Restyled 21.00

Nutmeg
Bowl, Cereal 15.00
Coffeepot 75.00
Creamer 20.00
Cup & Saucer 18.00
Mug 120.00
Plate, Bread & Butter,
　6 1/2 In. 12.00
Plate, Dinner, 10 In. 18.00
Salt & Pepper 30.00
Sugar, Cover 30.00

Oyster
Creamer, Stacking 25.00
Plate, Dinner, 10 In. 29.00

Parsley
Sugar & Creamer,
　Stacking 60.00

Pink Sherbet
Creamer 20.00
Plate, Bread & Butter,
　6 In. 7.00
Plate, Dinner,
　10 In. ...... 10.00 to 13.00
Plate, Salad, 8 In. 8.00
Sugar & Creamer,
　Stacking 50.00

Ripe Apricot
Plate, Bread & Butter,
　6 In. 7.00

IMPROMPTU is a 1956 shape designed by Ben Seibel. It was offered in solid-color Bridal White and seven original patterns. The china was guaranteed not to chip or break.

Bowl, Vegetable, Divided	20.00
Bowl, Vegetable, Oval	14.00
Compote, Fruit, Pyramids	7.00
Cup & Saucer	12.00
Plate, Dinner, 10 In.	9.00
Platter, 13 In.	35.00
Salt & Pepper	18.00

JOHNSON BROTHERS

Brothers Frederick and Alfred Johnson started their pottery business in Stoke-on-Trent, England, in 1883. The company made ironstone and semi-porcelain dinnerware with printed underglaze decorations. In 1968, Johnson Brothers became part of the Wedgwood Group (which became the Waterford Wedgwood Group in 1995).

FRIENDLY VILLAGE is made by Johnson Brothers, Ltd. of Hanley, England, now part of the Waterford Wedgwood Group. The pattern has been made since 1953 and is still being made. It is decorated with a black transfer design tinted in pastel colors and features scenes of rural life.

Bowl, 8 1/4 In.	16.00
Butter, Cover	38.00
Cookie Jar, Series 3, 9 1/2 x 6 In.	31.00
Dish, Christmas Tree, 14 In.	39.00
Pickle, 8 x 5 1/2 In.	30.00
Plate, Dinner, Hayfield, 10 1/2 In.	25.00
Plate, Dinner, Sugar Maples, 10 1/2 In.	9.50
Plate, Dinner, Well, 10 1/2 In.	16.00
Plate, Salad, Covered Bridge, 7 1/2 In.	9.75
Plate, Village Street, 10 1/2 In.	18.50
Platter, Harvest Time, 13 1/2 x 11 In.	25.00
Sugar, Cover	20.00
Sugar & Creamer, Cover	35.00
Tidbit, 3 Tiers, 3 Scenes	30.00

LEIGH

Crescent China Company, located in Alliance, Ohio, became Leigh Potteries in 1926. The factory made dinnerware, kitchenware, and a semiporcelain line of decorative pottery called

Leigh Art Ware. The company closed in 1931.

GREEN WHEAT pattern is decorated with separate wheat stalks.

Bowl, Fruit	6.00
Creamer	30.00
Cup & Saucer	19.00
Gravy Boat	40.00
Plate, Bread & Butter, 6 In.	4.00
Sugar, Cover	40.00

METLOX

Metlox Potteries was founded in 1927 in Manhattan Beach, California. The company originally made ceramic fittings for neon signs. Metlox's first dinnerware was made in 1931. In 1958, the company bought molds and rights to the trademark *Vernonware* from Vernon Kilns. The factory closed in 1989.

ANTIQUE GRAPE is a pattern introduced by Metlox Potteries in 1964. The firm had been making a pattern called Sculptured Grape with a raised grapevine border in natural colors. Antique Grape is the same shape but, according to a company brochure, has "carved grapes and leaves raised on a soft beige antique finish against a warm white background." It was made until at least 1975.

Bowl, Vegetable, Cover,
2 Qt. 130.00
Bowl, Vegetable, Round,
8 1/2 In. 55.00
Creamer 36.00
Cup 18.00
Cup & Saucer 21.00
Plate, Salad, 7 1/2 In. 12.00
Platter, Oval, 9 5/8 In. . . . 57.00
Platter, Oval, 12 1/2 In. . . 69.00
Sugar, Cover 48.00

AUTUMN BERRY was pictured in the 1979 Metlox brochure. The pattern features brown leaves and berries.

Bowl, Cereal, 6 5/8 In. . . 19.00
Plate, Dinner, 10 3/4 In. . . 26.00
Platter, Oval,
11 3/4 In. . . . . 51.00 to 69.00
Sugar, Cover 48.00

CALIFORNIA AZTEC is made on the freeform shape. It is white with a wiggly black line as the design. It was introduced in 1955.

Cup 6.00
Gravy Boat, 9 1/2 In. 35.00
Plate, Dinner, 10 In. 10.00
Plate, Salad, 7 1/2 In. 7.50
Saucer 4.00

CALIFORNIA DEL REY was in the 1955 Metlox brochures. It is made on the Confetti shape. California Del Rey is blue and white; California Confetti is pink and white. Both patterns look like bits of confetti were dropped on the plates. Pieces like pitchers and sugar bowls are white on the inside, solid color on the outside.

Cup & Saucer 10.00
Plate, Dinner, 10 In. 10.00
Platter, 13 In. 35.00
Sugar & Creamer,
Cover 40.00

CALIFORNIA IVY was one of the most popular patterns made by Metlox. It was introduced in 1946. The pattern was named for its ivy vine border.

Bowl, Vegetable, Round,
9 In. 35.00

Creamer 18.00
Cup & Saucer 12.00
Gravy Boat, Underplate,
9 In. 35.00
Pitcher, Water, Ice Lip . . . 75.00
Sugar, Cover 25.00
Tumbler, 13 Oz. 30.00

CALIFORNIA PEACH BLOSSOM features sprigs of pink blossoms. It was introduced in 1952.

Bowl, Cereal 8.00
Bowl, Fruit 5.00
Bowl, Salad 75.00
Bowl, Vegetable, Round . 50.00
Butter Chip 12.00
Casserole, Cover 55.00
Coffee Server 50.00
Cup 9.00
Plate, Bread & Butter 4.00
Plate, Dinner, 9 1/2 In. . . 10.00
Plate, Salad, 7 1/2 In. . . . 10.00
Platter, 13 In. 57.00
Relish, Divided 25.00
Salt & Pepper 25.00
Tumbler 19.00

CALIFORNIA PROVINCIAL dinnerware pictures a maroon, green, and yellow rooster in the center. It has a border made up of a wavy line and dots. It was made beginning in 1950. A similar design, with a different border, was called Red Rooster.

Bowl, Fruit, 6 In. 22.00
Butter, Cover Only 30.00
Canister Set, 4 Piece . . . 225.00
Creamer 43.00
Cup & Saucer . . 12.00 to 27.00
Mug 35.00
Plate, Bread & Butter,
6 3/8 In. 12.00
Plate, Dinner, 10 In. 34.00
Platter, Oval, 11 In. 105.00
Sugar, Cover 26.00

CALIFORNIA TEMPO is featured in the 1961 catalog. It is a solid-color pattern made with yellow, blue, or chartreuse on the front, walnut brown on the back.

Bowl, Fruit, 5 In. 8.00
Bowl, Vegetable, Round . 23.00
Cup & Saucer 12.00
Plate, Dinner,
  10 1/4 In. . . . . 15.00 to 21.00
Platter, 13 1/4 In. 25.00

COLORSTAX is a pattern that was made to mix and match. Pieces were made in solid colors and could be bought in any combination. Chocolate, Fern Green, Forest Green, Midnight Blue, Sand, Sky Blue, Terra-Cotta, and White were used. These 1970s dishes were dishwasher, oven, and microwave safe.

COLORSTAX

Apricot
Creamer 12.00
Cup & Saucer 8.00
Plate, Salad, 8 In. 8.00

Sky Blue
Salt & Pepper,
  2 x 2 3/4 In. 12.00

DELLA ROBBIA shape was made in 1965. Vernon Della Robbia, seen in the 1974 catalog, was this shape with a brown, green, and beige border of leaves and flowers.

Bowl, Cereal, 7 1/8 In. . . 19.00
Bowl, Fruit, 6 1/2 In. 15.00
Bowl, Vegetable,
  Cover 130.00

Bowl, Vegetable,
  Divided 69.00
Bowl, Vegetable, Oval . . . 50.00
Bowl, Vegetable,
  Round 39.00
Casserole, Cover, 2 Qt. . . 84.00
Creamer 27.00
Cup & Saucer 20.00
Gravy Boat 69.00
Mug, 10 Oz. 19.00
Plate, Bread & Butter,
  6 1/2 In. 9.00
Plate, Dinner,
  10 5/8 In. 24.00
Platter, Oval,
  9 5/8 In. . . . . 36.00 to 43.00
Platter, Oval, 11 1/8 In. . . 73.00
Sugar, Cover 36.00

GIGI was introduced in 1978. The pattern has dark green, blue, red, and yellow flowers that have a hand-painted look.

Bowl, Cereal 19.00
Bowl, Vegetable,
  Round 55.00
Cup & Saucer 21.00
Platter, Small 57.00

HOMESTEAD PROVINCIAL is one of the Poppytrail patterns by Metlox Potteries. The designs are based on Early American folk art themes. Homestead Provincial is dark green and burgundy. Other patterns are the same design but in different colors. Colonial Homestead is red and brown, and Provincial Blue is blue.

Bowl, Fruit, 6 In. 12.00
Bowl, Vegetable, 10 In. . . 32.00

Bowl, Vegetable, Cover,
  10 In. 90.00
Coaster 16.00
Creamer, Cover,
  Handles 22.50
Cup & Saucer . . 12.00 to 15.00
Pepper Mill 34.00
Plate, Bread & Butter,
  6 1/2 In. 10.00
Plate, Dinner,
  10 In. . . . . . . 15.00 to 25.00
Plate, Salad, 7 1/4 In. . . . 12.00
Platter, 11 3/4 In. 25.00
Saltshaker 17.00
Saucer, 6 In. 5.00
Soup, Dish, 8 1/2 In. 22.00
Sugar 18.00

MARGARITA was featured in the 1971 brochure. It is a hand-painted golden-yellow pattern on a burnt orange background.

Bowl, Cereal, 6 1/4 In. . . 16.00
Bowl, Vegetable, Round,
  9 In. 48.00
Plate, Dinner, 10 1/4 In. . . 22.00
Plate, Salad, 7 3/4 In. . . . 11.00
Platter, 13 In. 47.00

PEPPER TREE is a 1957 pattern decorated with a leaf pattern in bronze-green and sun-gold.

Bowl, Vegetable, Round,
  9 1/2 In. 48.00
Creamer 29.00
Cup & Saucer 17.00
Gravy Boat 71.00
Platter, Medium, 11 In. . . 69.00
Soup, Dish 17.00

POPPYTRAIL (or Poppy Trail) was a mark used on many pieces made by Metlox Potteries. Solid-color wares and hand-decorated pieces were made. Listed here are solid mix-and-match pieces marked *Metlox Poppytrail*. This is the 1934 pattern known to the company as the 200 Series. The original eight colors were Canary Yellow, Cream, Delphinium Blue, Old Rose, Poppy Orange, Rust, Sea Green, and Turquoise Blue. Later, seven pastel colors were added: Opaline Green, Pastel Yellow, Peach, Petal Pink, Powder Blue, Satin Ivory, and Satin Turquoise.

Cream
Bowl, Crimped Edge,
2 x 11 In. 10.00

Pastel Yellow
Chop Plate, 13 1/2 In. . . . 25.00

Petal Pink
Plate, 9 In. 8.50

Satin Ivory
Chop Plate, 13 In. 20.00

Satin Turquoise
Plate, 9 In. 8.50

Sea Green
Bowl, Low,
12 1/4 x 9 In. 45.00

PROVINCIAL BLUE is a Metlox Potteries pattern that was made from 1950 to about 1968. It is decorated with blue scenes of farm life. A similar pattern, Homestead Provincial, features the designs in other colors.

Butter, Cover 68.00
Mug, No Cover 30.00
Pepper Mill 45.00
Salt Mill 45.00

PROVINCIAL FRUIT pattern was made in 1965. It is part of the Poppytrail line. Another pattern called Provincial Fruit was made by Purinton, but it is not listed here.

Butter 43.00
Plate, Dinner, 10 1/2 In. . . 22.00
Plate, Salad, 7 1/2 In. 11.00

RED ROOSTER is a pattern in the Poppytrail line made beginning in 1955. It is easy to identify because the center design is a large red rooster. Some of the pieces look as if they have rivets. California Provincial is a very similar design with a different border. Another similar pattern is called Rooster Bleu.

Ashtray, Large 35.00
Bowl, Fruit,
6 In. . . . . 12.00 to 13.00
Bowl, Salad, Large 79.00
Bowl, Vegetable,
Cover 115.00
Bowl, Vegetable,
Round 50.00
Butter 65.00
Butter, Cover 80.00
Coffeepot 98.00
Cookie Jar 90.00
Cookie Jar, Wooden
Cover 125.00
Cup, 6 Oz. 15.00
Dish, Hen On Nest, Cover,
Medium 98.00
Dish, Hen On Nest, Cover,
Small 72.00
Eggcup 25.00
Gravy Boat 50.00
Pitcher 72.00
Plate, Bread & Butter,
6 1/2 In. 11.00
Plate, Dinner,
10 In. . . . . . . 13.00 to 14.00
Plate, Salad,
7 1/2 In. . . . . . 11.00 to 14.00
Platter, Turkey,
22 1/2 In. 249.00
Salt & Pepper, 4 In. 18.00
Saucer, 6 1/8 In. 3.00

Soup, Dish, 8 In. 19.00
Teapot 78.00

SAN FERNANDO is a Vernonware pattern made by Metlox beginning in 1966. It is amber and golden brown decorated with a scroll design. Some pieces have a brown exterior and amber interior.

Bowl, Cereal, 6 7/8 In. . . 16.00
Bowl, Vegetable, Oval,
11 1/4 In. 48.00
Cup & Saucer 17.00
Plate, Bread & Butter,
6 5/8 In. 8.00
Plate, Salad, 7 1/2 In. 11.00
Platter, Oval, 9 3/4 In. . . . 47.00
Soup, Dish 17.00

SCULPTURED DAISY was made in 1964 as part of the Poppytrail line. The pattern features raised white daisies and green leaves.

Bowl, Cereal, 7 1/4 In. . . 19.00
Bowl, Fruit, 6 1/2 In. 16.00
Bowl, Vegetable, Cover,
1 Qt. 65.00
Bowl, Vegetable,
Divided 69.00
Bowl, Vegetable, Round,
10 In. 47.00
Butter, Cover 40.00
Coffeepot 86.00
Creamer 31.00
Cup & Saucer . . 10.00 to 17.00
Gravy Boat 74.00
Plate, Dinner, 10 1/2 In. . . 10.00
Plate, Salad, 7 1/2 In. 12.00
Platter, Oval, 9 1/2 In. . . . 51.00
Platter, Oval, 11 In. 81.00
Platter, Round 69.00

Salt & Pepper 22.00
Sugar, Cover 40.00

SCULPTURED GRAPE is a pattern made by Metlox Potteries as part of the Poppytrail line from 1963 to 1975. The pattern has a raised grapevine colored blue, brown, and green.

Bowl, Salad 70.00
Bowl, Vegetable, Divided,
    9 1/2 In. 40.00
Bowl, Vegetable, Round,
    8 1/2 In. ..... 25.00 to 47.00
Butter, Cover 55.00
Creamer 32.00
Cup & Saucer 20.00
Platter, Oval, 9 5/8 In. ... 57.00
Sugar, Cover 43.00

SCULPTURED ZINNIA is a pattern made from 1964 to 1980 as part of the Poppytrail line. The Sculptured Zinnia shape was made in three color variations named Lavender Blue, Memories, or Sculptured Zinnia.

Bowl, Vegetable, Round,
    9 1/2 In. 50.00
Creamer 32.00
Cup & Saucer 21.00
Plate, Bread & Butter,
    6 3/8 In. 9.00

❖

When you pack teapots to move, do not tape the lid to the pot. The tape may leave a stain and the lid may chip if it is handled roughly or just bumps around while being moved in a car.

❖

Platter, Oval, 12 1/2 In. ... 51.00
Saltshaker 23.00
Soup, Dish 21.00
Teapot, Cover 69.00

TRUE BLUE is a 1974 Vernonware pattern. It has scalloped edges and fluted details. There is a blue floral design on an off-white background.

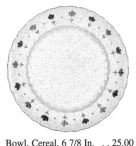

Bowl, Cereal, 6 7/8 In. ... 25.00
Bowl, Soup, 7 In. 32.00
Bowl, Soup, Rim,
    8 1/8 In. 16.00
Bowl, Vegetable, Round,
    9 1/4 In. 30.00
Creamer 18.00
Cup & Saucer .. 15.00 to 25.00
Plate, Bread & Butter,
    6 5/8 In. 12.00
Plate, Dinner, 10 3/4 In. ... 35.00
Plate, Salad,
    7 1/2 In. ..... 16.00 to 30.00
Platter, Oval, 13 3/4 In. ... 28.00
Saucer, 6 1/4 In. 5.00

VINEYARD is a pattern shown in the 1974 brochure. It is decorated with a border of grapevine leaves in fall tones with blue grapes.

Bowl, Cereal, 6 7/8 In. ... 19.00
Bowl, Fruit, 6 In. 15.00
Bowl, Vegetable,
    Divided 69.00
Creamer 27.00
Cup & Saucer 20.00
Gravy Boat 82.00
Plate, Bread & Butter,
    6 5/8 In. 9.00
Plate, Dinner, 10 3/4 In. ... 26.00
Sugar, Cover 48.00

WOODLAND GOLD is from the 1970s. It features leaves in fall colors.

Bowl, Cereal, 5 5/8 In. ... 16.00
Bowl, Fruit, 5 3/8 In. 14.00
Creamer 29.00
Cup & Saucer 17.00
Gravy Boat 71.00
Plate, Dinner, 10 1/4 In. ... 22.00
Platter, Oval, 11 In. 69.00
Soup, Dish 17.00
Sugar, Cover 41.00

NORITAKE

Noritake porcelain was made in Japan after 1904 by Nippon Toki Kaisha. The best-known Noritake pieces are marked with the M in a wreath for the Morimura Brothers, a New York City distributing company. This mark was used until 1941.

AZALEA pattern by Noritake was made for Larkin Company customers from 1918 to 1941. Larkin, the soap company, was in Buffalo, New York. Each piece of the white china was decorated with pink azaleas and green leaves.

Bowl, Fruit, 5 1/4 In. 10.00
Bowl, Oatmeal,
  5 1/2 In. 20.00
Bowl, Vegetable, Handles,
  9 1/4 In. 55.00
Bowl, Vegetable, Oval . . . 52.00
Creamer . . . . 12.00 to 22.00
Cup & Saucer . . 11.00 to 23.00
Gravy Boat, Underplate,
  9 x 6 In. 42.00
Pickle . . . . 18.00 to 24.00
Plate, Bread & Butter,
  6 1/2 In. . . . . . . 7.50 to 10.00
Plate, Dinner, 10 In. 25.00
Plate, Salad,
  7 1/2 In. . . . . . 10.00 to 20.00
Plate, Serving, Handles,
  9 3/4 In. 35.00
Platter, 10 1/4 In. 54.00
Platter, 11 3/4 In. 55.00
Soup, Dish,
  7 1/2 In. . . . . . 22.00 to 25.00
Sugar, Cover . . . 15.00 to 24.00
Sugar & Creamer, Cover . 45.00

TREE IN THE MEADOW is another pattern made for the Larkin Company in the early 1900s.

Bowl, Shrimp 225.00
Coffeepot, 6 1/2 In. 350.00

PADEN CITY

Paden City Pottery was founded in 1907 by George Lasell in Paden City, West Virginia. Early cookware items were made of red clay. Beginning in the 1920s, the company made dinnerware, floral items, and kitchenware and is credited as being the first to use an underglaze decal. Paden City Pottery closed in 1963.

AMERICAN ROSE is also called American Beauty. It has a lacy gold border and a large pink rose and green leaves in the center.

Cup & Saucer . . . 8.00 to 15.00
Plate, Bread & Butter,
  6 In. 10.00
Plate, Dinner, 9 In. 16.00

JONQUIL pattern has pastel flowers and a border of yellow sprays of flowers.

Bowl, Vegetable, Oval . . . 30.00
Cup & Saucer 15.00
Plate, Dinner, 9 In. 20.00
Plate, Luncheon, 8 In. . . . 10.00
Platter, Large 45.00

MIMION is a shape made in the 1950s. It was decorated with solid colors.

Dark Green
Cup & Saucer 15.00
Gray
Plate, Bread & Butter,
  6 In. 5.00
Green
Bowl, Cereal 10.00
Plate, Dinner,
  10 In. 10.00

PURINTON

Purinton Pottery

Purinton Pottery Company was incorporated in Wellsville, Ohio, in 1936. The company moved to Shippenville, Pennsylvania, in 1941 and made a variety of hand-painted ceramic wares. By the 1950s, Purinton was making dinnerware, souvenirs, cookie jars, and florist wares. The pottery closed in 1959.

APPLE was made by Purinton in the early 1940s. It was designed by William Blair. The hand-decorated pattern features an apple colored red with yellow and brown highlights. The stems and leaves are green, blue, and dark brown. The trim colors are red, cobalt blue, or blue-green.

Chop Plate, Scalloped
  Border, 12 In. 58.00
Cookie Jar, Wooden Cover,
  Square 150.00
Cruet, Oil 80.00
Jug, Dutch, 2 Pt.,
  5 3/4 In. 30.00
Jug, Kent, Pt., 4 1/2 In. . . 45.00
Sugar, Cover 55.00
Tumbler, 5 In. . . 22.00 to 27.00

FRUIT was made from 1936 to about 1950. It pictures a variety of large fruits.

Canister Set, Round 115.00
Cruet, Oil, Square,
  5 In. 50.00
Jug, Dutch, 2 Pt.,
  5 3/4 In. 70.00
Jug, Kent, 4 1/2 In. 20.00

INTAGLIO has an incised design on a colored background of Black, Blue, Brown, Coral, Golden Brown, Green, or Turquoise. It was made from 1936 to 1959.

Brown
Bowl, Serving, Oval,
  11 1/4 In. 22.00
Cup 10.00
Plate, Dinner, 9 3/4 In. . . 18.00
Platter, Oval, 12 1/2 In. . . 22.00
Saucer 3.00
Sugar, Cover 20.00

NORMANDY PLAID is a red plaid pattern made from 1936 to 1959.

Creamer 18.00
Tumbler, 12 Oz., 5 In. . . . 20.00

PENNSYLVANIA DUTCH, a popular pattern made from 1936 to 1959, is decorated with red and blue plaid tulips around the border. The design was inspired by the furniture and pottery made and used by the Pennsylvania Dutch community in the nineteenth century.

Cookie Jar, Wooden Cover,
  Square 350.00
Cruets, Oil & Vinegar,
  Square 85.00
Plate, Lap, Tea & Toast,
  8 1/2 In. 75.00
Platter, 11 In. 57.00

RED WING

Red Wing Pottery, Red Wing, Minnesota, was a firm started in 1878. The company first made utilitarian pottery. In the 1920s art pottery was made. Many dinner sets and vases were made before the company closed in 1967.

BOB WHITE was made from 1956 to 1967. It was one of the most popular dinnerware patterns made by the factory. The pattern, a modern hand-painted design, shows a stylized bird and background.

Bowl,
  Vegetable . . . . 30.00 to 32.00

Bowl, Vegetable, Oval . . . 65.00
Casserole, Cover 55.00 to 70.00
Cookie Jar 135.00
Creamer . . . . . . 18.00 to 28.00
Cup . . . . 7.00 to 10.00
Cup & Saucer 25.00
Gravy Boat, Cover 49.00
Pitcher, Ice Lip, 112 Oz.,
    11 1/2 In. 46.00
Pitcher, Water, 60 Oz.,
    6 7/8 In. . . . . . 37.00 to 62.00
Plate, Bread & Butter,
    6 In. 8.00
Plate, Dinner, 10 1/2 In. . . 12.00
Plate, Salad,
    8 1/2 In. . . . . 19.00 to 25.00
Platter, Oval, 13 In. 70.00
Salt & Pepper, Bird,
    Small 45.00
Server, Large 65.00
Soup, Dish . . . . . 16.00 to 22.00
Sugar, Cover 27.00

CAPISTRANO is a design picturing modern yellow-breasted swallows flying near black foliage. It was made from 1953 to 1967.

Bowl, 10 x 4 1/2 In. 37.00
Casserole, Cover, Basket
    Weave Texture, 9 In. . . 26.50
Coffeepot 36.00
Plate, Hors D'Oeuvre,
    10 1/2 x 7 In. 31.00
Tidbit, Handle, 8 In. 10.50

DAMASK is a china pattern introduced in 1964. It is a modern shape with a gray background and a large center design of yellow-beige flowers.

Don't put pottery or porcelain with crazed glaze in the dishwasher. It will crack even more.

Bowl, Cereal 7.00
Bowl, Vegetable, Oval . . . 20.00
Bowl, Vegetable,
    Square 35.00
Butter, Cover 20.00
Casserole, Cover 35.00
Coffeepot, Cover 45.00
Creamer 25.00
Cup & Saucer 12.00
Gravy Boat, Underplate . . 25.00
Plate, Dinner, 10 1/2 In. . . 14.00
Platter, Medium 25.00
Salt & Pepper 25.00
Sugar, Cover . . . 25.00 to 35.00
Tray, 3 Tiers 45.00

LEXINGTON or Lexington Rose features a large red rose and green leaves in the center of the piece. The dinnerware shape was introduced in 1941.

Plate, Dinner, 10 1/2 In. . . 20.00
Salt & Pepper 25.00

LOTUS was made in the Concord shape introduced in 1941. A large lotus flower in pale cream with black leaves is shown on the plates.

Cup & Saucer 10.00
Plate, Dinner, 10 1/2 In. . . 25.00
Plate, Salad, 8 1/2 In. 15.00

LUTE SONG is a pattern decorated with stylized pictures of musical instruments in pastel colors. Unlike most Red Wing patterns, the dishes are china, not pottery. Lute Song was one of eight patterns made in 1960.

Bowl, Vegetable, Round,
    8 1/2 In. 35.00
Plate, Dinner, 10 1/4 In. . . 17.00
Platter, Oval, 13 In. 50.00

MAGNOLIA has a white magnolia with pale green leaves on the plate. It was introduced in 1947.

Bowl, 8 In. 20.00
Bowl, Fruit, 6 In. 6.00
Casserole, Cover 35.00
Cup & Saucer . . 10.00 to 16.00
Plate, Bread & Butter,
    6 1/2 In. 5.00
Plate, Dinner,
    10 1/2 In. . . . 12.00 to 14.00
Plate, Salad,
    8 1/2 In. . . . . . . 8.00 to 9.00
Platter, Small 30.00
Salt & Pepper . . . 15.00 to 20.00
Saltshaker 7.00
Soup, Dish 10.00
Sugar, Cover 35.00
Sugar, Open 30.00
Sugar & Creamer, Cover . 25.00

MAJESTIC is a solid-color pattern introduced in 1960.

Bowl, Fruit, 5 7/8 In. 10.00
Cup & Saucer 25.00

Plate, Bread & Butter,
6 1/2 In. 10.00
Plate, Dinner, 10 1/2 In. . . 20.00
Plate, Salad, 7 1/2 In. 18.00
Soup, Dish 18.00

MERRILEAF has a design of translucent beige and gray-green leaves and wheat. It is a china pattern made about 1960.

Bowl, Cereal 7.00
Bowl, Vegetable,
Divided 19.00
Plate, Dinner, 10 1/2 In. . . 9.00
Plate, Salad, 8 1/2 In. 6.00

RANDOM HARVEST is a dinnerware pattern that is colorfast and ovenproof. It was made in the 1960s. The design is hand painted in brown, copper, coral, green, and turquoise on a flecked dish.

Bowl, Vegetable,
Divided, 10 In. 45.00
Gravy Boat, Underplate . . 40.00

TAMPICO pattern, on the Futura shape, is decorated with browns, greens, and pinks picturing watermelon slices. This modern design was introduced in 1955. Many other patterns were also made on Futura bodies.

Creamer 24.00
Plate, Dinner,
10 1/2 In. . . . . 15.00 to 22.00
Plate, Salad, 8 1/2 In. 15.00

TOWN & COUNTRY was designed by Eva Zeisel in 1947 and was made until 1954. Pieces

are decorated with glossy or matte glaze. Sets were sold in mixed colors. Colors include Chalk White, Chartreuse, Dusk Blue, Forest Green, Gray, Metallic Brown, Rust, and Sandy Peach. Pieces have been reissued in Black, Lime, and White.

Chalk White
Casserole, Cover,
10 x 8 x 4 3/4 In. 191.00
Chartreuse
Salt & Pepper,
4 1/2 & 3 In. 83.00
Dusk Blue
Bowl, 13 In. 145.50
Syrup 128.00
Teapot 350.00
Forest Green
Relish, 9 In. 18.00
Salt & Pepper 58.00
Rust
Mixing Bowl, 9 3/4 x
7 7/8 x 4 3/4 In. 168.00
Pitcher, 2 Pt., 6 3/4 In. . . . 79.00
Salt & Pepper, 3 In. 50.00
Syrup, 6 In. 41.00
Sandy Peach
Baker, 10 1/2 In. 28.00
Relish, 7 x 5 x
2 1/4 In. 25.00

TWEED TEX is a white, solid-color pattern made on the Anniversary shape about 1953.
Creamer 25.00
Cup & Saucer 25.00

REGAL CHINA

FINE CHINA

Regal China Corporation was founded in Antioch, Illinois, around 1938. The company was bought by Royal China and Novelty Company in the 1940s. Regal made Jim Beam bottles, cookie jars, kitchen canisters, and salt and pepper shakers called Huggers or Snuggle Hugs designed by Ruth Van Tellingen Bendel. The company closed in 1992.

VELLUM is decorated with various decals of pastel flowers. Some have a metallic trim.

Bowl, Serving, Oval,
9 1/2 In. 18.00
Cup & Saucer 14.00
Gravy Boat,
Underplate 16.00
Plate, Salad, 8 1/4 In. 12.00
Soup, Dish, 8 1/2 In. 16.00

ROSEVILLE

Roseville Pottery Company was organized in Roseville, Ohio, in 1890. Another plant was opened in Zanesville, Ohio, in 1898. Many types of pottery were made until 1954. Later lines were often made with molded decorations, especially flowers and fruit. Most pieces are marked *Roseville*. Only a few dinnerware patterns were made. Many reproductions made in China have been offered for sale the past few years.

RAYMOR is a stoneware made by the Roseville Pottery in 1952 and 1953. It was designed by Ben Siebel. Pieces were made in Autumn Brown, Avocado Green, Beach Gray, and Terra Cotta (rust) in either a plain or mottled version and in Contemporary White. Some Avocado pieces are mistakenly called black. Later, Chartreuse and Robin's Egg Blue were added to the line.

OVENPROOF
PAT. PEND.

Autumn Brown
Bean Pot, Cover, 10 In. . . 45.00
Bowl, Salad 85.00
Corn Server, Individual,
12 1/2 In. 75.00
Ramekin, Cover, Individual,
No. 156 . . . . 45.00
Beach Gray
Ramekin, Cover, Individual,
No. 156 . . . . 45.00
Trivet, Round, 4-Footed,
6 In. 40.00

Robin's Egg Blue
Celery & Olive Dish,
15 1/4 In. 225.00

ROYAL

Royal China Company moved from Omaha, Nebraska, to Sebring, Ohio, in 1933. The company made semiporcelain dinnerware, cookware, and advertising premiums. Jeannette Glass Corporation bought the factory in 1969. Royal changed ownership several times before closing in 1986.

COLONIAL HOMESTEAD was made from about 1951 and was offered by Sears, Roebuck & Company all through the 1960s. It was designed by Gordon Parker.

UNDERGLAZE *Evan* 195
PATENTED
MADE IN U.S.A.

Ashtray 15.00
Bowl, Cereal,
6 3/8 In. . . . . . 14.00 to 26.00
Bowl, Fruit,
5 3/4 In. . . . . . . 8.00 to 10.00
Bowl, Vegetable,
9 In. . . . . 16.00 to 20.00
Butter, Cover,
1/4 Lb. . . . . . . 35.00 to 45.00
Casserole,
Cover . . . . . . 75.00 to 85.00
Chop Plate, 12 In. 24.00
Creamer . . . . . . 18.00 to 20.00
Cup . . . . 3.00 to 7.00
Cup & Saucer . . 12.00 to 15.00
Gravy Boat 25.00
Gravy Boat,
Underplate . . . 26.00 to 45.00
Mug 30.00
Pie Plate, 10 In. 40.00
Plate, Bread & Butter,
6 In. . . . . 4.00 to 8.00
Plate, Dinner,
10 In. . . . . . . 17.00 to 19.00
Plate, Luncheon,
9 In. . . . . 10.00 to 25.00
Plate, Salad, 7 1/4 In. 18.00
Platter, Oval,
13 x 10 In. 35.00
Platter, Round, 13 In. 40.00
Platter, Tab Handle,
10 1/2 In. 12.00
Salt & Pepper 24.00
Saucer, Center
Ring . . . . 3.00 to 8.00
Snack Plate, 9 In. 50.00
Soup, Dish,
8 1/4 In. . . . . . 8.00 to 15.00
Sugar, Cover . . . 12.00 to 15.00
Teapot, Drop Spout,
Cover 60.00
Teapot, Flat Spout,
Cover 90.00

CURRIER & IVES was made from 1949 until about 1983. It was designed by Gordon Parker and is based on the old Currier & Ives prints. Early pieces were date coded. It is white with a blue, brown, green, or pink decal decoration. The pattern was popular as a store premium. Some serving pieces were made by Harker Pottery Company.

Blue

Ashtray, 5 1/2 In. 18.00
Ashtray, Central Park . . . 12.00
Bowl, Cereal,
   Schoolhouse In Winter,
   6 1/4 In. . . . . . 15.00 to 18.00
Bowl, Dessert, 5 1/2 In. . . . 4.00
Bowl, Fruit,
   5 1/2 In. . . . . 4.00 to 5.00
Bowl, Vegetable,
   9 In. . . . . 24.00 to 28.00
Bowl, Vegetable,
   Deep, 10 In. 40.00
Bowl, Vegetable,
   Family Welcome, Dad
   Is Home, 10 In. 24.00
Bowl, Vegetable, Maple
   Sugaring, 9 In. 16.00
Butter, Cover 42.00
Butter, Road, Summer,
   1/4 Lb. 55.00
Butter, Road, Winter 30.00
Cake Plate, 10 In. 50.00

Casserole, Fashionable
   Turnouts . . . . 70.00 to 115.00
Chop Plate, Winter In
   The Country, Getting
   Ice, 12 In. . . . . 24.00 to 45.00
Coffeepot, Cover, After
   Dinner 5.00
Creamer, American Express
   Train . . . . 8.00 to 16.00
Cup, Star Of The
   Road . . . . 3.00 to 4.00
Cup & Saucer . . . . 5.00 to 5.50
Gravy Boat, Underplate, Road,
   Winter . . . . 25.00 to 48.00
Hostess Plate, 7 3/8 In. . . 20.00
Ladle 45.00
Mug, Fashionable
   Turnouts 30.00
Mug, Star Of The Road . . 20.00
Pie Baker, 10 In. 38.00
Pie Plate, Sleigh Race,
   10 In. 18.00
Pie Plate, Snowy Morning,
   10 In. . . . . . . 18.00 to 25.00
Pie Plate, Road, Winter,
   10 In. . . . . . . 18.00 to 35.00
Plate, Bread & Butter, Harvest,
   6 In. . . . . 4.00 to 11.00
Plate, Dinner, Old Grist Mill,
   10 In. . . . . 6.00 to 12.00
Plate, Luncheon, Old Grist Mill,
   9 In. . . . . 18.00 to 20.00
Plate, Salad,
   7 1/4 In. . . . . . 14.00 to 18.00
Platter, Rocky Mountains, Tab
   Handles, 10 1/2 In. 14.00
Platter, Snowy Morning,
   13 In. . . . . . . 50.00 to 100.00
Platter, Winter Wonderland,
   Oval, 13 x 10 In. 35.00
Salt & Pepper . . . 38.00 to 50.00
Saucer, Low Water In
   The Mississippi,
   6 In. . . . . 2.00 to 3.00
Soup, Dish, Early Winter,
   8 1/2 In. . . . . . . 9.00 to 12.00
Sugar, Cover . . . 20.00 to 25.00
Sugar, On The
   Mississippi . . . 14.00 to 16.00
Teapot . . . . . . 135.00 to 150.00
Teapot, Clipper Ship
   Dreadnought 80.00
Teapot, Knob Cover . . . 135.00
Tumbler, 3 1/2 In. 11.00

Tumbler, 4 3/4 In. 13.00
Tumbler, 5 1/2 In. 16.00
Underplate, For Gravy Boat,
   Water Well 15.00

Brown
Pie Plate, American Farm
   Scene, 10 In. 18.00

Green
Bowl, Salad, 7 1/4 In. . . . 15.00
Pie Plate, 10 In. 18.00
Salt & Pepper 35.00

Pink
Bowl, Fruit 16.00
Chop Plate, 12 In. 15.00
Creamer 20.00
Plate, Bread & Butter,
   6 In. 10.00
Plate, Dinner, 10 In. 28.00
Teapot 55.00

FAIR OAKS is a transfer-decorated pattern that is primarily brown on white. It pictures a stone house with a red roof amid green trees. A boy and his dog are herding cows in the foreground. The pattern has its own oak-leaf-shaped mark. It was made after the 1940s.

Bowl, Cereal, Tab
   Handles 30.00
Soup, Dish, 8 1/4 In. 15.00

MEMORY LANE is a rose on white transfer-decorated pattern. It pictures a log cabin in the woods. It has its own oak-leaf-shaped mark.

Ashtray	12.00
Berry Bowl, 5 3/4 In.	3.00
Bowl, Cereal, 6 3/8 In.	20.00
Bowl, Vegetable, 9 In.	16.00
Bowl, Vegetable, 10 In.	25.00
Butter, Cover	35.00
Casserole	65.00
Chop Plate, 12 In.	30.00
Creamer	8.00
Cup	3.00 to 4.00
Gravy Boat	25.00
Mug	35.00
Pie Plate, 10 In.	35.00
Plate, Bread & Butter, 6 1/2 In.	5.00
Plate, Dinner, 10 In.	6.00 to 8.00
Plate, Luncheon, 9 In.	25.00
Plate, Salad, 7 1/4 In.	18.00
Platter, Oval, 13 x 10 In.	35.00
Platter, Tab Handles, 10 1/2 In.	12.00
Salt & Pepper	25.00
Saucer	2.00

❖

Keep basement windows locked.

❖

Soup, Dish, 8 1/4 In.	6.00
Sugar, Cover	15.00
Teapot, Cover	90.00
Underplate, For Gravy Boat	18.00

OLD CURIOSITY SHOP is a 1940s pattern. It has a green scenic center design and an elaborate border. The Cavalier shape was used.

Ashtray, 5 1/2 In.	12.00 to 18.00
Bowl, Cereal, Tab Handles, 6 3/8 In.	15.00 to 40.00
Bowl, Fruit, 5 1/2 In.	3.00 to 4.00
Bowl, Vegetable, 9 In.	16.00
Bowl, Vegetable, 10 In.	24.00
Butter, Cover	22.00
Cake Plate, Handles, 10 1/2 In.	35.00
Casserole, Cover	90.00
Chop Plate, 12 In.	30.00
Creamer	7.00 to 8.00
Cup	3.00 to 4.00
Cup & Saucer	5.00
Gravy Boat	22.00
Ladle	45.00

Pie Plate, 10 In.	50.00
Plate, Bread & Butter, 6 1/2 In.	3.00 to 4.00
Plate, Dinner, 10 In.	6.00 to 7.00
Plate, Luncheon, 9 In.	24.00
Plate, Salad, 7 1/4 In.	10.00 to 18.00
Platter, Oval, 13 x 10 In.	35.00
Platter, Round, 13 In.	55.00
Platter, Tab Handles, 10 1/2 In.	12.00
Saucer	2.00
Soup, Dish, 8 1/4 In.	8.00
Sugar, Cover	15.00
Sugar & Creamer, Cover	18.00
Teapot, Cover	90.00
Underplate, For Gravy Boat	12.00

SUSSEX is a brown transferware pattern sometimes called Royal Sussex. It has flowers in the center and a border.

Cup & Saucer	4.00
Plate, Bread & Butter, 6 1/2 In.	4.00
Plate, Dinner, 10 In.	9.00

SALEM

Salem China Company produced white granite and semiporcelain dinnerware in Salem, Ohio, from 1898 to 1967. Many of Salem's patterns made in the 1930s and 1940s were designed by Viktor Schreckengost or his brother, Don. The company has been a distributor of dinnerware made in Japan and England from 1968 to the present.

DEBUTANTE was designed by Don Schreckengost.

Bowl, Fruit, 5 1/2 In.	13.00
Creamer	25.00
Cup & Saucer	18.00
Gravy Boat	35.00
Plate, Bread & Butter, 6 In.	10.00
Plate, Dinner, 10 In.	18.00
Platter, Small	40.00
Soup, Dish, Rimmed	18.00
Sugar	35.00

ENGLISH VILLAGE was made to resemble the old blue and white Staffordshire transfer-decorated plates. Various scenes are pictured. The plates have a floral border. Pieces have a special mark.

Bowl, Cereal	14.00
Bowl, Fruit, 5 1/2 In.	12.00
Bowl, Vegetable, Round, Open	40.00
Creamer	25.00
Plate, Bread & Butter, 6 In.	10.00
Plate, Dinner, 10 In.	15.00 to 23.00
Platter, Small	40.00
Saucer	4.00

GODEY PRINTS, also called Godey Fashions, was based on the prints in the Lady's Book by Louis Antoine Godey. There are at least three different pic-

tures. The dinnerware is made on the Victory shape designed by Victor Schreckengost in 1938.

Bowl, Cereal	13.00
Bowl, Fruit, 5 1/2 In.	12.00
Bowl, Fruit, Ribbed, 5 1/2 In.	9.00
Bowl, Vegetable, Oval, Open	25.00
Bowl, Vegetable, Round, Open	25.00
Plate, Bread & Butter, 6 In.	10.00
Plate, Bread & Butter, Ribbed, 6 In.	9.00 to 10.00
Plate, Dinner, 10 In.	17.00
Plate, Dinner, Ribbed, 10 In.	15.00
Plate, Salad, 7 1/2 In.	12.00
Plate, Salad, Ribbed, 7 1/2 In.	12.00
Platter, Small	45.00
Saucer	4.00

LACE BOUQUET has gold or platinum trim.

Bowl, Fruit, Platinum Trim, 5 1/2 In.	5.00
Bowl, Vegetable, Cover Gold Trim	25.00
Cup, Platinum Trim	7.00
Cup & Saucer, Platinum Trim	10.00
Plate, Dinner, Platinum Trim, 10 In.	9.00
Saucer, Platinum Trim	5.00

PRIMROSE is a dinnerware of modern design decorated with stylized green leaves and pink flowers.

ovenproof
Primrose

Bowl, Fruit, 5 1/2 In.	13.00
Bowl, Vegetable, Oval, Open	30.00
Creamer	15.00
Cup	9.00
Cup & Saucer	11.00
Plate, Bread & Butter, 6 In.	8.00
Plate, Dinner, 10 In.	14.00
Plate, Salad, 7 1/2 In.	12.00
Sugar, Cover	25.00

SILVER ELEGANCE is an ironstone pattern with platinum trim made in England or America.

Bowl, Fruit, America, 5 1/2 In.	13.00
Cup, America	5.00
Cup & Saucer, America	13.00
Plate, Dinner, America	15.00
Soup, Dish, England	8.00

SYMPHONY was designed by Viktor Schreckengost about 1940. It has embossed concentric circles around the edges of the plates and bottoms of the teapots. It has its own mark with a music bar and a treble clef.

❖

Check the supports on wall-hung shelves once a year. Eventually a heavy load will cause the items to "creep," the metal brackets will bend, and the shelf will fall.

❖

Bowl, Cereal 14.00
Bowl, Fruit, 5 1/2 In. 12.00
Bowl, Vegetable, Round,
   Open 25.00
Cake Plate 25.00
Creamer 20.00
Cup 12.00
Cup & Saucer 15.00
Gravy Boat 30.00
Plate, Bread & Butter,
   6 1/2 In. 10.00
Plate, Dinner, 10 In. 16.00
Plate, Salad, 9 In. 12.00
Salt & Pepper 25.00
Soup, Dish, Rimmed 18.00
Sugar, Cover 30.00

WHIMSEY has a nosegay of five-petaled flowers and leaves and platinum trim.

Creamer 18.00
Cup & Saucer . . 16.00 to 19.00
Plate, Bread & Butter,
   6 In. . . . . 10.00 to 12.00
Plate, Dinner, 10 In. 20.00
Saucer 8.00
Sugar 10.00
Sugar, Cover 23.00

SHAWNEE

Shawnee
U.S.A.

Shawnee Pottery was started in Zanesville, Ohio, in 1937. The company made vases, novelty ware, flowerpots, planters, lamps, cookie jars, and dinnerware. Shawnee produced pottery for George Rumrill during the late 1930s. The company closed in 1961.

CORN KING is an unusual pattern. Dishes are three-dimensional representations of ears of corn. This novel idea became a popular reality when Corn King pattern was sold by Shawnee in 1946. The green and yellow pieces ranged from dinner plates to small salt and pepper shakers. Corn King has darker yellow corn kernels and lighter green leaves than a later pattern called Corn Queen.

Bowl, Cereal,
   No. 94 . . . . 20.00
Bowl, No. 5 . . . . 16.00
Bowl, No. 6 . . . . 24.00 to 36.00
Bowl, No. 8 . . . . 30.00
Bowl, Vegetable, No. 95,
   8 7/8 In. 120.00
Butter, Cover, No. 72 . . . 61.00
Casserole, Individual,
   No. 73 . . . . 79.00
Casserole, No. 74,
   11 In. . . . . 40.00 to 65.00
Cookie Jar, No. 66 . . . . . 141.00
Corn Holder,
   No. 79 . . . . 16.00 to 33.00
Corn Holder, No. 79,
   Set Of 4 . . . . 50.00
Cover, For Large
   Casserole 13.00
Creamer,
   No. 70 . . . . . . 12.00 to 26.00

Cup & Saucer . . 25.00 to 50.00
Jar, Utility,
   No. 78, 14 Oz. 47.00
Mixing Bowl,
   No. 5, 5 In. 26.00
Mixing Bowl, No. 6,
   6 1/2 In. . . . . . 20.00 to 48.00
Mug, Coffee, No. 69,
   8 Oz. 70.00
Pepper Shaker, 4 In. 10.00
Pitcher, No. 71, 40 Oz. . . 15.00
Plate, No. 68,
   9 3/4 In. . . . . . 20.00 to 49.00
Plate, No. 93,
   7 1/2 In. . . . . . 10.00 to 13.00
Platter, No. 96,
   11 3/4 In. . . . . 50.00 to 56.00
Salt & Pepper, No. 76,
   3 1/4 In. 15.00
Salt & Pepper, No. 77,
   5 1/4 In. 30.00
Saucer 26.00
Snack Set 51.00
Sugar, No. 78 . . . . 25.00
Sugar &
   Creamer . . . . . 21.00 to 60.00
Teapot, Individual,
   No. 65 . . . . 125.00 to 200.00
Teapot, Miniature 153.00
Teapot, No. 75 . . 86.00 to 96.00

CORN QUEEN is similar to Corn King pattern. The shapes are the same, but the corn kernels are a lighter yellow. It was made from 1954 to 1961.

Bowl, No. 6, 6 1/2 In. . . . 32.00
Bowl, Vegetable, No. 95,
   9 In. 78.00
Cookie Jar,
   No. 66 . . . . . 125.00 to 195.00
Creamer, No. 70 . . . . 45.00
Plate, No. 68, 10 In. 20.00

Salt & Pepper, No. 76,
  3 1/4 In. 20.00
Salt & Pepper, No. 77,
  5 1/4 In. 11.00
Sugar, Cover, No. 78 . . . . 16.00

SOUTHERN POTTERIES
See Blue Ridge

STANGL

Stangl Pottery traces its history back to the Fulper Pottery, Flemington, New Jersey. In 1910, Johann Martin Stangl started working at Fulper. He bought into the firm in 1913, became president in 1926, and in 1929 changed the company name to Stangl Pottery. The pottery made dinnerwares and a line of bird figurines. The company went out of business in 1978.

AMBER GLO is a pattern made in 1954. It was designed by Kay Hackett. The flames are orange, the background gray.

Bowl, Vegetable, 8 In. . . . 24.00
Coffee Warmer,
  4 5/8 x 3 1/4 In. 18.00
Cup & Saucer 11.00
Server, Metal Handle 20.00
Soup, Dish, 7 1/2 In. 12.00
Soup, Dish, Tab Handle,
  5 1/2 In. 11.00
Tray, Condiment, 4 Indentations
  For Bottles 22.00

APPLE DELIGHT was made from 1965 to 1974. The pattern features a dark border and red and yellow apples as a center design.

Bowl, Dessert 9.00
Plate, Dinner, 10 In. 17.00
Plate, Salad, 7 In. 9.00
Saucer 3.00
Soup, Dish 15.00

CARNIVAL is a pattern decorated with abstract stars. It was made from 1954 to 1957.

Pitcher, 1 Pt.,
  4 3/4 In. 50.00
Sugar Bowl,
  Cover 30.00

COLONIAL is a solid pattern line. Colonial Blue, Persian Yellow, and Silver Green were introduced in 1924. Rust, Tangerine, and Surf White were added in 1935. Aqua Blue was added in 1937 and the white was renamed Satin White. Some sets of dishes were sold in mixed colors.

Aqua Blue
Bowl, 5 In. 10.00
Plate, Bread & Butter,
  6 In. 2.00
Plate, Dinner,
  10 In. 10.00
Relish 15.00
Sugar, Cover 10.00

Silver Green
Cup & Saucer 15.00
Plate, Dinner, 10 In. 15.00
Plate, Salad, 7 In. 10.00
Saucer 4.00

Tangerine
Cup & Saucer 15.00
Plate, Dinner,
  10 In. 15.00

Plate, Salad, 7 In. 10.00
Sugar, Cover 10.00

COUNTRY GARDEN has a decoration of three raised flowers. The pattern was made from 1956 to 1974.

Bowl, 5 1/2 In. 15.00
Bread Tray 40.00
Plate, Dinner, 10 In. 15.00

FRUIT & FLOWERS pattern, No. 4030, was made from 1957 to 1974. The design shows a mixed grouping of flowers, leaves, grapes, and fanciful shapes. Pieces have a colored border.

Bowl, 8 1/4 x 2 1/4 In. . . . 36.00
Bowl, Salad, 10 In. 38.00
Eggcup 15.50
Plate, Bread & Butter,
  6 In. 6.50
Plate, Dinner, 10 In. 10.50
Plate, Salad, 8 In. 20.50
Platter, Kidney Shape,
  10 x 14 In. 30.00
Sugar & Creamer 31.00
Teapot 45.00
Tidbit, 2 Tiers 21.00

If a white powder forms on a piece made of lead or glasses or pottery decorated with a lead glaze, immediately remove the piece from your house. The powder is poisonous. Consult an expert conservator if the piece is valuable and should be saved. Do the ecologically correct thing if you must dispose of the piece.

GARDEN FLOWER was offered from 1947 to 1957. The design featured a different flower on each piece. These include pink Bleeding Hearts, blue Balloon flowers, purple Campanula, yellow Calendula, blue Flax, blue Morning Glory, pink Phlox, pink Rose, yellow Sunflower, and yellow Tiger Lily.

Bowl, Cereal, 5 1/2 In. . . 14.00
Bowl, Fruit, 5 1/2 In. 8.00
Bowl, Vegetable, Cover . . 90.00
Bowl, Vegetable,
  Round 30.00
Chop Plate, 14 1/2 In. . . . 30.00
Creamer 25.00
Cup & Saucer 18.00

Custard Cup 11.00
Plate, Bread & Butter,
  6 In. 5.00
Plate, Dinner, 10 In. 16.00
Plate, Luncheon, 9 In. . . . 22.00
Plate, Salad, 8 In. 9.00
Salt & Pepper 25.00
Sugar, Cover 35.00
Teapot, Cover 75.00

GARLAND pattern was made from 1957 to 1967. The border is a garland of green leaves and red flowers. The piece is gray, and there may be a grouping of flowers and leaves on the side of sugar bowls or pitchers.

Bowl, 8 In. 25.00
Bowl, Cereal, Tab
  Handles 14.00
Bowl, Salad, 12 In. 45.00
Bread Tray 18.00
Chop Plate 25.00
Coffeepot 68.00
Cup & Saucer 12.00
Gravy Boat, Underplate . . 20.00
Plate, Bread & Butter,
  6 In. 6.00
Plate, Dinner, 10 In. 13.00
Plate, Salad,
  8 In. . . . . 9.00 to 10.00
Ramekin, Cover Held . . 32.00

GOLDEN BLOSSOM, made from 1964 to 1974, is decorated with brown blossoms and orange leaves.

Bowl, Vegetable, Oval . . . 30.00
Bowl, Vegetable,
  Round 30.00
Chop Plate 30.00
Creamer 25.00
Cup & Saucer 15.00
Plate, Bread & Butter,
  6 In. 5.00
Plate, Dinner, 10 In. 16.00
Plate, Salad,
  8 In. . . . . 9.00 to 10.00
Saucer 6.00
Soup, Dish 15.00
Sugar, Cover 35.00

GOLDEN HARVEST was made from 1953 to 1973. The pattern pictured yellow flowers on a gray background.

Bowl, Fruit, 5 1/2 In. 8.00
Bowl, Vegetable, Cover,
  8 In. 90.00
Creamer 25.00
Cup 14.00
Cup & Saucer 17.00
Plate, Bread & Butter,
  6 In. 5.00

Plate, Dinner,
  10 In. . . . . . . 12.00 to 16.00
Platter, 11 1/4 In. 26.00
Sugar, Cover 35.00

MAGNOLIA pattern has a center design of a burgundy magnolia flower. The pattern, No. 3870, was made from 1952 to 1962.

Bowl, Fruit, 5 1/2 In 8.00
Bowl, Vegetable, Cover,
  8 In. 80.00
Bowl, Vegetable, Round,
  8 In. . . . . 25.00 to 30.00
Coffeepot 98.00
Creamer . . . . 18.00 to 20.00
Cup 9.00
Cup & Saucer . . 15.00 to 17.00
Plate, Bread & Butter,
  6 In. . . . . 5.00 to 8.00
Plate, Dinner,
  10 In. . . . . . . 15.00 to 18.00
Plate, Salad,
  8 In. . . . . 9.00 to 12.00
Platter, Round 30.00
Salt & Pepper 25.00
Sugar, Cover 30.00

ORCHARD SONG was made by Stangl Pottery from 1962 to 1974.

Bowl, Salad 55.00
Bowl, Vegetable, Oval,
  Open 35.00
Coffeepot 72.00
Cup & Saucer 10.00
Gravy Boat, Underplate . . 35.00
Plate, Dinner, 10 In. 10.00
Platter, Large 45.00
Soup, Dish 10.00

PRELUDE is a pattern with a stylized flower design. It was made from 1949 to 1957.

Cup & Saucer 10.00
Plate, Salad, 8 In. 9.00
Sugar, Cover 18.00

PROVINCIAL is a bordered plate with a floral center made from 1957 to 1967.

Bowl, Fruit, 5 1/2 In. 10.00
Plate, Bread & Butter,
  6 In. 5.00
Plate, Dinner, 10 In. 15.00
Plate, Salad, 8 In. 10.00

SINGLE BIRD is a carved pattern that pictures a fanciful bird on a branch and a wide border on plates.

Charger,
  12 In. . . . . . . 95.00 to 100.00
Teapot . . . . . 105.00 to 120.00

TOWN & COUNTRY pattern was made in a variety of colors in the 1970s. The design looks like the sponged stoneware made in the nineteenth century. Black, Blue-Green, Brown, Honey Beige, and Yellow were used.

Blue-Green
Plate, Salad, 8 1/2 In. 20.00
Saucer 7.00

WHITE DOGWOOD was made from 1965 to 1974. It pictured a white dogwood flower. Stangl also made patterns called Dogwood and Colonial Dogwood.

Cup 12.00
Plate, Bread & Butter,
  6 In. 4.00
Plate, Dinner, 10 In. 14.00
Plate, Salad, 8 In. 7.00

WILD ROSE was made from 1955 to 1973. The pattern shows a group of single roses and leaves. It has a thin border.

Bowl, Cereal, 5 1/2 In. . . 15.00
Bowl, Vegetable,
  8 In. 25.00
Cup 12.00
Cup & Saucer 12.00
Plate, Bread & Butter,
  6 In. 6.00
Plate, Dinner, 10 In. 15.00
Platter, Round 20.00
Sugar & Creamer,
  Cover 25.00

STEUBENVILLE

Steubenville Pottery Company operated in Steubenville, Ohio, from 1879 to 1959. The company made granite ware, semiporcelain dinnerware, and toilet seats. When the Ohio factory closed, the molds and equipment were moved to a Canonsburg, Pennsylvania, factory that continued to use the Steubenville mark in the 1960s.

AMERICAN MODERN, designed by Russel Wright, was the most popular dinnerware pattern made in the 1950s. It was made by Steubenville from 1939 to 1959. The original dishes were made in Bean Brown (a shaded brown), Chartreuse, Coral, Granite Gray, Seafoam (blue-green), and White. The brown was replaced with Black Chutney (dark brown) during World War II. Cantaloupe, Cedar Green, and Glacier Blue were added in the 1950s. Matching linens and glassware were made. Wright designed dinnerware in modern shapes for many companies, including Iroquois China Company, Harker Pottery Company, Steubenville Pottery, Paden City Pottery (Justin Tharaud and Sons), Sterling China Company, Edwin M. Knowles China Company, and J.A. Bauer Pottery Company

Bean Brown

Cup	23.00
Plate, Bread & Butter, 6 In.	15.00
Plate, Dinner, 10 In.	29.00
Plate, Salad, 8 In.	28.00
Saucer	15.00

Black Chutney

Bowl, Vegetable, 10 In.	55.00
Cup	10.00
Gravy Boat	55.00
Mug	125.00
Plate, Bread & Butter, 6 In.	8.00 to 10.00
Plate, Dinner, 10 In.	12.00 to 20.00

Cedar Green

Casserole, Cover	55.00

Chartreuse

Bowl, Fruit, Lug, 6 1/4 In.	15.00
Bowl, Vegetable, Divided	85.00
Cup & Saucer	17.00
Gravy Boat	35.00
Mug	75.00
Plate, Dinner, 10 In.	15.00
Plate, Salad, 8 In.	10.00
Soup, Dish	15.00

Coral

Bowl, Fruit, Lug, 6 1/4 In.	15.00
Bowl, Vegetable, Cover, Tab Handles	75.00
Bowl, Vegetable, Open, 10 In.	30.00

Casserole, Cover, Stick Handle	50.00
Celery Dish	22.00 to 35.00
Chop Plate, 13 In.	45.00
Coaster-Ashtray	15.00
Coffeepot, After Dinner	125.00
Creamer	15.00
Cup & Saucer	13.00
Gravy Boat	30.00
Pitcher, Water	100.00
Plate, Bread & Butter, 6 In.	5.00
Plate, Dinner, 10 In.	10.00 to 13.00
Plate, Salad, 8 In.	15.00
Platter, 13 3/4 In.	45.00
Relish	30.00
Saucer	3.00
Sherbet	23.00
Soup, Dish, Lug	20.00
Sugar, Cover	20.00

Glacier Blue

Cup	25.00

Granite Gray

Bowl, Fruit, Lug	15.00
Bowl, Salad	95.00
Bowl, Vegetable, 10 In.	80.00
Creamer	10.00 to 15.00
Cup	8.00
Cup & Saucer	13.00
Gravy Boat	24.00
Pitcher, Water	100.00
Plate, Bread & Butter, 6 In.	5.00
Plate, Dinner, 10 In.	13.00
Plate, Salad, 8 In.	15.00
Relish	30.00
Salt & Pepper	20.00
Saucer	3.00
Soup, Dish, Lug	20.00
Spoon, Salad	48.00
Stack Set Insert	85.00
Sugar, Cover	20.00

Seafoam

Creamer	20.00
Cup & Saucer	15.00
Gravy Boat	55.00
Pickle	35.00
Plate, Bread & Butter, 6 In.	8.00

Plate, Dinner, 10 In.	15.00
Plate, Salad, 8 In.	20.00
Platter, 13 1/4 In.	75.00
Sugar	10.00

White

Creamer	30.00
Cup	8.00
Cup & Saucer	34.00
Gravy Boat	75.00
Sugar, Open	20.00

FAIRLANE was made from 1959 to 1962. It is a white dinnerware decorated with pink wildflowers with blue petals at the bottom and green leaves..

Bowl, Cereal, 6 In.	5.00 to 11.00
Bowl, Fruit, 5 1/2 In.	4.00
Cup	4.00 to 7.00
Plate, Dinner, 10 In.	11.00 to 12.00
Plate, Salad, 7 1/4 In.	6.00
Platter, Medium	20.00

WOODFIELD dishes are shaped like leaves and are colored in many of the shades used for American Modern dishes, made by Steubenville. Full dinner sets were made.

Dove Gray

Ashtray	16.00
Bowl, Salad, Round, 11 In.	24.00
Bowl, Smooth Edge, 5 1/2 In.	15.00
Bowl, Vegetable, Oval, 10 1/2 In.	10.00
Chop Plate, 13 1/2 In.	24.00
Cup, Flat	8.00
Cup, Footed	8.00
Cup & Saucer, Flat	11.00
Cup & Saucer, Footed	11.00
Pitcher, 9 1/2 In.	75.00
Plate, Bread & Butter, 6 1/2 In.	3.50
Plate, Dinner, 10 1/2 In.	14.00
Plate, Salad, 8 1/2 In.	8.50 to 9.00
Platter, Oval, 13 1/2 In.	25.00
Relish, 9 1/2 In.	38.00
Salt & Pepper	28.00
Snack Plate, 8 1/2 In.	7.00
Snack Set, 8 1/2 In.	10.00
Teapot, Cover	58.00

Jungle Green

Saucer	18.00

Salmon Pink

Snack Set, 8 1/2 In.	10.00 to 20.00

After washing a teapot, dry it as well as possible. Then put a sugar cube in the teapot to absorb the remaining water.

SYRACUSE

SYRACUSE China
1871

The Farrar Pottery was established in 1841 in Syracuse, New York, by W. H. Farrar. It soon became the Empire Pottery Company, and in 1871 it was acquired by Onondaga Pottery Company. In 1891 the firm started to make Syracuse China. The name of the company was changed to Syracuse China Corporation in 1966. The Corporation merged with Canadian Pacific Investments, Ltd. in 1978. The Susquehanna-Pfaltzgraff Company bought it in 1989. It was purchased by Libbey, Inc. in 1995. The company closed its consumer division in 1970 and stopped making household dinnerware.

APPLE BLOSSOM pattern has gold trim and a design of asymmetrical apple tree branches and blossoms in pink and green. It was made from about 1950 to 1966.

Bowl, Vegetable, Round	95.00
Creamer	52.00
Cup & Saucer	30.00
Gravy Boat	50.00
Plate, Bread & Butter	12.00 to 25.00
Plate, Dinner, 10 In.	32.00 to 48.00
Plate, Salad, 7 1/2 In.	12.00 to 27.00
Platter, Medium	50.00 to 88.00
Soup, Cream, Underplate	41.00 to 54.00
Soup, Dish	30.00

ARCADIA, made from 1928 to 1932, is decorated with garlands of roses. Dishes are ivory with gold trim.

Cup & Saucer	41.00
Plate, Dinner, 10 In.	41.00
Plate, Salad, 7 1/2 In.	20.00

ATHENA, made from 1937 to 1970, has a black ropelike border and gold trim.

Bowl, Vegetable	85.00
Creamer	61.00
Cup & Saucer, Espresso	32.00 to 33.00
Plate, Bread & Butter	14.00
Plate, Dinner, 10 In.	43.00
Plate, Salad, 7 1/2 In.	19.00
Soup, Dish	33.00
Sugar, Cover	75.00

AVALON has a wide gray band, a picture of a gardenia in the center, and gold or platinum trim. It was made from 1937 to 1970.

Plate, Bread & Butter,
Gold Trim 21.00
Plate, Salad, Gold Trim,
7 1/2 In. 25.00
Soup, Cream, Underplate,
Gold Trim 41.00

BARBADOS, a pattern made
from 1968 to 1970, is a rimless
shape glazed dark brown.

Plate, Bread & Butter . . . 12.00
Plate, Dinner, 10 In. 18.00
Salt & Pepper 25.00

BAROQUE pattern has a fluted
rim and a gray inner rim design.
It was made from 1950 to 1966.

Bowl, Fruit 34.00
Plate, Salad, 7 1/2 In. 11.00
Saucer 10.00
Soup, Cream,
Underplate 35.00

BELAIRE features a lily-of-the-
valley flower in the center.
Many pieces have platinum
trim. The pattern was produced
from 1953 to 1970.

Bowl, Vegetable, Oval . . . 79.00
Plate, Dinner, 10 In. 27.00
Plate, Salad, 7 1/2 In. 18.00

BELCANTO pattern has a border of small leaves and platinum trim. It was made from
1966 to 1970.

Plate, Bread & Butter . . . 15.00
Plate, Salad, 7 1/2 In. 22.00

BELMONT features a border
made of groups of geometric
designs. The dinnerware, made
from 1966 to 1970, has platinum trim.

Plate, Bread & Butter . . . 14.00
Plate, Dinner, 10 In. 43.00
Plate, Salad, 7 1/2 In. 19.00

BRACELET is a pattern introduced in 1941. It is a white dinnerware with gold trim.

Bowl, Fruit 34.00

Creamer . . . . 67.00 to 68.00
Cup & Saucer . . 42.00 to 50.00
Gravy Boat . . . 135.00 to 146.00
Plate, Bread & Butter . . . 17.00
Plate, Dinner,
10 In. 54.00
Plate, Salad,
7 1/2 In. 34.00
Platter, Medium 95.00
Platter, Small 70.00
Sugar 81.00

BRIARCLIFF pattern was introduced in 1938 and continued in
production until 1969. It is decorated with pastel yellow, pink,
and blue flower clusters.

Bowl, Cereal 41.00
Bowl, Vegetable, Oval . . . 94.00
Creamer 41.00
Cup & Saucer 38.00
Plate, Bread &
Butter . . . . 14.00 to 21.00
Plate, Dinner, 10 In. 34.00
Plate, Salad, 7 1/2 In. 20.00
Platter, Medium 75.00
Platter, Small 114.00
Saucer 9.00

BRIDAL ROSE, made from
1953 to 1970, has pink roses
and gray leaves scattered on the
platinum-trimmed pieces.

Bowl, Cereal 38.00
Cup & Saucer 40.00

CARVEL has a gray lacey border and gold trim.

Bowl, Vegetable 54.00
Platter, Medium 88.00
Sugar, Cover 48.00

CELESTE has a rim with scattered blue leaves. It has platinum trim. It was made from
1954 to 1969.

Bread Plate 15.00
Creamer 65.00
Cup & Saucer 39.00
Plate, Salad, 7 1/2 In. 22.00
Sugar, Cover 88.00

CHAMPLAIN, made from 1950
to 1966, is trimmed with gold.
The rim is fluted and the design
is green leaves.

Cup & Saucer 42.00
Plate, Dinner, 10 In. 54.00

CORALBEL, made from 1937
to 1970, has green and platinum
lines as an inner border. The
center of the plate is decorated
with green and pink flowers
that resemble lilies-of-the-
valley.

Creamer 55.00
Cup & Saucer . . 22.00 to 37.00
Gravy Boat 28.00
Plate, Dinner,
10 In. . . . . 12.00 to 40.00
Plate, Salad,
7 1/2 In. . . . . . 12.00 to 27.00
Platter, Small 75.00
Soup, Dish 15.00

DIANE features encrusted gold
trim and an inner gold border. It
was made from 1937 to 1970.

Bowl, Vegetable, Round 183.00
Coffeepot 305.00
Plate, Bread & Butter . . . 41.00
Plate, Dinner, 10 In. 88.00

EVENING STAR has scattered
"stars" made of lines. The dinnerware has platinum trim.

Bowl, Fruit 12.00
Bowl, Vegetable,
Oval 42.00
Cup & Saucer 30.00
Plate, Bread & Butter . . . 10.00
Plate, Dinner, 10 In. 25.00

Plate, Salad, 7 1/2 In. 16.00
Sugar, Cover 30.00

FINESSE has an off-center decoration of sprigs of gray and
pink. It was made from 1956 to
1970.

Creamer 18.00
Cup & Saucer 13.00
Gravy Boat 82.00
Plate, Salad,
 7 1/2 In. . . . . . . 8.00 to 12.00
Saucer . . . . 4.00 to 5.00
Sugar, Cover . . . 22.00 to 48.00

FUSAN has blue trim and a bor-
der of oriental-looking flowers.
Bowl, Vegetable, Cover . . 81.00
Platter, Medium 70.00

GARDENIA was made from
1950 to 1966. It has a fluted
rim, gold trim, and a border of
large gardenias.
Bread Plate . . . . 14.00 to 23.00
Plate, Bread & Butter . . . 37.00
Plate, Dinner, 10 In. 46.00
Plate, Luncheon,
 8 In. 34.00
Saucer 9.00
Soup, Cream,
 Saucer 51.00
Sugar, Cover 81.00

GOVERNOR CLINTON was
made from 1937 to 1970.
Dishes have gold trim, an inner
trim line, and a center decoration of three vertical leaves.
Bowl, Cereal 27.00
Soup, Cream, Underplate . 27.00

INDIAN TREE pattern is a version of the classic Indian tree
design of the nineteenth century. It was made in the appropriate Imari colors of red-rust
and blue.
Bouillon, Underplate,
 Pink Scalloped 37.00
Bowl, Cereal, Pink
 Scalloped 27.00

JEFFERSON was made from
1937 to 1970. It has a gold laurel border and gold trim.

Bowl, Dessert 27.00
Chop Plate, 13 In. 115.00
Gravy Boat 95.00
Plate, Dinner, 10 In. 42.00
Plate, Salad, 7 1/2 In. 27.00
Platter 90.00

LADY MARY pattern has a pur-
ple-blue flower cluster border
and platinum trim. It was made
from 1937 to 1970.
Bowl, Vegetable, Oval . . . 61.00
Creamer 41.00
Plate, Bread & Butter . . . 21.00
Plate, Dinner, 10 In. 27.00
Platter, Small 41.00
Sugar, Cover 48.00

LYRIC has inner and edge plat-
inum trim. The design pictures
a leaf sprig and dots. It was
made from 1952 to 1970.
Bowl, Vegetable, Round 100.00
Creamer 72.00
Cup & Saucer . . 39.00 to 40.00
Plate, Bread & Butter . . . 15.00
Plate, Dinner,
 10 In. . . . . . . 40.00 to 50.00
Plate, Salad,
 7 1/2 In. . . . . . 22.00 to 27.00
Platter, Small 126.00
Sugar, Cover 88.00

MANDARIN was made on the
Governor Winthrop shape from
1922 to 1935. It has a floral border and center.
Bowl, Fruit 15.00

Plate, Bread & Butter . . . 10.00
Plate, Dinner, 10 In. 24.00
Plate, Salad, 7 1/2 In. 14.00
Soup, Cream,
 Underplate 25.00

MAYFLOWER was made from
1956 to 1970. The pattern has a
wide border of maroon flowers.
Creamer 36.00
Sugar, Cover 48.00

MEADOW BREEZE has a pale
gray-blue border and curving
thin leaves and twigs of brown
and gray-blue for a center
design. It has platinum trim.
The pattern was made from
1952 to 1970.
Cup & Saucer 43.00
Gravy Boat 174.00
Plate, Dinner, 10 In. 54.00
Plate, Salad, 7 1/2 In. 34.00
Sugar, Cover 75.00

MINUET has a gray-blue border
with small white blossoms on a
vine. There is also platinum
trim. It was made from 1955 to
1970.

Creamer 70.00
Cup & Saucer 43.00
Plate, Dinner, 10 In. 45.00
Plate, Salad, 7 1/2 In. 27.00
Sugar, Cover 75.00

MONTICELLO has gold trim
and a plain, wide rim. It was
made from 1928 to 1952.
Bowl, Cereal 12.00
Cake Plate 40.00

Creamer 15.00
Cup & Saucer 42.00
Gravy Boat 162.00
Plate, Salad, 7 1/2 In. 14.00
Saucer 11.00
Sugar, Cover . . . . 9.00 to 19.00

NORDIC dinnerware has a border made of spearlike spikes facing toward the center. The pattern, made from 1956 to 1970, was decorated in blue and red.

Gravy Boat, Underplate . . 50.00
Platter, Large 75.00
Platter, Medium 50.00

OLD COLONY has gold trim and a gold inner rim on a plain shape.

Bowl, Fruit 7.00
Bowl, Vegetable 20.00
Cup & Saucer 10.00
Plate, Bread & Butter 6.00

PENDLETON pattern is made with a red and blue vine border, an inner red rim, and gold trim. It was made from 1938 to 1969.

Bowl, Fruit 34.00
Plate, Bread & Butter . . . 17.00
Plate, Salad, 7 1/2 In. 24.00

POLARIS was made from 1952 to 1970. It has platinum trim and a design of stars made of lines on the rim and parts of the center.

Plate, Bread & Butter . . . 12.00
Platter, Large 80.00

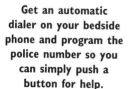

Get an automatic dialer on your bedside phone and program the police number so you can simply push a button for help.

QUEEN ANNE pattern has a dark blue border and gold encrusted trim. The very formal looking dinnerware was made from 1937 to 1970.

Cup & Saucer 88.00
Dish, Square 54.00

RHAPSODY has a fluted rim, gold trim, and decorations of branches of blooming trees. It was made from 1950 to 1966.

Cup & Saucer 26.00
Plate, Bread & Butter . . . 14.00
Plate, Dinner, 10 In. 22.00
Plate, Salad, 7 1/2 In. 18.00
Platter, Small 50.00

ROSALIE was made from 1938 to 1969. It has a single rose and leaves in the center of the plate, a scalloped edge, and gold trim. It was made from 1938 to 1969.

Creamer 55.00
Plate, Bread & Butter . . . 10.00
Soup, Cream,
   Underplate 55.00
Sugar, Cover 30.00

SANTA ROSA is decorated with bunches of red roses and other flowers and gold trim. It was made from 1938 to 1969.

Bowl, Cover, Round . . . 100.00
Bowl, Vegetable,
   Cover 105.00
Bowl, Vegetable, Oval . . . 50.00
Creamer . . . . . . 40.00 to 50.00
Cup & Saucer . . 28.00 to 30.00
Gravy Boat 50.00
Plate, Bread & Butter . . . 14.00

Plate, Dinner,
   10 3/8 In. 25.00
Plate, Salad,
   8 In. . . . . 18.00 to 20.00
Platter, 12 In. 50.00
Platter, 14 In. 60.00
Soup, Dish 24.00
Sugar, Cover 50.00

SELMA, made from 1928 to 1952, has a border of roses and leaves in small bunches and a small bunch of flowers in the center. It is a gold-trimmed pattern.

Bowl, Dessert 11.00
Cup & Saucer 30.00
Plate, Bread & Butter . . . 14.00
Plate, Dinner, 10 In. 30.00
Plate, Salad, 7 1/2 In. 20.00

SERENE is an undecorated pattern made from 1956 to 1970.

Creamer 42.00
Gravy Boat, Underplate . . 24.00
Plate, Dinner, 10 In. 14.00
Sugar, Cover 53.00

SHERWOOD was made from 1940 to 1970. The design has a formal berry and leaf border in blues and dark yellow. It has gold trim.

Bowl, Vegetable, Oval . . 170.00
Creamer . . . . . . 41.00 to 71.00
Cup & Saucer . . 38.00 to 42.00
Gravy Boat 88.00
Plate, Bread & Butter . . . 17.00
Plate, Dinner,
   10 In. . . . . . . 41.00 to 51.00
Plate, Salad,
   7 1/2 In. . . . . . 15.00 to 25.00
Platter, Medium . 47.00 to 88.00
Soup, Cream,
   Underplate . . . 35.00 to 60.00
Soup, Dish 48.00
Sugar, Cover 48.00

SPLENDOR has a center design of a green sprig, and a green-gray rim with platinum trim. It was made from 1952 to 1970.

Gravy Boat, Underplate . . 50.00
Platter, Large 75.00

STANSBURY was introduced in 1938 and discontinued in 1969. The pattern features trailing flowers in pale pinks, green, and grays. It has gold trim.

Bowl, Fruit 34.00
Bowl, Vegetable,
   Oval 110.00
Plate, Bread & Butter . . . 17.00
Soup, Dish 42.00

SUZANNE pattern has a border strewn with pink, blue, and yellow flowers. The edge has gold trim. It was introduced in 1938 and discontinued in 1970.

Bowl, Fruit 32.00
Bowl, Vegetable,
   Oval . . . . 88.00 to 93.00
Creamer 71.00
Cup & Saucer . . 42.00 to 49.00
Gravy Boat 136.00
Plate, Bread &
   Butter . . . . . . 16.00 to 25.00
Plate, Dinner, 10 In. 54.00
Plate, Salad, 7 1/2 In. 24.00
Platter, Large 193.00
Platter, Medium 88.00
Soup, Cream 32.00
Sugar, Cover 86.00
Underplate, For Soup,
   Cream 27.00

VICTORIA was made from 1939 to 1970. The center of the plate pictures a realistic rose with buds and leaves. A few small buds are placed on the border. The ivory plate has a fluted shape and gold trim.

Bowl, Fruit 22.00
Bowl, Vegetable,
   Oval . . . . 88.00 to 93.00
Creamer 79.00
Cup & Saucer . . 30.00 to 42.00
Gravy Boat 162.00
Plate, Bread &
   Butter . . . . . . 14.00 to 15.00
Plate, Dinner, 10 In. 54.00

Plate, Salad,
   7 1/2 In. . . . . 24.00 to 30.00
Platter, Medium 165.00
Sugar, Cover . . . 40.00 to 95.00

WAYNE was made from 1937 to 1970. It has a gold-encrusted border. There are four types, plain or with a colored band of blue, green, or maroon.

Maroon

Bowl, Fruit 34.00
Bowl, Vegetable, Oval . . . 88.00
Gravy Boat,
   Underplate 130.00
Plate, Dinner, 10 In. 48.00
Platter, Medium 88.00
Relish 34.00

WAYSIDE is an asymmetrical pattern with a cluster of grapes, pears, and apples with leaves on one side of the plate. It was made from 1962 to 1970.

Cup 29.00
Cup & Saucer 32.00
Platter, Small 103.00

WEDDING RING is a white dinnerware with platinum trim. It was made from 1960 to 1970.

Cup & Saucer 48.00
Plate, Salad, 7 1/2 In. 34.00

WOODBINE was made from 1956 to 1970. The decoration features an off-center branch of pink and green maple leaves.

Creamer 27.00
Cup & Saucer 17.00
Gravy Boat 71.00

Plate, Bread & Butter 8.00
Plate, Dinner, 10 In. 16.00
Sugar, Cover 41.00

TAYLOR, SMITH & TAYLOR

Taylor, Smith & Taylor produced dinnerware in Chester, West Virginia, from 1901 to 1981. The company produced an extensive number of patterns. In 1973, Anchor Hocking purchased the company and started marking the dinnerware *Anchor Hocking*.

AUTUMN HARVEST was made on the Versatile shape.

Bowl, Fruit,
   5 1/8 In. . . . . . . 7.00 to 12.00
Bowl, Vegetable, Cover . . 40.00
Butter, Cover 30.00
Cup 7.00
Cup & Saucer 19.00
Plate, Bread & Butter,
   6 In. . . . . 5.00 to 10.00
Plate, Dinner, 10 In. 9.00

Plate, Salad, 7 1/2 In. 14.00
Soup, Dish 18.00

AZURA pattern has a border of large and small daisies. It is ovenproof and detergent safe.

Plate, Bread & Butter,
6 In. 7.00
Plate, Salad, 7 1/2 In. 14.00

BLUE BONNET pattern pictures a group of blue bonnet flowers in an off-center arrangement. It is a 1960s pattern.

Bowl, Cereal 6.00
Bowl, Fruit 6.00
Creamer 8.00
Cup 4.00
Cup & Saucer 6.00
Plate, Dinner,
10 1/4 In. . . . . . 6.00 to 9.00
Platter, Small 15.00
Salt & Pepper 15.00
Sugar, Cover 10.00

BONNIE GREEN has a colorful rooster and stylized flowers center.

Bowl, Dessert 7.00
Plate, Bread & Butter,
6 In. 9.00
Plate, Dinner, 10 In. 15.00
Saucer 3.00

BOUTONNIERE has a group of blue flowers that resemble bachelor buttons as the design.
Bowl, Cereal 7.00
Bowl, Dessert . . . . 5.00 to 7.00
Creamer 14.00
Cup & Saucer . . . 7.00 to 11.00

Gravy Boat,
6 1/2 In. 10.00
Plate, Bread & Butter,
6 In. . . . . 4.00 to 7.00
Plate, Dinner,
10 In. . . . . 7.00 to 10.00
Platter, 13 1/2 In. 22.00
Platter, Small . . . 16.00 to 19.00
Saucer 3.00
Sugar, Cover . . . . 8.00 to 20.00

BUTTERCUP pattern has a border of buttercups.

Plate, Dinner, 10 In. 9.00
Plate, Salad, 7 1/2 In. 7.00
Saucer 3.00
Soup, Dish 9.00

CATHAY is a modern pattern that has a wide border of abstract designs in blue and green. The pattern is marked *Taylorstone, Cathay.*

Bowl, Fruit 5.00
Platter, Medium 15.00

CLASSIC HERITAGE is a simple pattern with white interiors, sage green exteriors or rims, and gold trim.

Bowl, Fruit 8.00
Cup & Saucer 12.00
Plate, Dinner, 10 In. 15.00

ECHO DELL pattern has a wide border of flowers in greens and yellows.

Bowl, Cereal 13.00
Chop Plate 30.00
Creamer 20.00
Cup 12.00

Cup & Saucer 16.00
Plate, Dinner, 10 In. 15.00
Sugar, Cover 30.00

GOLDEN JUBILEE has gold encrusted trim or gold bands.

Bowl, Cereal 16.00
Bowl, Fruit 13.00
Bowl, Vegetable,
Oval 36.00
Coffeepot, Cover 63.00
Creamer 34.00
Plate, Bread & Butter,
6 In. 13.00
Plate, Dinner, 10 In. 24.00
Plate, Salad, 7 1/2 In. . . . 16.00
Platter, Medium 42.00
Sugar, Cover 38.00

INDIAN SUMMER has a border of rust and yellow chrysanthemums with sprays of leaves. Pieces are marked with the pattern name and instructions that say *detergent proof.*

Bowl, Vegetable 30.00
Creamer . . . . 8.00 to 20.00
Cup & Saucer 6.00
Gravy Boat 30.00
Ladle 8.00
Plate, Dinner, 10 In. 17.00

Dishes that can be used in a microwave or conventional oven can be used in a convection oven.

Saucer 4.00
Sugar, Cover 30.00

JAMACIA is decorated with leaves.

Bowl, Cereal 12.00
Bowl, Fruit 8.00
Plate, Bread & Butter,
　6 In. 5.00

LAZY DAISY is a pale green dinnerware with a border of realistic white daisies and leaves.

Bowl, Fruit 8.00
Bowl, Vegetable 30.00
Creamer 30.00
Cup & Saucer 17.00
Plate, Luncheon, 8 In. . . . 9.00
Plate, Salad, 7 1/2 In. 15.00
Platter, Medium 40.00
Saucer 5.00
Soup, Dish 19.00
Sugar, Cover 25.00

LU-RAY has a slightly speckled, solid-color glaze. It was made from 1938 to 1961. Pastel colors include Chatham Gray, Persian Cream (yellow), Sharon Pink, Surf Green, and Windsor Blue.

Persian Cream
Cup & Saucer 25.00
Plate, Bread & Butter,
　5 In. 5.00
Plate, Dinner, 10 In. . . . 30.00
Platter, 11 1/2 In. 60.00
Sauceboat, Underplate . . . 45.00
Saucer 10.00

Sharon Pink
Bowl, Fruit 15.00
Pitcher, Footed 145.00
Saucer . . . . 5.00 to 10.00

Surf Green
Bowl, Fruit 15.00
Bowl, Vegetable, Oval,
　10 1/2 In. 30.00
Platter, Medium 75.00
Saucer 10.00
Saucer, After Dinner 18.00

Windsor Blue
Bowl, Fruit 15.00
Cup & Saucer 28.00
Gravy Boat 40.00
Plate, Bread & Butter,
　6 In. 5.00
Salt & Pepper 25.00
Saucer, After Dinner 18.00
Soup, Dish 29.00

MOULIN ROUGE pattern features a single branch of roses with a pink rose and bud and gray leaves.

Creamer 15.00
Cup & Saucer 14.00
Plate, Bread & Butter,
　6 In. 5.00
Plate, Dinner, 10 In. . . . 14.00
Sugar, Open 20.00

PEBBLEFORD was made on the Versatile shape, which included a plain round coupe shape. It has a speckled glaze in Burnt Orange, Granite Gray, Honey (beige), Marble White,

Mint Green, Pink, Sand (pumpkin), Sunburst Yellow, Teal, and Turquoise. Every piece was made in every color. There are two different styles of teapots and sugar bowls.

Granite Gray
Plate, Dinner, 10 In. 15.00
Pink
Bowl, Vegetable, 9 In. . . . 14.00
Plate, Dinner, 10 In. 5.00
Sand
Platter, 13 1/2 In. 25.00
Turquoise
Bowl, Vegetable, 9 In. . . . 14.00
Plate, Dinner, 10 In. 5.00

PLATINUM BLUE pattern has a plain blue border with platinum trim.

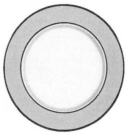

Bowl, Vegetable 20.00
Plate, Dinner, 10 In. . . . 10.00
Plate, Salad, 7 1/2 In. 7.00

REVEILLE pattern pictures a red rooster in a Pennsylvania Dutch design. It was made about 1960. Some small pieces like saucers do not show the rooster.

Don't put a message on your answering machine indicating when you will return.

Plate, Bread & Butter,
  7 In. . . . . 4.00 to 6.00
Plate, Dinner,
  10 In. . . . . . . 13.00 to 18.00
Platter, 13 1/2 In. 30.00
Platter, 15 In. 17.00
Saucer . . . . 4.00 to 5.00
Soup, Dish 8.00

RIVIERA has a wide border that includes leaflike shapes and curling lines.
Plate, Bread & Butter 5.00
Plate, Dinner 11.00

TAVERNE dinnerware was made by Taylor, Smith & Taylor of Chester, West Virginia. Matching serving pieces were made by the Hall China Company of East Liverpool, Ohio, in the 1930s. A rolling pin was made by Harker Pottery Company. The silhouetted figures eating at a table are very similar to those seen on the pattern Silhouette, but there is no dog in this decal. In some of the literature, Taverne is called Silhouette. Reproductions using the Taverne decoration have been made. These, unlike the originals, are marked *Limited Edition.*

Bowl, Cover, 9 1/2 In. . . . 38.00
Platter,
  13 1/4 x 9 1/2 In. 15.00

VISTOSA is a solid-color dinnerware made about 1938. The plates have piecrust edges, and the other pieces have some bands or ridges. The glaze colors are Cobalt Blue, Deep Yellow, Light Green, and Mango Red. Pieces were marked with the name *Vistosa* and the initials *T.S. & T. Co. U.S.A.*

Cobalt Blue
Bowl, Fruit 18.00
Deep Yellow
Bowl, Fruit 18.00
Platter, 13 In. 60.00
Light Green
Bowl, Fruit 18.00
Mango Red
Bowl, Fruit 10.00
Cup & Saucer 20.00
Nappy 80.00
Plate, Dinner, 10 In. . . . 25.00

WILD QUINCE is part of the Ever Yours line.

Plate, Bread &
  Butter, 6 In. 5.00
Plate, Dinner, 10 In. . . . 10.00

WOOD ROSE is part of the Ever Yours line.

Cup & Saucer 12.00
Plate, Dinner, 10 In. . . . 19.00
Salt & Pepper 12.00
Saucer 6.00

UNIVERSAL

Universal Potteries, Inc. operated in Cambridge, Ohio, from 1934 to 1976. The company made semi-porcelain dinnerware and kitchenware until 1956, when production switched to decorative tile. See Harmony House for additional patterns and information.

BALLERINA was a very modern shape and had solid-color glazes. It was made from 1947 to 1956. A later line was decorated with abstract designs. The original solid-color Ballerina dinnerware was offered in Dove Gray, Jade Green, Jonquil Yellow, and Periwinkle Blue. In 1949, Chartreuse and Forest Green were added. By 1955,

Burgundy, Charcoal, and Pink were added, while some other colors had been discontinued. There was also a line called Ballerina Mist, which had a pale background and decal decorations. It may be marked with the backstamp *Ballerina* or *Ballerina Mist*.

Chartreuse
Bowl, Vegetable, 9 In. 7.00
Pitcher, Ball, Ice Lip 31.00

Decal
Bowl, Wood Vine,
7 In., ... 11.75
Casserole, Cover, Moss Rose,
5 1/2 In. . . . . . 25.00 to 35.00
Pitcher, Ball, Moss Rose,
7 1/2 In. 26.00
Platter, Tab Handle, Moss Rose,
11 5/8 x 10 3/4 In. 5.75
Platter, Tabbed, Iris,
10 1/2 In. 20.50
Refrigerator Dish, Cover
Harvest 10.00

Jade Green
Cake Plate 25.00
Soup, Lug, 6 1/2 In. 3.50

CATTAIL (CAT-TAIL) pattern dishes were found in many

homes in America in the 1940s. Sears, Roebuck & Company featured the pattern from 1934 to 1956. It was made by Universal Potteries. The red and black cattail design was used for dinnerware and matching tinware, kitchenware, glassware, furniture, and table linens. Another pattern by Universal was also called Cattail. It has a realistic green and brown design. The red and black pieces are listed here.

Bowl, Cover, 8 In. 25.00
Bowl, Metal Holder,
Cover, Bakelite Handle,
9 1/2 x 3 1/2 In. 49.00
Butter 15.00
Casserole, Cover,
8 5/8 In. 10.50
Cup 6.00
Cup & Saucer 9.00
Grease Jar 22.00
Pitcher, Ball 43.00
Pitcher, Water 35.00
Plate, Bread & Butter,
6 In. 3.00
Plate, Dinner,
9 In. . . . . 4.50 to 7.50
Platter, 11 In. 12.50

Saucer 3.00
Soup, Dish, 8 In. 10.00
Sugar, Cover 16.00

VERNON KILNS

Vernon Kilns was the name used by Vernon Potteries, Ltd. The company, which started in 1931 in Vernon, California, made dinnerware and figurines until it went out of business in 1958. The molds were bought by Metlox, which continued to make some patterns. Collectors search for the brightly-colored dinnerware and the pieces designed by Rockwell Kent, Walt Disney, and Don Blanding.

BROWN EYED SUSAN was made by Vernon Kilns from 1946 to 1958. It has yellow flowers and a brown border.

Cup & Saucer 18.00
Plate, Bread & Butter,
6 1/2 In. 10.00

Plate, Dinner, 10 1/2 In. . . . 23.00
Plate, Salad, 7 1/2 In. 15.00
Sauceboat 32.00

CALICO is one of the plaid patterns made from 1949 to 1958. It is pink and blue plaid with a blue border. Other plaids are Gingham (green and yellow), Homespun (cinnamon, green, and yellow), Organdie (brown and yellow), Tam O'Shanter (rust, chartreuse, and dark green), and Tweed (yellow and gray-blue).

Casserole, Chicken Pie, Cover,
Stick Handle, 4 In. 70.00
Creamer 20.00
Gravy Boat 40.00
Soup, Dish, 8 In. 25.00

CASA CALIFORNIA, made in 1938, has a center decoration of blues and green or browns and yellows with a matching border.

Coffeepot 90.00
Plate, Salad, 7 1/2 In. 9.00

CASUAL CALIFORNIA, a very popular solid-color dinnerware,

was made from 1947 to 1956. It was made in Acacia Yellow, Dawn Pink, Dusk Gray, Lime Green, Mahogany Brown, Mocha Brown, Pine Green, Sno-white, and Turquoise Blue.

Dawn Pink
Butter 25.00

Lime Green
Casserole, Chicken Pie, Cover,
Stick Handle, 4 In. 40.00
Cup & Saucer 8.95
Pitcher, Streamline,
2 Qt., 11 In. 60.00
Salt & Pepper 13.00

Mahogany Brown
Pitcher, Streamline,
1 Qt. 50.00
Soup, Dish, 8 3/8 In. 15.00
Tumbler, 14 Oz. 18.00

Mocha Brown
Pitcher, Streamline,
1/4 Pt. 22.00
Pitcher, Streamline,
1/2 Pt. 22.00
Tumbler, 14 Oz. 18.00

CHINTZ is a floral decorated pattern made about 1942 and again in 1950. The pattern, in red, blue, yellow, green, and maroon, resembled the English dinnerware patterns of the early nineteenth century. Many English manufacturers made unrelated overall patterns now called Chintz by collectors.

Bowl, 9 1/4 In. 10.50
Gravy, Footed 13.00
Tidbit, Handles,
10 1/2 In. 47.50

CORAL REEF was designed by Don Blanding for Vernon Kilns

in 1938. The tropical fish in the design are colored blue, mustard, and maroon on a cream background.

Chop Plate, 14 In. 138.50
Plate, Maroon & Cream,
8 1/2 In. 50.00

CORONADO, made from 1935 to 1939, was used as a grocery promotion. It was glazed Blue, Brown, Dark Blue, Light Green, Orange, Pink, Turquoise, or Yellow.

Turquoise
Cup 8.00
Plate, Bread & Butter,
6 1/2 In. 7.00

Yellow
Plate, Bread & Butter,
6 1/2 In. 7.00

EARLY CALIFORNIA is a solid-color line of dinnerware made in the late 1930s. The dishes, in Blue, Brown, Green, Orange, Pink, Turquoise, or Yellow, were made to be used as mix-and-match sets. The dishes are marked with the name of the pattern.

Brown
Creamer 15.00
Cup & Saucer 12.00
Orange
Plate, 8 1/2 In. 7.00
Pink
Chop Plate, 12 In. 32.00
Creamer, Round, 3 In. . . . 15.00
Yellow
Platter, 12 1/2 x 8 In. 12.00

GINGHAM is one of the plaid patterns made from 1949 to 1958. It is green and yellow plaid with a dark green border. Other plaids are Calico (pink and blue), Homespun (cinnamon, green, and yellow), Organdie (brown and yellow), Tam O'Shanter (rust, chartreuse, and dark green), and Tweed (yellow and gray-blue).

Bowl, Fruit 16.00
Cup 10.00
Cup & Saucer 21.00
Plate, Luncheon,
  9 1/2 In. . . . . . 11.00 to 13.00
Plate, Bread & Butter,
  6 In. 3.50
Plate, Salad, 7 In. 6.00
Salt & Pepper 43.00
Saucer 3.00

HAWAIIAN FLOWERS was a well-known Vernon Kilns tableware designed by Don Blanding. It was first made from 1938 to 1942. It has an overall pattern of cream-colored lotus flowers and leaves on a solid-color background of blue, maroon, mustard, or pink.

Blue
Bowl, 8 In. 22.50
Mug, Handles, 4 In. 22.25
Maroon
Chop Plate, 12 In. 160.50

HEAVENLY DAYS was made from 1956 to 1958. Pieces are decorated with aqua, mocha, and pink geometric designs.

"Heavenly Days"

Gravy Boat 20.00
Pitcher, Qt. 28.00
Plate, Bread & Butter,
  6 In. 8.00
Platter, 11 In. 18.00

HOMESPUN is a cinnamon, green, and yellow plaid pattern with a reddish brown border made from about 1948 to 1958.

Other related plaids are Calico (pink and blue), Gingham (green and yellow), Organdie (brown and yellow), Tam O'Shanter (rust, chartreuse, and dark green), and Tweed (yellow and gray-blue).

Chop Plate, 12 In. 36.00
Cup & Saucer 13.00
Eggcup, Double 25.00
Mug, Straight Sides,
  9 Oz., 3 1/2 In. 28.00
Plate, Bread & Butter,
  6 1/2 In. 8.00
Teacup 11.00

LEI LANI was made from 1938 to 1942 and again from 1947 to 1955. The pattern features a maroon-printed lotus flower.

Chop Plate, 12 1/2 In. . . 100.00
Plate, Dinner, 10 1/2 In. . . 20.00
Sugar & Creamer 75.00

LOLLIPOP TREE is a pattern that features abstract pastel lollipops. It was made from 1957 to 1958.

Cup 10.00
Plate, Bread & Butter,
  6 In. 11.00
Platter, 13 1/2 In. 55.00

❖

Put a wide-angle viewer in a solid outside door so you can see who is there before opening the door.

❖

MAY FLOWERS was made from 1942 to 1955. The pieces picture a large floral spray.

Bowl, Serving, Round,
9 In. 33.00
Bowl, Serving, Oval,
10 In. 33.00
Platter, Oval,
13 1/2 In. 43.00
Sugar, Cover,
Short 25.00
Teacup 18.00

ORGANDIE is one of several different plaid patterns made in the 1940s and 1950s. It is an overall brown pattern with a yellow and brown plaid border. Other related plaids are Calico (pink and blue), Gingham (green and yellow), Homespun (cinnamon, yellow, and green), Tam O'Shanter (rust, chartreuse, and deep green), and Tweed (yellow and gray-blue). Organdie was originally the name for a group of plaid designs made in 1937 that are not listed here. One of these was Coronation Organdy (gray and rose).

Bowl, Fruit, 5 1/2 In. 4.50
Bowl, Serving, Round,
9 In. 20.00
Casserole, Cover,
8 In. 45.00
Chop Plate,
12 In. . . . . . . 24.00 to 29.00
Cup & Saucer . . . 8.00 to 13.00
Eggcup, Double 30.00
Gravy Boat, Handle 20.00
Mug 20.00
Pitcher, Milk 19.00
Plate, Bread & Butter,
6 1/2 In. 3.50
Plate, Dinner,
10 1/2 In. 15.00
Plate, Luncheon,
9 1/2 In. 10.00
Plate, Salad, 7 1/2 In. 8.00
Platter, 12 1/2 In. 24.00
Platter, Oval, 10 In. 15.00
Salt & Pepper 10.00
Soup, Dish, Rimmed,
8 1/2 In. 15.00
Tumbler 22.00

RAFFIA is a pattern made about 1950. It is green brushed with brownish red to give a textured effect. Barkwood and Shantung are the same pattern in different colors.

Bowl, Vegetable,
Divided 18.00
Creamer 5.00
Cup & Saucer 7.00
Sugar, Cover 8.00

SHADOW LEAF has red and green flowers on a green swirled background. It is the same design as Trade Winds,

but in different colors. It was made from 1954 to 1955.

Cup 8.00
Pitcher, Medium 24.00

TAM O'SHANTER is one of many plaid patterns made between 1949 and 1958. It is a rust, chartreuse, and dark green plaid with forest green border. Other related plaids are Calico (pink and blue), Gingham (green and yellow), Homespun (cinnamon, yellow, and green), Organdie (brown and yellow), and Tweed (yellow and gray-blue).

Bowl, 7 In. 6.00
Bowl, 8 1/2 In. 8.00
Bowl, Salad, Deep 15.00
Bowl, Salad, Individual,
5 In. 5.00
Butter Pats 16.00
Chicken Pie Server,
Cover, Stick Handle,
4 In. . . . . 16.00 to 27.00
Cup & Saucer 13.00
Mug, 9 Oz. 8.00
Pitcher, Juice, Streamline,
Qt., 8 1/2 In. 55.00
Plate, Bread & Butter,
6 In. 4.50
Plate, Dinner, 10 1/2 In. . . 5.00
Platter, Oval, 12 In. 20.00
Soup, Dish, Rim,
8 1/2 In. 15.00

TICKLED PINK is a pattern made from 1955 to 1958. It features small squares and crosses in pink and charcoal on most pieces. Cups, lids, and a few serving pieces are made of solid pink. The pattern and name rights were purchased by Metlox Potteries in 1958 and Tickled Pink continued to be produced.

Chowder, 6 In. 14.00
Creamer, 4 1/4 In. 10.00
Cup 6.00
Plate, 7 In. 8.00
Plate, 10 In. 12.00

TWEED is one of the plaid patterns. It was made between 1950 and 1955. It is a yellow and gray-blue plaid with a border. Other related plaids are Calico (pink and blue), Gingham (green and yellow), Homespun (cinnamon, yellow, and green), Organdie (brown and yellow), and Tam O'Shanter (rust, chartreuse, and dark green).

Bowl, Vegetable, Round,
    8 7/8 In. 38.00
Chop Plate, 13 3/4 In. . . . 50.00
Pitcher, Streamline, 1 Pt.,
    6 In. 70.00
Plate, Bread & Butter,
    6 1/2 In. 6.50
Plate, Dinner, 10 1/2 In. . . 20.00
Platter, Oval, 12 1/2 In. . . 40.00
Salt & Pepper 27.00
Soup, Dish,
    8 1/4 In. . . . . . . 20.00 to 26.00

W. S. GEORGE

W. S. George ran the Ohio China Company in

the 1890s. He purchased the East Palestine Pottery Company in East Palestine, Ohio, in 1903 and renamed it the W. S. George Pottery Company. It closed about 1960.

PEACH BLOSSOM pattern has several sprays of peach blossoms scattered on the border.

Bowl, Cereal 7.00
Creamer 8.00
Cup & Saucer . . . . 7.00 to 8.00
Plate, Bread & Butter,
    6 In. 6.00
Plate, Dinner, 10 In. 10.00
Plate, Luncheon,
    9 In. 8.00
Plate, Salad, 8 In. 7.00
Soup, Dish 8.00

RADISSON was made from the 1920s to the 1940s. The shape has a scalloped age. Pieces are decorated with small groups of flowers or bands of color, or are undecorated with or without gold trim.

Bowl, Fruit 8.00
Cup & Saucer 10.00
Plate, Bread & Butter 5.00
Plate, Dinner 15.00
Soup, Dish 18.00

WATT

Watt Pottery was started in 1922 in Crooksville, Ohio, by William J. Watt and his sons. They made oven-safe k#510 ware in 1935. Most of its dinnerwares were not made until the 1950s. It was destroyed by fire in 1965. Pieces were usually marked with an impressed number indicating shape.

AMERICAN RED BUD, also called Bleeding Heart or Teardrop, was decorated with hanging red buds, green leaves, and brown stems. It was introduced in the mid-1950s.

Baker, Square, Cover,
    No. 84 . . . . 800.00
Salt & Pepper, Barrel,
    No. 46 . . . . 300.00

❖

To remove old gummed labels, use Bestine solvent found at artist supply stores.

❖

APPLE is the most popular Watt pattern. It is sometimes called Red Apple. Dinnerware sets and kitchenware were made beginning in 1952. The company burned to the ground in 1965.

Bowl, Chip 'n Dip,
No. 110, No. 120 .... 300.00
Bowl, Spaghetti, No. 39,
13 In. 150.00
Creamer, No. 62,
2-Leaf ..... 105.00 to 125.00
Mixing Bowl, No. 05,
3-Leaf 70.00
Pitcher, No. 15 .... 110.00
Pitcher, No. 16 .... 100.00

AUTUMN FOLIAGE was made from 1959 to 1965. It has brown leaves on brown stems. It is also called Brown Leaves.

Bowl, No. 63 .... 41.00
Bowl, No. 64 .... 33.00
Bowl, No. 65 ... 31.00 to 36.00
Pitcher, No. 15 .. 31.00 to 58.00
Sugar, Cover, No. 98 .... 86.00

DUTCH TULIP was introduced in 1956. The design shows a black stylized tulip with green and red leaves on a cream-color dinnerware.

Casserole, Cover, French
Handle, No. 18 ..... 325.00
Casserole, Cover,
No. 67 .... 200.00

ROOSTER was introduced in 1955. It was made until at least 1958. Pieces picture a black, green, and red rooster standing in green grass.

Bowl, Cover, No. 5 .... 183.00
Creamer,
No. 62 ..... 125.00 to 144.00
Mixing Bowl, No. 7 ..... 59.00
Pitcher, No. 15,
5 1/2 In. 145.00
Pitcher, Refrigerator,
Ice Lip, No. 69 ...... 200.00

STARFLOWER was made in the early 1950s in several variations. One type has either four-petal or five-petal red flowers with green leaves on a cream background. Other variations have two or three green leaves. Similar patterns with different names were made in several color combinations.

Cookie Jar, No. 21 ..... 91.00
Creamer, No. 62, Mountain
Lake, Minn. 175.00
Mixing Bowl, No. 7 ..... 23.00
Mixing Bowl, No. 8 ..... 22.00

Pitcher, Ice Lip,
No. 17 .... 125.00
Pitcher, No. 16 .... 93.00
Salt & Pepper, Barrel,
No. 45 & No. 46 .... 177.00
Salt & Pepper, Hourglass,
No. 117 & No. 118 ... 100.00

TULIP pattern was sold in Woolworth stores. It was made about 1963. The pattern features a red and a blue tulip with green leaves.

Creamer, No. 62 ...... 175.00
Pitcher, No. 16 .... 185.00

WILLOW

Willow pattern pictures a bridge, figures, birds, trees, and a Chinese landscape. The pattern was first used in England by Thomas Turner in 1780 at the Caughley Pottery Works. It was inspired by an earlier Chinese pattern. The pattern has been copied by makers in almost every country. It was made in the United

States by Homer Laughlin China Company, Sebring, and others. Pieces listed here are blue unless another color is mentioned. Blue and pink willow were made by the Royal China Company of Sebring, Ohio, from the 1940s through the 1960s.

Ashtray, Royal China ... 15.00

Berry Bowl, Royal China, 5 1/4 In. 6.00

Berry Bowl, Royal China, 6 1/4 In. 12.00

Bowl, Buffalo Pottery, 5 1/2 In. 50.00

Bowl, Cereal, Homer Laughlin, 5 In. 10.00

Bowl, Cereal, Marked USA 11.00

Bowl, Cereal, Royal China, 6 1/4 In. 32.00

Bowl, Fruit, Homer Laughlin, 5 1/2 In. 10.00

Bowl, Homer Laughlin, 5 In. 19.00

Bowl, Japan, 5 3/4 In. 8.00

Bowl, Vegetable, Open, Round, Homer Laughlin 30.00

Bowl, Vegetable, Royal China, 9 In. 20.00

Bowl, Vegetable, Royal China, 10 In. 14.00

Butter, Cover, Royal China 50.00

Casserole, Cover, Royal China 70.00

Chop Plate, Royal China, 12 In. 24.00

Coffeepot, Cover, Japan 70.00

Creamer, Japan 25.00

Creamer, Miniature 17.00

Creamer, Royal China ... 10.00

Cup, Handle Design, Royal China 16.00

Cup, Marked USA 5.00

Cup, Royal China 4.00

Cup & Saucer, Marked USA 7.00

Gravy Boat, Royal China ...... 20.00 to 30.00

Grill Plate, Royal China, 11 1/2 In. .... 25.00 to 30.00

Pepper Shaker, Japan 16.00

Plate, Bread & Butter, Homer Laughlin, 6 In. 10.00

Plate, Bread & Butter, Royal China, 6 1/2 In. 4.00

Plate, Buffalo Pottery, 6 3/8 In. 28.00

Plate, Buffalo Pottery, 9 1/4 In. 40.00

Plate, Dinner, Buffalo Pottery, 10 1/4 In. 100.00

Plate, Dinner, Homer Laughlin, 10 In. 10.00

Plate, Dinner, Marked USA, 10 In. 8.00

Plate, Dinner, Royal China, 10 In. 8.00

Plate, Japan, 6 1/4 In. 7.00

Plate, Luncheon, Royal China, 9 In. 14.00

Plate, Salad, Marked USA, 7 1/4 In. 7.00

Plate, Salad, Royal China, 7 1/4 In. 14.00

Platter, Buffalo Pottery, Oval, 8 3/4 In. 140.00

Platter, Buffalo Pottery, Oval, 14 1/8 In. 220.00

Platter, Oval, Royal China, 13 x 10 In. 30.00

Platter, Serving, Oval, 12 3/4 In. .... 37.00 to 47.00

Platter, Tab Handles, Royal China, 10 1/2 In. 24.00

Relish, Buffalo Pottery, 8 3/8 In. 80.00

Saltshaker, Handle Design, Royal China 10.00

Saucer, Homer Laughlin, 6 In. 5.00

Saucer, Royal China, 6 In. 3.00

Snack Plate, Royal China, 9 In. 40.00

Soup, Dish, Cream, Homer Laughlin ..... 16.00 to 19.00

Soup, Dish, Royal China, 8 1/4 In. 10.00

Sugar, Cover, Buffalo Pottery 140.00

Sugar, Cover, Japan 35.00

Sugar, Cover, Royal China 12.00

Teapot, Drop Spout, Design, Royal China 120.00

Teapot, Flat Spout, Royal China 70.00

CERAMIC DINNERWARE

Clubs and Publications

CLUBS

Blue & White Pottery Club, *Blue & White Pottery Club* (newsletter), 224 12th St. NW, Cedar Rapids, IA 52405.

Currier & Ives Dinnerware Collectors, *Currier & Ives Dinnerware Collectors' Newsletter,* 29470 Saxon Rd., Toulon, IL 61483.
Web site: www.royalchinacollectors.org

Eva Zeisel Collectors Club, *Eva Zeisel Times* (newsletter), P.O. Box 9086, Calabasas, CA 91372-9086.
Web site: www.evazeisel.org

Fiesta Collector's Club, *Fiesta Collector's Quarterly* (newsletter), P.O. Box 471, Valley City, OH 44280.
Web site: www.chinaspecialties.com

Franciscan Collectors Club, *Franciscan Newsletter,* 8400 5th Ave. NE, Seattle, WA 98115.
Web site: www.gmcb.com

Frankoma Family Collectors Association, *Pot & Puma* (newsletter), *Prairie Green Sheet* (newsletter), P.O. Box 32571, Oklahoma City, OK 73123-0771.
Web site: www.frankoma.org

Hall China Collector Club, *Hall China Collector Club Newsletter,* P.O. Box 361280, Cleveland, OH 44136.

Homer Laughlin China Collectors Society, *The Dish* (magazine), P.O. Box 26021, Crystal City, VA 22215-6021.
Web site: www.hlcca.org

International Willow Collectors, 503 Chestnut St., Perkasie, PA 18944.
Web site: www.willowcollectors.org

McCoy Lovers, *NMXxpress* (newsletter), 8934 Brecksville Rd., Suite 406, Brecksville, OH 44141.
Web site: hometown.aol.com/nmxpress

National Autumn Leaf Collectors Club, *N.A.L.C.C.* (newsletter), P.O. Box 900968, Palmdale, CA 93590-0968.

Web site: nalcc.org

Novelty Salt & Pepper Shakers Club, *Novelty Salt & Pepper Shakers Club Newsletter,* P.O. Box 677388, Orlando, FL 32867-7388.

Web site: members.aol.com/spclub1234/index.htm

Red Wing Collectors Society, *Red Wing Collectors Society Newsletter,* P.O. Box 50, Red Wing, MN 55066.

Web site: www.redwingcollectors.org

Stangl/Fulper Collectors Club, *Stangl/Fulper Times* (newsletter), P.O. Box 538, Flemington, NJ 08822.

Web site: www.stanglfulper.com

Watt Collectors Association, *Watt's News* (newsletter), P.O. Box 30561, Winston-Salem, NC 27130.

PUBLICATIONS

The Daze (newspaper), 10271 State Rd., Box 57, Otisville, MI 48463.

Web site: www.thedaze.com

The Harker Arrow (newsletter), 69565 Crescent Rd., St. Clairsville, OH 43950.

Web site: users.1st.net/colbert/ harker/harker.htm

***Kovels on Antiques and Collectibles* (newsletter), P.O. Box 420347, Palm Coast, FL 32142-0347.**

Web site: www.kovels.com

Lu-Ray Relay (newsletter), P.O. Box 3512, Arlington, VA 22203.

National Blue Ridge Newsletter, 144 Highland Dr., Blountville, TN 37617-5404.

Purinton News & Views (newsletter), P.O. Box 153, Connellsville, PA 15425.

Snack Set Searchers (newsletter), P.O. Box 908, Hallock, MN 56728.

Willow Review (magazine), P.O. Box 41312, Nashville, TN 37204.

CERAMIC DINNERWARE

References

China Identification Kit. Replacements, Ltd. Privately printed, continuously updated. (P.O. Box 26029, Greensboro, NC 27420).

Chipman, Jack. *Collector's Encyclopedia of California Pottery.* 2nd edition. Paducah, Kentucky: Collector Books, 1998.

Cunningham, Jo. *Collector's Encyclopedia of American Dinnerware.* Revised edition. Paducah, Kentucky: Collector Books, 1999.

————. *The Best of Collectible Dinnerware.* Atglen, Pennsylvania: Schiffer Publishing Ltd., 1995.

Duke, Harvey. *Official Price Guide to Pottery and Porcelain.* 8th edition. New York: House of Collectibles, 1995.

Eva Zeisel: Designer for Industry. Exhibition catalog. Chicago: University of Chicago Press, 1984.

From Kiln to Kitchen: American Ceramic Design in Tableware. Springfield, Illinois: Illinois State Museum, 1980 (out of print).

Gates, William C., Jr., and Dana E. Ormerod. "The East Liverpool, Ohio, Pottery District: Identification of Manufacturers and Marks." *Historical Archaeology* 16 (1982). Washington, D.C.: The Society for Historical Archaeology (out of print).

Keller, Joe and David Ross. *Russel Wright Dinnerware, Pottery & More: An Identification and Price Guide,* Atglen, Pennsylvania: Schiffer Publishing Ltd., 2000.

Kerr, Ann. *Collector's Encyclopedia of Russel Wright Designs.* 2nd edition. Paducah, Kentucky: Collector Books, 1998.

————. *Russel Wright Dinnerware: Designs for the American Table.* Paducah, Kentucky: Collector Books, 1985 (out of print).

Kovel, Ralph and Terry. *Kovels' Antiques & Collectibles Price List.* 33rd edition. New York: Three Rivers Press, 2001.

————. *Kovels' Know Your Collectibles.* New York: Crown Publishers, 1981, updated 1992.

————. *Kovels' New Dictionary of Marks—Pottery & Porcelain: 1850 to the Present*. New York: Crown Publishers, 1986.

Lehner, Lois. *Lehner's Encyclopedia of U.S. Marks on Pottery, Porcelain & Clay*. Paducah, Kentucky: Collector Books, 1988.

Piña, Leslie. *Pottery: Modern Wares 1920–1960*. Atglen, Pennsylvania: Schiffer Publishing Ltd., 1994.

Snyder, Jeffrey B. *Depression Pottery*. Atglen, Pennsylvania: Schiffer Publishing Ltd., 1999.

Venable, Charles, et al. *China & Glass in America, 1880-1980: From Tabletop to TV Tray*. Dallas, Texas: Dallas Museum of Art, 2000.

BAUER

Snyder, Jeffrey B. *Beautiful Bauer: A Pictorial Study with Prices*. Atglen, Pennsylvania: Schiffer Publishing Ltd., 2000.

Chipman, Jack. *Collector's Encyclopedia of Bauer Pottery: Identification & Values*. Paducah, Kentucky: Collector Books, 1998.

Tuchman, Mitch. *Bauer Classic American Pottery*. San Francisco, California: Chronicle Books, 1995.

BLUE RIDGE

Newbound, Betty and Bill. *Southern Potteries Incorporated: Blue Ridge Dinnerware*. 3rd edition. Paducah, Kentucky: Collector Books, 1989.

Ruffin, Frances and John. *Blue Ridge China Today: A Comprehensive Identification and Price Guide for Today's Collector*. Atglen, Pennsylvania: Schiffer Publishing Ltd., 1997.

————. *Blue Ridge China Traditions*. Atglen, Pennsylvania: Schiffer Publishing Ltd., 1999.

COORS

Carlton, Carol and Jim. *Collector's Encyclopedia of Colorado Pottery*. Paducah, Kentucky: Collector Books, 1994.

Schneider, Robert. *Coors Rosebud Pottery*. Privately printed, 1984 (P.O. Box 10382S, Pike Place Station, Seattle, WA 98101).

FRANCISCAN

Enge, Delleen. *Franciscan: Embossed Hand Painted*. Privately printed, 1992 (121 E. El Roblar Dr., Suite #10, Ojai, CA 93023).

————. *Franciscan Ware*. Paducah, Kentucky: Collector Books, 1981.

Enge, Delleen, and Merrianne Metzger. *Franciscan: Plain & Fancy*. Privately printed, 1996 (121 E. El Roblar Dr., Suite #10, Ojai, CA 93023).

Page, Bob, and Dale Frederiksen. *Franciscan: An American Dinnerware Tradition.* Privately printed, 1999 (Replacements, Ltd., P.O. Box 26029, Greensboro, NC 27420).

Snyder, Jeffrey B. *Franciscan Dining Services: A Comprehensive Guide with Values.* Atglen, Pennsylvania: Schiffer Publishing Ltd., 1996.

FRANKOMA

Bess, Phyllis and Tom. *Frankoma and Other Oklahoma Potteries.* 3rd edition. Atglen, Pennsylvania: Schiffer Publishing Ltd., 2000.

Schaum, Gary V. *Collector's Guide to Frankoma Pottery: 1933–1990.* Gas City, Indiana: L-W Book Sales, 1997.

HALL

Cunningham, Jo. *Autumn Leaf Story Price Guide.* Privately printed, 1979 (P.O. Box 4929, Springfield, MO 65808).

Duke, Harvey. *Superior Quality Hall China: A Guide for Collectors.* Privately printed, 1977 (12135 N. State Rd., Otisville, MI 48463).

Miller, C. L. *Jewel Tea Sales and Houseware Collectibles with Value Guide.* Atglen, Pennsylvania: Schiffer Publishing Ltd., 1995.

―――. *The Jewel Tea Company: Its History and Products.* Atglen, Pennsylvania: Schiffer Publishing Ltd., 1994.

Whitmyer, Margaret and Kenn. *Collector's Encyclopedia of Hall China.* 2nd edition. Paducah, Kentucky: Collector Books, 1994.

HARKER

Colbert, Neva W. *Collector's Guide to Harker Pottery U.S.A.: Identification and Value Guide.* Paducah, Kentucky: Collector Books, 1993.

HOMER LAUGHLIN

Cunningham, Jo. *Homer Laughlin: A Giant Among Dishes, 1873–1939.* Atglen, Pennsylvania: Schiffer Publishing Ltd., 1998.

―――. *Homer Laughlin China: 1940s & 1950s.* Atglen, Pennsylvania: Schiffer Publishing Ltd., 2000.

Fiesta, Harlequinn Kitchen Kraft: The Homer Laughlin China Collectors Association Guide. Atglen, Pennsylvania: Schiffer Publishing Ltd., 2000.

Gonzalez, Mark. *Collecting Fiesta, Lu-Ray & Other Colorware.* Gas City, Indiana: L-W Book Sales, 2000.

Homer Laughlin China Company: A Fiesta of American Dinnerware. Newell, West Virginia: Homer Laughlin China Co., 1985.

Huxford, Sharon and Bob. *Collector's Encyclopedia of Fiesta.* 8th edition. Paducah, Kentucky: Collector Books, 1998.

Jasper, Joanne. *The Collector's Encyclopedia of Homer Laughlin China: Reference & Value Guide.* Paducah, Kentucky: Collector Books, 1993.

Nossaman, Darlene. *Homer Laughlin China: An Identification Guide.* Revised edition. Privately printed, 1994 (5419 Lake Charles, Waco, TX 76710).

Racheter, Richard. *Post 86 Fiesta: Identification and Value Guide,* Paducah, Kentucky: Collector Books, 2001.

Snyder, Jeffrey B. *Fiesta: The Homer Laughlin China Company's Colorful Dinnerware.* 2nd edition Atglen, Pennsylvania: Schiffer Publishing Ltd., 1999.

HULL

Hull, Joan Gray. *Hull Shirt Pocket Price List.* 3rd edition. Privately printed, 1998 (1376 Nevada SW, Huron, SD 57350).

———. *Hull: The Heavenly Pottery.* 7th edition. Privately printed, 2000 (1376 Nevada SW, Huron, SD 57350).

Roberts, Brenda. *Roberts' Ultimate Encyclopedia of Hull Pottery.* Privately printed, 1992 (Rte. 2, Highway 65 S., Marshall, MO 65340).

———. *Collectors Encyclopedia of Hull Pottery.* Paducah, Kentucky: Collector Books, 1990.

———. *Companion Guide to Roberts' Ultimate Encyclopedia of Hull Pottery.* Privately printed, 1992 (Rte. 2, Highway 65 S., Marshall, MO 65340).

Snyder, Jeffrey B., *Hull Pottery, Decades of Design.* Atglen, Pennsylvania: Schiffer Publishing Ltd., 2001.

Supnick, Mark and Ellen. *Collecting Hull Pottery's Little Red Riding Hood.* Gas City, Indiana: L-W Book Sales, 1998.

JOHNSON BROTHERS

Finegan, Mary J. *Johnson Brothers Dinnerware Pattern Directory & Price Guide.* Privately printed, 1993. (Marfine Antiques, P.O. Box 3618, Boone, NC 28607).

E. M. KNOWLES

Gonzalez, Mark. *Collecting Fiesta, Lu-Ray & Other Colorware.* Gas City, Indiana: L-W Book Sales, 2000.

McCOY

Hanson, Bob, Craig Nissen, and Margaret Hanson. *McCoy Pottery,* Volume 2. Paducah, Kentucky: Collector Books, 1999.

Snyder, Jeffrey B. *McCoy Pottery.* Atglen, Pennsylvania: Schiffer Publishing Ltd., 1999.

METLOX

Gibbs, Carl, Jr. *Collector's Encyclopedia of Metlox Potteries: Identification and Values.* Paducah, Kentucky: Collector Books, 1995.

NORITAKE

Brewer, Robin. *Noritake Dinnerware: Identification Made Easy.* Atglen, Pennsylvania: Schiffer Publishing Ltd., 1999.

Melvin, Florence, and Rodney and Wilma Bourdeau. *Noritake Azalea China: A Reference in Color for Collectors.* Privately printed, 1975 (Red White and Blue Shop, 2 Starr St., Danbury, CT 06810).

Spain, David. *Noritake Collectibles, A to Z.* Atglen, Pennsylvania: Schiffer Publishing Ltd., 1997.

———. *Collecting Noritake, A to Z: Art Deco & More.* Atglen, Pennsylvania: Schiffer Publishing Ltd., 1999.

Stevenson, Ferne and David. *Noritake Azalea China.* Privately printed, 1987 (730 North 5th St., Hamburg, PA 19526).

Van Patten, Joan. *Collector's Encyclopedia of Noritake.* Paducah, Kentucky: Collector Books, 1984.

PURINTON

Bero-Johnson, Jamie, and Jamie Johnson. *Purinton Pottery with Values.* Atglen, Pennsylvania: Schiffer Publishing Ltd., 1997.

Dole, Pat. *Purinton Pottery.* Privately printed, 1984 (P.O. Box 4782, Birmingham, AL 35206).

———. *Purinton Pottery.* Book 2. Privately printed, 1990 (142 W. Salisbury St., P.O. Box 308, Denton, NC 27239-0308).

Morris, Susan. *Purinton Pottery.* Paducah, Kentucky: Collector Books, 1994.

RED WING

Dollen, B. L. *Red Wing Art Pottery Identification & Value Guide, 1920s–1960s.* Paducah, Kentucky: Collector Books, 1997.

Dollen, B. L. and R. L. *Collector's Encyclopedia of Red Wing Art Pottery.* Paducah, Kentucky: Collector Books, 2001.

Reiss, Ray. *Red Wing Art Pottery.* Volume 2. Chicago: Property Publishing, 2000.

———. *Red Wing Art Pottery, Including Pottery Made for RumRill: Classic American Pottery from the 30s, 40s, 50s & 60s.* Chicago: Property Publishing, 1996.

———. *Red Wing Dinnerware Price and Identification Guide.* Chicago: Property Publishing, 1997.

Simon, Dolores. *Red Wing Pottery with RumRill*. Paducah, Kentucky: Collector Books, 1980.

ROSEVILLE

Bassett, Mark. *Introducing Roseville Pottery*. Atglen, Pennsylvania: Schiffer Publishing Ltd., 1999.

Bomm, Jack and Nancy. *Roseville in All Its Splendor*. Gas City, Indiana: L-W Book Sales, 1998.

Huxford, Sharon and Bob. *The Collectors Encyclopedia of Roseville Pottery*. Paducah, Kentucky: Collector Books, 1976, updated values 1993.

Mollring, Gloria and James. *Roseville Pottery Collector's Price Guide*. 6th edition. Privately printed, 2000 (Gloria Mollring, P.O. Box 22754, Sacramento, CA 95822).

ROYAL

Aupperle, Eldon R. *A Collector's Guide for Currier & Ives Dinnerware*. Privately printed, 1996 (29470 Saxon Rd., Toulon, IL 61483).

SHAWNEE

Curran, Pamela Duvall. *Shawnee Pottery: The Full Encyclopedia with Value Guide*. Atglen, Pennsylvania: Schiffer Publishing Ltd., 1995.

Mangus, Jim and Bev. *Shawnee Pottery: An Identification & Value Guide*. Paducah, Kentucky: Collector Books, 1994.

Supnick, Mark E. *Collecting Shawnee Pottery*. Gas City, Indiana: L-W Book Sales, 2000.

Vanderbilt, Duane and Janice. *The Collector's Guide to Shawnee Pottery*. Paducah, Kentucky: Collector Books, 1992.

STANGL

Duke, Harvey. *Stangl Pottery*. Radnor, Pennsylvania: Wallace-Homestead, 1993.

Rehl, Norma. *Collectors Handbook of Stangl Pottery*. Privately printed, 1979 (P.O. Box 556, Milford, NJ 08848) (out of print).

———. *Stangl Pottery*. Part 2. Privately printed, 1982 (P.O. Box 556, Milford, NJ 08848) (out of print).

Runge, Robert C., Jr. *Collector's Encyclopedia of Stangl Dinnerware*. Paducah, Kentucky: Collector Books, 2000.

STERLING

Sterling Vitrified China. Catalog. East Liverpool, Ohio: Sterling China Company, 1991.

STEUBENVILLE
Kerr, Ann. *Steubenville Saga*. Privately printed, 1979 (P.O. Box 437, Sidney, OH 45365) (out of print).

SYRACUSE
Reed, Cleota, and Stan Skoczen. *Syracuse China*. Syracuse, New York: Syracuse University Press, 1997.

TAYLOR, SMITH & TAYLOR
Gonzales, Mark. *Collecting Fiesta, Lu-Ray & Other Colorware*. Gas City, Indiana: L-W Book Sales, 2000.

Meehan, Kathy and Bill. *Collector's Guide to Lu-Ray Pastels*. Paducah, Kentucky: Collector Books, 1995.

UNIVERSAL
Smith, Timothy J. *Universal Dinnerware and Its Predecessors*. Atglen, Pennsylvania: Schiffer Publishing Ltd., 2000.

VERNON KILNS
Nelson, Maxine. *Collectible Vernon Kilns: An Identification & Value Guide*. Paducah, Kentucky: Collector Books, 1994.

———. *Versatile Vernon Kilns*. Book 2. Paducah, Kentucky: Collector Books, 1983.

WATT
Morris, Sue and Dave. *Watt Pottery: An Identification and Value Guide*. Paducah, Kentucky: Collector Books, 1993.

Thompson, Dennis, and W. Bryce Watt. *Watt Pottery: A Collector's Reference with Price Guide*. Atglen, Pennsylvania: Schiffer Publishing Ltd., 1994.

WILLOW
Lindbeck, Jennifer A. *A Collector's Guide to Willow Ware*. Atglen, Pennsylvania: Schiffer Publishing Ltd., 2000.

Rogers, Connie. *Willow Ware Made in the U.S.A.: An Identification Guide*. Privately printed, 1996, prices 2000 (1733 Chase Ave., Cincinnati, OH 45223).

PLASTIC
DINNERWARE

PLASTIC DINNERWARE

Introduction

Plastic dishes were first made in the late 1920s. American Cyanamid Corporation developed a urea formaldehyde material that was similar to the British plastic called Beetleware. The earliest American Beetleware was given away as premiums with products like Wheaties and Ovaltine. American Beetleware was inexpensive to produce, but it didn't stand up to normal use. The dishes faded and cracked after repeated contact with water.

The formula for melamine was originally discovered in 1834 by a Swiss scientist. The plastic wasn't used for dishes until 1937, when a food company used it to make trays for serving hot meals to factory workers. During World War II, the U.S. Navy bought more than a million pounds of melamine to make injection-molded dishes. American Cyanamid was the major producer of the powder that was used in the injection molding process.

In 1944 American Cyanamid commissioned designer Russel Wright to create a line of melamine dishes for the average home. Wright's first design was called Meladur. By the 1950s, melamine dishes, commonly called Melmac, were advertised as an "accident-proof" substitution for pottery dinnerware. In the 1953 Sears catalog, the price for a 16-piece set of Melmac was almost twice as much as a similar 16-piece set of semi-porcelain dinnerware.

Melamine dishes scratched and stained easily and the dinnerware wasn't truly unbreakable. By the late 1970s, Melmac lost its popularity.

Collectors pay most for items by well-known designers like Russel

Wright and Joan Luntz. The dinnerware is usually sold in sets or mixed lots. "Mixed color" listings in this section refer to mixed sets of solid-colored dishes. "Speckled" means the plastic itself has dots of different colors. "Decal" refers to printed decorations, usually on solid white dishes.

AZTEC

The Aztec Company was located in St. Louis, Missouri. The design of the medium-weight dinnerware line suggests the line was produced in the mid-1950s. Dishes are in deep colors, including Brown, Gray, Green, Mustard Yellow, Salmon, and Turquoise; and pastel colors, including Blue, Pink, White, and Yellow. Some colors are speckled, and a Beige set with a floral pattern was made. Dishes are marked *Aztec* and *Melamine Dinnerware*.

Brown
Bowl, Vegetable, 2 Handles,
  12 In. . . . . 11.00 to 12.50

❖

It is said creativity comes from a messy, cluttered environment. It inspires ideas. Remember that the next time you rearrange your collectibles. Now we realize that our son's childhood bedroom was a clue to his future in a creative business.

❖

Green
Salad Set, Open Handles,
  9 Piece 65.00
Salmon
Sugar & Creamer, Cover . . 2.50

BOONTONWARE

The Boonton Molding Company, of Boonton, New Jersey, made heavyweight Melmac dishes in 1948 for institutional use. In 1951, designer Belle Kogan worked with the company to produce dinnerware for the home. Later patterns, like Crown Patrician, Normandy Rose, and Somerset, are lighter weight. The company's ads listed the colors Butter Yellow, Charcoal, Cranberry Red, Forest Green, Golden Yellow, Oyster White, Pewter Gray, Powder Blue, Seafoam Green, Shrimp Pink, Stone Gray, Tawny Buff, and Turquoise Blue. Decals, including Normandy Rose, were used on white dishes. Mixing bowls were made in speckled colors. The company continued to make dinnerware until 1977. Dishes are marked *Boonton, Boontonware, Boontonware Belle,* and *Melmac.*

Butter Yellow
Bowl, Vegetable, Cover,
  2 Sections 35.00
Dinner Set, Plates, Bowls,
  Cups, Saucers, Tumblers,
  55 Piece 250.00
Platter, 14 1/2 In. 20.00
Cranberry Red
Bowl, Vegetable, Cover,
  2 Sections 13.00
Mixing Bowl, Fluted,
  7 3/4 In. 8.00
Decal
Dinner Set, Normandy
  Rose, Plates, Cups,
  Saucers, 16 Piece 27.00
Forest Green
Butter, Cover 5.05
Plate, Dinner, 10 In. 5.00
Golden Yellow
Bowl, Vegetable,
  2 Sections, 8 1/4 In. 5.00
Platter, 14 1/2 In. 20.00
Mixed Color Set
Breakfast Set, Plates,
  Bowls, Mugs, Sugar,
  Creamer, 28 Piece 40.00
Oyster White
Bowl, Vegetable,
  Cover, 2 Sections,
  8 In. . . . . 10.00 to 13.00
Seafoam Green
Platter 2.50
Shrimp Pink
Bowl, Vegetable,
  2 Sections, 9 In. 5.00
Butter, Cover 9.00
Salt & Pepper 8.00
Sugar, White Cover 5.50
Speckled Rose
Mixing Bowl, Fluted, Nesting,
  4 & 2 Qt., 2 Piece 27.00
Stone Gray
Bowl, Vegetable,
  2 Sections 3.00
Turquoise Blue
Bowl, Vegetable,
  2 Handles, 8 1/4 In. 8.50
Bowl, Vegetable, Oval,
  14 1/2 In. 10.50
Butter, Cover 6.50
Dinner Set, 46 Piece 41.00

Dinner Set, Plates, Cups,
  Saucers, Creamer, Sugar,
  14 Piece 10.50

BROOKPARK

Brookpark dinnerware
was made by International
Molded Products, of
Cleveland, Ohio, from
1950 to 1962. The Arrow-
head line was designed by
Joan Luntz in 1950 and
won a Good Design
Award from the Museum
of Modern Art. Modern
Design dinnerware, also
designed by Luntz, fea-
tures square dishes.
Brookpark's dinnerware
was made in Black, Bur-
gundy, Chartreuse, Emer-

ald, Pearl Gray, Pink,
Stone, Turquoise, White,
and Yellow. In 1956,
Brookpark introduced the
Fantasy line, the first
decal-decorated melamine
dinnerware. Other deco-
rated lines are Bluebells,
Contemporary, Delicado,
Dual-Tone, Elegance,
Flower Box, Gaiety,
Golden Pine, Magic Car-
pet, Only a Rose Pavilion,
Pink Hyacinth, Town and
Country, and Tropicana.
Desert Flower is a Brook-
park line with an im-
pressed floral decoration.
Mixing bowls were made
in speckled colors. Dishes
are marked *Brookpark,
Efficiency Ware, Ever Ware,
International Molded Plastics
Inc.,* and with pattern
names.

Arrowhead
Dinner Set, Chartreuse,
  Plates, Bowls, Cups,
  Saucers, 85 Piece 104.00
Dinner Set, Mixed Colors,
  Plates, Bowls, Cups,
  Saucers, 24 Piece 26.00
Saucer, Stone 1.50
Sugar & Creamer, Cover,
  Emerald 4.00

Mixed Color Set
Mixing Bowl Set, Pink,
  Blue, Yellow, Nesting,
  8-11 In., 3 Piece 51.00

Modern Design
Bowl, Burgundy,
  4 1/2 In. 5.00
Cup & Saucer, Burgundy . . 5.00
Dinner Set, Pink & Black,
  Plates, Bowls, Cups,
  Saucers, 58 Piece 177.00
Place Setting, Black,
  4 Piece 13.00
Place Setting, Burgundy,
  4 Piece 4.50
Place Setting, Chartreuse,
  4 Piece 7.50

Platter, Black, 9 1/4 In. . . 15.00
Sugar & Creamer, Cover,
  Chartreuse 10.00
Sugar & Creamer, Cover,
  Turquoise . . . . . 9.00 to 10.00

Speckled
Mixing Bowl, Blue, Nesting,
  11 3/4 & 8 1/4 In.,
  2 Piece 13.50
Mixing Bowl, Green,
  11 1/2 In. 18.00
Mixing Bowl, Red, White,
  Blue, 11 1/2 In. 17.50

COLOR-FLYTE

Color-Flyte and Color-
Flyte Royale medium-
weight dishes were made
by Branchell (a division of
Lenox Plastics) in St. Louis,
Missouri, and San Fran-
cisco, California, beginning
in 1952. It was sold by
door-to-door salesmen.
The dinnerware was pro-
duced in mottled colors:
Glade Green, Glow Cop-
per, Mist Gray, and Spray
Lime. Royale colors were
Charcoal Gray, Flame
Pink, Gardenia White, and
Turquoise Blue. Some of
the plates were sold with
decal decorations, includ-
ing Golden Grapes,
Golden Harvest, Lady Fair,
Rosedale, Sweet Talk, and
Tip Top. The dishes are
marked *Branchell, Color-
Flyte, Melmac,* and *Royale.*

Glade Green

Bowl, Vegetable, Oval   . . . 7.00
Plate, Salad, 7 1/2 In. 4.00
Sugar & Creamer,
  Cover 22.00

Glow Copper

Bowl, Salad, 7 In. 3.50
Bowl, Tab Handle, 6 In.,
  6 Piece 10.50
Butter, Cover 25.00
Fork & Spoon, Salad 9.50
Gravy Boat 8.50
Platter, 9 3/4 In. 9.00
Sugar & Creamer,
  Cover 22.00
Tumbler, Juice, 4 Piece . . 11.00
Tumbler, Water, 4 Piece . 15.50

Mist Gray

Bowl, Salad, 7 In. 3.50
Bowl, Vegetable, Oval   . . 4.00
Bowl, Vegetable, Oval,
  2 Sections, 10 1/2 In. . . 22.00
Butter, Cover 20.00
Luncheon Set, Plates,
  Tumblers, Cups,
  Saucers, 16 Piece 26.00
Platter, Oval, 9 3/4 In. 4.00

Mixed Color Set

Dinner Set, Plates,
  Cups, Saucers,
  16 Piece   . . . . . 11.00 to 20.00
Dinner Set, Plates, Cups,
  Saucers, Sugar, Creamer,
  28 Piece 41.00
Tumbler Set, Juice,
  3 1/2 In., 8 Piece 54.00

Spray Lime

Bowl, Vegetable,
  10 1/2 In. 7.00
Bowl, Vegetable, Oval,
  8 In. 3.00

Always put plastic dishes on the top rack of the dishwasher. Test any old dishes to be sure they will not warp or melt in the dishwasher.

Cup & Saucer, 4 Sets 12.50
Gravy Boat   . . . . . 7.50 to 15.50
Platter, Oval,
  9 3/4 In. . . . . 4.00 to 8.00

HARMONY HOUSE

Harmony House melamine dishes were made by Plastic Masters, of New Buffalo, Michigan, for Sears, Roebuck & Company. The Talk of the Town line first appeared in the 1953 catalog and was produced in Chartreuse, Dawn Gray, Mint Green, and Victorian Red. Other solid-color lines are Avalon (Blue, Ivory Pink, and Yellow), Catalina (Bronze Green, Inca Gold, Malibu Coral, and Spice Beige), Catalina Translucent (Light Federal Gold, Light Malibu Coral, Ming Blue, and Parchment Beige), New Talk of the Town (Clay Beige, Frosty Pink, Medium Federal Gold, and Medium Sage Green), and Today (Aquamarine, Dawn Gray, Spice Beige, and Sunshine Yellow). Many decal-decorated patterns, like Autumn Leaves, Crocus, Floral Lace, Frolic, Golden Spears, Mademoiselle, Patio Rose, and Pro-

vince, were introduced after 1957 and continued to be made through the 1960s. Dishes are marked *Harmony House, Melmac,* and with pattern names.

Avalon

Cup, Pink 1.50
Sugar & Creamer, Pink   . . 9.00

Catalina

Bowl, Dessert,
  Inca Gold 4.00
Sugar & Creamer, Inca
  Gold 6.00
Sugar & Creamer, Malibu
  Pink 15.00

Talk Of The Town

Plate, Frosty Pink, 10 In. . . 4.00
Salad Set, Clay Beige,
  Bowls, Dressing Server,
  6 Piece 6.50
Sugar & Creamer, Frosty
  Pink 9.00

Today

Sugar & Creamer,
  Aquamarine 4.00

HOLIDAY

Holiday medium-weight dinnerware was manufactured by Kenro Company of Fredonia, Wisconsin. Kenro also produced the Debonaire pattern. The speckled dishes came in Blue, Pink, Red, Salmon, Turquoise, White, and Yellow. Decorated patterns included Gale Art,

Orchid Spray, and Seneca. An op-art black-and-white checkered set was designed by Tom Strobel and produced in a limited edition. Dishes are marked *Holiday by Kenro.*

Salmon
Ice Bucket, Cover, Handle,
Lining 9.00

Yellow
Platter, 13 3/4 In. 6.00

INSULATED PLASTIC

In the mid-1950s, the plastics industry introduced colorful insulated (thermal) tumblers, pitchers, mugs, and dishes. The drinking items were advertised as preventing condensation, thus avoiding rings on the furniture. The mugs, pitchers, and serving dishes could keep drinks and food hot or cold. One popular, unmarked design features a woven straw insert, similar to burlap, between a layer of Lucite and opaque colored plastic. Marked lines include Bolero by Thermo-Temp, Cornish, Raffiaware by Thermo-Temp, Sunfrost, Therm-O-Bowl by Reinecke, Thermo-Serv by West Bend, and Vacron.

When using antiques on a holiday table, be careful. Wax from candles can stain a cloth. Dishes may be stained from cranberry or other fruits. Flower containers are easily water stained. Vases and plants often stain wood; be sure to use a coaster or dish. Greens draped on pictures or marble can stain.

Bolero
Pitcher, Cover,
Turquoise 6.00
Tumbler, Orange,
6 1/2 In. 3.50
Tumbler, Pink, 5 In. 2.50
Tumbler Set, Mixed Colors,
5 In., 6 Piece 10.50

Cornish
Bowl, Salad, Cover,
Yellow 10.00
Creamer, Yellow 4.00

Raffiaware
Beverage Set, Mixed
Colors, Pitcher, Mugs,
7 Piece 20.00
Bowl Set, Mixed Colors,
Covers, Stand, 5 In.,
9 Piece 20.00
Mug, Turquoise,
3 1/2 In. 3.00
Salad Set, Green Bowl,
Fork, Spoon 10.00
Sherbet, Tan 4.00
Sherbet Set, Mixed Colors,
8 Piece 13.00
Sherbet Set, Salmon,
6 Piece 10.00
Snack Set, Mixed Colors,
Trays, Mugs, 8 Piece . . . 4.50
Tumbler Set, Mixed Colors,
Stand, 9 Piece 14.00

Straw Weave
Beverage Set, Mixed Colors,
Mugs, 9 3/4-In. Pitcher,
5 Piece 42.00
Bowl, Cover, Pink 3.00
Bowl Set, Mixed Colors,
5 In., 8 Piece 28.00
Ice Bucket, Beige, Box . . . 9.00
Mug Set, Mixed Colors,
3 3/4 In., 6 Piece 9.00
Mug Set, Mixed Colors,
4 1/2 In., 4 Piece 6.00
Tumbler Set, Mixed Colors,
6 In., 6 Piece 6.50

Vacron
Bowl, Yellow 3.00
Mug, Pink 4.00
Tumbler, Dark Pink,
Small 3.00

LENOX PLASTICS

Lenox Plastics Inc. worked in Los Angeles, California, and St. Louis, Missouri, and was the parent company of Branchell (see Color-Flyte). The style of the medium-weight dishes suggests they were made in the late 1950s or early 1960s. Decorated lines included Americana, Andover, Aztec Green, Concept, Contempra, Deluxe, and Regency. The dishes are marked *Lenox Plastics, Lenoxware,* and with pattern names.

Andover
Dinner Set, Turquoise
Floral, Bowls, Plate, Cups,
Saucers, Box 18.00

Aztec Green
Dinner Set, Plates, Bowls,
Cups, Saucers, Platter,
34 Piece . . . . . 20.00 to 25.00

Lenoxware
Hostess Set, White, Plates
With Wells, Cups, Box,
8 Piece 20.00

MALLO-WARE

P.R. Mallory Plastics Inc. of Chicago, Illinois, made Mallo-Ware. The medium-weight dinnerware was produced in Avocado, Beige, Burgundy, Chartreuse, Gold, Gray, Light Blue, Light Green, Pink, White, Yellow, and a decorated line called Moonglow. Dishes are marked *Mallo-Ware, Melmac,* and with shape numbers.

Avocado
Bowl, Tab Handles, 5 In. . . 4.00
Sugar & Creamer 5.00

Beige
Bowl, Fruit, 5 1/4 In. 2.00

Burgundy
Dinner Set, Plates, Cups,
Saucers, Bowls,
15 Piece 26.00

Chartreuse
Platter 4.50

Light Blue
Bowl, Tab Handles, 9 In. . . 5.50
Breakfast Set, Bowls, Cups,
Saucers, 10 Piece 10.00

Mixed Color Set
Salad Set, 7 Piece 50.00
Tumbler Set, 4 1/2 In.,
10 Piece 34.00

Pink
Bowl, Tab Handles, 9 In. . . 5.50
Platter 4.50

PROLON

Prolon Plastics was a division of Prophylactic Brush Company of Florence, Massachusetts. Early Prolon dishes are heavier and were probably created for institutional use. Later styles, like Beverly, Cadence, and Florence, are lighter weight and more graceful. The Florence dinnerware line, designed by George Nelson Associates, won the House Beautiful Classic Award in 1955. Colors include Burgundy, Dark Green, Dawn (beige-gray), Gray, High Noon (mustard yellow), Lime Green, Midnight (black), Olive Green, Rust Red, Sunset (red), Turquoise, White, and Yellow. Decorated lines include Artiste, Bazaar, Designers, Grant Crest, Hostess, Potpourri, Vista, and World of Color. Dishes are marked *Melmac, Prolon, Prolon Ware,* and with pattern names. Institutional dinnerware marked *Prolon* is still being made by Lincoln Foodservice Products Inc. in Fort Wayne, Indiana.

Florence
Bowl, Vegetable, Burgundy,
2 Handles, Oval, 11 In. . . 8.00
Dish, Sunset, Rectangular,
10 In. 11.00
Lunch Set, Sunset, Plates,
Bowls, Cups, Saucers,
10 Piece 61.00
Platter, Sunset, 10 1/4 In. . . 6.00
Sugar & Creamer, Cover,
Sunset 1.50

Grant Crest
Bowl, Salad, Charcoal,
7 In. 3.00
Bowl, Salad, Turquoise,
7 In. 3.00
Bowl, Vegetable, Turquoise,
9 In. 4.00

ROYALON

Royalon Inc. of Chicago, Illinois, was a subsidiary of Royal China Inc. of Logansport, Indiana. Royalon's lines included Brookpark by Royalon, Candlelight, Hallmark, Roymac, Windsor, and World's Fair House. The lines were made in Beige, Pink, Purple, Turquoise, White, and Yellow, and were decorated with decals like Aristocrat, Crescendo, Jasmine, Romance, San Marino, and Violets. The Shenandoah line is decorated with apples. Dishes are marked *Melmac, Romac, Royalon,* and with pattern names.

Decal

Dinner Set, Shenandoah,
Plates, Cups, Saucers,
Platter, 25 Piece 28.00
Plate, Bread & Butter,
Blue & Purple Violets,
6 1/4 In. 2.00
Plate, Shenandoah,
9 3/4 In., 4 Piece 10.00

Purple

Bowl, Cereal,
6 1/4 In. 2.00
Bowl, Dessert,
5 In. 2.00
Creamer 2.00
Cup 1.00
Dinner Set, Floral Decal,
Plates, Bowls, Cups,
Saucers, 38 Piece 31.00
Gravy Boat ...... 2.00 to 6.00

RUSSEL WRIGHT

Designer Russel Wright was a pioneer in melamine dinnerware. In 1945 he worked with American Cyanamid on prototype dishes for institutional use.¹ His first line was Meladur, which was marked with his signature from 1949 to 1953. Wright's Residential line was made for domestic use by Northern Industrial Chemical Company, Boston, Massachusetts, and received the Good Design Award from the Museum of Modern Art in 1953 and 1954. Residential dishes are opaque with a mottled effect created by overlapping two colors. Original colors are Black Velvet (black with aluminum dust), Copper Penny (brown with copper dust), Gray, Lemon Ice, and Sea Mist. Additional colors are Light Blue, Salmon, and White. The Home Decorators line was introduced in 1954 and came in Blue, Pink, Salmon, White, and Yellow with Bow Knot and Leaf decorations. Flair was introduced in 1959 in solid colors and with Arabesque, Golden Bouquet, Ming Lace, Spring Garden, and Woodland Rose decorations. Wright's Ideal Adult Kitchen Ware for children and for "refrigerator-to-table" use is also listed here, although the dishes are made of polyethylene, not melamine. Dishes are marked *Russel Wright, Northern,* and with pattern names.

Home Decorators

Creamer, Yellow 8.00
Cup & Saucer, Pink 8.00
Plate, Pink, 6 In. 6.50
Plate, Salad, Pink 8.00
Platter, Pink 20.00
Tumbler Set, Mixed
Colors, 10 Piece 180.00

Ideal Adult Kitchen Ware

Creamer, Coral, Child's .. 13.00
Cup, Granite Gray,
Child's 8.00
Cup, Yellow, Child's 8.00
Gravy Boat, Coral,
Child's 15.00
Pickle, Chartreuse,
Child's 15.00
Plate, Dinner, Chartreuse,
Child's 5.00
Plate, Dinner, Seafoam
Green, Child's 8.00
Platter, Meat, Chartreuse,
Child's 20.00
Saucer, Bean Brown,
Child's 8.00
Saucer, Seafoam Green,
Child's 5.00
Saucer, White, Child's 8.00
Sugar, Cantaloupe,
Child's 13.00
Sugar, Coral, Child's 10.00
Sugar, Cover, Coral,
Child's 15.00
Teapot, Cantaloupe,
Child's 30.00
Teapot, Coral, Child's ... 25.00

Meladur

Plate, Dinner, Yellow ... 10.00
Plate, Salad, Yellow 8.00

Residential

Bowl, Vegetable, Salmon,
9 In. 20.00
Creamer, Lemon Ice 15.00
Cup, Salmon 6.00
Cup & Saucer, Black
Velvet 18.00
Cup & Saucer, Light
Blue 8.00
Cup & Saucer, Salmon ... 8.00
Cup & Saucer, Sea Mist .. 8.00
Plate, Dinner, Salmon,
10 1/2 In. 8.00

If you have an alarm system, program a strobe light attached to the outside of the house to go on if there is a break-in attempt. The light will frighten the burglar and will make it easy for the police to find the house.

Plate, Salad, Salmon,
  7 1/2 In. 5.00
Plate, Sea Mist, 6 In. 4.50
Platter, Light Blue 20.00
Platter, Salmon,
  14 1/2 In. . . . . 25.00 to 30.00
Soup, Dish, Lug,
  Light Blue 15.00
Tumbler, Salmon, 10 Oz.,
  3 1/4 In. 23.00

SPAULDING

Spaulding Ware was manufactured by American Plastics Manufacturing Corporation in Chicago, Illinois. The dinnerware was made in solid and mottled colors, including Brown, Gray, Light Blue, Mustard Yellow, Pink, Red, and Turquoise. Some plates are decorated with decals. Dishes are marked

Genuine Melamine, Melmac, Spaulding, and *Spaulding Ware.*

Bowl, Vegetable, Mustard
  Yellow, 2 Sections,
  11 1/2 In., 2 Piece 12.50
Bowl, Vegetable, Red,
  11 1/2 In. 28.50

STETSON

Stetson Chemicals had factories in Lincoln and Chicago, Illinois. The company made various lines, including Contour, Riviera, and Sun Valley. The dinnerware was made in Butterscotch, Light Green, mottled Orange, Pink, Turquoise, White, and Yellow. The dishes are marked *Melmac, Stetson,* and with pattern names.

Decal
Dinner Set, Roses, Plates,
  Bowls, Cups, Saucers,
  Sugar, Creamer, Platter,
  47 Piece 50.00
Sun Valley
Bowl, Vegetable, Pink,
  2 Sections, 9 In. 5.00
Bowl, Vegetable, Turquoise,
  2 Sections, 9 In. 5.00

Sugar & Creamer, Turquoise,
  Cover 18.00

TEXAS WARE

Texas Ware heavyweight dinnerware was made by Plastics Manufacturing Company in Dallas, Texas. The most common items are the speckled mixing bowls. Dallas Ware was an institutional line. Rio Vista was introduced in 1952 in Bone White, Chinese Red, Ebony Black, Sage Green, Stone Gray, and other colors. San Jacinto was introduced in 1953 and was made in Bone White, Dresden Blue, Dusty Rose, Jonquil Yellow, Sage Green, Sandalwood, and Sea Green. In 1957 Plastics Manufacturing Company introduced the first tone-on-tone items. The San Jacinto line won a Good Design Award from the Museum of Modern Art for Gray on White, Sandalwood on White, White on Sage Green, and Yellow on Dusty Rose items. Decal decorations included Angles, Autumn Leaves, Avant Garde, Bon Vivant, Bouquet, Classics, Epicure, Flourish, Happenings, Marco Polo, Park Avenue, Shasta Daisy, Trend, and Westwood. Dishes are marked *Plastics Manufacturing Company, PMC, Texas Ware,* and with pattern names. Plastics Manufacturing Company is still in business.

Chinese Red

Dinner Set, Plates, Bowls,
Mugs, 16 Piece 21.00

Decal

Dinner Set, Bouquet, Plates,
Bowls, Mugs, Tumblers,
Box, 32 Piece 27.00

Dinner Set, Park Avenue,
Plates, Bowls, Cups, Saucers,
Platter, Box, 45 Piece . . 27.00

Dusty Rose

Sugar & Creamer 8.50

Jonquil Yellow

Dinner Set, Plates, Bowls,
Mugs, Platter,
34 Piece 10.00

Sugar & Creamer 9.00

Rio Vista

Butter Chip, Pink,
3 1/4 In., 8 Piece 8.50

Plate, Luncheon, Gray,
7 In., 8 Piece 5.00

Sea Green

Bowl, Fruit, 5 1/2 In. 3.00

Saucer 1.50

Speckled

Bowl, Green, 5 1/4 In.,
4 Piece 17.00

Mixing Bowl, Brown,
No. 118, 10 In. 12.00

Mixing Bowl, Brown,
No. 125, 11 1/4 In. 21.00

Mixing Bowl, Coral,
No. 125, 11 1/4 In. 29.00

Mixing Bowl, Gray,
No. 111, 8 In. 15.00

Mixing Bowl, Green,
9 In. 9.00

Mixing Bowl, Pink,
No. 111, 8 In. 9.50

Mixing Bowl, Pink,
No. 125, 11 1/4 In. 15.00

WATERTOWN

Watertown Manufacturing Company was located in Watertown, Connecticut. The company's lines included Balmoral, Lifetime Ware, Monterey, and Woodbine. Woodbine, introduced in 1952, was the first plastic dinnerware with a raised design. The heavyweight dinnerware was made in Beige, Ber-

muda Coral, Black, Canyon Yellow, Caribbean Blue, Chartreuse, Cocoa, Grenada Green, Light Blue, Palisades Gray, Pink, Red, Sahara Sand, and Yellow. Decal decorations include Cathay, Country Gardens, Promenade, Puffs, and Wheat. Dishes are marked *Watertown* and with pattern names.

Lifetime Ware

Dinner Set, Mixed Colors,
Plates, Bowls, Serving
Pieces, 41 Piece 40.00

Sugar, Cover, Grenada
Green 3.50

WESTINGHOUSE

Westinghouse Electric Corporation, Bridgeport, Connecticut, made medium to heavyweight dinnerware called Calais, Darien, Newport, and Ovation. The lines were made in Pink, Turquoise, White, and Yellow, and with decal decorations. Dishes are marked *Genuine Melmac, Westinghouse,* and with pattern names.

Ovation

Bowl, Vegetable, White,
2 Sections, 9 In. 10.50

Bowl, Vegetable, Yellow,
2 Sections, 9 In. 22.00

Sugar & Creamer, Yellow,
Cover 18.00

PLASTIC DINNERWARE

References

Goldberg, Michael J. *Collectible Plastic Kitchenware and Dinnerware, 1935–1965.* Atglen, Pennsylvania: Schiffer Publishing Ltd., 1995.

Wahlberg, Holly. *1950s Plastic Design: Everyday Elegance.* Atglen, Pennsylvania: Schiffer Publishing Ltd., 1999.

Zimmer, Gregory R., and Alvin Daigle, Jr. *Melmac Dinnerware.* Gas City, Indiana: L-W Book Sales, 1997.

Ceramic Dinnerware
Patterns and Factories Index

This is an alphabetical list of the dinnerware patterns and factories listed in this book. Factory names are in capital letters.

Kovels' Library

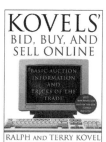

0-609-80571-1

0-609-80312-3

0-609-80757-9

0-609-57806-0

0-609-58840-4

0-609-88381-3

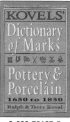

0-609-70137-5

0-609-55914-5

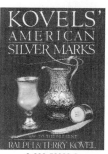

0-609-56882-9

0-609-80417-0

0-609-60168-7

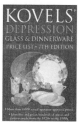

0-609-80640-8

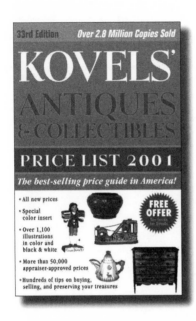

Kovels Order Form

SEND ORDERS & INQUIRIES TO:
Crown Publishers, Inc.
c/o Random House, 400 Hahn Road
Westminster, MD 21157
ATT: ORDER DEPT.

SALES & TITLE INFORMATION:
1-800-733-3000
FOR ORDER ENTRY:
FAX# 1-800-659-2436
WEBSITE: www.randomhouse.com

NAME_____

ADDRESS _____

CITY & STATE _____ ZIP _____

Please send me the following books:

ITEM NO.	QTY.	TITLE	PRICE	TOTAL
0-609-80571-1	___	Kovels' Antiques & Collectibles Price List, 33rd Edition	PAPER $15.95	_____
0-517-70137-5	___	Dictionary of Marks—Pottery and Porcelain	HARDCOVER $17.00	_____
0-517-55914-5	___	Kovels' New Dictionary of Marks	HARDCOVER $19.00	_____
0-517-56882-9	___	Kovels' American Silver Marks	HARDCOVER $40.00	_____
0-609-80757-9	___	Kovels' Bid, Buy, and Sell Online	PAPER $14.00	_____
0-609-80312-3	___	Kovels' Bottles Price List, 11th Edition	PAPER $16.00	_____
0-609-80640-8	___	Kovels' Depression Glass & Dinnerware Price List, 7th Edition	PAPER $16.00	_____
0-517-57806-9	___	Kovels' Know Your Antiques, Revised and Updated	PAPER $17.00	_____
0-517-58840-4	___	Kovels' Know Your Collectibles, Updated	PAPER $16.00	_____
0-517-88381-3	___	Kovels' Quick Tips: 799 Helpful Hints on How to Care for Your Collectibles	PAPER $12.00	_____
0-609-60168-7	___	The Label Made Me Buy It: From Aunt Jemima to Zonkers	HARDCOVER $40.00	_____
0-609-80417-0	___	Kovels' Yellow Pages: A Collector's Directory of Names, Addresses, Telephone and Fax Numbers, E-Mail, and Internet Addresses to Make Selling, Fixing, and Pricing Your Antiques and Collectibles Easy	PAPER $18.00	_____

___ TOTAL ITEMS   TOTAL RETAIL VALUE _____

CHECK OR MONEY ORDER ENCLOSED
MADE PAYABLE TO CROWN PUBLISHERS
or telephone 1-800-733-3000
(No cash or stamps, please)

CHARGE: ☐ MasterCard ☐ Visa ☐ American Express
Account Number (include all digits) Expires: MO.___ YR.___

Shipping & Handling
Charge (per order) $5.50
Please add applicable
sales tax.   _____

TOTAL AMOUNT DUE

$_____

_____

_____
Signature

PRICES SUBJECT TO CHANGE
WITHOUT NOTICE.
If a more recent edition of a price list
has been published at the same price,
it will be sent instead of the old edition.

Thank you for your order

BUSINESS REPLY MAIL

FIRST CLASS   PERMIT NO. 191   FLAGLER BEACH, FL

POSTAGE WILL BE PAID BY ADDRESSEE

KOVELS ON ANTIQUES AND COLLECTIBLES

P.O. BOX 420349

PALM COAST, FL   32142-9655